Race and Arab Americans
Before and After 9/II

Arab American Writing

OTHER TITLES IN ARAB AMERICAN WRITING

The Cairo House: A Novel
SAMIA SERAGELDIN

A Community of Many Worlds:
Arab Americans in New York City
MUSEUM OF THE CITY OF NEW YORK

Does the Land Remember Me?
A Memoir of Palestine
AZIZ SHIHAB

Hayati, My Life: A Novel
MIRIAM COOKE

Letters from Cairo
PAULINE KALDAS

The New Belly Dancer
of the Galaxy: A Novel
FRANCES KHIRALLAH NOBLE

Post Gibran: Anthology
of New Arab American Writing
MUNIR AKASH and KHALED MATTAWA, eds.

Remember Me to Lebanon: Stories
of Lebanese Women in America
EVELYN SHAKIR

The Situe Stories
FRANCES KHIRALLAH NOBLE

Swimming Toward the Light: A Novel
ANGELA TEHAAN LEONE

Race and Arab Americans Before and After 9/11

FROM INVISIBLE CITIZENS TO VISIBLE SUBJECTS

EDITED BY

AMANEY JAMAL AND **NADINE NABER**

Syracuse University Press

First Edition 2008

08   09   10   11   12   13   6   5   4   3   2   1

Mohamad El-Hindi Books on Arab Culture and Islamic Civilization
are published with the assistance of a grant from the M.E.H. Foundation.

The paper used in this publication meets the minimum requirements
of American National Standard of Information Sciences—Permanence
of Paper of Printed Library Materials, ANSI Z39.48-1984∞™

For a listing of books published and distributed by Syracuse University Press,
visit our Web site at SyracuseUniversityPress.syr.edu.

ISBN-13: 978-0-8156-3152-1 (cl.)   ISBN-10: 0-8156-3152-9 (cl.)
ISBN-13: 978-0-8156-3177-4 (pbk.)   ISBN-10: 0-8156-3177-4 (pbk.)

Library of Congress Cataloging-in-Publication Data

Race and Arab Americans before and after 9/11 : from invisible citizens to visible subjects /
edited by Amaney Jamal and Nadine Naber. — 1st ed.
p. cm.
Includes bibliographical references and index.
ISBN-13: 978-0-8156-3152-1 (cloth : alk. paper)
ISBN-13: 978-0-8156-3177-4 (pbk. : alk. paper)
1. Arab Americans—Race identity.   2. Arab Americans—Civil rights.
3. Arab Americans—Social conditions—20th century.   4. Arab Americans—
Social conditions—21st century.   5. September 11 Terrorist Attacks, 2001—Influence.
6. United States—Race relations.   7. Racism—United States.
I. Jamal, Amaney A., 1970–   II. Naber, Nadine Christine.
E184.A65R33 2007
305.8992'7073—dc22   2007039522

Contents

Figures and Tables

Acknowledgments

FOR SEVERAL DECADES, a shared sense of urgency over the realities of anti-Arab racism and discrimination in the United States has inspired intense discussion and debate among our colleagues in Arab American Studies. This book was inspired by conversations that took place among colleagues in this field, including many contributors to this book, about the relevance of the concept of "race" to Arab American Studies. It was particularly inspired by a panel held at the annual meetings of the Middle East Studies Association in 2002, "Arab American Engagements with Race in the United States," organized by Sarah Gualtieri. At this conference, Suad Joseph encouraged us to develop an edited volume on Arab Americans and "race." Without her support, this book would not exist. We are indebted to her for her guidance and encouragement. We are also indebted to those scholars who have come before us who have paved the way for research on "race" and Arab Americans.

We have learned a great deal from the work of each of the contributors to this volume. We would like to take this opportunity to thank the contributors for their thoughtful and insightful contributions.

Special thanks to Mary Selden Evans, executive editor at Syracuse University Press for her enthusiasm and dedication to thus project. Her commitment to this book has been invaluable and immensely appreciated. We would also like to thank Syracuse University Press for giving our volume a home. Marcia Hough and the staff at Syracuse University Press have been wonderful to work with. Further, we would like to thank the two reviewers who evaluated the manuscript and D. J. Whyte, Syracuse's copy editor, for their invaluable contributions to this book.

We are particularly grateful to Emily Weigel, Matthew Stiffler, Lee Ann Wang, and Jessi Gan for their exceptional research assistance in editing, proofreading, and formatting several parts of this book.

We would also like to thank the following people for their unconditional support throughout the process of completing this project: Atef Said, Evelyn Alsultany, Andrea Smith, Sarita See, Lillian Boctor, Eman Desouky, Lara Deeb, Maylei Blackwell, Barbara Aswad, Zeina Zaatari, the Naber family, Renda Dabit, the Anthropology Writing Group at the University of Michigan (Rebecca Hardin, Julia Paley, Damani Patridge, Miriam Ticktin, Elizabeth Roberts), Elizabeth Cole, Nidal, Manal, Randa and Eman Jamal, Helmi, Asma, Lina, and Ayah Saud, and Khalid, Souha, Ranya, and Jamal K. Jamal.

Contributors

Sawsan Abdulrahim is assistant professor in the Faculty of Health Sciences at the American University in Beirut. Her research focuses on the socioeconomic aspects of health behavior, and her work has been based on the Arab immigrant community in the United States. She is currently carrying out research on the health of African migrant workers in Lebanon.

Evelyn Alsultany is assistant professor in the Program in American Culture at the University of Michigan. Her research focuses on representations of Arab and Muslim Americans in the U.S. mainstream media. She is coeditor (with Nadine Naber and Rabab Abdulhadi) of "Gender, Nation, and Belonging," a special issue of the *MIT Electronic Journal of Middle East Studies on Arab American Feminisms*. She has published essays in *American Quarterly* and in *The Arab Diaspora* (2006).

Louise Cainkar is a sociologist and assistant professor of social welfare and justice at Marquette University. Her current research focuses on Arab and Muslim American experiences after 9/11 in metropolitan Chicago. Her recent publications have appeared in *City and Society,* the *Journal of American Ethnic History, Ameraisa Journal, Contexts, Anthropology and Education Quarterly,* and the *Bulletin of the Royal Institute for Interfaith Studies.*

Benjamin D'Harlingue is a member of the Cultural Studies Graduate Group at the University of California, Davis, where he also has taught classes in Women and Gender Studies. Benjamin's current research is on the intersections of haunting, tourism, and colonial legacies.

Sarah M. A. Gualtieri holds a joint appointment in the Departments of History and American Studies and Ethnicity at the University of Southern California.

She is a historian of Middle Eastern migration, whose research and writing focuses on questions of race, gender, and national identity. Her articles and reviews are published in *Arab Studies Quarterly,* the *Journal of American Ethnic History,* the *Journal of Religion, Radical History Review,* and *Comparative Studies in South Asia, Africa and the Middle East.*

Michelle Hartman is assistant professor of Arabic literature and languages at the Institute of Islamic Studies, McGill University, as well as chair of the Women's Studies Advisory Committee. Her book *Jesus, Joseph and Job: Reading Rescriptings of Religious Figures in Lebanese Women's Fiction* appeared in 2002. She has published articles on Arab and Arab American engagements with the question of "race" in journals such as the *International Journal of Middle East Studies (IJMES),* the *Journal of Arabic Literature (JAL), Journal of Multi-Ethnic Literatures of the United States (MELUS),* and *Black Arts Quarterly.*

Amaney Jamal is assistant professor of politics at Princeton University. Jamal's first book, *Barriers to Democracy,* explores the role of civic associations in promoting democratic effects in the Arab world. Her second book examines patterns of citizenship in the Arab world. Jamal is a principal investigator of the Arab Barometer Project; co–principal investigator of the Detroit Arab American Study, a sister survey to the Detroit Area Study; and senior advisor on the Pew Research Center Project on Islam in America, 2006.

Suad Joseph is professor of anthropology and women and gender studies at the University of California, Davis, and director of the Middle East/South Asia Studies Program. She is general editor of the *Encyclopedia of Women and Islamic Cultures.* Her edited books include *Gender and Citizenship in the Middle East* (Syracuse, 2000) and *Intimate Selving in Arab Families* (Syracuse, 1999). Her coedited books include: *Building Citizenship in Lebanon* (1999, with Walid Moubarak and Antonine Messarra), *Women and Citizenship in Lebanon* (1999, with Najla Hamadeh and Jean Said Makdisi), and *Women and Power in the Middle East* (2001, with Susan Slyomovics).

Nadine Naber is assistant professor in the Department of Women's Studies and Arab American Studies (an emerging Ethnic Studies Program within the Program in American Culture at the University of Michigan, Ann Arbor). Nadine is coeditor, with Rabab Abdulhadi and Evelyn Alsultany, of *Gender, Nation, and Belonging*, a special issue of the *MIT Electronic Journal of Middle East Studies on Arab American Feminisms*. She is also a coeditor of the book *The Color of Violence*, for INCITE! Women of Color Against Violence. She has published articles in the *Journal of Cultural Dynamics*, the *Journal of Asian American Studies*, the *Journal of Ethnic Studies*, the *Journal of Feminist Studies*, *The Muslim World*, and *Meridians: Feminism, Race, Transnationalism*.

Jen'nan Ghazal Read is assistant professor in the Department of Sociology at the University of California, Irvine. She has published a book, *Culture Class and Work among Arab American Women*, and numerous articles, including "More of a Bridge than a Gap: Gender Differences in Arab-American Political Engagement" *(Social Science Quarterly)* and "Racial Context of Origin, Black Immigration, and the U.S. Black/White Health Disparity" *(Social Forces)*.

Andrew Shryock is Arthur F. Thurnau Professor of Anthropology at the University of Michigan. Shryock is the author of *Nationalism and the Genealogical Imagination: Oral History and Textual Authority in Tribal Jordan* (1997); editor, with Nabeel Abraham, of *Arab Detroit: From Margin to Mainstream* (2000); and editor of *Off Stage/On Display: Intimacy and Ethnography in the Age of Public Culture* (2004). In other media, Shryock was a producer and narration writer for the film *Tales from Arab Detroit* (1995), and he has been a curator of several public exhibitions, including A Community Between Two Worlds: The Arab Americans of Greater Detroit (1996, 1997–2000) and Building Islam in Detroit: Foundations, Forms, Futures (2005, 2006).

Alvin Ka Hin Wong is a first-year graduate student in the cultural studies section of the Literature Department at the University of California, San Diego. His main research interests are transnational Chinese cultural studies, queer theory, and postcolonial theory.

Race and Arab Americans
Before and After 9/11

Introduction

Arab Americans and U.S. Racial Formations

NADINE NABER

UP UNTIL THE HORRIFIC ATTACKS of September 11, 2001, several Arab American writers used the trope "invisibility" to refer to the place of Arab Americans within dominant U.S. discourses on race and ethnicity. A common theme in this literature was that while most government definitions classify Arab Americans as "white," popular U.S. discourses tend to represent "Arabs" as different from and inferior to whites. Exemplifying this perspective, Helen Samhan referred to the racialization of Arab Americans within U.S. government racial schemas as "white, but not quite" (1999); Joanna Kadi argued that Arab Americans are the "most invisible of the invisibles" (1994); Therese Saliba published the essay "Resisting Invisibility: Arab Americans in Academia and Activism" (1999); and Nada Elia used the trope "the white sheep of the family" to analyze the ways in which Arab American women have been positioned among U.S. women of color feminist movements (2002).

Some scholars have argued that the aftermath of September 11 consolidated the racialization of the category "Arab/Middle Eastern/Muslim" as a signifier of

I am indebted to my graduate student Matthew Stiffler. His commitment, dedication, and intellectual contributions to this chapter have been truly invaluable. I am grateful to those who provided feedback on this chapter, including Evelyn Alsultany, Catherine Squires, Elizabeth Cole, Joe Gone, Andrea Smith, and Amaney Jamal. This introduction was developed in conversation with several colleagues to whom I am indebted, including Andrew Shryock, Louise Cainkar, Sarita See, and Minoo Moallem. Many thanks to Kent Ono and Kali Akuno, who encouraged me to pursue research on "race" and Arab Americans in the 1990s.

nonwhite Otherness[1] or that a "racialization of Islam" has underlain the post-9/11 backlash against persons perceived to be Arab, Middle Eastern, South Asian, and/or Muslim. Exemplifying this perspective, Minoo Moallem argues that "In the wake of the horrific events of September 11th, 'Islamic fundamentalism,' a discourse which has been decades in the making, has finally come into its own. The representation of Islamic fundamentalism in the West," she contends, "is deeply influenced by the general racialization of Muslims in a neo-racist idiom, which has its roots in cultural essentialism and a conventional Eurocentric notion of 'people without history.' Islamic fundamentalism has become a generic signifier used constantly to single out the Muslim other, in its irrational, morally inferior, and barbaric masculinity and its passive, victimized, and submissive femininity" (2002, 298).

Alongside the proliferation of hate crimes against persons perceived to be Arab, Muslim, or South Asian after the attacks of September 11, 2001, educational institutions, government officials, and nonprofit organizations fervently reached out to Arab, Muslim, and South Asian communities with a series of diversity initiatives. In this sense, the "invisible citizens" became "visible subjects."[2] In the aftermath of September 11, 2001, a series of essays referred to Arab Americans with terms such as "no longer invisible" (Cainkar 2002a) or as having "hyper-visibility" (Alsultany 2006). The terms of "visibility" have required that an individual or community be "seen" as a potential victim of racism in order to be "included" in liberal multicultural diversity initiatives. Yet they have promoted "tolerance" through the condemnation of hate crimes while remaining silent on the federal government's targeting of Arab, South Asian, and Muslim immigrants (without evidence of criminal activity). Similarly, within months following September 11, most media coverage of the backlash focused on individual hate crimes that took place in the public sphere while downplaying attacks against those targeted by state violence at detention centers, airports, immigration and naturalization service centers, and the workplace. In this sense, the terms upon which Arab Americans became "hyper-visible" within dominant public U.S. discourses on multiculturalism after 9/11 paralleled the rhetoric of the Bush administration and

1. See Volpp (2003, 147) and Naber (2000), who write about the construction of the category Arab/Middle Eastern/Muslim.

2. See Kien Lee (2002) for an analysis of how communities across the United States have initiated activities to build solidarity with Arabs, Muslims, and other Middle Easterners.

the corporate media that distinguished between "good Arabs or Muslims" and "bad Muslims."[3] Mahmood Mamdani argues that within official U.S. discourse after 9/11, "'bad Muslims' were clearly responsible for terrorism . . . 'good Muslims' were anxious to clear their names and consciences of this horrible crime . . . and unless proved to be 'good,' every Muslim was presumed to be 'bad'" (2004, 15). Government policies, such as the PATRIOT Act, special registration, and FBI investigations put the logic of "good Muslim/bad Muslim" into practice by targeting noncitizens as "potential terrorists" or "bad Muslims," and distinguishing them from "citizens" or "good Muslims."[4] Within liberal discourses on tolerance and diversity, the privileging of individual hate crimes over the institutionalization of state violence facilitated official U.S. narratives that sought to reduce the post-9/11 backlash against persons perceived to be Arab, Middle Eastern, Muslim, or South Asian to the acts of a "few bad apples" and to cover up the systematic institutionalized nature of the violence. The Abu Ghraib torture case is but one example in which the "few bad apples" argument served to overshadow state accountability in promoting violence against persons perceived to be Arab or Muslim. In this case, the Bush administration argued that the abuses were isolated acts committed by low-ranking personnel—even though authorities either ordered or implicitly condoned the abuses (Mayer 2005; Hersh 2004).

The aftermath of 9/11 not only illustrated what critical race scholars have been arguing for decades—that "visibility" is a power-laden project that has the effect of silencing critiques of state violence and the structural inequalities that produce hatred and racism—but also revealed the objectification that often accompanies "inclusion." Moallem and Boal argue that multiculturalism "consistently evades engagement with three pressing issues: the enduring heritage of Eurocentrism, the question of justice, and the connections between national and

---

3. Here I build on Mamdani (2004) and Alsultany's (2005) analyses of Good Muslim/Bad Muslim.

4. Here I build upon Volpp's analysis of the ways that racism has operated within the context of the post-9/11 backlash in terms of a binary opposition between the "citizen" and the "terrorist" (2003). I also build upon Kent Ono's analysis of "potential terrorist." Ono argues that "'potential terrorists' serves as a useful concept to begin to address political and media discourses that produce a creative, if fictional, 'network' or interconnection along racial, gender, national, sexual, political, and ideological lines. Hate crimes, surveillance by the repressive apparatus of the state, and surveillance and disciplining technologies have erected a powerful discursive barrier to full participation in society by those marked as 'potential terrorist'" (2005, 443).

global domains." Multiculturalism, they argue, "contrives to efface all historicity in its consumption of the present" (1999, 244).[5] After decades of silence on Arab American issues in U.S. academia, September 11 sparked discourses on the "new targeted communities" that framed attacks against persons perceived to be "Arab," "Muslim," or "South Asian" in the public sphere as a "new" crisis—as if September 11 was a dividing line of history; as if the only "targeted communities" were Arabs and Muslims; and as if the Bush administration's anti-Arab, anti-Muslim state policies were not located within complex histories of European colonialism and U.S.-led imperialism in Arab homelands and decades of state-sponsored harassment of Arab American individuals, particularly those who are politically active. Along with discourses on "the new targeted communities" came an increased interest in and funding for Middle East and Islamic studies, partly owing to the intelligence needs of the U.S. war machine. In the 1990s, I learned of several cases in which academic advisors told their Ph.D. students specializing in Arab American Studies that they were committing academic suicide because they would never land academic jobs in this area. Perhaps the heightened interest in Arab American studies on university campuses and the growing number of tenure-track positions in this field has diminished the need for such concerns.

This book transgresses the liberal multiculturalist "add on" approach that has tended to dominate official academic and popular discussions on Arab Americans since 9/11. It highlights the heterogeneity of Arab American histories and the shifting and contradictory historical contexts through which Arab Americans have engaged with immigration, assimilation, and racialization. It also locates the attacks of September 11, 2001, as a turning point, as opposed to the starting point, of historics of anti-Arab racism in the United States. As many essays in this volume demonstrate, September 11 was a turning point in that representations of "terrorism" and "Islamic fundamentalism" have increasingly replaced other representations (i.e., the rich Arab oil sheikh and belly-dancing harem girls) and have become more fervently deployed in anti-Arab state policies and everyday patterns of engagement than ever before.

---

5. Here I am building on Moallem and Boal's definition of U.S. liberal multiculturalism: "[M]ulticultural nationalism operates on the fault line between a universalism based on the notion of an abstract citizenship that at the same time systematically produces sexualized, gendered, and racialized bodies, and particularistic claims for recognition and justice by minoritized groups" (1999, 245).

The multiple, shifting, and contradictory lenses through which Arabs and Arab Americans have been regarded in the United States before and after September 11, 2001, have sparked significant debate about the importance of "race" to Arab American studies and the place of Arab Americans within racial justice movements.[6] In conversation with these debates, contributors to this book engage with several questions: Is "race" a useful concept for exploring the relationship between U.S.-led war in Arab homelands and the marginalization of Arabs in the diaspora? What are the theoretical and political implications of bringing Arab American studies into conversation with the study of "race" in the United States? Are whiteness studies relevant to Arab American studies? What is the relationship between Islamaphobia and "race" and "racism"? What are the transformative possibilities for organizing around the rubric of racial justice for Arab American scholars and activists?

THE POLITICS OF NAMING

The meaning of the term "Arab" is contested. Commonly used among scholars is the definition of "Arab" as a cultural and linguistic term that includes persons from countries where the primary language is Arabic. Another definition, influenced by the Arab nationalist movements that emerged in resistance to Ottoman rule and European colonization, assumes that Arab is also a national identity and that Arabs share a language and a common cultural and imagined national community. Since 1945, nations for which the primary language is Arabic have combined to form the Arab League, and the members of the Arab League are considered the Arab nations, including Algeria, Bahrain, Djibouti, Egypt, Iraq, Jordan, Kuwait, Lebanon, Libya, Morocco, Oman, Palestine, Qatar, Saudi Arabia, Somalia, Sudan, Syria, Tunisia, the United Arab Emirates, and Yemen. Although U.S. popular cultural representations often conflate the categories "Arab" and "Muslim," not all Arabs are Muslim and not all Muslims are Arabs. The top six countries with the largest Muslim population are Indonesia (170.3 million), Pakistan (136 million),

---

6. Between January 2002 and January 2003, I conducted a research study on the increased emergence of Arab- and Arab American–related issues within racial justice, immigrant rights, and anti-war movements. My research demonstrated that efforts to insure the representation of Arab and Arab American activists within these movements substantially increased after September 11, 2001 (Naber 2002).

Bangladesh (106 million), India (103 million), Turkey (62.4 million), and Iran (60.7 million).[7] None of these countries is considered Arab. Arab countries include a diversity of linguistic, ethnic, and religious groups. Religious groups include, but are not limited to, Christians, Jews, and Druze. Non-Arab ethnic minorities include, but are not limited to, Kurds, Amazighs, and Armenians.

Before turning to the issue of Arab Americans and "race," it is crucial to recognize the complexities that come with efforts to classify Arab immigrants and Arab Americans. The religious, ethnic, and linguistic diversity of the Arab region gives at least some insight into why the federal government as well as Arab individuals and communities have found reaching a consensus over *who* is an Arab and what constitutes Arabness to be a particularly arduous task. Suad Joseph writes: "There are Palestinians, Iraqis, Kuwaitis, Yemenis, Saudi Arabians, Bahreinis, Qataris, Duabis, Egyptians, Libyans, Tunisians, Moroccans, Algerians, Sudanese, Eritreans, and Mauritanians; there are Maronites, Catholics, Protestants, Greek Orthodox, Jews, Sunnis, Shi'a, Druze, Sufis, Alawites, Nestorians, Assyrians, Copts, Chaldeans, and Bahais; there are Berbers, Kurds, Armenians, bedu, gypsies, and many others with different languages, religions, ethnic, and national identifications and cultures who are all congealed as Arab in popular representation whether or not those people may identify as Arab" (Joseph 1999a, 260).

Ever since the late 1880s, when the first significant group of Arab immigrants came to the United States, the terms of Arab identity have been contested and shifting.[8] The first significant group of immigrants were from the Ottoman provinces of Syria, Mount Lebanon, and Palestine. According to Samhan, the federal government classified them along with other Ottoman subjects as originating from "Turkey in Asia" (1999, 216). Immigration reforms that were passed in 1893 led to the classification of Arabic-speaking immigrants as "Syrians" after 1899 (216). Several scholars have argued that these identity categories diverged from the familial, village, or religious modes of categorization through which early immigrants tended to identify (Majaj 2000, 321). The end of the Ottoman Empire in 1917 and the emergence of distinct Arab nations that are often referred to collectively as the "Arab world" marked another shift in the identity terms deployed by

---

7. Islamic Web (n.d.).

8. Although Arab immigration to the United States predates the nineteenth century, the first significant group came to the United States in the late 1880s. See Kayyali (2006) for a description of Arab immigration to the United States before 1880.

both the federal government and Arab individuals and communities. For example, Naff argues that for early immigrants from Mount Lebanon, an area formerly located within the Ottoman province of Syria, the term "Lebanese" was given political legitimacy in the 1920s as a national label or identity and was adopted by most immigrants originating in Mount Lebanon (1985, 2).

Alongside the collapse of the Ottoman Empire, and particularly during the 1950s and 1960s, Arab nationalism emerged as a framework for resisting European colonization and intervention in the Arab region. While Arab nationalist tendencies proliferated among Arab immigrants for decades, widespread in Arab American studies literature is that the 1967 Arab-Israeli war marked a watershed for members of the Arab American community who were "dismayed and extremely disappointed to see how greatly one-sided and pro-Israeli the American communications media were in reporting on the Middle East" (Suleiman 1999, 10).[9] Michael Suleiman adds that this war "reinforced and strengthened their sense of an Arab identity" and sparked the emergence of a pan-ethnic Arab American identity (ibid.).

On the level of federal government racial categories, a 1978 classification scheme located Arabs within the broader rubric of "persons originating in Europe, the Middle East, and North Africa" (Samhan 1999). In 1997, the Office of Management and Budget, based on a collaboration with various Arab American community organizations, noted a lack of consensus about the definition of an Arab ethnic category and suggested that further research be done to improve data on this population group. Census 2000 added the classification "Arab ancestry" within a separate part of the census to obtain specific information about persons from the Middle East and North Africa who identify an Arab ancestry. The federal government and the major national Arab American community organizations have yet to reach a consensus on the appropriate term for naming

9. Hani Bawardi (2006) critiques dominant narratives in Arab American studies that have argued that no Arab American political organizations existed before 1967. Bawardi argues that an Arab American national identity existed ever since the first period of early immigration to the United States in the late 1880s and early 1900s, particularly through the involvement of Arab immigrants within transnational Arab organizations that were unequivocally anti-imperialist, anti-colonialist, and anti-Ottoman. Davidson argues that a "determined lobbying and educational effort on behalf of the Palestinians" did arise "after the issuance of Balfour Declaration and sought to organize around, persuade about, and debate the issue of Palestine within the Arab-American community and American society at large" (1999, 229).

immigrants from Arabic-speaking countries. Within the field of Arab American Studies, scholars have tended to refer to immigrants from the Ottoman province of Syria before 1920 as Syrian and the post–World War II immigrants as Arabs or Arab Americans.

Some Arab and Arab American activists have contested the terms "Arab" or "Arab American" as rubrics for organizing identity. They have argued that these terms are nationalist in scope and therefore exclusionary toward non-Arab minorities in the region.[10] Feminist and queer activists in particular have proposed the geographic-based term "Southwest Asian and North African" (often referred to as SWANA) as an alternative that includes non-Arab minorities, transcends patriarchal and homophobic nationalisms, and opens up possibilities for alliance building between people from Arab nations and other nations in the region, such as Iran, who share a similar history in the context of U.S. imperialism and war in the region. This perspective also contends that SWANA is a useful alternative to the term "Middle East," a Eurocentric term produced in the context of European expansion and conquest. Others have privileged religious identities such as "Muslim" or "Muslim American" over the nation-based label "Arab American" on the grounds that their primary loyalty is one rooted in faith and the divine. In some contexts, scholars have documented an interplay between an increased relevance of a "Muslim American" compared to an "Arab American" identity alongside the post-1980s rise of global Islamic movements as mechanisms for resisting Western imperialism (Naber 2006; Cainkar 2004c). While these examples are not exhaustive, they represent the diversity and historically and politically specific ways in which identity categories are imagined and performed.

Scholars have tended to study Arab immigration to the United States in two periods, pre- and post–World War II, and have argued that the first large influx of Arab immigrants were predominantly Christians from Mount Lebanon and came from Greater Syria at the turn of the twentieth century (Naff 1985; Suleiman 1999; Shakir 1997; Aswad 1974; Elkholy 1969). In this literature, a general consensus is that early migrants came to the United States out of economic necessity and for personal advancement. Repeatedly cited within accounts of Arab American histories are two economic setbacks of the mid-1800s in Mount

---

10. The organization SWANABAQ (South West Asian and North African Bay Area Queers) based in San Francisco exemplifies efforts to create more inclusive rubrics for organizing identities based on shared cultural and political histories that are not nationalist in scope.

Lebanon, coupled with the demographic pressures of an exploding population that tended to inspire the early migration: the opening of the Suez canal, which sidetracked world traffic from Syria to Egypt so that Japanese silk became a major competitor to the Lebanese silk industry, and the invasion of Lebanese vineyards by the phylloxera pest, which nearly destroyed the vineyards (Khater 2001, 59; Suleiman 1999, 2). The more contentious debates within the study of early migration are over the extent to which Christian oppression under Ottoman rulers and the concomitant presence of Western missionaries ignited Arab Christian migration in the early years.[11]

The majority of historical accounts argue that before World War II most migrants were poor, uneducated, unskilled workers who were illiterate in Arabic and English and that the most common occupation among early migrants was pack peddling, although mill work and factory work were also common among early immigrants (Shakir 1997; Naff 1985; Khater 2001; Hooglund 1987). Naff argues that in some cases, pack peddling became a means toward eventually owning a dry-goods store and that peddling routes also led to established settlements of Syrians. Hooglund has added that industrial cities in the eastern and midwestern states, such as Fall River, Massachusetts; Pittsburgh; Detroit; and Michigan City, Indiana, attracted large numbers of Syrian immigrants to work in steel mills and textile factories, and on the railroads. Although early immigrants tended to identify as sojourners who hoped to acquire wealth and return to their country of origin, the majority eventually became permanent U.S. residents (Abraham 1995; Suleiman 1994).[12]

11. Alixa Naff (1985), Albert Hourani (1992), Najib Saliba (1992), Charles Issawi (1992), Samir Khalaf (1987), Michael Suleiman (1999), Barbara Aswad (1974), Evelyn Shakir (1997), and Akram Khater (2001) list demographic pressures in Mount Lebanon, economic setbacks such as the declining silk industry, the newly developed intellectual class's distaste for Ottoman rule, the presence of American Protestant missionaries, and the looming conscription of Christians into the Ottoman army among the causes of increased emigration. Several scholars have labeled the idea that religious persecution was a major factor in the decision to emigrate a "myth" that can be traced to "mainly . . . the post–World War II studies on Arabs in America" and the rhetoric of advocates for a "French-ruled, Maronite-dominated Lebanese entity" (Naff 1985, 86–88). Khalaf (1987) and Shakir (1997) contend that the missionary presence influenced emigration, while Khater (2001) and Naff (1985) do not emphasize the Protestant missionaries' role in emigration.

12. It is estimated that by 1916, 100,000 Arabs had immigrated to the United States (Naff 1985, 2), and by 1924, the Arab population in the U.S. reached 200,000. Scholars approximate

Post–World War II immigration and displacement to the United States was more diverse than in the early years. As Michael Suleiman explains, immigrants came from nearly every Arabic-speaking country and included nearly equal numbers of Christians and Muslims (1999, 9). While early Arab immigrants were primarily Christian and from Greater Syria, post–World War II immigrants have included Arabs from Gulf States and from North Africa as well as a greater number of Muslim immigrants, adding a greater variation in appearance and skin color, cultural patterns, and religious groupings. Post–World War II immigrants and refugees have also been more diverse in terms of socioeconomic class. Moreover, post–World War II immigration has included more individuals and communities who have come to the United States because of displacement by war, colonialism, neocolonialism, and imperialism than before.[13] Increasing U.S. economic and military intervention in the Arab world since World War II has underscored a deepening continuity between U.S.-led war in the Arab region, processes of immigration and displacement from the Arab region to the United States, and the escalating targeting of Arab immigrants and Arab Americans. This book asks: How have these diverse histories mapped onto a society like the United States, which has been obsessed with organizing social difference along the lines of "race"?

THE EMERGENCE OF RACIAL CLASSIFICATION
IN THE UNITED STATES

While there is no consensus among scholars about the meaning of race before European colonization in the Western hemisphere, there is a consensus that a significant shift in the concept of race took place between the fifteenth and

---

that 195,000 were Christians and 5,000 were divided between Muslims and Druze—of this Christian population, the Maronites claimed 90,000, the Greek Orthodox 85,000, the Greek Catholic 10,000, Protestants 5,000—and 5,000 were unaccounted for (Hitti, cited in Ansara 1958, 12).

13. See McAlister (2001) for an overview of U.S. expansion in the Middle East and the capitalist search for new markets abroad after World War II, in which she refers to Lebanese immigration in the context of the Lebanese civil war, Palestinian displacement to the United States in the context of Israeli occupation, the displacement of Iraqi refugees in the context of U.S.-led war on Iraq, Yemeni immigration in the context of civil war in Yemen, and general worsening of economic conditions in the region during this period and beyond. There is also a note on U.S. interests in the region before World War II.

eighteenth centuries (Rodriguez 2000, 34; Baker 1998, 1). This perspective contends that efforts aimed at racial classification that were based upon scientific racism emerged in Western Europe and the United States during this period. Attempts to categorize humans into different varieties or types developed in the context of the rise of biology, anthropology, and other sciences in their Western European form; late eighteenth- and early nineteenth-century European "Enlightenment" concepts of observation, classification, progress, and romanticism; the rise of capitalism; and European expansion and colonialism.[14] Baker argues that between the sixteenth and eighteenth centuries, the term "race" consisted of folk classifications that were interchangeable with concepts like nation, type, variety, or stock, which were perceived to reflect inherent natural, biological differences that were not malleable and "merged with the Anglican and Puritan belief in the sacredness of property rights and the individual" (1998, 11). The idea that religious and cultural differences were based upon biological differences helped to justify the colonization of Native American land and the reduction of African Americans to chattel slavery. Rana argues that as "Catholic Spain . . . undertook the benevolent role of sending missionaries to spread the work of a Christian God to heathens in the Americas. . . , notions of race were being consolidated through ideas of nation and religion" (Rana 2007, 153). He adds that the Spanish, who developed a schema for distinguishing between Christians and "infidel Muslims" after having just finished a war driving Muslims out of the Iberian peninsula, transferred the concept of "religious infidel" onto what they defined as "heathen Indians" in their conquest on the other side of the Atlantic (154).

Ideologies of religious difference inherited from Spain thus shaped racial ideologies in the United States and the concomitant efforts to destroy Native American land and people (Shohat and Stam 1994, 60–91). As the significance of slavery to the capitalist economy increased, religion was used to justify the classification of Native Americans and African Americans as "pagan" and "soulless." In the eighteenth century, amid the institutionalization of slavery and the diminished legitimacy of religion as a justification for racism, biological, zoological, and botanical scientific theories became essential to the formation of racial thinking. By the second half of the eighteenth century, scholars formed "an elaborate system to classify races into a rigid hierarchical scheme" (Baker 1998, 14). A North American scientific system, coupled with the colonizers' popular thinking

14. See Bernal (1987) and Baker (1998, 11).

about racial hierarchies, coincided with political goals and economic interests. This process institutionalized racial inferiority and socially structured racial categories as well as the idea that "negroes and Indians were savages not worthy of citizenship or freedom" (Baker 1998, 14). By the latter half of the nineteenth century, the construction of race reached its full development within the legal apparatus of the United States, and various state governments conspired with science to legitimize structural inequality by sanctioning it in law. Colonialism thus produced the conditions for social and political institutions, such as slavery, that were justified through racial theory (Gossett 1997, 17).

That the racial categorization of Native Americans and African Americans took on contrasting form illustrates that the terms upon which racial categories have operated are malleable and shifting, depending on historical and political circumstances. In the nineteenth century, for example, a minimum "blood quantum" was required to be granted racial classification as Native American. Prior to this period, membership in Native American tribes did not require a particular degree of "blood." Moreover, in 1860, the census first began counting untaxed Indians. According to Rodriguez, until 1940, the federal government classified Native Americans as "Indians." The federal government used the term "American Indians" for the next twenty years and the term "Indians (Amer.)" between 1970 and 1990 (Rodriguez 2000, 88). Native Americans who paid taxes were counted as white until all Indians were first counted separately in the 1860 census. They were then classified as a "not-white, not-Negro group within the 'other races' category, along with the Chinese" (88). Since the 1970s, Indians have been classified along with Eskimos and Aleuts in a separate "race" category, "Native American Indian." The 2000 census used the category "American Indian" or "Alaska Native" (88). Annette Jaimes uses the term "bureaucratic racism" to refer to the federal and state process that determines who may or may not be recognized as Indian. She argues that such federal policies are a result of the five-hundred-year heritage of colonialist ideological and legal constructions of American Indians and the U.S. government's treatment of indigenous populations as a colonized people in their own homelands. By determining how the government classifies American Indians, bureaucratic racism makes it increasingly difficult for an individual of intertribal descent to claim recognition as Indian. Such policies, Jaimes argues, have been designed to break up communal land, co-opt indigenous land for non-Indian usage, and sustain the process of colonization (1996, 49–53).

In the context of the Jim Crow laws of the South that were established in the late nineteenth century after reconstruction and lasted until the 1960s, African Americans were classified according to "blood" ancestry.[15] In the early 1900s, the "one-drop rule" was adopted as a written law in several states. This law determined that a single drop of "black blood" makes a person black and sought to facilitate segregation and prevent miscegenation. Despite the extent of racial mixing, one drop of "black blood" rendered a person "black," whereas for Native Americans, racial mixing had the effect of excluding a person from classification as Native American. As Jack Forbes puts it, "with any mixture of blood, the 'Indian' is supposed to disappear. . . . White North Americans are always finding 'Blacks' and they are always losing 'Indians,' or so it would seem" (1990, 2). Andrea Smith explains that while white supremacy equates blackness with slaveability as a justification for the commodification of blacks as property in a capitalist system, it requires that Native Americans must "always be disappearing, in order to allow non-indigenous peoples rightful claim over this land" (2007). Thus classification of those who did not qualify to be Native American and were classified as white did not necessarily signify privilege or a decrease in their vulnerability to racism, but it facilitated erasure by contributing to efforts aimed at denying Native Americans claims to their indigenous ancestry and to their land.

Within the context of immigration to the United States, "race" has been a central framework for locating immigrants along a continuum from black to white and thereby determining the degree to which they deserved or did not deserve citizenship (Ong 2003, 11). The classification of diverse communities with a shared language, birthplace, or geographic origin within a fixed, homogenous identity category has intersected with and facilitated restrictive immigration

15. See Finkleman (2006) for more information on the "black codes" that were enforced from 1865 to 1866. For African Americans, the end of the nineteenth century entailed an intensification of racist laws and racial violence. In states such as Texas, Louisiana, Mississippi, Alabama, Georgia, Florida, South Carolina, North Carolina, Virginia, Arkansas, Tennessee, Oklahoma, and Kansas, elected, appointed, or hired government authorities began to require or permit discrimination. The following forms of racism were crucial during this period: *Plessy v. Ferguson* (1986), which upheld racial segregation; voter suppression in the southern states; the denial of economic opportunity; and private acts of violence and mass racial violence against African Americans, often encouraged by government authorities. "Jim Crow" was the term used to refer to the interplay between law, public and private acts of discrimination, the denial of economic opportunity, and antiblack violence in the southern states.

policies and racial exclusion. The United States passed its first nationalization law in 1790, granting naturalization to aliens who were classified as "free white persons." This "racial prerequisite to citizenship endured for over a century and a half—remaining in force until 1952" (Rodriguez 2000, 1). In every census thereafter, the U.S. population was racially classified, even though the racial categories used and the terms upon which they were deployed were constantly changing. At the turn of the twentieth century, the U.S. racial classification system and decisions about whether or to what extent particular individuals should be granted the right to citizenship were based upon scientific racism, or the deployment of science to explain differences and hierarchies between perceived racial groups. Scientific racism emerged in continuity with centuries of colonization of Native American land and the enslavement of African Americans that were justified through constructed racial hierarchies. Scientific racism was also invoked to rationalize the exclusion of Asian immigrants and the colonization of the Philippines, Guam, and Puerto Rico, among other territories.[16]

Although the census is not the only site for defining the rules through which race and racism operate, it provides a useful example of how "race" can often appear to reflect some underlying scientific reality and how the meaning of "race" in the United States has changed depending on historical and political circumstances. In 1790, the census divided the population into the racial categories "free whites," "slaves," and "all other free persons" (American Indians) (Prewitt 2002, 7). In 1820, the census added "free colored persons" to the racial scheme. After the Civil War, the census used the categories mulatto, quadroon, and octoroon, based on the proliferation of interest in "shades of color"; these categories were dropped in the early 1900s. During that period, the census included Asians within its racial categories. This practice often entailed a conflation of race and nation or meant that race would be determined according to one's nation or country of origin. In 1890, the census distinguished between Japanese and Chinese. The census added Hindus, a religious group, to be counted as a racial group in 1920 through a conflation of religion and race. The census first used the term Mexican in 1930 but dropped it shortly after, when the Mexican government contested the classification of Mexicans as a "race" (Prewitt 2002, 7). During this

16. For research on the relationship between racism and legislation limiting the opportunities for citizenship for particular immigrant groups, see Hing (2004); Ono and Sloop (2002); and Ngai (2004).

period, classification separated those entitled to civic participation from those whose classification was cause for exclusion. As Prewitt argues, "the slave system, the relocation of Indians to reservations, implementation of the separate but equal doctrine, denial of citizenship to Asians, racist immigration quotas in the 1920s, and Japanese-American internment are familiar chapters in this story. From 1790 until the civil rights movement, policy designed to protect the numerical and political supremacy of Americans of European ancestry used a classification system that assigned individuals to a discrete racial group" (2002, 8).

The early 1900s were characterized by intensified nativism in which racism permeated nationalism in the form of anti-immigrant sentiment that distinguished between "Americans born in the United States" and "immigrants."[17] Anti-immigrant nativism took shape in the context of white supremacist reactions to the increase in the number of new immigrants and those who had been brought to the United States through conquest, territorial expansion, and exploitative labor policies as well as the desire to protect the numerical, political, and economic supremacy of Americans of European ancestry.[18] Groups classified as non-European (such as Mexicans, Caribbean Islanders, Native Hawaiians, Pacific Islanders, Native Alaskans, and Asians) were added to the landscape of U.S. racial and immigrant politics through conquest, imperial war, territorial expansion, and the need for cheap immigrant labor.[19] In the late nineteenth and early twentieth centuries, public officials had instituted a policy that required immigration officers to document the "race" of new immigrants. According to Roediger, "they used a supplemental form providing information on 'color,' 'country and province of birth,' 'mother tongue,' and 'religion' to define the 'race' of those arriving." For example, Roediger explains, "Russian birth plus Yiddish mother tongue plus Jewish religion equaled 'Hebrew race'" (2005, 16).[20] In 1903, the racial classification process privileged "stock or blood" over language,

17. See Hingham (1994) for an analysis of anti-immigrant nativism in the early 1900s.

18. Anti-immigrant sentiment took on different forms in different parts of the U.S. Anti-immigrant nativism was intensified in places that included larger numbers of new immigrants (Hingham 1994).

19. For example, between 1850 and 1880, in the context of American expansion into Asia and Asian immigration to the United States, the Chinese population in U.S. increased fifteen-fold.

20. Roediger adds, "The resulting data were sometimes grouped under the heading 'Race' and sometimes under 'Race or People.' In 1903, new passenger lists added a 'Race or People' heading 'to be determined by the stock from which they spring and the language they speak'" (2005, 16).

though the process for how to arrive at such a determination remained uncertain (Roediger 2005, 16). Yet what remained clear was that white state actors had the power to make such decisions.

In the late 1800s and early 1900s, previous racial thinking and patterns of white supremacy had inspired a related attack on European newcomers. The increase in anti-immigrant sentiment, including anti-Semitism, at this time was inspired, in part, by the increase in immigration from Europe that was Mediterranean, Slavic, and Jewish, which placed whiteness more easily into question than it had for German, Irish, and Scandinavian immigrants. Anti-immigrant nativists who had targeted those who were unquestionably considered nonwhite, such as Japanese, were working toward attaching similar provisions to immigration measures that would affect those with questionable ancestry, which in the early 1900s included southern Europeans. According to Roediger, "[I]n 1898, just as the Spanish-American War and the validation of segregation in *Plessy v. Ferguson* helped solidify Deep South–style white supremacy nationally, collecting 'race' statistics among European immigrants took a decisive step forward." Roediger explains that "Powderly, the U.S. commissioner-general of immigration, along with AFL veteran Edward F. McSweeney, devised a new system of enumerating by race" between 1898 and 1902 (2005, 15). This system classified new immigrants by race and gave "clues to their characteristics and their resultant influence upon the community of which they are to become members."[21] At this time, Southern Europeans were classified as belonging to a semi-Asiatic ancestry and were therefore deemed "questionable."

Roediger explains, "the division of European immigration into Teutonic, Iberian, Celtic, and Slavic 'races or peoples or more properly subdivisions of race' during critical years was, as Perlmann puts it, 'partly political' in that it 'provided a way of distinguishing racially the old [mostly northern and western European immigration] from the new immigration'" (2005, 17). Roediger suggests that the term "new immigration" was remarkable for its ability to describe recent arrivals as racially different. In his view, it was a term encompassing history and biology, culture and stock. The division between Europeans into "races" (from superior Nordics of northwestern Europe to the inferior southern and eastern races of Alpines, Mediterraneans, and Jews) was based on intersections between class and

---

21. This statement was made by Joel Perlmann in his important study of "'federal race classifications' from 1898 to 1913" (cited in Roediger 2005, 15).

race in that southern and eastern European immigrants tended to be workers or "the lower classes" who were also considered to be the "lower races" among Europeans (and the upper classes, mostly northern and western Europeans, were considered "racially pure" and therefore, superior) (Sacks 1994, 80–82).

In the early twentieth century, scientific racism coupled with eugenics, or the idea of "breeding for a 'better' humanity" (Sacks 1994, 80), rationalized the hierarchical ranking of the human population. It also rationalized legislation supporting racial segregation, miscegenation, and the restriction of immigration from Asia, Africa, and southern and eastern Europe. Between 1907 and 1920, the federal government began collecting data on naturalization. While over one million people obtained citizenship under racially restrictive naturalization laws that required northwestern European ancestry for whiteness and therefore citizenship, many others were rejected (Haney-López 1996, 1). This racial prerequisite requirement emerged from the histories of African slavery, the colonization of Native Americans, and the exclusion of Asian immigrants in which exclusion from citizenship was explained in racial terms. By the 1920s, eugenics consolidated the process by which questions about immigration and citizenship became questions about biology and solidified the notion that "real Americans were white and real whites came from northwest Europe" (Sacks 1994, 81). Scientific racism inspired the process that excluded and expelled Chinese in 1882, for example, and then closed the door to immigration by virtually all Asians and most southern Europeans in 1924 (Sacks 1994). Bill Ong Hing argues that after Chinese exclusion, the demands of agricultural labor in Hawaii and California inspired efforts to attract Japanese workers, yet by the turn of the century, there emerged a proliferation of adverse sentiment toward Japanese laborers (2004, 41). This adversity emerged in the context of Japan's victories over China in 1895 and Russia in 1905 and the concomitant perception of Japanese as potential enemies (42). Filipinos came to the United States in the context of a process of U.S. colonization that was justified by the notion that "they are unfit for self-government" and "in need of Christianizing." This colonialist rhetoric translated into the notion that "they are unfit to become American" upon immigration to the United States. As the Philippines became a U.S. colony, Filipinos thus became noncitizen nationals of the United States. Efforts to exclude Filipinos proliferated, particularly after World War I, when they began immigrating in significant numbers (2004, 44). Between 1911 and 1917, two thousand Asian immigrants immigrated to the United States, and over seventeen hundred were denied entry on the grounds that they were classified as nonwhite (45). Although lower courts classified them as whites under the citizenship laws of 1790 and 1890, the 1923 Supreme Court case *United States v. Bahgat Singh Thind* (261 U.S. 204) entailed the reversal of this racial stance and determined that "Indians, like Japanese would no longer be considered white persons—and are therefore ineligible to become naturalized citizens." In this context, the 1917 act of Congress extended Chinese exclusion laws to all Asians, and only Filipinos and Guanamanians, persons whose homelands were colonized by the United States and under U.S. jurisdiction, were exempt for this exclusion (Hing 2004, 46).

The broader U.S. context of anti-immigrant nativism following World War I produced the conditions for greater prohibitions on immigration. The Immigration Act of 1924, or the National Origins Act, Asian Exclusion Act, or Johnson-Reed Act, limited the number of immigrants who could be admitted from any country to 2 percent of the number of people from that country who were already living in the United States in 1890, according to that year's census. It excluded immigration to the United States of Asian laborers, specifically Chinese immigrants who did not agree to work, and Chinese prostitutes, and had the effect of preventing Japanese Americans from legally owning land. It superseded the 1921 Emergency Quota Act. The law was aimed at further restricting the southern and eastern Europeans who had begun to enter the country in large numbers beginning in the 1890s, as well as East Asians and Asian Indians, who were prohibited from immigrating entirely. It set no limits on immigration from Latin America. The act halted "undesirable" immigration with quotas. It barred specific origins from the Asia-Pacific Triangle that included Japan, China, the Philippines, Laos, Siam (Thailand), Cambodia, Singapore (then a British colony), Korea, Vietnam, Indonesia, Burma (Myanmar), India, Ceylon (Sri Lanka), and Malaysia. It barred these immigrants because their "race" was deemed undesirable. Among the arguments advanced in support of this act were those that stressed the racial superiority of Anglo-Saxons and the unassimilability of foreigners (Hing 2004, 46). The quotas remained in place with minor alterations until the Immigration and Naturalization Act of 1965. For eugenicists, "admitting 'degenerate breeding stock' seemed one of the worst sins the nation could commit against itself"; "environment could never modify an immigrant's germ plasm"; and "only a rigid selection of the best immigrant stock could improve rather than pollute endless generations to come" (Hingham 1994, 151). Early Arab immigration to the United States in the late 1800s and early 1900s thus emerged within a broader context in which definitions of "race" assumed that differences in moral character and intelligence between social groups were based in biology and nature (Banton 1977). In the 1930s, the U.S. census distinguished southern and eastern Europeans from northwestern Europeans also on the basis of the eugenicist racial distinctions of this period (Sacks 1994, 82).

Many scholars have compared the backlash against Arab immigrant communities after the attacks of September 11, 2001, to Japanese internment during World War II, particularly in terms of the similar processes by which Japanese and Arabs, Muslims, and South Asians have been targeted within the United States in the context of U.S.-led war in their homelands and the similarities between state and media discourses that represented them as culturally degenerate, menacing and sinister, and threatening to the nation in the process of legitimizing war and racism. In the case of Japanese internment, on December 7, 1941, Franklin D. Roosevelt issued Proclamation 2525, which was directed at Japanese "alien enemies" and legitimized the interment of over 120,000 Japanese Americans and the separate incarceration of Japanese aliens according to the Alien Enemy Act. Four years later, another proclamation, 2655, justified "alien removal," which provided that subjects deemed dangerous to public peace and safety would be subject to an order to depart or deportation (Hing 2004, 221).

Several scholars of Latino/a and Asian American studies have contended that assumptions about national origin have figured into histories of anti-Asian and anti-Latino/a racism. A prominent perspective within Asian American studies is that for Asian Americans, racial formation has been "defined not primarily in terms of biological racialism but in terms of institutionalized legal definitions of race and national origin" (Lowe 1996, 10). In their analysis of immigration legislation that has specifically targeted Latinos (such as Proposition 187), Ono and Sloop argue that a "racist discourse emerges that uses suspicion of the other as a strategy for the preservation of the self" (2002, 41).[22] This discourse, they argue, constructs a binary between citizens and documented immigrants versus those who are not, producing an intensified sense of "fear" of the undocumented other

22. Ono and Sloop argue that such laws are constructed as "the proper mechanism to stem the tide of criminality intrinsic to undocumented immigrants and to protect the citizen against 'others' who are either potentially or already criminal." They add that the biologistic racialization of Mexicans and Mexicanos and Chicanas and Chicanos in this discourse focus on them as more prone to criminality and violence than other groups (2002, 34).

(2002, 41). In her comparison between Asian and Mexican engagements with "race," Ngai argues that the legal racialization of these ethnic groups' national origin casts them as permanently foreign, unassimilable to the nation and ultimately, alien in the eyes of the nation (2004, 8). The divergent contexts through which various immigrant communities have engaged with European and U.S. constructs of "race" illustrate that "race" has operated as an unquestionable facet of virtually all immigrant histories in the United States and that "race" operates according to multiple, shifting logics depending on the context. How then, have dominant U.S. racial schemas positioned "the Arab" and how have Arab immigrants and Arab Americans been required to engage with "race" and "racism"?

"RACE" AND ARAB AMERICANS IN THE EARLY YEARS: 1880–1940

Several scholars have analyzed the position of Arabs and Arab Americans within U.S. racial schemas in terms of what Edward Said (1978) has termed "Orientalism," or the academic, political, and literary discourses on Arabs, Islam, and the Middle East originating in England and France and appearing later in the United States. Said argues that Orientalism constructs a binary opposition between East and West and attributes an immutable "essence" to the East or Orient. Orientalism, according to Said, continues to permeate Western media, government policies, and academia and operates as a discursive, ideological justification for Western colonial and imperial projects in the Middle East. Said's framework is useful for conceptualizing the ways in which Arabs and Arab Americans have been positioned within U.S. racial schemas.

On the level of immigration policy, the multiple and shifting terms for categorizing immigrants from Arabic-speaking countries have coincided with and facilitated a complex and contradictory process through which Arab immigrants have been brought into the U.S. racial classification system. In 1909, in the context of Jim Crow segregation laws of the southern and border states and the first significant period of Arab immigration to the United States, a federal court case in Georgia granted Syrian Costa George Najour the right to naturalization on the basis that he was considered to belong to the white or Caucasian race (Hassan 2002). Judge Newman, presiding over the case, explained, "I consider the Syrians as belonging to what we now recognize and what the world recognizes, as the white race. . . . The applicant comes from Mt. Lebanon, near Beirut. He is not particularly dark, and has none of the characteristics or appearances of the Mongolian race, but so far as I can see and judge, has the appearance and characteristics of the Caucasian race."[23] In 1914, in a South Carolina case, a Judge Smith denied Syrian immigrant George Dow a petition to become a U.S. citizen on the basis that "'Syrians might be free white persons, [but] not that particular free white person to whom the act of congress had donated the privilege of citizenship' in 1790—a privilege he ruled was intended for persons of European descent" (quoted in Samhan 1999, 217).[24] In the case of George Dow, the judge argued that whiteness is not a matter of physical appearance, linguistic, or ethnographic racial classifications but is one of geography. Since Dow was perceived to be "Asiatic," the judge argued that he was not European and, therefore, not white. This decision, although it affirmed the notion that "race" is a social construction and that particular actors have created what "race" is, was reversed in 1915 on scientific, congressional, and legal grounds.[25] The cases of Najour and Dow took place in a broader U.S. context in which anti-immigrant sentiment and nativism were not only rampant but were justified by a concept of "race" that operated to legitimize the classification of the human population in terms of beliefs about biological and civilizational evolution.

Other immigrants also participated in public debates over the racial identity of the Syrians.[26] Kalil A. Bishara, for example, representing a particular perspective among Maronite Christian immigrants in *The Origin of the Modern Syrian* (Bishara 1914), carefully detailed the genealogy of Syrians in ancient history, arguing that no group that was not Caucasian "had ever pitched a tent or set up a pillar" in Syria (Bishara 1914, 24). In this treatise, Bishara attempted to demonstrate that Syria has been "the rendez-vous of world powers . . . and they all were Caucasians" (39). In the conclusion of this piece, it becomes clear that Bishara identified Christianity as a key feature contributing to Syrians' whiteness and

23. See Haney-López (1996).

24. For further discussion of this case, see Hassan (2002); Suleiman (1999); Majaj (2000); Joseph (1999a).

25. See Haney-López (1996, 206) for further analysis on the reversal of this case.

26. While these debates tended to be highlighted in scholarly discussions about early Syrian immigrants and "race," less cited are examples of individuals who expressed less secure relationships to whiteness, those who were targeted by anti-immigrant sentiment. Also less visible in dominant scholarly discourses are the narratives of those who were critical of European and U.S. foreign policy, particularly those who were involved in transnational alliances organized around a commitment to the liberation of Palestine (Bawardi 2006).

hence their eligibility for American citizenship. Bishara also concedes that although Syrians are geographically "Asiatic," as Syria lies in the "near East," the "'Asiatic exclusion laws' [were] clearly meant to be a synonym of 'Mongolians' . . . who have a peculiar type of civilization of their own so radically different from our Christian civilization" (40). Bishara agreed that Syrians may be technically "Turks" or "Asiatic," but not so much as to "debar the Syrian" from American citizenship. In this case, historical conflations of religion, civilization, geographic origin, and "race" operated to justify the "whiteness" of early Arab immigrants.

Yet the association between racial superiority and a European origin inspired further investigation into Syrian origins, leading to the eventual appeal of the Dow case based on a report that said, "'they belong to the Semitic branch of the Caucasian race and are widely different from their rulers, the Turks, who are in origin, Mongolian'" (quoted in Naff 1985, 257). Although this case was appealed and established the "legal precedent that 'Syrians' meet the racial prerequisite for naturalization," it did not mark an official shift in the racial classification of Syrian immigrants during this period (Hassan 2002). In 1923, the Supreme Court denied a Syrian petition for naturalization on the grounds that Syria fell under a 1917 restrictive immigration act—which bars immigration for natives from most countries east of the Persian Gulf. Later, it was proven that Syrians do not fall within those wartime restrictions (Samhan 1999, 217).

Lisa Majaj explains that Arab American studies scholars have tended "to view the prerequisite controversy as an anomalous period in a relatively straightforward Arab American history of assimilation" (Majaj 2000, 323). However, Majaj argues that while connections between non-European, non-Christian, and nonwhite identity persisted within official U.S. policy and popular discourses, so too did the potential exclusion of Arabs, particularly those who were not Christian. To illustrate this point, Majaj turns to two naturalization cases from this period, including the 1942 case of the Yemeni Muslim applicant Ahmed Hassan, who was denied naturalization based on his non-European and non-Christian heritage, and the 1944 case in which an Arab applicant was granted naturalization based on the idea that Arabs could be considered white because they have been "*transmitters* of western civilization" (Majaj 2000, 324). On the one hand, "while the credibility of whiteness was periodically called into question by government authorities and public opinion," on the other hand, Arab American proximity to whiteness facilitated efforts to qualify for citizenship (see chapter 5 by Sarah

Gualtieri). In this sense, I use the term "racialization of ambiguity" to refer to the position of early Arab immigrants on the level of the federal government until the 1940s, when the U.S. Census Bureau took the position that "Arab-Americans were to be treated like Italian-Americans, Greek-Americans and some other European immigrant communities" (Hassan 2002, 4).

Providing a survey of the histories of U.S. popular representations of "the Arab" is beyond the scope of this chapter. Yet a brief account of a few key moments within these representational histories illustrates that images of Arabs in U.S. popular culture are numerous, constantly changing, and predate the first significant period of Arab immigration to the United States. It also demonstrates the ways in which government discourses have tended to overlap with or parallel popular representations. Some scholars have argued that images of "the Arab" are rooted in images of the "Muslim" as a dark and evil Other that were transposed from the Byzantines to western Europeans and European colonists during the period of the rise of Islam and, later, to the Americas (Suleiman 1989, 257). Others have contended that an analysis of the historical fascination with the Holy Land is critical to understanding representations of the "Arab" in U.S. popular culture (Little 2002; McAlister 2001). One perspective is that the Puritan fascination with the Holy Land entailed "a profound ambivalence about the 'infidels'—mostly Muslims but some Jews" (Little 2002, 9). Rana contends that this fascination has permeated U.S. popular imagination ever since the early days of European colonization in the United States four centuries ago, when representations of Native Americans paralleled representations of Muslims and Jews (Little 2002, 9; Rana 2007). He adds that Native Americans were interpellated through stereotypes of Muslims that proliferated during the Spanish contact and configured Indians as Muslims. He argues that this stereotype served as part of an ideological justification for holy war and imperial expansion (Rana 2007; Matar 2000, cited in Rana).[27]

---

27. According to Junaid Rana, "Throughout the sixteenth century into the seventeenth and eighteenth, ideas of racial difference were encapsulated through religious difference, and in the case of Native Americans and Muslims, sexual difference. In this configuration Muslims and Native Americans were classified as racially other—that is, barbaric, depraved, immoral, and sexually deviant. The stereotype of the Muslim as represented in literary and theological documents imagined the 'Turk' as 'cruel, tyrannical, deviant, and deceiving,' and the 'Moor' as 'sexually overdriven and emotionally uncontrollable, vengeful, and religiously superstitious'" (Rana 2007, 154).

In the eighteenth century, biographies of the Prophet Mohammed that depicted the "Islamic messenger of God as the founder of a wicked and barbarous creed that had spread from Arabia to North Africa by offering conquered peoples a choice between conversion and death" proliferated in the United States (Little 2002, 10). Little contends that "the revolutionary statesmen who invented America in the quarter-century after 1776 regarded the Muslim world, beset by oriental despotism, economic squalor, and intellectual stultification, as the antithesis of the republicanism to which they had pledged their sacred honor" (10). Literary representations of Muslims as polluted, autocratic Orientals who had fallen from grace continued throughout the eighteenth and nineteenth centuries.[28] Nineteenth-century representations of Arabs and Muslims were shaped in part by missionaries, tourists, and merchants who sailed from America into the eastern Mediterranean who perceived Arab governments and societies through the Eurocentric lenses of backwardness and inferiority (10). In their travel writings, some missionaries represented Islam as inferior to Protestantism and the Orient as a place ruled by despots, prone to cruel displays of power and self-indulgence, barbarism, and captivity and closely associated with tyranny and slavery. McAlister argues that by the end of the nineteenth century, "the Holy Land images were the most popular subject for the more than five million stereographs produced in the United States" (2001, 17). She adds that representations of the Holy Land "saturated the culture, combining Orientalist themes of exoticism with the complex nexus of adoration and appropriation that most Protestant Americans felt for the land they claimed as spiritual heritage" (18).

In the antebellum period and early decades of the nineteenth century, Orientalist imagery proliferated in the United States in the form of "paintings, prints, decorative arts, advertisements, photographs, films, fashion, and a variety of performing arts" (Edwards 2000, 16). Within the first few decades after

---

28. Little (2002) argues that "No one probably did more to shape nineteenth-century U.S. views of the Middle East than Mark Twain, whose darkly humorous account of his calamitous tour of the Holy Land sold nearly one hundred thousand copies in the two years after it was published in 1869." In *Innocents Abroad* Twain homogenized the local population as "Muslims" and referred to them as "a people by nature and training filthy, brutish, ignorant, unprogressive and superstitious." He also called the Ottoman Empire, "a government whose three graces are tyranny, rapacity and blood." The Arabs of Palestine, according to Twain, were "mired in dirt, rags, and vermin," and "do not mind barbarous ignorance and savagery" (1984, 516, 106, 431, 433).

the Civil War, particularly through Holy Land imagery, while "the Orient" was conceived as a traditional and monolithic culture, it also emerged as a place upon which "Americans" could project a Protestant narrative. Yet by the end of the nineteenth century, the Orient was "remodeled for new consumers" (Edwards 2000, 16). Representations of the Orient at the Chicago World's Fair of 1893, where the Orient was constructed "as different and exotic, complete with mosque, bazaar, harem, and belly dancers to titillate Victorian Americans" are indicative of this shift (Little 2002, 13).[29]

Representations of an exotic and exceptionally different and mysterious Orient reinforced dominant discourses that constructed the categories "East" and "West" in the binary terms of civilized Americans versus a belittled, demeaned, and sexualized Orient (Edwards 2000, 16). In the early twentieth century, the Orient was increasingly represented in terms of sexualized imagery in U.S. popular culture. In the entertainment industry in general, and in Hollywood films in particular, the Orient emerged as an exotic site for the fulfillment of Western desires that could not be enacted in "America"—where a restrictive Production Code forbade "scenes of passion" and policed through camouflage, restriction, and the denial of the free flow of energy (Edwards 2000, 39; Shohat and Stam 1994, 158). The "recurrent figure of the veiled woman" emerged as a central representation within mid-twentieth-century U.S. popular culture as a symbol of "mysterious inaccessibility" that has come to "allegorize the availability of Eastern land for Western penetrating knowledge and possession" (Shohat and Stam 1994, 148–49).[30] Also critical within early-twentieth-century Hollywood imagery of the Orient was the "rape and rescue trope," by which virginal white women, and at times dark women, are rescued from dark men. For Shohat and Stam, the 1921 film *The Sheik* exemplifies representations of Arab women who "quite literally fight over their Arab man while the white woman has to be lured, made captive, virtually raped to awaken her repressed desire" (156). The rape-and-rescue fantasy, they argue, "catalyzes the narrative role of the Western liberator as integral to the colonial rescue fantasy. In the case of the Orient, it also carries theological overtones of the inferiority of the polygamous

29. Also see Timothy Mitchell's *Colonising Egypt* (1988) for analyses on representations of Arabs in the context of World Fairs.

30. See Amira Jarmakani (2004) for further analysis of representations of the "veil" within U.S. popular culture.

Islamic world to the Christian world as encapsulated by the celibate priest or the monogamous couple" (156). In this sense, religion coupled with civilizational discourses support the construction of "the Arab" as different from and inferior to white Americans.

Images of Arabs in Hollywood in the early twentieth century were often reified in popular magazines such as *National Geographic* (Steet 2000; Little 2002). According to Little, not only did *National Geographic*, a magazine that reached millions of homes by the late 1920s, represent a heightened binary between "East" and "West," it also represented Muslims as fanatics who are radically anti-Western and misogynistic, and simultaneously exotic, erotic, and mysterious (Steet 2000). Perhaps the trajectory of "the Arab" in U.S. popular culture until the mid–twentieth century set the stage for the contradictory reactions that the first significant group of Arab immigrants encountered upon immigration to the United States in the late 1800s and the gradual intensification of anti-Arab racism in the decades that followed.

CHANGING CONCEPTS OF "RACE" IN THE UNITED STATES

Shifts in the meaning of "race" in the United States in the 1950s and 1960s have had important implications for racial classification on the level of the federal government that "were felt well beyond the arena of demographics into the civic, political and economic life of the country" (Samhan 1999). The 1950s marked a fundamental shift in core anthropological and sociological theories and ideas about "race" that illustrated that race is a social construction and is not scientifically meaningful. Many civil rights scholars and activists who agreed with this position in principle rejected the idea of doing away with the "race" concept altogether.[31] Such concerns reflected the view that while democratic principles adopted as a consequence of the civil rights movement were meant to apply equally to all citizens, racial discrimination obstinately continued. These shifts paralleled the emergence of a general liberal consciousness in the United States that "supported the opinion that racial segregation . . . had no objective

---

31. Shifts in dominant U.S. meanings of "race" developed in continuity with centuries of resistance against racism and a watershed moment in the fields of anthropology and sociology in which several scholars demonstrated that race cannot be biologically determined but is socially determined and constantly changing (Sanjeck 1994, 6).

scientific basis" (Sanjeck 1994, 7). Yet despite repeated refutations of biological definitions of "race," race and racism have continued to permeate institutionalized structures for organizing difference in the United States. Faye Harrison captured this contradiction between scientific arguments and the realities of racism by stating that while "race" no longer exists, "racism" persists (1995, 47). Harrison argues, "despite its uneven development and varying systematization, racism is characterized by an international hierarchy in which wealth, power and advanced development are associated largely with whiteness or 'honorary whiteness'" (50).

The civil rights movement produced a period of intense conflict in which the "very *meaning* of race was politically contested" (Omi and Winant 1994, 2). Controversies over race during this period opened up new possibilities for exploring racial discrimination (as opposed to biological races) as measurable and institutionalized and embedded in unequal social and economic structures, such as patterns of segregation, rates of income, and university admissions. As principles of nondiscrimination were translated into affirmative action, one approach for advancing the goals of the civil rights movement was to compare the percentage of the population that had access to particular jobs, higher education, or desirable housing. Because statistical proportionality cannot be assessed without a count of how many members of various racial and ethnic groups live in the United States, the census had a central role to play in such efforts. Pointing to the significance of census categories, Helen Samhan explains that "these categories also permeated most record-keeping and application procedures in the public sector, and private sector activity subject to federal state or local statutes to monitor civil rights. Forms used by schools, health professionals, social service agencies and most businesses eventually conformed to the federal standards" (1999, 214–15).

Inspired by the civil rights movement, a new period of racial measurement was institutionalized in the 1950s and 1960s that purported to respond to the persistence of racism. Affirmative action is but one example of policies that relied on racial classification as a mechanism that would guarantee civil rights and equal access to social and economic resources. Samhan argues that "the new impetus for racial classification as a civil rights check transformed dramatically the role of the census, which acquired a political importance that it never had in the past" (1999). According to this later-twentieth-century deployment of "race," racial classification, a tool previously deployed to deny rights, emerged as a mechanism for measuring the representation of various groups within civil society and their access to social and economic resources. Disproportionate representation implied "a glass ceiling or other racially based barriers to full access that had to be eliminated" (Prewitt 2002).

Since the civil rights era, the U.S. census has continued to rely upon racial classification as a mechanism for counting various populations, producing knowledge about the relationship between particular groups and their access to social and economic resources and monitoring the health and welfare needs of a diverse population. While evaluating the civil rights–based approach to racial discrimination is beyond the scope of this introduction, it is important to note its alleged benefits and drawbacks. Since the 1964 Civil Rights Act, the alleged purpose of deploying civil rights–based categories is to create the "ability to monitor the health and welfare needs of a diverse population, protect civil rights, and attempt to narrow the socioeconomic gaps among the citizenry" (Samhan 1999, 215). Affirmative action reflects the deployment of a civil rights framework. Supporters of affirmative action argue that it rectifies the effects of past discrimination by providing opportunities for groups historically discriminated against. Some opponents (with right-wing, liberal, and even leftist political leanings) have argued that race-based preferential treatment toward "unqualified" racial minorities and women causes "reverse discrimination." Other critics who have defended the continuation of affirmative action have argued that while it has assisted a small percentage of people of color, particularly those from middle- and upper-class backgrounds, economic conditions have increasingly excluded people of color from productive jobs and universities. This position contends that affirmative action alone cannot adequately address the enduring legacies of slavery and colonization and that affirmative action should not replace efforts to create alternatives to government programs and regulations. An alternative, although often overlapping position has been that the use of racial categories to safeguard civil rights often ignores the intersection between racism and colonization and assumes that racial discrimination is a distinct axis of oppression that operates separately from colonialism. Several Native American scholars and activists have argued that racism and colonization are inseparable and that the affirmative action–based approach had the effect of disregarding Native American struggles for racial justice and sovereignty over indigenous land. As Andrea Smith contends, "many Natives would argue that the affirmative action–based paradigm does not apply to them because it collapses Natives into the category of race while occluding colonialism. For instance, it implies that Natives want citizenship when in fact, some would argue that citizenship has been forced upon them" (2007). Similar debates have been taken up in Arab American studies. Some have argued that Arab American marginalization and exclusion from the national body are the problem and that citizenship and inclusion are the solution. Yet others have contended that many Arabs are "here" because the United States went to war "over there," and therefore ending U.S.-led imperialism should be part of the solution.

Beyond the realm of official government racial classification, government policy and official public discourse on "race" have also been malleable and constantly shifting, depending on the historical and political moment. Omi and Winant explain that the racial minority movements of the 1960s began to diminish in power and that the 1970s brought a period of racial quiescence (1994, 12). They also state that in the 1970s, "while racial oppression had hardly vanished, conflicts over race receded as past reforms were institutionalized" (2). These shifts paralleled new patterns in fields such as anthropology, where "'ethnicity' came to center stage, and the realities of race and racism were pushed aside" (Sanjeck 1994, 8). Although the term "ethnicity" has taken on various meanings in different historical moments, ethnicity paradigms that emerged after the 1960s are rooted in early-twentieth-century critiques of racial biologism (Omi and Winant 1994, 15), which emerged out of the fields of anthropology and sociology Although early-twentieth-century approaches defined ethnicity in terms of the "result of a group formation process based on culture and descent," later ethnicity theory questioned the validity of primordial notions of identity and argued that concepts such as "culture" and "descent" were social constructs (Omi and Winant 1994, 15). One of the most salient critiques of ethnicity theory is that it is strictly based in the experiences of European (white) immigrants and privileged the experiences of migration, cultural contact, and assimilation, or the incorporation and separation of ethnic minorities, and turns a blind eye toward the historical experiences of minority groups who are classified or treated as nonwhite, for whom experiences of cultural contact and engagements with assimilation and Americanization are not only struggles over culture but are constituted by racism and racial exclusion (Omi and Winant 1994, 15–16). By ignoring institutionalized racial inequality, the ethnicity paradigm of the 1970s promoted a "pull yourself up by your bootstraps" model that assumed that climbing the economic ladder was simply a matter of hard work and dedication. Furthermore, Omi and Winant argue that in the 1980s, issues of race were revived once again "in the form of a 'backlash' to the political gains of racial minority movements of the past. Conservative popular movements, some academics, and the Reagan administration have joined hands to attack the legacy and logic of earlier movement achievements" (1994). The significance of such movements is that they have the effect of evading the realities of racism and their complicity in racist policies by appealing to the notion of a "colorblind society" (Omi and Winant 1994, 2).

Approaches to Arab American studies that refer to Arab Americans as an "ethnic/cultural" group while ignoring the realities of anti-Arab racism and the structural inequalities that shape Arab American experiences illustrate the limitations of ethnicity theory. Operating simultaneously with the structures of "race" that shape government discourses and practices are those that operate in the context of civil society and popular culture. Several scholars have argued that "concepts of race structure both state and civil society" and that "race continues to shape both identities and institutions in significant ways" (Omi and Winant 1994, vii; Lipsitz 1998). Moreover, many scholars have gone beyond analyzing "race" only in terms of experiences of racial discrimination, exclusion, and marginalization and have focused on how "race" also operates to grant access to social and economic privileges, advantages, and opportunities. This analysis has often emerged within the field of whiteness studies. Writing on "whiteness," George Lipsitz argues that "white supremacy is an equal-opportunity employer; nonwhite people can become active agents of white supremacy as well as passive participants in its hierarchies and rewards" (1998, viii). Whiteness studies have opened up important possibilities for conceptualizing the multiple, contradictory ways that Arab Americans have tended to self-identify vis-à-vis U.S. racial categories. As several essays in this volume illustrate, some Arab Americans have passed as "white," others have not had the privilege of passing, yet others have self-identified according to explicit nonwhite racial/ethnic categories.

ANTI-ARAB RACISM AFTER WORLD WAR II

The period in which the meaning of "race" shifted in the United States was also a period of growing anti-Arab discourses and policies coupled with an escalation in pan-ethnic Arab American political activism. Whereas several scholars use the term "racism" to explain the logic underpinning Arab American marginality

(Salaita 2006; Naber 2000; Stockton 1994; Abraham 1989), others contend that terms such as political exclusion are more accurate for describing the marginalization of Arab Americans after World War II more generally and after September 11 more specifically (see chapter 3 by Andrew Shryock). I use the term anti-Arab racism to locate Arab American marginalization within the context of U.S. histories of immigrant exclusion (e.g., the history of Asian exclusion, anti-Mexican racism, and Japanese internment) in which the racialization of particular immigrants as different than and inferior to whites has relied upon culturalist and nationalist logics that assume that "they" are intrinsically unassimilable and threatening to national security (Naber 2006). I would argue that anti-Arab racism represents a recurring process of the construction of the Other within U.S. liberal politics in which long-term trends of racial exclusion become intensified within moments of crisis in the body politic, as in the contexts of World War II and the aftermath of September 11, 2001. Anti-Arab racism after World War II emerged in an interplay of U.S. military, political, and economic expansion in the Middle East, anti-Arab media representations, and the institutionalization of government policies that specifically target Arabs and Arab Americans in the United States. Since World War II, the proliferation of anti-Arab government policies and perceptions of "the Arab" as nonwhite Others within U.S. popular culture has coincided with the increasing significance of oil as a commodity to the global economy and the United States' expanding interest in military and economic intervention in the Middle East. After 1945, U.S. policy makers and oil companies joined forces in exerting pressure on the Arab world in a political strategy that Douglas Little refers to as "What was best for Exxon and Texaco seemed also what was best for America, and vice versa" (Little 2002, 4). These geopolitical interests set the stage for the 1970s U.S.-Arab oil wars that contributed to the production of the image of the "greedy Arab oil sheikhs" within the United States and the strengthening of the United States' alliance with Israel in geopolitics. At that time, McAlister argues, the United States was vying to consolidate its position of superiority in global politics, particularly in terms of attaining control over the world's oil resources.[32] The U.S.-Arab oil wars took place in the aftermath of the 1960s, when the U.S. government was

---

32. McAlister refers to four contending forces, or "primary interests," that informed both foreign policy and public discussion of the Middle East: U.S. attempts to achieve control over oil, American support of Israel, religious loyalties, and a strategic position in global politics (2001, 35).

intent on building allies in the Arab region (e.g., Iran and Saudi Arabia) in a two-fold, interconnected struggle against the Soviets in the context of the Cold War, and pan-Arab nationalist regimes under leaders such as Nasser in the Arab world who were connected to the Soviet Union's hegemony in the region. The American conflict with Arab nationalists took shape post-1945 when the U.S. government saw Arab nationalists as similar to the National Liberation Front in the context of Vietnam and supported Israel's attempt to defeat them. Moreover, as U.S. involvements abroad had expanded dramatically, the 1967 Arab-Israeli war signified a turning point in the impact of U.S. involvement in the Arab region on Arab diasporas in the United States. The 1967 war marked the U.S. state's confirmed alliance with Israel as well as an intensification of U.S. military, political, and economic intervention in the Arab region, anti-Arab media representations, and anti-Arab discrimination and harassment within the United States. According to Said (1978), it also marked the intensification of representations of Islam as a signifier of evilness and Otherness, which was exacerbated in the aftermath of the Iranian revolution, when hegemonic discourses on the "Arab Other" in the United States increasingly deployed the assumption that all Arabs are Muslim and that Islam is an inherently backward and uncivilized religion.[33] In the aftermath of the Iranian revolution (post-1979) in particular, the process by which "Islam" had gained an increasingly global appeal as a framework for expressing political sentiments took on local form in the United States. Government policies that were directed at individuals who were associated with a constructed "Arab enemy" came to be directed at a constructed "Arab Muslim" enemy. Thus particularly since the 1970s, government and media discourses on "the Arab" tended to be constituted by a conflation of the categories "Arab" and "Muslim" and a refashioning of European discourses that portrayed Islam as homogenous, uncivilized, and culturally backward, and violently misogynistic toward women.

33. Said argues that throughout the Middle Ages and in the early part of the Renaissance in Europe, "Islam was believed to be a demonic religion of apostasy, blasphemy, and obscurity" and Mohammed was believed to be a false prophet and an agent of the devil (Said 1981, 5). He also points out that since the end of the eighteenth century, Orientalist thinking has reduced Islam to a monolith that belongs to the Orient and is constituted by a "very special hostility and fear" (4) and that for hundreds of years, "only Islam seemed never to have submitted completely to the West; and when, after the dramatic oil-price rises of the early 1970's, the Muslim world seemed once more on the verge of repeating its early conquests, the whole West seemed to shudder" (5).

The 1960s and 1970s inspired among many Arabs and Arab Americans the sense that the state and media had waged a war against them.[34] Arab American activists and scholars responded by establishing several Arab American organizations, many that were pan-ethnic in character, such as the Organization of Arab Students in 1967; the Arab American University Graduates (1968); and the National Association of Arab Americans (1972).[35] In particular, the 1967 Arab-Israeli war ignited an "Arab American awakening."[36] Pan-Arab American activism during this period emerged within a broader context of the civil rights movement and third-world liberation movements in the United States. The following quote by Gary Awad (1981) captures a sentiment that many Arab American activists expressed in the late 1960s and 1970s: "The shock for Arab Americans was not so much the defeat of Egypt, Jordan, and Syria in 1967, but the way it was received in the West and especially in the United States, where strong, derogatory racial overtones in the media toward the Arab contributed significantly, for the first time, to a growing political and ethnic awareness in the American Arab community."[37]

From the 1970s to the 1990s, several events, coupled with an increasing convergence between U.S. and Israeli policy, further facilitated the expansion of U.S. control in the Arab world: the 1970s U.S.-Arab oil wars; the 1980s Iranian

34. Community activist Abdeen Jabara, quoted in an *Los Angeles Times* article, expressed a similar view: "In 1967, the view in this country was that the United States had won a war against the dirty Arabs."

35. Other organizations included Najda: Women Concerned about the Middle East (1960), Pal-Aid International (1967); U.S. Organization for Medical and Educational Needs (1961); and the American Arab Association (1961).

36. In the 1970s, a series of newspaper articles on Arab Americans reflected this sense of a "community awakening," including a *Los Angeles Times* article, "Mideast War Spurs Unprecedented Formation of Arab Groups in the U.S." (Nelson 1973). Arab American efforts to counter European and U.S. support for European Jewish settlement in Palestine did not begin in the aftermath of 1967 but have persisted since the turn of the twentieth century (Bawardi 2006).

37. Civil rights lawyer Abdeen Jabara's 1977 Community Day Speech in Dearborn, Michigan, exemplifies this perspective about anti-Arab attitudes. He states, "These attitudes frequently govern how people act in employing Arab Americans, promoting Arab Americans, renting or selling homes or apartments to Arabs, or in characterizing Arabs in the local media. . . . It was the July 1967 war in the Middle East that had the effect of galvanizing what had been a dormant giant. Second and third generation Arab Americans were confronted with a historic challenge to their self-identification."

revolution; U.S. intervention in Lebanon in 1982; the U.S. bombing of Libya in 1986; the 1990s Gulf War; the U.S. bombing of Sudan and Afghanistan in 1998; and continued U.S. support of Israel and the bombing of Iraq.[38] U.S. political, military, and economic expansion in the region paralleled a rise in the institutionalization of government policies and law enforcement that specifically targeted Arabs and Arab Americans. In 1972, Nixon's Operation Boulder marked the beginning in a series of FBI policies that entailed the harassment of individuals of Arab descent in general and Arab students in particular, who were targeted by the state and denied their constitutional rights, specifically those related to free speech. Based on presidential directives, it authorized the FBI to harass individuals of "Arabic speaking descent" with phone calls and visits without evidence of criminal activity, based on the assumption that they might have a relationship with "terrorist activities" in Palestine and Israel (Akram 2002, 5).[39] According to Susan Akram, "Later investigations, both by the press and by organizations in the Arab-American community, confirmed that 'Operation Boulder' was initiated as a result of pressure from Zionist groups both within the U.S. and from Israel to silence Arab-Americans from voicing opposition to U.S. and Israeli policies in the Middle East" (5). Operation Boulder specifically targeted Arabs with U.S. citizenship, resident aliens of Arab descent, non Arab Americans sympathetic to Arab causes, as well as the relatives, neighbors, friends, and employers of Arab individuals (American Arab Anti-Discrimination Committee 1986). Also during the 1970s, several government agencies, including the Federal Bureau of Investigation, the Justice Department, and the Immigration Department, carried out a wide-ranging campaign of investigation and surveillance of Arab Americans through tactics such as spying and wiretapping that were ordered from the White House under the guise of uncovering the activities of persons potentially involved in sabotage (Hussaini 1974). A consensus among Arab American activists and scholars is that the purpose of such government policies has been to intimidate, harass, and discourage Arab American resistance to U.S. policies in the Arab world. As Susan Akram put it, "One of the factors with the greatest impact on the targeting of Arabs and Muslims is what might best be termed 'institutionalized racism' in government

38. See Rashid Khalidi (2004) for further analysis of U.S. expansion in the Middle East.

39. Writing on Operation Boulder, Susan Akram argues that, at that period of time, no acts of terrorism conducted by a person of Arab descent had been committed in the U.S. (2002).

and law enforcement, in collaboration with institutions and think-tanks having a specific ideological or foreign policy agenda driven by anti-Arabism" (Akram 2002, 5).

In 1978, Operation Abscam, in which FBI director William Webster had agents pose as rich Arabs and try to bribe politicians and elected officials, sought to create the impression that Arabs are a threat to American politics. In the 1970s, the Department of Energy (DOE) printed thousands of bumper stickers stating: "The Faster You Drive, The Richer They Get . . . Driving 75 Is Sheik; Driving 55 Is Chic" (Shehadeh 2000). The titles of a series of newspaper articles published in the 1970s illustrate a perceived rising anti-Arab sentiment during this period, including a *Los Angeles Times* article, "Mideast War Spurs Unprecedented Formation of Arab Groups in U.S." (Nelson 1973); a *Washington Post* article, "Arab Americans Sue Marriott Corporation Alleging Job Discrimination" (Valente 1977); and a *Rochester Democrat and Chronicle* article, entitled, "Arab American Fed Up with Situation Here" (Oct. 28, 1973, 1E). The significance of organized efforts by pro-Israeli groups in shaping public opinion and facilitating the targeting of Arab and Arab American activists and their allies cannot be underestimated. Some pro-Israeli groups have adopted a strategy that seeks to maintain a unified pro-Israel position and to quell criticism of Israeli state policy by demonizing its critics. The myth that any criticism of Israel is anti-Semitic has been integral to these concerted efforts (Marshall 1993). Hatem Hussaini argues that since 1968, several pro-Israeli groups have pressured Congress and the White House to take action against Arabs and Arab Americans critical of Israel (1974, 216).

The case of the L.A. 8 exemplifies the government's deliberate unconstitutional targeting of Arab American activists and the process by which the social construction of "the Arab" as a potential terrorist and the unsubstantiated conflation of Arab American activists and terrorism have legitimized violations of Arab and Arab American rights. The L.A. 8, seven Palestinians and one Kenyan, were targeted for removal, technically a civil proceeding, on grounds that they allegedly had raised money for the PFLP, the Popular Front for the Liberation of Palestine, in 1987. The initial charges involved their distribution of *Al-Hadaf,* the PFLP magazine—a publication available in public libraries, on college campuses, and even at the U.S. Library of Congress. Since the beginning of this case, the government admitted none of the L.A. 8 had committed a criminal or terrorist act. The L.A. 8 case epitomizes the government's deliberate unconstitutional targeting of Arab American activists · and the process by which the social construction of "the Arab" as a potential terrorist has legitimized U.S. imperial ambitions in the Arab world and violations of Arab and Arab American rights in the United States. Since January 1987, when the eight were arrested, the case has bounced from immigration court, through federal district courts, up to the U.S. Supreme Court and back again, with side visits to individual immigration status hearings.[40] During the L.A. 8 court proceedings, a Justice Department contingency plan was revealed that provided a blueprint for the mass arrest of ten thousand alien terrorists and undesirable Arabs within the United States.[41] Several scholars and activists have argued that it "is doubtful that the contingency plan and mass arrest of the [L.A. 8] would have occurred if not for the provocation of B'nai Brith's Anti-Defamation League (McDonnel 1987, 7). In this case, the ADL admitted that it provided names of the defendants to the FBI early in 1985, stating that they were distributing "Arab propaganda." According to the ADL, anyone speaking out in support of Palestinians is a terrorist and should be arrested by the FBI and deported by the INS. As ACLU attorney Mark Rosenbaum put it,

40. Peter King (2005) wrote that one event in particular sparked their arrest. "The event—a night of ethnic food, folk dances and political speeches delivered in Arabic—would be attended by an estimated 1,200 men, women and children, most of them immigrants from the Middle East. It had been promoted as a festival to celebrate the 18th anniversary of the Popular Front for the Liberation of Palestine, a Marxist-oriented faction of the Palestine Liberation Organization. The underlying purpose, organizers said, was to generate donations for 'the homeland,' in particular to provide medical care and schooling in Palestinian refugee camps." According to King, "The charges against the L.A. 8 have been reworked at least three times since, reflecting changes in immigration and anti-terrorism laws, some of which were tailored to be applied retroactively to this case. . . . Two of the eight, Khader Musa Hamide and Michel Ibrahim Shehadeh, are scheduled for trial in immigration court in July of 2005 with the government seeking to deport them under a provision of the PATRIOT Act that forbids giving material support to terrorist organizations."

41. See *Sacramento Bee* (Jan. 24, 1991, cited in Joseph 1999a). Suad Joseph explains that the *Sacramento Bee* carried a story, reproduced in little of the national press. This story reported that U.S. Representative Norman Mineta "pointed to a 1978 contingency plan the FBI and the Immigration and Naturalization Service drew up to detain Arab Americans at a camp in Oakdale, Louisiana, in the event of war with certain Arab states. Mineta said that the plan could still be initiated to 'round up' Arab Americans" (1999a).

"'What the U.S. government is saying to Arabs is Shut Up or Get Out of This Country'" (quoted in McDonnel 1987, 7).[42]

Historical shifts in U.S. imperial ambitions in the Middle East paralleled shifts in corporate media representations of "the Arab." Jack Shaheen's research has demonstrated that since the 1970s, the corporate media has increasingly portrayed persons associated with the category "Arab/Middle Eastern/Muslim" as not only culturally backward, uncivilized, exotic, or potentially dangerous, but also as potential enemies of the U.S. nation (1984, 2001). For example, the 1970s brought images of rich oil sheikhs threatening the U.S. economy alongside images of harems and belly dancers and the 1980s brought cartoons that portrayed Palestinians as "rats malevolently entering a house or caught in a trap, or as fleas infesting a region and being exterminated" (Stockton 1994, 133). The 1980s and 1990s brought an intensification of images of Arab terrorists, as in the films *True Lies* (1994), *The Siege* (1998), *Back to the Future* (1985); and *GI Jane* (1988). Elsewhere, I have argued that three media types have reinforced the idea of an "Arab/ Middle Eastern/Muslim" enemy of the nation (Naber 2000). The first media type associates a constructed image of "Arab/Middle Eastern/Muslim" men with violent misogyny. The second media type associates "Arab/Middle Eastern/Muslim" women with passivity and victimhood in comparison to white American women, who are idealized to represent equality, democracy, and justice. The third media type is what Therese Saliba refers to as the "absent Arab women" (1994), which juxtaposes excessively patriarchal Arab men and white women who were once victimized by Arab men—but are now "free," leaving Arab women completely absent from the scene. These media types illustrate the significance of gender to media representations that operate to legitimize the binary "us vs. them"/ "Americans vs. Arabs" that proliferates within dominant U.S. discourses.

President Clinton's counterterrorism bill of 1994 further legitimized the federal government's targeting of Arabs in the United States. This bill called for the federal government's deportation of noncitizens based on evidence known only to the government. In some cases, defendants and defense attorneys did not receive a summary of the evidence. A 1998 *New York Times* article stated that there were more than two dozen immigrants around the country who were

42. Also see Hasso (1987) for more information on the implications of this case for Arab Americans.

facing deportation or exclusion from the United States largely on the basis of secret evidence that they were not permitted to see and that came from people who were unidentified. The article added that all twenty-five men accused in these cases are of Arab descent or are Muslims (Smothers 1998).

The history of anti-Arab hate crimes documented by several Arab American organizations illustrates the ways in which popular cultural discourses have taken on local form in the public sphere (ADC 1992). The unsettled murder of Alex Odeh, the West Coast regional director of the American Arab Anti-Discrimination Committee (ADC) in 1986, when a pipe bomb exploded as he unlocked and opened his office door, and the 1986 murder of Ismail al-Faruqi, a Palestinian American Islamic scholar who was outspoken in his views about Palestine, and his wife, Lois Lamya al-Faruqi (ADC 1986), exemplify the multiple registers through which anti-Arab racism has operated.

THE AFTERMATH OF SEPTEMBER 11, 2001

The aftermath of the September 11 attacks against the Pentagon and the World Trade Center consolidated the conflation of the categories "Arab," "Middle Eastern," and "Muslim" and the notion of an "Arab/Middle Eastern/Muslim" enemy of the nation (Volpp 2003). Right-wing, neoconservative think tanks coupled with Washington-based opinion and policy makers have covered up historical and political realities such as the United States' imperial ambitions in the Middle East by constructing the "war on terror" as a "clash of civilizations" that "will be the latest phase in the evolution of conflict in the modern world" (Said 2002, 571). In this sense, Americans are constructed to be on the side of good and persons perceived to be "Arab/Middle Eastern/Muslim" (and/or South Asian) are positioned on the side of evil.

Discourses such as the "clash of civilizations" have justified U.S.-led war in Muslim majority countries and the racial profiling, detentions, deportations, and torture of Arabs and Arab Americans (as well as other individuals perceived to be associated with "potential terrorists") without evidence of criminal activity. According to Louise Cainkar, "the US government's domestic legislative, administrative, and judicial measures implemented after September 11th have included mass arrests, secret and indefinite detentions, prolonged detention of 'material witnesses,' closed hearings and use of secret evidence, government eavesdropping on attorney client conversations, FBI home and work visits, wiretapping, seizures of property, removals of aliens with technical visa violations, and mandatory special registration" (2003, 1). Cainkar adds that "at least 100,000 Arabs and Muslims living in the United States have personally experienced one of these measures" and that "of thirty-seven known US government security initiatives . . . twenty five either explicitly or implicitly target Arabs and Muslims in the United States" (1).

The case of Maher Hawash is an acute example of the intensified institutionalization of anti-Arab violence in the United States after 9/11. Hawash is a U.S. citizen originally from Palestine. On March 20, 2003, FBI agents and members of the Portland Joint Terrorism Task Force arrested him in the parking lot at Intel Corporation, where he worked, under the material witness law, a law the U.S. Department of Justice has deliberately used to secure the indefinite incarceration of persons it planned to interrogate as potential terrorist suspects without probable cause after September 11 (ACLU 2003). According to the ACLU, at least seventy Muslim men have been arrested based on this law "for little more than attending the same mosque as a September 11 hijacker or owning a box-cutter." Federal agents have arrested these men at gunpoint, held them in solitary confinement, and subjected them to the harsh and degrading conditions of high-security prisons where they have been verbally harassed and in several cases, physically abused. In cases such as these, federal government discourses have rendered men perceived to be Arab, Middle Eastern, Muslim (and/or South Asian) as "potential terrorists."

The difference between the 1914 case of George Dow (who was marked as nonwhite and eventually became "white") and the 2003 case of Maher Hawash (a U.S. citizen who eventually became "a potential terrorist") represents the process by which state discourses have transformed "the Arab" over time, from proximity to whiteness to a position of heightened Otherness. While this trajectory in no way captures the experiences of *all* Arabs living in the United States during the early years or more recently, it reflects a pattern within dominant U.S. discourses such as corporate media and federal government discourse, and the process by which the "Arab," who was once positioned as white, but not quite, has come to signify Otherness more than ever before. Whether and to what extent the framework of "race" or "racism" is useful for explaining this trajectory is one of the questions explored in this book.

THE IDEA to develop this project emerged after we attended the annual meetings of the Middle East Studies Association (MESA) in 2002. Historically, Middle East studies have been dominated by an area-studies approach that constructs an undeniable link between seemingly fixed and authentic cultural patterns, peoples, and specific places of origin and elides the histories and experiences of communities stretched across national borders (Lavie and Swedenburg 1996, 1).[43] Reproducing an area-studies logic, MESA's agenda and conference programs have historically positioned discussions on Arab diasporas in general, and Arab Americans in particular, as marginal to "real" Middle East studies. In the aftermath of September 11, 2001, however, the Bush administration's unrelenting repetition of the concept of absolutely evil terrorists who know no borders or boundaries and are to be found anywhere and everywhere in the world required Middle East studies to take the fluidity of national boundaries seriously. At the MESA 2002 meetings, the number of papers presented on Arab American issues was significantly greater than in previous years. Moreover, while dominant trends within Arab American studies before September 11 tended to avoid theorizations of the significance of "race" to Arab Americans, several papers at MESA's 2002 meetings highlighted the multiple ways that Arab Americans have engaged with "race." This shift within Arab American studies paralleled the disproportionate increase in hate crimes and U.S. government violence against Arab immigrants and Arab Americans (and persons perceived to be Muslim) after September 11. This book was inspired by previous scholarship on "race" within Arab American studies and a panel organized by Sara Gualtieri entitled, "Arab American Engagements with Race" at the MESA 2002 meeting. It seeks to expand the possibilities for comparative research and teaching on "race" that take the specificities of Arab American histories and experiences seriously and to place research on Arab homelands into conversation with research about Arab diasporas. We intentionally included diverse perspectives to provide readers with a glimpse into some of the central debates on "race" that we have encountered within Arab American studies.

43. See Moallem (2005, 16–20) and Ella Shohat (2001) for a critique of Middle East studies from a transnational feminist post-colonial studies perspective. Also see Howell and Shryock (2003) for an analysis of the limitations of transnational identity among Arab Americans after September 11.

Focusing on various historical moments and social locations, this book puts a variety of analytical possibilities on the relevance of racial formation theory to Arab American studies into conversation with each other and seeks to open up more spaces for future research and discussion in this area. One of the themes that our contributors take up involves whether and in what ways "race" matters (or does not matter) to conceptualizations of Arab immigrant exclusion and Arab American marginality. Contributors writing on this theme agree that Arabs and Arab Americans have been increasingly marginalized since 9/11, yet they theorize the significance of "race" to this trajectory differently.

Louise Cainkar, in her essay, "Thinking Outside the Box," contends that "the exclusion of Arabs in the United States is a racial project with global goals." She argues that "Arab inferiority has been constructed and sold to the American public using essentialist constructions of human difference in order to manufacture public consent for global policies." Cainkar's analysis is based on ethnographic research on the impact of 9/11 on Arabs and Muslims in Chicago. Her research demonstrates a relationship between racialization and the imposition of collective guilt on Arabs and Muslims and the impact of racialization on the process of self-identification among Arab and Muslim interviewees.

Andrew Shryock's essay, "The Moral Analogies of Race," is based on findings generated by the Detroit Arab American Study (DAAS), a face-to-face survey of more than a thousand Arabs and Chaldeans. He effects a "tactical retreat from the domain of activist rhetoric and critical race theory" on the grounds that the language of "race" does not capture the reality that "almost all government policy pertaining to Arabs in the United States, be it positive, neutral, or negative, is based on identifications rooted in nationality, religion, institutional affiliations, and a set of complex (usually stereotypical and fantastic) assumptions about the political behaviors of people who can be identified in these ways." He adds that the language of race is ahead of, behind, or at odds with trends prevalent "in the [Arab American] community."

Amaney Jamal's essay, "Civil Liberties and the Otherization of Arab and Muslim Americans," also uses data gathered in the Detroit Arab American Study. From her perspective, the racialization of Arab Americans involves an interplay between domestic politics and geopolitical realities that relationally justify arguments for denying Arabs and Muslims in the United States their civil rights. She adds that in this case, racism deploys an "us" versus "them" logic that transcends racism based on phenotype toward a racism based on the representations of culture and values as inherently inferior and, ultimately, evil.

Another theme our contributors explore is the relationship between Arab American studies, ethnic studies, and whiteness studies. Several authors destabilize the dichotomy often reproduced within Arab American studies that assumes that either Arab Americans are assimilable ethnics for whom "race" does not matter or Arab Americans are vulnerable to racism and therefore "race" matters.

Using a "critical whiteness framework," which places whiteness at the forefront of her analysis, Sawsan Abdulrahim, in her essay "'Whiteness' and the Arab Immigrant Experience," argues that whether Arab Americans identify as white or nonwhite, they are engaging in racial formation. Focusing on the local contexts of Detroit and Dearborn, Michigan, she investigates how Arab immigrants engage with whiteness. For Abdulrahim, this approach requires abandoning the "race-neutral language of assimilation" and "resisting the tendency to situate Arab Americans solely as racialized victims."

Sarah Gualtieri, in "Strange Fruit?" also explores the significance of whiteness to Arab American studies through a historical interrogation of Syrian-Arab whiteness at the beginning of the twentieth century. She focuses specifically on the lynching of Syrian immigrant N. G. Romey in 1929 and contends that on the one hand, Arab American identification with whiteness in the early years provided them the privilege of distinguishing themselves from blacks and Asian Americans. On the other hand, she explains, it did not settle the question of Arab American racial status because whiteness, for Arab Americans, was unstable and ambiguous at best.

In "Grandmothers, Grape Leaves, and Kahlil Gibran," Michelle Hartman traces discourses on race and ethnicity within three leading Arab American anthologies. She argues that these anthologies explicitly or implicitly locate themselves in relation to one of three canons: the "mainstream American canon," largely white to this day, consisting of figures like Whitman, Longfellow and Frost; other racialized or "ethnic" literatures such as African American, Latino, and Native American; and the Arabic literary canon, including such lionized figures as Mahmoud Darwish, Taha Hussain, and Nazik al-Mala'ika.

The theme of the racialization of religion is also central to this book. Several contributions illustrate that conceptualizing Arab American engagements with "race" necessitates an analysis of the intersections between race and religion.

For Evelyn Alsultany, in "The Prime-time Plight of the Arab Muslim American after 9/11," the conflation of the categories Arab, Muslim, and terrorist is a racial configuration in that it assigns derogatory meaning to particular bodies distinguished by ethnicity, nationality, biology, or geography, as well as legitimizing discourses. Alsultany examines the ways in which TV dramas that portray Arab Americans after 9/11 participate in the process of legitimizing racism against Arabs through story lines that support exceptionalism. It is through this process that the categories Arab and terrorist came to be conflated, consolidated, and interchangeable. Thus racism toward Arabs and Muslims is configured as legitimate and racism toward other groups illegitimate.

In "Arab Americans and Muslim Americans in the *New York Times*," Suad Joseph, Benjamin D'Harlingue, and Alvin Ka Hin Wong examine the racializing effects of representations of Arab Americans in the *New York Times* in the aftermath of September 11, 2001. They argue that racialization entails a process by which Arabs and Muslims are represented in "collective," essentialized identities that are characterized by intersections of race, religion, and nation in ways that are mutually constitutive. According to Joseph, D'Harlingue, and Ka Hin Wong, these intersections produce "a thin veil separating the hearts and heartbeats of Arab and Muslim Americans from globalized Islamic fanaticism and terrorism, making Arab Americans and Muslim Americans high-risk citizens and subtly justifying indiscriminate violation of their civil rights."

My essay, "Look, Mohammed the Terrorist Is Coming!" is based on ethnographic research on the impact of the aftermath of 9/11 on Arab Americans in San Francisco, California. I argue that federal government discourses and policies on the "domestic war on terror" have constituted particular persons as enemies within the nation. Yet at the same time, a wide range of identities have been associated with terrorism and Islamic fundamentalism, including Arab Christians, Iranian Jews, Latinos/as, and Filipinos/as, among others, illustrating that dominant U.S. discourses on "Islam" and "Muslims" are not only malleable and fluid but are arbitrary, fictional, and imaginary at best. I contend that the post-9/11 backlash has been characterized by an intersection between two racial logics, cultural racism and nation-based racism. I also call for an intersectional approach to the study of anti-Arab racism that takes the linkages between multiple axes of oppression such as class, gender, and sexuality seriously.

Jen'nan Ghazal Read, in "Discrimination and Identity in a Post-9/11 Era," compares the racial and ethnic identities of Muslims and Christians and their experiences of discrimination after 9/11. She argues that despite the varieties of racial identifications among Arab American Christians and Muslims, Arab American Muslims are more likely to experience racial discrimination. Her data are derived from a survey questionnaire she administered to 355 Arab American congregants at an Arab church and an Arab mosque in central Texas in 2002.

SIX YEARS have passed since the attacks of September 11, 2001. Although the Bush administration has lost much of its credibility in the context of the disastrous war on Iraq, the endless "war on terror"—characterized, in part, by an intensification of anti-Arab/anti-Muslim (and anti-South Asian) racism and acts of hatred and violence in the public sphere—continues to expand. By opening up new conversations on Arab American engagements with whiteness, racialization, immigration, and citizenship, we hope this book will also contribute to expanding the possibilities for social justice and transformation during these times of enduring violence and war. While many of the contributors take up the issue of "race" and racism out of a shared sense of concern and urgency regarding the realities of the post-9/11 environment, we do not share a consensus on whether and to what extent the targeting of Arabs and Arab Americans can and should be referred to as a form of "racism." Some argue that "race" is a useful concept for conceptualizing Arab and Arab American experiences of marginalization and discrimination, and they illustrate that racism can be signified by multiple, shifting, and overlapping axes of difference, such as culture, religion, or nation, depending on the context. Others contend that "race" is not the appropriate framework for understanding this experience at all.

Several contributors point to the significance of "race" as a framework for conceptualizing not only Arab and Arab American experiences of marginalization, but also Arab and Arab American experiences vis-à-vis whiteness and the social and economic privileges associated with whiteness. In placing Arab American studies in conversation with the field of whiteness studies, these authors illustrate that "race" does not only operate to structure anti-Arab discrimination, exclusion, or marginalization but also provides many Arabs and Arab Americans with the "rewards of whiteness" (Lipsitz 1998, 4), including access to social and economic privileges and opportunities. Moreover, the essays in this book privilege different (yet often overlapping) sites of analysis, ranging from a focus on state policies and the reproduction of official state discourses in the public sphere to a focus on the corporate media and the realm of subjective, individual engagements with "race." The range of viewpoints expressed in this book are shaped in part by the different ways in which each author conceptualizes the concepts of "race" and "racism" and the different theoretical lenses about "race" through which we see the world. In this sense, this book presents multiple approaches to and conclusions about "race," and "race" reemerges as a site of contestation where no one has the final word.

Thinking Outside the Box

Arabs and Race in the United States

LOUISE CAINKAR

ARABS HAVE HAD A UNIQUE EXPERIENCE with race in America. In their one-hundred-plus-year history in the United States, their social status has changed from marginal white status to a more subordinate status that shares many features common to the experiences of people of color. Just as one can document and measure the process of becoming white (Omi and Winant 1994; Roediger 1991) a downgrading of the social status of Arabs in the United States through racial formation processes is measurable in public policies; in mainstream representations; in social patterns of discrimination, separation, and exclusion; and in self-identification. Although the early Arab American experience (1880–1930) was largely similar to that of white ethnics as measured by structural rights, such as land ownership, employment, voting, and naturalization (although there are some localized exceptions; see Cainkar forthcoming), and social patterns, such as freedom of movement and residential and marital commingling among whites, the Arab American experience since the late 1960s has been decidedly different. After that point in time, dominant themes of the Arab American experience have been exclusion, prejudice, discrimination, stereotyping, and selective policy enforcement, themes evidenced in scholarly research produced during this period (e.g., Suleiman 1999; McCarus 1994; Suleiman and Abu-Laban 1989; Cainkar 1988; Shaheen 1984, 2001; Abraham and Abraham 1983; Bassiouni 1974; Hagopian and Paden 1969). Indeed, the most important pan-Arab American organizations founded since the 1960s—the Association of Arab American University Graduates, the American Arab Anti-Discrimination Committee (ADC), the Arab American Institute, and the National Association of Arab Americans—had reversing these conditions and dismantling the propositions of innate cultural difference that lay at their root as primary organizational objectives. One of the first historic studies of Arab American communities commissioned by an Arab American organization noted:

> At a time when the United States is more receptive to cultural pluralism, and ethnicity is no longer socially unacceptable, Arab Americans remain primary targets of defamatory attacks on their cultural and personal character. Thus, much of the activity of the Arab-American community has been directed at correcting the stereotypes that threaten to produce a new wave of anti-Arab racism in the United States and endanger the civil and human rights of the Arab-American community. (Zogby 1984, 21)

The racialization processes experienced by Arab Americans differ in both historical timing and pretext from that of other groups in the United States. Historically afforded some of the benefits and protections of whiteness, such as in their eligibility for homestead lands and legal and voting rights, the exclusion of Arab Americans from social and political perquisites postdates the historic exclusions of other negatively racialized groups. It cannot therefore be perfectly tied, in its genesis, to ideas about race and the superiority of whiteness that have existed since the founding of the United States. Rather, the fall of Arabs from the graces of marginal whiteness is traceable to the emergence of the United States as a global superpower. This sociopolitical relationship, although not framed in racial terms, is acknowledged in some of the earlier scholarship on Arab Americans. For example, Suleiman and Abu-Laban note that the source of bias against Arabs in the United States relates "more to the original homeland and peoples than to the Arab-American community" (1989, 5), nonetheless producing substantial negative domestic repercussions. In the 1984 Zogby report noted above, domestic "images of greedy oil sheiks and bloodthirsty terrorists" are tied to political and economic events in the Middle East. More to the point, Fay states that "the source of today's defamation of Arab-Americans might be described as the domestic counterpart of the Arab-Israeli conflict" (1984; 22). My research on Palestinians in the United States (Cainkar 1988) showed how adopting an American identity was fraught with conflict for Palestinian Americans, who were portrayed by the media as a culturally barbaric group and treated by the U.S. government as the enemy within. How can one be American and America's enemy at the same time? The Palestinian case exposed the racialized nature of the challenge: the Soviet, Cuban, and Sandinista enemies were about governments and ideologies, the Arab enemy was about innate cultural dispositions to violence.

The domestic transformation of Arabs from marginal white to subordinate status was facilitated by the flexibility of whiteness and the historic and "observable" racial liminality of Arabs (a concept that can be extended to South Asians). In the decades prior to 1920, Arab whiteness was contested by local court clerks and judges trying to block their naturalization in locations such as Detroit, Buffalo, Cincinnati, St. Louis, and parts of the South (e.g., Georgia and South Carolina) (Samhan 1999). These experiences, however, were neither universal nor indicative of the totality of the early Arab American experience and can be counterposed, for example, by the freedom of movement experienced by Arabs engaged in commerce. These disparate experiences highlight the notion that race is socially constructed and that racial projects are embedded in local social relationships (Gualtieri 2004). But at its core, the social exclusion of Arabs in the United States has been a racial project because Arab inferiority has been constructed and sold to the American public using essentialist constructions of human difference. In the 1990s, when Islamist challenges to American global hegemony became more powerful than Arab nationalism, these constructions were extended to Muslims and became grander; they became civilizational. Seen as recently as 1943 as persons who shared "in the development of our civilization" by the Immigration and Naturalization Service (INS), affirming their whiteness and justifying their eligibility for naturalization, by the 1990s the "clash of civilizations" view (Huntington 1996), positioning Arabs (and Muslims) as the cultural Other, had become an accepted scholarly perspective. The seemingly race-neutral lens of essentialized cultural and religious differences was evoked after blatant racism had lost its power as an effective hegemonic tool (a consequence of the civil rights movement, according to some critical race theorists). Nonetheless, all the components of a racial project were there: the assertion of *innate characteristics* held by all members of a *group*. Power then comes into play when positive or negative valence is attached to innate characteristics and dominant societal institutions are utilized to inform, reward, control, and punish based on these determinations. Because race remains one of the fundamental tools for claiming rewards and organizing discipline in American society, and is something Americans know and understand, these notions of essential human difference have been corporealized, as if they were about color. Thus, race became the operant reference category for a woman opposing the construction of a mosque in her suburb when she testified: "I have no ill remorse for the Muslim race at all. I wish we could all live in peace, but . . . "[1] The corporealization is also evident in the actionable but sloppy phenotypic category "Arabs, Muslims, and persons assumed to be Arabs and Muslims," terms without which one cannot accurately describe hate incidents in the United States after the 9/11 attacks.

The racialization of Arabs is thus tied to larger global policies of the U.S. government. The domestic aspect of this project is in the manufacture of public consent—needed to support, finance, and defend these policies. For this reason, the most noted features of Arab exclusion in the United States are tactical: persistent, negative media representations; denial of political voice; governmental and nongovernmental policies targeting activism; and distortions of Arab and Muslim values, ways of life, and homelands ("civilizational" distortions). All of these actions are tied to the disenfranchisement of dissenting voices and delegitimation of Arab claims so as to assert information hegemony.

Since the darkening of Arabs began in earnest after the beneficiaries of the U.S. civil rights movement had been determined and the categories of "nonwhite" and "minority" had been set, Arabs have experienced the double burden of being excluded from whiteness *and* from mainstream recognition as people of color. They are still officially white and ineligible for affirmative action (Samhan 1999). This exclusion also has been evident in political mobilizations and in multicultural pedagogy. Political exclusion of Arab voices has been reinforced in mainstream civil society institutions by issue control, through which organizational leadership silences discussion of issues that challenge U.S. policies in the Arab world if their assertion is deemed to hinder other organizational objectives. In pedagogy, Arabs have been excluded from race and ethnic studies, and when mentioned, often treated differently than other groups (Cainkar 2002b). Consider the following quote from a race and ethnic studies textbook that implies that unlike other groups, Arabs are responsible for their own stereotyping:

Perhaps more serious (than discrimination faced by Muslim women) is the persistence of negative stereotyping that has plagued Middle Easterners in the US. The activities of *Arab terrorists* in the ME and elsewhere *have created* a

---

1. Field notes, Orland Park, Illinois, mosque hearing, Apr. 2004.

sinister image of Arab and other Middle Eastern groups—an image that was greatly exacerbated by the attack on the World Trade Center in 2001. (Emphasis added) (Marger 2003, 165)

The isolation of Arab Americans and their organizations from mainstream vehicles of dissent left them with few powerful allies from the 1960s onward (although they have had some local successes), allowing their challenges to hostile media representations, textbook biases, and selective policy enforcement to be ignored without a price.[2] Perpetuation and reinforcement of stigmatized views and political isolation of Arab Americans left them open targets for collective punishment after the 9/11 attacks on the United States.

Because the formation of Arabs as a unique racial group (separate from whites as well as others) was a racial project with timing and purpose different from historic American racism, its objective manifestation also differs from that of traditionally subordinated groups: African American, Latinos, Asians, and Native Americans. Its impact is not well measured by indexes of income, occupation, education, and residential segregation because the racialization project intervened in the ongoing trajectories of historically successful Arab American communities and because a large percentage of post–World War II Arab immigrants arrived in the United States with significant amounts of human capital. These facts have allowed Arabs to overcome some of the economic outcomes that usually correlate subordinate status; at the same time, they mask deep impacts on Arab American communities with low levels of human capital.

For similar historic reasons, some Arabs may see themselves as white (especially if they have benefited or seek to benefit from historical whiteness) while others may not, and Arab American communities may vary in their political alliances and understandings around race. Arab Americans may have racial options (a variation of Waters's [1990] concept of ethnic options) that members of other groups do not possess, but these options do not alter their grounded realities as a negatively stigmatized group. For these reasons of experience and aspiration, a person's racial identity may change over the course of his/her lifetime. Racialization and racial identity formation should be seen as unfolding and ongoing processes for Arab Americans.

2. See Fay (1984, 23), where she discusses the isolation of Arab Americans and ADC's efforts to establish ties to other ethnic and racial groups to forge antiracist alliances.

The ways in which Arabs, Muslims, and persons assumed to be Arabs and Muslims were held collectively responsible after the 9/11 attacks should alone provide convincing evidence that their racial denouement had been sufficiently sealed before the attacks occurred.[3] The public attribution of collective responsibility required an understanding that collective status trumps the individual. This phenomenon is reserved for persons from cultures represented as backward or barbaric, where persons operate in Durkheimian mechanical solidarity "in so far as they have no action of their own, as with the molecules of inorganic bodies. . . . In societies where this type of solidarity is highly developed, the individual is not his own master" (Giddens 1972, 139). Allegations of primitive culture correspond to Western racism as they have historically been used to describe communities of color. Inherently lazy, violent, familialistic, and unassimilable groups have been held responsible for their own bad fates, not the structure that denied them rights, as they were seen to block progress in the name of manifest destiny and the white man's burden. In contrast, a primary correlate of whiteness is the attribution of modernity, rationality, and individuality, including individual culpability. When someone who is white does something interpreted as wrong or reprehensible, it is depicted by the organs of power as an individual act, one that has no reflection on the values and beliefs of other members of the group. On the other hand, the virtues of whiteness that are positive are presented as shared characteristics. Thus, during World War II, Japanese in the United States were interred as potential enemies, but neither Germans nor Italians were so treated. Hitler, Mussolini, and their agents are portrayed as deviants and outliers, not reflections on white, European, or Christian culture. But the violent act of any Arab or Muslim is rendered to represent entire societies and cultures and is portrayed as a mechanical, civilizational act. These racialized ways of thinking require a priori stigmatization and cultural constructions.

Widespread acceptance and use of the "clash of civilizations" thesis by scholars, filmmakers, publishers, the media, the Christian right, and certain members of the U.S. government cemented the racialization of Arabs and Muslims and established the preconditions for collective backlash after 9/11. Because the

---

3. I am speaking domestically here, but the wars in Iraq and Afghanistan and other features of the war on terror (Guantanamo, torture, renditioning, disappearances) suggest that a global collective responsibility has been imposed.

majority of backlash has been perpetrated by whites, the backlash can be viewed as actions defining the boundaries of whiteness (Cainkar 2004a). Research conducted in Chicago shows that those who perpetrate these acts are often simultaneously displaying American flags, suggesting that these acts can also be viewed as symbolic attempts to define the boundaries of the nation, and who lies outside of it. While there is no doubt that concerns about personal safety and national security were behind some of the backlash and government policies that followed the 9/11 attacks, it is in their unbridled collective nature, their inclination to target anyone who appeared to be part of *the group,* that makes these responses racialized. Only members of groups that have been "othered" experience collective discipline and punishment, irrespective of any individual's relationship to a particular event, activity, or location.

The remainder of this chapter presents data collected in an ethnographic study of the impact of 9/11 on Arabs and Muslims in the Chicago metro area.[4] It amply demonstrates the imposition of collective guilt on Arabs and Muslims through public policies and popular actions, an outcome (not a beginning) of their racialization. It also demonstrates an achievement of the racialization project by showing that a majority of Arabs interviewed in the study do not think Arabs are white, although they are officially considered so, and know which box they are expected to check on forms. The various reasons Arabs give for this determination support a racialization thesis.

Arabs and Muslims in the United States have experienced, and continue to experience, collective punishment for the 9/11 attacks, irrespective of the fact that they did not perpetrate them. Their looks and names mark them as targets. At the same time, because "whiteness" bears the privilege of individual culpability, negative actions such as the abuse of Iraqi, Afghani, or other Arab or Muslim prisoners are represented as the work of lone "bad apples," thereby effectively circumventing the implication of higher-ups and the system they represent or an examination of the roots of these actions in cultivated racialized hatreds and essentialized, civilizational discourses. Applause-generating statements such as the following can be made by high-level military commanders without fear of discipline:

---

4. The Russell Sage Foundation funded the study of the impact of 9/11 on Arab Muslims in metropolitan Chicago.

Actually, it's a lot of fun to fight. You know, it's a hell of a hoot. I like brawling. You go into Afghanistan, you got guys who slap women around for five years because they didn't wear a veil. You know guys like that ain't got no manhood left anyway. So it's a hell of a lot of fun to shoot them. (Lt. Gen. James Mattis, quoted in NBCSanDiego.com 2005)

GOVERNMENT POLICIES AFTER 9/11

The United States government implemented a range of domestic policies in the name of national security and the war on terrorism after the attacks of September 11. Most of them were designed and carried out by the executive branch of government, bypassing public discussion or debate. Twenty-five of the thirty-seven known government security initiatives implemented between September 12, 2001, and mid-2003 either explicitly or implicitly targeted U.S. Arabs and Muslims (Tsao and Gutierrez 2003). These measures included mass arrests, secret and indefinite detentions, prolonged detention of "material witnesses," closed hearings, secret evidence, government eavesdropping on attorney-client conversations, FBI interviews, wiretapping, seizures of property, removals of aliens with technical visa violations, and mandatory special registration. At the very minimum, at least one hundred thousand Arabs and Muslims living in the United States personally experienced one of these measures.[5] Furthermore, the number of Arabs and Muslims able to study, work, and attend training, meetings, and conferences in the United States has plummeted (Cainkar 2004a). The profiling of Arabs and Muslims at U.S. airports, via special security checks and removal from airplanes, dampened their desire to travel domestically or abroad. A February 2002 article in *Arab-American Business* magazine provided special safety tips for Arab American travelers in a sidebar entitled "Flying While Arab." While many Arabs say these selective airport procedures have ended, others remain reluctant to fly.[6]

5. Some 83,000 persons living in the United States underwent call-in special registration, according to the Department of Homeland Security. At minimum, at least 20,000 additional Arabs and Muslims nationwide have been affected by one or more of the numerous post-9/11 national security initiatives.

6. Interview data from the study of the impact of 9/11 on Arab Muslims in metropolitan Chicago funded by the Russell Sage Foundation.

Government measures began with the roundup and detention of some twelve hundred citizens and noncitizens, most of Middle Eastern descent, directly after the September 11 attacks. While their names have not been revealed, the conditions under which persons were arrested and detained indicate profiling based on looks, names, and being in the wrong place at the wrong time. More than five hundred of these detainees were deported for visa violations, after long incarcerations waiting for security clearance; none was charged with connections to terrorism. (U.S. Department of Justice 2004). Subsequent measures included mandatory holds on all nonimmigrant visa applications submitted by men aged eighteen through forty-five from twenty-six countries, most of them Arab, subject to special security clearances; interviews with some five thousand individuals who came to the United States from Arab and Muslim countries after January 1, 2000, on nonimmigrant visas; and a second round of interviews with an additional three thousand persons. The Justice Department asked local police departments to participate in interviewing Arab residents of their towns, placing them in the position of monitoring persons they are supposed to protect.

In January 2002, the INS (now a division of the Department of Homeland Security) launched an initiative to track down and deport six thousand noncitizen males from (unnamed) Middle Eastern countries who had been ordered deported but had never left the United States. Although they are less than 2 percent of the estimated 314,000 so-called "absconders" in the United States, Middle Easterners were the government's target. In a meeting with members of Chicago's Arab American community, government officials claimed that they were not engaging in racial profiling, as other communities would be approached next.[7] They never were. In June 2002 the Department of Justice issued an internal memo to the INS and U.S. Customs requesting that they seek out and search all Yemenis, including American citizens, entering the United States. Yemeni Americans were removed from planes and boarding lines, waiting hours for security clearances. In July 2002, the INS announced that it would begin enforcing section 265(a) of the Immigration and Naturalization Act, which requires all aliens to register changes of address within ten days of moving. There

---

7. Statement made by U.S. Attorney Fitzpatrick at a public meeting with Chicago region federal government officials and members of Chicago's Arab and Muslim community. Burbank, Ill., Mar. 2002.

is nothing to prevent the selective enforcement of this rule. In fact, in one region, an INS official openly stated that this rule was not intended to be enforced for everyone.[8] In North Carolina, a Palestinian legal immigrant stopped for driving four miles over the speed limit was detained for two months and finally charged with a misdemeanor for failing to report his address change. The INS sought his deportation. A local immigration judge later ruled that he could not be deported for this technical infraction because he did not willfully break the law.

On August 12, 2002, Attorney General Ashcroft announced the implementation of the special registration program requiring tens of thousands of foreign visitors from Arab and Muslim countries to be fingerprinted, photographed, and registered. The domestic call-in part of the program required nonimmigrant males aged sixteen to sixty-four from twenty-three Muslim-majority countries, plus heavily Muslim Eritrea (and North Korea) to report and register with the U.S. immigration authorities during a specified time frame, be fingerprinted, photographed, and questioned, and thereafter submit to routine reporting.[9] Credit cards, licenses, and other documents were photocopied and sometimes not returned. Registrants were checked against lists for terrorist connections. Persons cleared of terrorist connections but found to be in violation of their visas or out of (immigration) status were jailed, required to post bond, and issued removal orders (deportation).

The INS produced flyers to advertise the call-in program. "This notice is for you" was splayed across the top, reminiscent of the notices posted for Japanese living in the western United States during World War II. The arrest and detention of hundreds of registrants, mostly Iranians, in southern California during the first period of special registration sparked national protest, as persons seeking to comply voluntarily with government rules were handcuffed and led off to jail for visa violations. Some reported verbal abuse and body-cavity searches. Men were confined to rooms holding fifty or more people, in leg shackles, and

8. National Immigration Forum national conference call, Aug. 15, 2002. Participation at the offices of the Illinois Coalition for Immigrant and Refugee Rights.

9. "Nonimmigrant aliens" includes all immigrants who are inspected by the INS upon entry to the United States and are not U.S. citizens, permanent residents, applicants for permanent residency, or applicants for asylum. The rule for special registration excluded nonimmigrants who are diplomats, persons working with international organizations, and a few other narrow categories of nonimmigrants (categories A and G).

forced to sleep on concrete floors.[10] Most of these detainees were working tax-payers with families who had otherwise lived lawfully in the United States for decades. Many had pending applications for permanent residency. Eventually, most of the detainees were released on bail, but the INS started removal proceedings at the same time. As a result of this initial handling of special registrants, the INS allowed persons found out of status, but cleared of terrorism, to post bail until their removal hearing.

The domestic call-in part of the program ran for nine months. In May 2003, after stating for months that the program was not targeting certain groups because it would eventually be expanded to all visiting aliens, the government announced its phasing out. According to the Department of Homeland Security, 82,880 Arabs, Muslims, and others from the selected countries had been "specially" registered through domestic call-in. Of these, 13,434 were issued removal orders for visa violations, all of them affirmatively cleared of terrorism or terrorist connections.[11] Another 127,694 persons were registered at their port of entry; none were found to have connections to terrorists. Of the more than 200,000 Muslims, Arabs, and persons from Muslim-majority countries registered, less than 50 were found to have criminal records. The rounding up for removal of more than 14,000 persons for visa violations—a highly select group comprising less than 1 percent of the estimated 3.2 to 3.6 million persons living in the United States while "out of status" and the 8 million undocumented—has few historic precedents in the United States. It far outnumbers the 556 foreign nationals deported for their political beliefs during the infamous 1919 Palmer Raids, but modestly compares to the 3.8 million Mexicans deported during Operation Wetback in the 1950s (Gourevitch 2003). The purpose of special registration, according to the executive associate commissioner of the Office of Field Operations of the INS, was to facilitate the "monitoring" of aliens whose residence in the United States warranted it "in the interest of national security" (U.S. Immigration and Naturalization Service n.d.). The U.S. Department of Homeland Security (2003), which took over immigration functions from the now-defunct INS, referred to special registration (using its NSEERS acronym) as a "pilot project focusing on a smaller segment of the nonimmigrant alien population deemed to be of risk

10. Reuters, Dec. 18, 2002.

11. Carol Hallstrom (Department of Homeland Security, Community Relations), in personal communication with the author, Chicago, June 2004.

to national security." These statements make explicit the government's view that Arabs and Muslims *as a group* are considered a security risk for the United States. This view is found in other Bush administration programs, such as FBI director Mueller's January 2003 initiative to tie FBI field office goals for wire-tapping and undercover activities to the number of mosques in the field area.[12]

An examination of the legislative history upon which Attorney General Ashcroft legitimated special registration provides useful clues about its ideological and racial boundary making. Ashcroft cited legislative authority for this program that encompasses a history going back to the 1798 Alien and Sedition Acts, which were primarily aimed at restraining and deporting aliens living in the United States who were considered subversive. Ashcroft specifically cites as his authority the 1940 Smith Act, which was passed to strengthen national defense against communist and anarchist influences in the United States. The Smith Act was not aimed only at foreigners. It also prohibited American citizens from advocating or belonging to groups that advocated or taught the "duty, necessity desirability, or propriety" of overthrowing any level of government by "force or violence." It was the first peacetime federal sedition law since 1798 and was the basis for later prosecutions of persons alleged to be members of communist and socialist parties. The 2002 special registration program thus lies within the family of policies permitting the government to monitor, restrain, and remove persons whose political beliefs and ideologies it perceives as a threat.

On the other hand, because the special registration program named its targets by their countries of birth, not their beliefs, it shares features of the family of U.S. policies based on ideas about race (beginning with slavery, abolished in 1865, and Indian removal), such as the 1790 Naturalization Law, denying naturalized citizenship to nonwhites, repealed in 1952; the 1882 Chinese Exclusion Act, repealed in 1943; the Asia Barred Zone; and immigration quotas, enacted in 1921, revised in 1924 and 1952, and abolished in 1965, signaling the end of an era in which U.S. immigration policies were based principally on race. Although most of these laws referred to geographies and countries, their explicit purpose was racial. After 1965, it was considered against liberal democratic principles to discriminate blatantly in immigration policies by country of birth. But in 1981 the regulation of persons from certain "foreign states"

12. See, for example, Isikoff (2003). For a list of some of the earlier programs, see Louise Cainkar (2002a).

reemerged in immigration law when the attorney general was permitted to require "natives of any one or more foreign states, or any class of group thereof" to provide the government with address and other information upon ten days' notice. Interestingly, the Iran crisis of 1980 was specifically mentioned in the House Judiciary Committee report submitted for the 1981 law, thus connecting two reemergences: geographically based immigration procedures and political Islam (U.S. House Judiciary Committee 1981). Attorney General Ashcroft used this law to authorize call-in special registration.[13] Selective policies by country of birth emerged again in 1991 when Attorney General Dick Thornburgh required the special registration of persons holding Iraqi and Kuwaiti passports and travel documents. In sum, since the end of quotas and the dawn of the civil rights era, punitive or controlling special immigration policies based on country of birth or nationality have been applied solely to Arabs and persons from (non-European) Muslim-majority countries (with the exception of North Korea). These place-based discriminatory policies flourish at the nexus of assumptions about the relationship between "race" or national origin and culture and ideology. As they locate Arabs and Muslims and place them in subordinate status through laws and policies specially geared for them, they reinforce the appropriateness of maintaining essentialist ideas about members of these groups.

These programs link to the racialization of Arabs and Muslims because they give concrete meaning to essentialized, undifferentiated representations of Arabs and Muslims. The discourse of security risk and assumptions about the innate characteristics of persons who inhabit the grand categories of Arab and Muslim are institutionalized through homeland security and war-on-terror policies. These discipline and control programs tied to dominant institutions in American society establish boundaries of the nation inside the nation, effectively removing whole populations from legal protection. Operating in tandem with anti-Muslim discourses found throughout American society, these policies entrench the criminalization of Arabs and Muslims in the United States. Understanding that race is a historically located social construct that has no fixed meaning, that it differentiates between human beings using discourses of human essences, and that a racial project is one that creates or reproduces structures of domination based on these categories and understandings, we must ask: Can policies that target persons from two continents, three world regions, and

13. U.S. Public Law 97-116.

through their messiness incorporate persons from three major religions, be considered racist and part of a racialization project?[14] The answer, I believe, is yes, because the targets of these policies are categories of humans constructed on the basis of essentialized understandings. Implementation of these policies produces structural outcomes of inequality and further entrenches popular notions of a "terrorist" phenotype. This global project that includes multiple subordinate populations has been amalgamated into a civilizational racial project.

POPULAR SUPPORT FOR COLLECTIVE POLICIES

After the 9/11 attacks, public opinion polls showed broad support for the special treatment of Arabs, *as a group,* in the United States. A poll conducted in mid-September 2001 found respondents evenly divided over whether all Arabs in the United States, including American citizens, should be required to carry special identity cards (Smith 2001). Two late September Gallup polls found that a majority of Americans favored profiling of Arabs, including American citizens, and subjecting them to special security checks before boarding planes.[15] A December 2001 University of Illinois poll found that some 70 percent of Illinois residents were willing to sacrifice their civil rights to fight terrorism, and more than one-quarter of respondents said Arab Americans should surrender more rights than others.[16] A March 2002 CNN/Gallup/*USA Today* poll found that nearly 60 percent of Americans favored reducing the number of immigrants from Muslim countries. In August, a majority of the American public said that there were "too many" immigrants from Arab countries.[17] In December 2004, a Cornell University study found that nearly 50 percent of respondents in a national poll believed the U.S. government should curtail civil liberties for Muslim Americans (Nisbet and Shanahan 2004). These polls indicate that the essentialized representations of Arabs and Muslims, propagated by the media and film industry, uncontested in pedagogy, and reflected in government policies and actions, have been extremely effective in garnering public support for treating Arabs and Muslims as a special

14. "Essentialist" refers to a belief in real, true human essences, existing outside or impervious to social and historical context. See Omi and Winant (1994), 71.

15. *Chicago Sun-Times,* Oct. 2, 2001.

16. *News Sun* (Ill.), Dec. 20, 2001.

17. Gallup News Service, Aug. 8, 2002.

group possessing fewer rights than others. These views would not have emerged suddenly after 9/11 had they not been cultivated prior to the attacks. Otherwise, the hijackers would have been seen in ways similar to Timothy McVeigh, the Oklahoma City bomber, or to members of the Irish Republican Army—as extremists whose actions do not reflect on an entire race, religion, or civilization.

ARABS AND RACE FROM THE PERSPECTIVE
OF ARAB MUSLIMS IN METROPOLITAN CHICAGO

Data from interviews conducted with Arab Muslims in metropolitan Chicago as part of a post-9/11 ethnographic study provide insight into how Arabs view their place in the racial structure of the United States. One hundred and two study participants (see table 2.1 for sample demography) were asked: "There have been discussions about whether Arabs are white or not, with different points of view. Do you think Arabs are white, not white, or what?" Sixty-three percent of respondents said Arabs were not white, 20 percent said they were white, and another 17 percent gave equivocal responses. Study data indicate the elements of social life persons bring to bear on their assessment of the "racial place" of Arabs, which in theory could be phenotypical, experiential, observational, relational, local, national, or global.

Individuals who said Arabs were not white made this assessment on the basis (in order of frequency) of: their treatment in American society, skin color and other phenotypic criteria, the fact that Arabs are multiracial, cultural/historical differences from white Europeans, and Arab distinctiveness ("Arabs are Arabs"). Many invoked multiple criteria. A majority of persons who said Arabs are white and about one-third of persons who said Arabs were not white moved immediately into an unprovoked discourse about forms—especially census forms and job and school applications. In other words, the discussion of race became a discussion of categories and boxes and their views on these boxes and on the way that American society groups people by color. Arabs know that they are supposed to check the "white" box on forms, and a majority say they do so, even if they have serious problems with the concept, and even if they believe Arabs are not white.

Q: There have been discussions about whether Arabs are white or not, with different points of view. Do you think Arabs are white, not white, or what?

Table 2.1
Cainkar Study: Arab/Muslim Sample Statistics

Demographic	Percentage
Female	45
Income	
Poor/low income	18
Middle class	62
Upper middle class and wealthy	20
Age	
19–29	30
30–49	56
50 and over	14
Education	
High school or less	14
Some college or BS/BA	43
Postgraduate	42
Born in U.S.[a]	29
N	102

[a]Includes for sociological reasons persons who migrated to the United States before age ten.

> *A:* This confuses me every time I fill out an application. We are not white, black, Hispanic, or Asian. We are Arab. I put white. If there is another, sometimes I put that. But I put White because I know we are not other. (Jordanian-born female)

Most interviewees made a distinction between what they write on forms and what they see as their reality. In other words, Arab American responses on forms are social constructions in themselves, and must be understood as the products of a larger social context. This man speaks about how he writes "white," meanwhile knowing it's not "true."

> We used to report quarterly on affirmative action and I always asked my boss "what should I do?" Should I put myself as a minority or not?" He did not know either, so we called the company headquarters and they said you will be

considered white. But of course in real life we are not. As far as statistics go, that's what they say, legally. (Palestinian-born male)

Still, some insist on checking the "other" box. Most who do this do not know that persons who check "other" and can be determined to be Arab, or who write in "Arab," are recoded as white by the Census Bureau.

I always choose other. I'm not white and I'm not going to check white. (Puerto Rican–born male)

A large proportion of persons who said Arabs are white said they knew Arabs were white because they were told that was the case.

I was really surprised when I learned that we were Caucasian. (U.S.-born woman)

Geographically, Egypt is in Africa but they classify all the Arabs as white, so I write white. (Egyptian-born male)

Many Arab Americans see being required to participate in a project that socially constructs their identity in ways that match historic American ideas about race but denies their real experiences and refuses them minority benefits as yet another layer of discrimination.

I am resentful that I have to put down white. I don't look white. I am not treated as white. (1.5-generation female)

I felt I was at a disadvantage to have to check "white." I don't think it's fair because it is not who I am. I just don't feel that I'm a typical white American, you know, Anglo-Saxon, because if you look at me I'm not. I feel that I am a minority. Why should I be grouped with these people and not have a chance to obtain a scholarship? (Libyan-born female)

Sometimes you put other but what is other? Other could be anything. You feel like inferior, you know. Like the minority of the minorities. We're not defined. . . . Officially we are white but we're not white. Somebody can say I don't have to hire you because you are white and I have a lot of white people here. But you're not white! (Palestinian-born male)

Placement in the "white" category effectively hides the discrimination that Arab Americans face by removing them as subjects in the study of social inequalities.

If we were recognized as a minority it would be acknowledged that oppression and discrimination occur. Socially we are not accepted in white circles. (Chicago-born female)

ARABS ARE NOT WHITE: RESPONSES BASED ON HOW ARABS ARE TREATED IN AMERICAN SOCIETY

The largest response category among persons who said Arabs are not white (36 percent) revolved around how Arabs are treated in American society.[18] In other words, they saw their racial place as nonwhite because they do not benefit from the statuses, assumptions, and rewards that accrue to whiteness. These respondents note the political exclusion and discriminatory treatment in schools and among the public that Arab Americans experience. The overwhelming majority of interviewees who gave this type of response were born in the United States, suggesting that deep understanding of the relationship between race and inequality of experience are particularly American, formed as part of an American upbringing. Their responses, in that they invoke issues that existed before 9/11, support the thesis that the racial project excluding Arabs from the benefits of whiteness was in place long before 9/11.

We have always been told we should be classified as other, then white. But if I go to Mississippi with my brother named Ahmed, there is no way he'd be treated as white. (Chicago-born female)

Arabs are definitely not white. That categorization comes from the treatment of a community by the institutions of American society. Arabs in the schools face the same institutional racism as other students of color. (Chicago-born male)

18. Because these are open-ended ethnographic interviews, some persons offered responses that fall into multiple categories.

The issue is, are you part of a privileged group of people that can dominate others, and I do not think we are part of that. Arabs are not part of the white or European ruling structure. We are politically excluded. (U.S.-born female)

One interviewee sees Arabs claiming whiteness as a survival mechanism developed in an earlier era, but one that is no longer effective in today's cities and suburbs, where Arab Americans face dominant culture oppression.

There is a great proportion who are going to say white because when the court allowed them [Arabs] to come into this country, one of the most racialized societies in the world where there is a white/black dichotomy, identifying with white was a way of surviving. But as kids grow up in urban areas and in the suburbs, I think they reject whiteness as oppression. Many are gravitating toward the black experience and black culture as something closer to their experience. Young Arab kids growing up here definitely do not see themselves as white. (Jordanian-born male)

Since 9/11, the racial Otherness of the Arabs has been reconstructed as the foreign enemy, leading many Arab Americans to fear for their long-term safety in the United States.

You understand that there is racism even if it is not personally inflicted on you. Being a first-generation Egyptian American and Muslim is a difficult thing—to form an identity of your own and feel like an American and that you fit into this country when you feel you really don't anyway. So, there's always been this sort of racism. . . . That outlook was always there, it was just exaggerated [after 9/11] making you feel like the enemy. That you're the bad one, and you're definitely a foreigner and do not belong in this country. I'm just as much American as anyone else. I feel like maybe I need to get the hell out of this country because something bad is going to happen to our people here. (U.S.-born female)

ARABS ARE NOT WHITE: RESPONSES BASED ON SKIN COLOR
AND OTHER PHENOTYPIC CRITERIA

The second most common response (28 percent) among persons who said Arabs are not white was about skin color and other phenotypic features. Both U.S.- and non-U.S.-born respondents made such statements, although immigrants frequently spoke of how they learned about social systems organized around skin color only after arriving in the United States.

> You know it's funny, nobody ever discusses color once you step out of the United States. I think it only matters in this country. This country is very race conscious, color conscious I mean. My sister married a very dark man and when you look at him you would say he is black. We never thought that was unusual. . . . I complained about my hair once at school and they said oh, yeh, you have that Semitic hair. I never thought of my hair being Semitic. Sometimes the girls would say to me "well you are olive-skinned." I don't see myself that way. So, I think in their minds they have a perception of gradations of color, and I don't have that. (Jordanian-born female)

If not white, what color are Arabs? Some respondents tried to place themselves on a color chart, citing olive, brown, gray, or black.

> I'm not white, I am olive. To certain people it matters if you're white. (Chicago-born female)

> People look at me and they don't know what I am. They know I am not white or black. People think I am Hispanic. Brown is in the middle. (U.S.-born female)

> Clinically, Arabs have dispersed around the world enough to fall into both categories. Clinically they are a people of color. I consider myself gray (between white and black). (Palestinian-born male)

> I am from a country that is not white, for sure. (Sudanese-born male)

Arab Americans who say Arabs are not phenotypically white also point out that more than skin color enters the equation; there are also distinguishing facial features and types of hair.

> We don't look white. What matters in the U.S. is not Caucasian blood but skin color. This has a huge impact on us. And you see nappy hair, even if blue eyes and light skin. (Chicago-born female)

> In this suburb, it is lily white. We don't belong here. I am very aware of my skin color and looks. (Kuwaiti-born female)

Many respondents were extremely uncomfortable with the very concept of race and color. After stating that Arabs were not white, some respondents explained that they found the very idea of race useless, irrelevant, or offensive and some observed that racism is abhorred in Islam.

> We are definitely not white. But the whole idea of color makes no sense to me. My neighbor is black according to census forms but she is lighter than I am. There are Arabs that are lighter than white people. I don't think people should be classified like that, by color. I don't agree with it at all. If I was to classify myself, I would consider myself brown. I would not consider myself white. My youngest and oldest child would be white and my middle child brown. It does not work for me. (Kuwaiti-born female)

> You are not the color of your skin. It is ridiculous to try and categorize everybody into certain groups of skin color. You are who you are because of what sits in your heart and the experiences you have encountered in your life. (U.S.-born male)

> I don't feel comfortable classifying people by color anyway. It is against my ideology, my thinking, and my religion. (Egyptian-born male)

> We do not talk about this issue in our community. We feel that we are Muslims and that is what matters to us. (Palestinian-born male)

ARABS ARE NOT WHITE: THEY SPAN A RANGE OF GEOGRAPHIC REGIONS AND SKIN COLORS

The third most common response (24 percent) among persons who said Arabs are not white was that Arabs cannot be a racial group because the Arab world encompasses many geographic regions and skin colors. As such, it is not possible to assign a color to Arabs.

> I think Arabs should have a different category until things change. . . . If you look on the map, Arab countries cover two continents, and the white-white and dark black. If this is my cousin and he's dark, and he's from Africa, are you going to call him white? (U.S.-born female)

> It does not matter to me because in the Arab community we have white, black, and yellow. As Muslims, there is no difference between colors. (Palestinian-born male)

Arabs are distinct upon themselves, and the Arab world encompasses both black and white. (U.S.-born female)

Arabs are a race of colors, many colors. (Lebanese-born male)

ARABS ARE NOT WHITE: ARAB HERITAGE IS DIFFERENT
FROM CAUCASIAN/EUROPEAN

The fourth most common response (20 percent) among persons who said Arabs are not white was about culture and heritage. To these Arab Americans, being white means being Caucasian and European, and Arabs are neither.

I don't see myself as white. We have a different background. I think of Europeans. We are more African than European. (Lebanese-born male)

Most Arabs think Caucasians are Europeans. (Kuwaiti-born male)

For those who said being white means being European, then allowing your history to be subsumed into that of Europe means denying your own Arab culture and heritage.

White in my mind means European, but since I am not European, I feel like I am lying. Why should I write white? (Egyptian-born male)

I have a culture and heritage; being white denies that. (U.S.-born female)

Their history and culture is quite separate from Europe's. I find it a disgrace that the Arab people should be so blatantly insulted by the disregard of their history. (U.S.-born female)

The following comments from a young man living in a middle-class Chicago suburb show how Arab is counterposed to Caucasian/white/American at the grounded neighborhood level:

I was with a group of friends. These Americans, Caucasians, drove past us and yelled out remarks—racial remarks. They turned around and they ran at us and we started to fight. In Chicago Ridge everyone was Arabic mostly, our whole neighborhood was Arabic, so no white person or American would say something about us unless it was in school, but in Orland, it's a little different. Arabic are like, they are not the minorities over there.

Q: Have women been affected in any special way?

A: They've been affected because it's more hard for them to walk down the street especially if they are in more of a Caucasian neighborhood, people like to stare and talk like behind their backs and Arabic women might not like that but Arabic women can't say things back. Things like that. (Jordanian-born male who came to the United States at age one)

Seventeen percent of respondents gave what may be called equivocal responses to the race question, marking the difficulty they have with the very idea of race and of pigeonholing Arabs into a racial category. The following quote expresses this ambiguity as it reveals (along with some of the quotes above) the socially constructed nature of the way Arabs respond to the formulaic race question.

I don't really know. I think, for me, it's always been white because of what I look like. I consider myself white. That's probably a personal reflection because my skin color is white. I've always thought all Arabs were white. I've never really thought of them as being nonwhite. But, again, why do we say we're white, because we're not white. Like people say, "you put 'white,'" and I think that it just doesn't make sense. I don't know what white means in terms of technical definition. Is it people who live north of the equator? I don't know how the experts have defined it. If you ask anybody, they say to put white as a race. Do I think we're white? I don't think so. (Chicago-born female)

THE BOX MATTERS IN A SOCIETY BUILT ON RACE

Even though the race question was not formulated as a discussion of forms and categories, responses nearly always invoked them at some point, signaling both a learned relationship between racial identification and state categories and a deep tension between the Arab experience in the United States and the phenomenon of racial categorization, which may be ideological, religious, or experiential. Nonetheless, when asked whether racial identification matters, 30 percent of persons interviewed said racial position is important in American society, whether they like the concept or not, because it is used to determine one's benefits. As neither white nor nonwhite, Arabs accrue neither the benefits of whiteness nor the protections of minority affirmative action. They feel this exclusion is unfair and further indicates their subordinate status. While quite a few respondents said Arabs should have their own separate category, like Hispanics, since they do not fit into any existing categories, many think the whole discussion is absurd, except that American institutions work on these premises.

> Hmm. Does it matter? It might matter, actually, I'm not really sure. I guess if you're looking theoretical, it shouldn't matter, but when you look on social and political and all that stuff, I think it does matter because of the way institutions in our society run. If you have affirmative action at your university and you're African American, there are rights of having a qualified percentage. We probably wish it doesn't matter, but it does. On résumé applications, they look at what your application says. I think it would be foolish to think that they don't look at what your race is. (Chicago-born female)

The formation of Arabs as a unique racial group (separate from white) was a racial project with timing and purpose different from historic American racism, leaving Arabs in the position of having no racial category (box) that makes sense to most of them. Arabs were in the midst of a new racial formation process that rendered them nonwhite after the categories of race—white, black, Hispanic, Asian and Pacific Islander, and Native American—had been set. While a new multiracial category has been developed, Arab American claims asking for a special category have been declined by the Census Bureau. Although largely rejecting the concept of the racial box, Arabs know that in a racially constructed society, thinking inside the box matters.

Arab Americans may have racial options that members of other groups do not possess. Some may be able to decide from one moment or context to the next whether they are white or not, whether they will select the box as they have been told or think about skin color, or contemplate how they are treated. Their racial identity may change over their lifetime, based on their own experiences, preferences, and demands. Racial identity is an unfolding, ongoing, contextual, and socially constructed process for Arab Americans. As the research data show, when Arab Americans select the "white" box, it does not necessarily mean that they identify with whiteness. But when they check "other," they become lost, a group that is paradoxically hidden yet the object of social obsession. These options do not alter their grounded reality as a negatively stigmatized group; on the contrary, they offer proof of their racially subordinate status.

Study data from metropolitan Chicago show that the majority of Arab Muslims view their social position in American society as subordinate and translate that status to a nonwhite racial position in a race-based societal hierarchy. Unfortunately, one cannot conclude from these data if religious affiliation plays any role in this outcome because Arab Christians were not part of the study. It is notable, however, that religion and religious discrimination were rarely invoked in responses to this question, except in statements that Islam does not condone racial distinctions.

DISCRIMINATION AND SAFETY IN THE POST-9/11 ARAB MUSLIM EXPERIENCE

Prejudice, discrimination, and a compromised sense of safety are historically correlated with racial subordination in the United States. These experiences have ranged from lynching, mass removals, quarantining, law-enforcement profiling, and sentencing disparities, to inferior employment, housing, and educational opportunities. Study participants were asked if they had experienced discrimination since 9/11; 53 percent said yes and 47 percent said no. Among those who responded "yes," specific instances of discrimination were reported in the following social sectors: employment (39 percent), public space (22 percent), schools (11 percent), law enforcement (11 percent), commercial transactions (9 percent), government offices (9 percent), airports/airplanes (7 percent), and civil society institutions (6 percent). When one reads the interviews fully, however, one discovers that these responses are related to a specific interpretation of the meaning of the term discrimination, which is to be denied something or treated in a different way than others. For example, many people did not interpret hate speech as discrimination. The same applies to feeling unsafe or fearing removal from the United States, which came up many times in the interviews, or having to change one's name to avoid prejudice.

Q: Have you experienced what you would consider discrimination?
A: No. I have not done anything to trigger it. I have not flown on a plane or applied for a job, where someone could say I couldn't. I have done things to protect me. I got tired of these things. I served in the military. People

question your loyalty. I got veterans plates from the state. I thought it would make a difference if someone sees me, or the police, or going somewhere they would know there is such a thing as the Arab face and serving in the military. (Palestinian-born male)

Many respondents said they felt watched while conducting routine activities, such as loading their car trunks, but did not indicate that as discrimination. Others changed their normal life patterns to avoid placing themselves in situations in which they expected to experience discrimination, by eating separately or changing jobs. Many persons who used to travel domestically changed their travel patterns after the attacks; they either stopped traveling or drove to their destinations. These actions indicate that the policing and control of members of the group has moved inside the mind of the individual, what Hatem Bazian (2004) has called "virtual internment" and Nadine Naber (2006) has termed "internment of the psyche." In the following quotes, Arab Americans talk about changing their names and their friendship groups to avoid verbal harassment or abuse.

No. The only problem I have is my name "Osama." When people ask me, I say Sam. (U.S.-born male)

I changed my circle of friends from Caucasian small-town girls [at NIU] to Arabs and Muslims and people of other ethnic backgrounds. I stopped going to bars and clubs and anywhere people made ignorant comments. Caucasians lack tolerance. (U.S.-born female)

I can feel too much discrimination in people's eyes when they gaze or stare at me after realizing I'm Arabian. Actually my appearance is kind of tricky. I'm very white, so at the first glance people would think I'm American or belong to some other nationality, therefore, they treat me nicely. But, when I tell them I'm Arabian, their looks would change suddenly. . . . In the past, I gave my business card to customers to call me whenever they need a ride, but they never did. It is only after I changed my Arabian name to be American that I have started to receive many calls from my customers. (Palestinian-born male; taxi driver)

The overwhelming majority of study interviewees reported being verbally harassed after 9/11, although the harassment took different forms depending upon the context in which it occurred. Public spaces such as streets and shopping malls were primary sites of abusive behavior, where Arabs were marked as foreigners to be spit at, sneezed upon, and sometimes threatened with worse.

> Once, we were in our car, and because my wife wore the veil, some people spitted on us, swore and insulted us. Many times while walking down the street, we found ourselves subject to many insults such as turning someone's face, spitting and using rude expressions that we didn't understand. (Palestinian-born male)

> One lady said to me "If I had a gun I would shoot you." (Palestinian-born female)

> We were driving and some teenagers shouted to us, "go back to your country. We need to get rid of you guys, kill you off." (Chicago-born female)

The public schools emerged as another site of harassment after 9/11, but my research has consistently shown schools as sites of discrimination long before 9/11. Here the pedagogical bias against Arabs and Muslims emerges; dominant discourses that demonize them are located not only in the media; they are also taught in the schools.

> On 9/11 I was the only Arab in the class. We were watching TV and the teacher's way of dealing with me changed. He showed pictures of Osama bin Laden and said [pointing to the respondent], "Ask him if you have any questions." (Palestinian-born male, community college student)

> On a personal level my family was not harassed but kidded around a lot in school. Like you are an Arab, and therefore you must go to prison now? Camel jockey go home and this sort of verbal harassment. As well as the teachers, one of the teachers at —— school, right after 9/11 said something to the effect of the Muslims, their religion allows them to become terrorists. This is part of what they believe is jihad. Of course my son was extremely humiliated by such a statement and was not able to respond because it was a figure of, you know a teacher and educator. But he told me about it and I verified it from another Muslim student in the same class. Then I went to talk to the school. And then we started a whole series of workshops to educate educators about Islam and who are the Arabs and a basic 101. So that was on a personal level, it touched home. (Saudi-born female)

In many school settings, discrimination against Arabs and Muslims has become institutionalized. This institutionalization appears to be particularly true in schools where Arabs and Muslims are a significant minority population and may be located in the statements and actions of administrators and secretaries, as well as in the lunch talk of teachers, forming a kind of local school culture.

I remember specifically one of the administrators . . . we were doing a reenactment in case anything ever happened at the school like a terrorist attack. The public schools had to have some type of a plan and one of the administrators said, "Well, if a terrorist comes in, don't argue with that person about your religious ideology." Kind of insinuating there would be a Muslim as a terrorist. I kind of thought that was a bit of a discriminating remark, because you wouldn't have someone say . . . if you were contemplating that it was a racial issue, don't stand and discuss your race with that person, insinuating there would be a black American. So, I was a bit offended by that. So, remarks like that, I think, are, you know, I would define as discrimination. (U.S.-born female; teacher)

The day after 9/11 I was in the lunchroom and one of my colleagues said he saw a woman at the grocery store "with that thing on her head" and he wanted to hit her. Another colleague said "that would be stupid, they did not do it," and another colleague said "how do you know that, those people who did it were living here." I got up and left. I did not say anything. I was angry, and at the same time angry at myself for not having guts. After that, I was confiding in one of my friends what I felt and she said "if someone like you was next me on an airplane, I'd get nervous. (Egyptian-born 1.5 female; teacher)

I feel I'm discriminated against while at my children's school. The secretary there deals differently with Arabs. She never greets Arabic parents or smiles at them, while she always acts normally with other parents. (Kuwaiti-born female)

Many interviewees reported discrimination in the context of commercial transactions, especially in businesses located in primarily white suburban areas.

Shopping—people give an attitude, a look everywhere. Once I was with a friend at Kohls. I bought a lot of stuff. Expensive. The lady said after I paid for everything, she wants to check my stuff. She thought I stole. It was so embarrassing. I said bring your supervisor. She thought I'm afraid, that I don't speak the language. She started screaming at me. She called the supervisor. She checked. Everything was right. Asked cashier to apologize and she would not. I feel pressure is too high. She really embarrassed me. (Jordanian-born female)

I was at Linens and Things in Naperville with my friend and my curtain rod was hanging over the cart. I turned to the guy behind me to apologize for my rod (it did not touch him). I apologized and he said "turn around and don't talk to me." I said "someone woke up on the wrong side of the bed." He said "It's none of your business what side of the bed I woke up on. Why don't you wake up and go back where you came from." I was just floored. (Kuwaiti born female)

In addition to discrimination in public spaces and schools, some interviewees reported attacks on their homes.

Well, my van in front of my house was covered with eggs several times, about one or two months ago. I didn't report it . . . also some garbage was put in our mailbox, like ice cream cones and wrappers, stuff like that. . . . Once we called the police because it wasn't just the cars but also the house! They pelted the door with eggs, so I called the Oak Lawn police and he came and looked around. I showed him above the door and the van, and I wasn't happy with it and he said "Well, maybe these are kids" and I said, "Yeah, I know they aren't adults but they did it on purpose, not just because they were just having fun because it's only my house and my car." On the street, there are so many cars parked but only my cars were the ones hit. He said, "I recommend that you have a garage," and I said, "Yes, I do." He said I should put the cars in the garage and I asked him "Officer, what should I do with my door? Put it in the garage too?" (Palestinian-born male)

Discrimination was also reported in the context of work and applying for jobs. In the job application process, sometimes names triggered discrimination, other times it was triggered by looks.

Actually I face it personally like when I go fill out applications or go fill out papers because of my Arabic name—when you hear my name you know I am 100 percent Arabic of Arabic descent. When I write my name—it's like—I don't know like if they saw my name and some kid named "Mike" they're going to pick the "Mike" kid instead of me. Well I don't know for sure but I know where I went to a place that has 110 percent hiring and there was two kids with me—one of them Arabic and one of them white—and all three of us filled out the application and the white kid got the job. (Jordanian-born male, migrated at age one)

Besides the physical and verbal abuse, I applied for a job and I feel that it's not just that I'm imagining it. They said, "We don't know if we want someone who covers." Obviously, this is illegal but this was when I was going to school and I was trying to get a job in retail. For example, "It's not part of the image we want to have, especially now being a negative connotation and with you covering and the whole post-9/11 thing." In that regard, I have absolutely been discriminated against. But I always have. That just goes with being covered—I was always discriminated against pre-9/11 but especially post-9/11. I went to talk to the corporate manager of that retail chain and said it was uncalled for. They basically apologized and offered me a job but I didn't want to work there because of the bad experience I had and because I would probably be working with other people who probably felt the same way. Someone who's not working in the shop but at the headquarters is different. Originally, I did talk to a lawyer and they were going to go into it but I didn't go further than that. (Libyan-born female, migrated before age ten)

Discussions about Arab or Muslim terrorists were encountered by some interviewees in the daily context of work.

I have heard we should kill all Arabs/Muslims from people at work. (Egyptian-born male, migrated at age one)

Here in Chicago I would say not blatant, but right after 9/11 I took a job with a huge insurance brokerage firm and I was an underwriter for them and I basically assessed their risk for specific types of insurance coverage. And I had to deal a lot with the terrorism act that was made mandatory by Bush for all insurance policies. So when we were meeting about this and I was having to underwrite coverages and implement the terrorist act in there, there was . . . I dealt with a lot of bullshit comments and meetings from a lot of white people that were like you know how do we underwrite if . . . how are we supposed to underwrite if Ahmed or Mohammad get crazy and decide to throw another plane into a building and I am just like . . . I am sitting in this room and I am trying to maintain my composure and my managing director looks at me, she and I had a pretty good relationship, she was kind of like my mentor, she knows that I am just like brewing and steaming and she's like well first of all we shouldn't assume that it's going to be an Ahmed or a Mohammad you know and I quickly interjected, it could be a Timothy McVeigh, you know but either way you've got to underwrite it, figure out how to underwrite the risk that's involved. And everybody just kind of looked at me and I was just like it's the truth. (U.S.-born female)

One interviewee noted that discriminatory sentiments existed well before 9/11 and that they were more openly expressed in less diverse work environments:

I had more problems in my work after the Oklahoma City bombing than September 11. The Oklahoma City bombing wasn't Arab. I used to work in Ohio and I remember what happened in Oklahoma City, and it happened about noontime and I came back to the office and the guards who worked with me, they were joking and they asked me "where you been? You been to Oklahoma?" They told me what happened and they kind of put the finger on me like you guys did it, you know. I didn't feel comfortable, but the next day, when they found out who did it, things changed. I was working with another company two years after that, there was a guy who joked with me, I don't know if he was serious or if he was joking, he said, "if you want to bring a bomb here, just let me know, I'll leave the building before you come." I told him, "Listen, this is not a joke. Don't joke with me like that." This happened way after Oklahoma City and before September 11. I think the difference is the kind of people I work here with is different. In Ohio, there's not international or foreign people a lot. Most of the companies I worked with, I was the only one who had an accent. I'm the only one who's not white, you know. I look different and I have an accent and so on. Here in Chicago it's different . . . different nationalities, different languages. A lot of people have accents and people here, Americans and others, are used to that a lot. I feel more comfortable working in Chicago. (Palestinian-born male)

LACK OF SAFETY

Similarly, despite the fact that many interviewees said they had not experienced discrimination, a majority said that there are places where they do not feel safe in American society. A sense of lack of safety in public spaces appears to be gendered, as women, especially *muhajibaat* (women wearing headscarves) express this feeling significantly more than men. A large number of women interviewed, *muhajibaat* or not, report feeling afraid for their safety in certain types of public places. These places are almost always connected to whiteness. That is, while some men and women said they feel unsafe *as individuals* in neighborhoods associated with criminal activity, those who felt unsafe as *Arabs or Muslims* felt that way only in all-white or dominantly white areas. One woman said, "You won't find me in a park or a forest preserve"; another said, "Soccer moms scare me the most." Suburban shopping centers and malls were mentioned frequently as places where women endured stares and insults. The purpose of being made to feel uneasy, as they see it, is that Arabs and Muslims understand that they will not be granted the same rights and privileges that accrue to members of white society, including the privilege of being treated as an individual. Individuality lies at the opposite end of the pole to collective responsibility. The marking of these differences did not emerge as a result of the 9/11 attacks; the process was set in motion long before, creating the conditions for the attribution of collective guilt for the attacks.

Feeling unsafe is not limited to the public sphere. Interrogations, arrests, home invasions, and computer and property confiscations enacted by federal government authorities appear random, unfocused, and discriminatory to members of Arab and Muslim American communities. The government's use of secret evidence, closed hearings, arrests on terrorism charges that cannot be substantiated, eavesdropping on attorneys, and special registration have not built community confidence that Arab Americans will be treated fairly by the government or that the government's target is limited to terrorists and people who support them. Consequently, nearly everyone in the community feels vulnerable to a certain degree, even in their own homes. Thus, while some persons in the study said they felt safest in their homes, others said they felt the hidden eyes of surveillance, assumed their phones were tapped and computers monitored, and were concerned about the right of government agents to enter their homes at any time without permission or without leaving a trace.

Such matters of safety and security, where one is not safe even in one's home, are historically tied to racial subordination in American society: Native Americans lost their land and were placed in camps; African Americans were sold as property and segregated; Latinos were expropriated, attacked, and expelled in waves; and Asians were relegated to urban ghettos, denied property rights, and, in the case of Japanese, interred. The circle of closure that Arabs and Muslims feel is often not physically tangible, but many fear it could become so if another attack occurs. A majority of persons interviewed for this study said that they no longer feel secure in the United States and many fear a mass deportation, revocation of citizenship, or internment camps. Those with resources have adopted strategies to anticipate these potential outcomes: they have sent their children to universities in other countries and begun building homes in their countries of origin.

This feeling of "homeland insecurity" is exacerbated by the post-9/11 increase in discourses about civilizational differences between Arabs and Muslims and people with Western values. These ideas are published and broadcast in the mainstream American media and used as justifications for a range of government actions by neoconservative and Christian-right spokespersons, some of whom have described Islam as a religion outside the pale of human values and Muslims as "worse than Nazis" (Lee 2002). A booklet entitled *Why Islam Is a Threat to America and the West* (Lind and Weyrich 2002) argues that Muslims are a fifth column in the United States and "should be encouraged to leave." Televangelist Pat Robertson called Muslims potential killers on his *700 Club* TV program (Nimer 2003). Franklin Graham, who has called Islam an "evil and wicked religion," delivered the 2002 Good Friday homily at the Pentagon (Helal and Iftikhar 2003). While he was still in office, former attorney general Ashcroft stated in an interview with syndicated columnist Cal Thomas that "Islam is a religion in which God requires you to send your son to die for him. Christianity is a faith in which God sends his son to die for you."[19] Indeed, Arab and Muslim Americans feel quite uneasy about the close alliance between the Bush administration and the anti-Muslim Christian right in a country that espouses equality and religious pluralism.

CONCLUSION

The racialization processes experienced by Arab Americans differ in both historical timing and pretext from that of other groups in the United States. Unlike the historical argument of racial superiority and inferiority used to buttress the development of the United States as a country of white privilege, the fall of Arabs from the graces of marginal whiteness is traceable to the later emergence

---

19. See Mohamed Nimer (2003) and the American Arab Anti-Discrimination Committee (2003) for more documentation of these types of comments.

of the United States as a global superpower. The seemingly race-neutral lens of essentialized cultural differences and innate violence was promoted in the media and left to percolate by the educational system, thereby building support for government policies that targeted Arab Americans and justified their political exclusion. The cultural barbarism approach was effective and powerful because by the time it was needed to buttress U.S. foreign policies, blatant racism was no longer an effective hegemonic tool in the United States. The racial project that moved Arabs into subordinate status began clearly to mark the Arab American experience in the late 1960s and was the rationale behind the foundation of the most important pan-Arab American organizations. In the 1990s, when Islamist challenges to American global hegemony became more powerful than Arab nationalism, these essentialized constructions were extended to Muslims and became grander; they became civilizational. Both Arabs and Muslims were represented as persons of inherently different values and dispositions from "Americans." In time, American foreign policy ambitions also became grander, purporting to bring freedom to the subjects of Muslim civilization.

Race is something Americans know and understand and newcomers quickly learn. Despite all the efforts of the civil rights movement and affirmative action, race still has tremendous significance in American society. Like others in the United States, Arabs learn what their official racial group is. But many find a disjuncture between their assigned category (white) and their experiences, because race is understood as a phenomenon with experiential correlates. For decades, Arab Americans have faced challenges from the public over their beliefs, values, opinions, and culture, and over their claims that they were being disenfranchised in the pursuit of American foreign policies. Challenges have been based largely on notions that Arab American claims are invalid because the people making them are constitutionally different, flawed, less civilized, and more violent than others. The widespread display of this message, attesting to the notion of inherent differences among humans and representing Arabs as other than civilized people, has been an object of Arab American protest for more than thirty years. These representations of Arabs are embodied, displayed in images of dark haired, olive-skinned, hook-nosed, head-covered caricatures. Well in place before the 9/11 attacks, this corporealization came to life when "Arabs, Muslims, and persons assumed to be Arabs and Muslims" were physically attacked after 9/11. Notions of collective, civilizational responsibility justified imputing Arabs and Muslims with collective guilt for the attacks. As persons purportedly of a different civilization, the Arab/Muslim became counterposed to the American and to the white—Arab and Muslim Americans became the suspected, unsafe, and virtually circled.

The social and political exclusion of Arabs in the United States is an objectively verifiable racial project with global goals. Arab inferiority has been constructed and sold to the American public using essentialist constructions of human difference in order to manufacture public consent for global policies. The most noted features of Arabs' exclusion have been persistent negative media representations, denial of political voice, governmental and nongovernmental policies that target their activism, and civilizational distortions of Arab and Muslim values, ways of life, and homelands. Since the darkening of Arabs began in earnest after the beneficiaries of the U.S. civil rights movement had been determined and the categories of "nonwhite" and "minority" had been set, Arabs have experienced the double burden of being excluded from whiteness *and* from mainstream recognition as people of color. Their isolation from mainstream vehicles of dissent left them with few powerful allies to contest their treatment in American society, leaving them open targets for collective punishment after the 9/11 attacks on the United States. While many Arab American activists recognized long ago that their road to political inclusion and curtailment of discrimination is in alliance with people of color, their "untouchable" foreign policy issues and domestic economic relationships at the local level placed strains on these relationships. Perhaps one of the positive developments in the post-9/11 United States is the greater willingness of these groups to accept Arab Americans into their ranks.

THREE

The Moral Analogies of Race

Arab American Identity, Color Politics,
and the Limits of Racialized Citizenship

ANDREW SHRYOCK

THE 9/11 ATTACKS have resulted, so far, in U.S.-led invasions of two sovereign nation-states, the establishment of a massive government bureaucracy devoted to securing "the homeland," and the passing of draconian laws that infringe on civil liberties and basic human rights in the United States and abroad. While Americans at large are prone, in their assessments of 9/11 and its aftermath, to utter statements like "the world changed on that day" or "we will never be the same again," Arab Americans are likely to say that "things are the same as before, only worse." These formulas are already clichéd, but my sympathies lie with those who argue that the "war on terror" has managed only to render U.S. imperial policies in the Middle East more transparent, and prejudice against Arab and Muslim Americans more systematic, than they were in the past. I would also contend that many of the key sensibilities defining Arab American identity—what Nabeel Abraham (1989) once called its "mythos"—have been intensified by the trauma of 9/11. The sense of marginality, the ambivalence about inclusion in (or exclusion from) the cultural mainstream, desires for greater political influence in the United States, the fear of being scrutinized, spied on, and judged a threat to security—this "structure of feeling" has never been so firmly in place.

There are, however, novelties on the post-9/11 landscape. The one I will focus on in this essay is the growing perception that Arabs and Muslims in the United States are being "racialized," and that "racialization," as both an analytical tool and a political agenda, can help us understand what is happening to

Arabs and Muslims in America today. The best exemplars of this approach have appeared in the pages of *Middle East Report,* where several authors (e.g., Cainkar 2002a; Hassan 2002b; Aidi 2002, 2003; Bayoumi 2004) have portrayed the war on terror as a massive exercise in racialization. To "racialize" an identity, one must privilege its links to supposedly "innate" qualities of the human body; in turn, these essentialized attributes can be used to justify (or counteract) policies of discrimination. Analysts who track the racialization of Arab Americans, however, rarely depict the process in this literal sense. Most argue that "race," as commonly understood in the United States, does not explain how Arabs and Muslims are marked as Other. Salah Hassan (2002b) plays on this discontinuity in the following text:

> Although Arabs and other people from the Middle East are classified racially as white according to the US Census and most affirmative action forms, since the 1960s, the US government has unofficially constituted them as a distinct racial group by associating Arabs with terrorism and threats to national security. Unlike other racial constructs, such as blackness or Asian-ness, which are defined officially in opposition to whiteness, the contemporary racialization of Arabs appears to be linked to US foreign policy in the Middle East and its translation into the domestic context. US support of Israel and its occupation of Arab lands casts a shadow upon Arab-Americans, who are treated as perpetual foreigners and denied the rights of other citizens and immigrants.

I find this model of "racialization" fascinating, largely because (1) it privileges race language while transforming conventional meanings of "race"; (2) it differs, in tone and substance, from an older rhetoric (and well-established politics) of "ethnicity"; and (3) it is an intellectually complex discourse that reproduces many of the contradictions that shape American notions of citizenship, color, belonging, and allegiance to nation and state. Hassan highlights these contradictions when he claims that Arabs are handicapped by their official designation as "white" because they are treated like a stigmatized minority without having any of the advantages that come with official minority status. Correcting this misfit by providing Arab Americans with their own U.S. Census category, he argues, might only make things worse.

> The proposal to create a new minority category is grounded in the assumption that the position of Arabs within the political system will be enhanced

if they are so classified. It may be, however, that Arabs and others from the Middle East will simply secure an official position within the racial hierarchy that corresponds more accurately with their second-class status. In the present climate, one of the significant risks of elaborating a Middle East minority category is the possible convergence of ethnic classification and racial profiling. Moreover, as a number of critics of the census have noted, official classifications are one of the principal mechanisms that the state uses to manage minorities.

In the end, Hassan rejects calls for an official Arab category, but he has already argued (convincingly) that Arabs must adapt to a special status imposed on them de facto by the state, whose policies, both global and domestic, fix the location of Arabs in a nationalized politics of difference.

The language of racialization is functioning, for Hassan and others, as an alternative idiom—free of the old assimilationist/integrationist assumptions—in which to talk about the status of Arabs in America. Hassan's language reinforces the "structure of feeling" that predominates among Arab Americans insofar as it accentuates marginality; it challenges that structure, however, when it asks Arabs to interpret their "second-class status" in relation to a state-sanctioned (and peculiarly American) "racial hierarchy." The latter exercise is accomplished only with great difficulty. Arabs do not occupy a uniform location within or outside this "racial hierarchy." Arab Americanists have shown how flexible and contested the labels applied to Arabic-speaking immigrants have been over the last century (Samhan 1999; Naber 2000; Gualtieri 2001). Many Arabs and Muslims believe their "second-class status" is a political effect that should not be confused with the racism faced by black Americans and other historically oppressed people of color.[1] Indeed, most Arab Americans identify as "white." The federal government continues to "officialize" this identity and even imposes it on Arabs who do not necessarily think of themselves as "white." The 2000 U.S. Census reported that 80 percent of the Arab population claimed "white as their only race" (U.S. Bureau of the Census 2003). This finding is an artifact of coding

---

1. I often hear Arab Americans say they would face minimal discrimination in the United States were it not for the Arab-Israeli conflict. This belief motivates and sets ideological limits on attempts to build coalitions between Arab Americans and minority populations that, according to Hassan, are "defined officially in opposition to whiteness."

procedures individual respondents cannot control,[2] but it remains the case that many Arab Americans, especially descendents of earlier generations of Levantine immigrants, enjoy the benefits of "whiteness" and want to continue doing so. Newly arrived immigrants, by contrast, often do not understand where they fit in American racial typologies—"Are Arabs white?"—or they identify using terms most Americans define as "ethnic" or "national," not "racial": "I am Arab Lebanese," or "We are Palestinians," or "I am an Iraqi Catholic." Some Arab Muslims, especially those who espouse a color-blind faith, endorse ideologies that cannot give primacy to race: "There is no color in Islam."

All of this, I would argue, makes the racialization discourse compelling. The fact that many Arab Americans now believe antiterrorism policies have constituted them as "a distinct racial group" says a great deal about the trauma of 9/11, the experience of marginalization and stigma, and how these are reshaping identity politics among Arabs and Muslims in the United States. In the late 1960s, Arab scholars, activists, and their allies living in the United States helped establish "Arab American identity" as an ideological response to the 1967 Arab-Israeli War. Their efforts brought a diverse array of Arabic speakers and their children into a distinctly American brand of pan-ethnic politics. Likewise, the "racialization discourse" of today is articulated most eloquently by scholars, activists, and intellectuals; it is formulated in response to U.S. policies in the Middle East; and it is bringing Arab immigrants and formerly "ethnic" Arabs into a new, distinctly American brand of *racial* politics.

THE RESONANCE OF RACE

I have argued elsewhere that Arab American identity, like all "x-American" identities, is a creative blend of fact and fiction (Abraham and Shryock 2000). The label attained widespread acceptance not because it described everyone well or was appropriate to all contexts in which people live; rather, it attained the dominance it has today by virtue of its political resonance. "Arab-American," as an organizing concept, made sense on both sides of the hyphen. It represented a

---

2. I thank Louise Cainkar for alerting me to the U.S. Census coding procedures in which Arab respondents who check "some other race," then write in "Arab" (or an Arab nationality, or "Middle Eastern"), are recoded as "white." This recoding collapses into a single category all those who checked "white" and all those who were recoded as "white" but did not explicitly identify as such.

semantic collaboration between Arabs and other Americans. The identity narratives it made possible—basically, standard(ized) tales of "ethnicity"—were intelligible to millions of people at once. Arab Americans who lived through this period realized that the "political resonance" of the new identity was alluring, but incomplete. One had to *become* Arab American, rounding off the edges of older identifications to make them fit, acquiring new names (differently pronounced), new ways of telling a life story, and sometimes radically reorienting one's relationship to friends and family. Images of "awakening" and "conversion" are apt—and frequently invoked in Arab Americanist scholarship—to describe this phase shift (see Orfalea 1988; Naff 1985; Suleiman 1994). The current "political resonance" carried by the idea of a "racialized" Arab American identity is activating a similar process.

To understand what is happening, I will attempt a tactical retreat from the domain of activist rhetoric and critical race theory. The projects advanced in this domain are typically ahead of, behind, or at odds with trends prevalent "in the community." By invoking the phrase "in the community," I am not referring to a place that preexists theory or activist engagement. Quite the contrary, "the community" is indispensable shorthand for the mix of people, institutions, and interests that activists and scholars make it their business to represent, sometimes as "members," sometimes as "external observers." In my experience, views on race, ethnicity, and most other forms of identity are much broader and less consistent (logically and ideologically) "in the community" than among the intellectuals who analyze it. For a reliable sense of what the current range of Arab American views on race looks like, one needs to engage empirically and conceptually with a large, representative sample of individuals who have been asked, in fairly specific terms, what they think about their identities.

A sample of precisely this kind is now available for Arab Detroit, one of the oldest, largest, and most highly concentrated Arab communities in North America. In 2003, I was part of the team that conducted the Detroit Arab American Study (DAAS), a face-to-face survey of over a thousand Arabs and Chaldeans living in Wayne, Macomb, and Oakland counties (Baker et al., 2004). Funded by the Russell Sage Foundation, the DAAS was administered by the Institute for Social Research at the University of Michigan, which made full use of the complex sampling techniques and quantitative methodologies favored in policy-oriented "big social science." Because I am an ethnographer and oral historian by training, much of this apparatus was (and remains) a mystery to me,[3] but several of my colleagues on the team shared my interest in identity formation among Arab Americans, and the questions we devised for the survey have now been answered by 1,016 people, all of them randomly selected. The potential for knowing how "race," "ancestry," and "identity" are understood by Arabs in North America is greatly enhanced by this new (and, as statisticians would say, "robust") data set. Before discussing the data themselves, however, I would like first to discuss the ideological backdrop against which they are discernable as data about "race."

RACIALIZATION IS AMERICANIZATION

The study of race in the contemporary United States is tangled up, for now, in its own dichotomized orthodoxy. Most analysts agree that race is a "social construct," but the same analysts tend also to agree that race is defined as something real and is, as W. I. Thomas puts it, "real in its consequences." Arguments pitched too closely to either side of this orthodoxy—to a "reality of construction" or a "reality of consequence"—seem willfully at odds with what people think or do. The massive effort the U.S. Census puts into updating and analyzing its race categories—which divide roughly 300 million Americans into five groups and a residual slot for all "others," with the option of combining all six in multiple ways (U.S. Census 2001)—is proof enough that race is a creation of the political process. In 2000, census coders managed to define 98 percent of Americans as belonging to one of the six official categories, and of these only 6 percent were identified as belonging to "some other race"; only 2 percent of the population claimed to belong to more than one race. These figures suggest that there are "real consequences," socially and politically, for citizens who cannot be easily located, or cannot locate themselves, on the existing racial grid.

Although rarely as "neat" as U.S. Census models, popular discourses on race do have a prevailing logic and style, and all the contradictions that define scholarly and governmental approaches to race are equally present in everyday talk. Most Americans equate race with "the color of one's skin"—or the shape of

3. A thorough description of the methodology used in the DAAS, authored by Steve Herringa and Terry Adams, is available on the ISR website, at http://webuser.bus.umich.edu/way neb/DAASTechnicalReport.pdf. DAAS preliminary findings can be viewed at http://www.umich .edu/news/Releases/2004/Jul04/daas.pdf.

one's eyes, or the texture of one's hair—not with the "content of one's character." Yet race shapes life experiences, and most people assume that life experiences shape character. Race is thought to be "biological"; it exists apart from (and in spite of) any cultural or historical materials that might be associated with it. A person is "born" black in this worldview, even if cultural and historical factors make her an American citizen, a Dominican immigrant, a Baptist, and a resident of New York City. If this person had been adopted and raised by "white" American parents, she would remain, in some immutable sense, "black." This apparent fixity of types is contradicted, however, by the fact that most racial categories are historically new ("Asian" only recently replaced "Oriental," for instance), and the groups who "fit" in racial categories change markedly over time and space (Italians have not always been "white"; Punjabis, once "Aryan," are now "Asian"; our "black" Dominican Baptist is described as "blanca"/white on her Dominican passport). Nonetheless, terms like "white" and "Asian" make reference to "origins" and "ancestral populations" that are invariably portrayed as ancient. Finally, most Americans believe race is not a matter of personal choice (although being "white" or "black" or "Asian" requires constant effort, and divergences from racial norms will provoke anxiety and criticism). Because race is not freely chosen, belonging to a specific racial background should not, in itself, carry any negative or positive moral connotations (even though stereotypes are a fact of life, and racial groups seem clearly to be ranked).

Americans call unacceptable departures from this dominant ideology "racism," and polite society agrees that racism is bad, although everyone is assumed to have a race (and can now, officially, have more than one). We are encouraged to think of ourselves and others racially, and attempts to evade this task are often regarded with suspicion. Racialization, in this generic sense, is part of Americanization, and Arabs are expected to participate in this process, just as they are expected to vote, pay taxes, and learn English. The inconsistency with which Arab Americans associate themselves (or are associated) with existing racial categories is symptomatic of how Arabs are located in the politics of Americanization. The data from Detroit show that Arabs are ten times more likely than the general population to call themselves "other." Yet unlike many communities of color—and *like* Hispanics/Latinos[4]—Arabs are willing, in large

---

4. In the 2000 U.S. Census (2001), 48 percent of Latinos described themselves as "white," and 42 percent said they were "some other race." Few analysts develop the analogy, but it would seem

numbers, to identify as "white." These exceptional patterns are related to pre-vailing notions of "Arab Americanness," an identity that is not accepted by a substantial portion of "the community" it is said to describe.

THE DATA FROM DETROIT

The DAAS includes three questions that directly address issues of racial and ethnic identification. The first two acknowledge that "Arab American" is not the only identity label people in our sample use to explain who they are:

1. Do you feel the term "Arab American" describes you?

2. Is there any other term like "Arab American" that better describes you? (If respondents said "yes," they were asked to specify.)

Answers to these questions enabled us to determine how widespread "Arab American" identity is and what factors make it un/appealing to some respon-dents. The third question, explicitly oriented toward racial identities, is drawn from the U.S. Census:

3. What is your race? (Check all that apply): 1. White; 2. Black, African American, or Negro; 3. American Indian or Alaska Native; 4. Asian; 5. Pacific Islander; 6. Other (Specify).

Answers to this question were analyzed differently from answers provided to the U.S. Census. The DAAS did not "recode" write-in responses—"Arab," "Lebanese," "Palestinian"—as "white" when the respondent did not check the "white" box. A DAAS respondent who described herself as "other," then speci-fied that she was Iraqi, would not be returned to the "white" category (as she would be in the U.S. Census) but would remain as "other" (and Iraqi).

In answer to our first two identity questions, a solid majority (70 percent) of DAAS respondents were willing to call themselves "Arab American," while 30 percent wanted to be called something else. People offered roughly one hundred alternative identities when asked if there was "another term, like Arab American, that describes you better." Their responses included "just American," "Iraqi," "Egyptian Christian," "Arabic," "Lebanese American," "American Lebanese,"

---

that "Arabness," as a mixed cultural/linguistic identity, is similar to Latinidad as an overarching category in which levels of identification with "whiteness" vary. Viewing "Arab" in contradistinc-tion to "white," as opposed to "Anglophone," effectively prevents such analysis.

and other permutations of national, regional, and religious labels. Not a single person opted for an extant "racial" alternative: no one said white, black, Asian, or even "of color."

Christians were less likely than Muslims to accept the "Arab American" label. While 60 percent of Christians in the DAAS sample thought the term described them accurately, only 45 percent of Iraqi Christians did. Iraqi Christians in the Detroit area are mostly Chaldean Catholics, an Aramaic- and Arabic-speaking group whose leaders and organizations are known locally for insisting on their non-Arab status. Thirty percent of Christians from Lebanon and Syria (mostly Maronites) and Egypt (mostly Copts) wanted to be called something other than "Arab American." Muslim respondents, regardless of national origin, welcomed the term, with over 80 percent saying it described them. In general, half of Iraqis resisted the Arab American label, while overwhelming majorities from Yemen, Palestine, Jordan, Lebanon, and Syria embraced it. Citizenship and place of birth seem to have no bearing on whether a person identifies as Arab American. U.S. citizens and noncitizens accepted the label at a rate of 70 percent; the same is true of those born in the United States and those born abroad.

The DAAS also found strong, suggestive patterning in responses to our question about race. The 64 percent majority who identify as "white" were more likely to be Christian and to live in middle- and upper-middle-class suburbs, interspersed among a white majority. The 31 percent who identified as "other" were more likely to live in the heavily concentrated Muslim enclaves of Dearborn, Dearborn Heights, and adjacent neighborhoods in the City of Detroit. In the Dearborn area, 45 percent of respondents called themselves "other," compared to 25 percent who live elsewhere. While 73 percent of Christians identify as "white," only 50 percent of Muslims do. Religion and residence are not the only important variables. Arabs and Chaldeans born in America, and those with U.S. citizenship, are more likely to identify as "white" than noncitizens and those born abroad. Also, those who said the label "Arab American" does *not* describe them were more likely to identify as "white" (71 percent as compared to 60 percent among those who identified as Arab American).

The preference for "white" or "other" is nearly exclusive. Only 4 percent of Arabs and Chaldeans called themselves "Asian," and only two individuals (out of 1,016 surveyed) said they were "black." When asked to specify what kind of "other" they might be, most DAAS respondents suggested variants of "Arab" (43 percent), "Middle Eastern" (29 percent), or "Chaldean" (15 percent). A smaller number (9 percent) opted for a national identity, with "Lebanese" (4 percent) being the most common. Only eight individuals identified as Muslim; only two said they were Muslim only; and Christian identities were expressed using labels that, among Arabs, have strong ethnonational connotations (e.g., Copt, Maronite, Chaldean, Syrian Orthodox, and so on). In short, individuals who chose "other" were sending two clear messages: (1) they do not consider themselves "white," and (2) they do not accept the racial categories on offer in the U.S. Census. It is also worth noting that, in a control sample of 508 members of greater Detroit's general population, 68 percent of respondents identified as "white," a figure only 4 percentage points higher than the Arab sample. By contrast, only 3 percent of the general population described themselves as "other."

IDENTITY DIALECTS IN DETROIT

It is hard to say whether DAAS respondents think of "Arab American," "white," "Middle Eastern," or other identity labels primarily in terms of bodily difference, cultural inheritance, or political combinations of both. Opinions vary radically: "Arabs are people who speak Arabic," "Arabs are people who come from the Arab-majority countries," "To be an Arab, you've got to have some Arab blood in you," "If you identify as Arab, you're Arab," "If your dad's an Arab, so are you," "People who are part of the heritage and culture, who value it, are Arab." Over the years I have heard countless variations on comments like these. I have also learned, through adjustment to identity dialects spoken among Arabs in Detroit, that the terms "white" and "American" are powerfully linked in everyday usage. When an Arab American living in Dearborn says, "She married an American guy," or "His son acts like an American," or "Is he Arab or American?" the speaker is almost always using the term "American" to describe a "white person" or even a "white Christian person." If this were not the case, the appropriate marked term would likely be used: "She married a Jew," "His son acts black," "Is he Arab or Mexican?" This slipshod equation of generic "whiteness" with generic "Americanness" is scandalous in the accuracy with which it correlates color and social dominance. Predictably, it has produced a "politically correct" alternative, which is to divide all persons into "Arab" and "non-Arab," preserving the possibility that people located on both sides of this divide can be "American."

The link between America and whiteness remains strong, however, and the relationship of "Arabness" to either term is problematic. The hyphen (visible or deleted) in Arab-American is an iconic expression of this status, as is the tendency, common among Arabs in Detroit, to define "whiteness" as a quality Arabs can approximate—more convincingly than blacks or Asians, for instance—but cannot authentically embody, while authentic Arabness is somehow lessened or diluted by whiteness. "He thinks he's white," is a common putdown, and "halfies," with their white mothers (and, less often, their white fathers), are exposed to the flip side of this insult: "She thinks she's an Arab." It is true that most Arab Americans have no problem checking the "white" box on government forms, but these identifications are usually done in ways that place a strategic distance between "Arab whiteness" and other, more conventional kinds. As one Lebanese woman explained to me, when I asked why she checked "white" on her U.S. Census form: "Technically, I'm white. That's what I've been told. But it doesn't mean that I'm *white* white." Such views are common. They treat "Arab whiteness," quite explicitly, as a "technicality" (not a fact of nature), a quality dependent on "what others say" (not what one believes about oneself), and somehow insufficient (not fully or "really" what it seems to be). When Arabs in Detroit say "I'm not white," or even "I'm not *white* white," they are marking their position against a set of racial identities that render their claims to citizenship and national belonging insecure.

Given all this, it is fairly easy to conclude that "racial features" and biologized conceptions of "race"—at least as most Americans understand them—cannot explain how Arabs deploy the range of identities now available to them. The DAAS found that Arab Americans who called themselves "white" were generally perceived to have lighter complexions by their interviewers (most of whom were also of Arab background); those who identified as "other" were perceived, on average, to be darker. Yet many respondents identified against their phenotype. Over a quarter (27 percent) of respondents described as "light or very light" called themselves "other," while 42 percent of respondents described as "dark or very dark" said they were "white." Even though 64 percent of the sample identified as white, just under half (49 percent) were judged to have "light" or "very light" skin. In fact, some of the most significant predictors of "whiteness" had nothing to do with complexion: if a person was interviewed in Arabic (over 40 percent were); was older, more highly educated, Christian, or American born; or lived outside Dearborn's Arab/Muslim enclaves (as 71 percent of the sample did), they were more likely to call themselves "white."

I would argue that Arabs—and, even more so, Muslims—in the United States are not discerned principally (by themselves or others) in relation to a color chart, much less a color line, but in relation to political boundaries and presumed loyalties that place Arabs and Muslims *outside* the American "racial hierarchy," with its recognizable patterns of abuse and redress. The post-9/11 intensification of color politics among Arab Americans is an elaborately coded response to this exclusion, and like most tactical responses, it reveals a great deal about "the rules" of race(ism), pluralism, and citizenship in the United States. To understand the code, one must first get beneath its fetishization of color terminology, the "unstable currency" on which the political economy of racism, and antiracism, is based.

SPINNING THE COLOR WHEEL

The instability of "color" as a racial typing mechanism for Arab Americans is based largely on the fact that "white," "black," and "of color" are not literal references to pigmentation; as Arab (and other) Americans change their class, political, and linguistic identities, their "color," perceived and professed, can change as well.[5] Real phenotypic variation also destabilizes rigid color typologies. Arabs are not uniformly light or dark in their complexions. Indeed, Arabs "look like" a wide variety of people. Greek, Mexican, Pakistani, Italian, Cuban, Iranian, Bulgarian, Somali, Turk, Venezuelan, Israeli, French, or Portuguese: an Arab in the United States might be taken (or mistaken) for a person from any of these backgrounds on first sight. Compare this to the relative ease with which Americans sort each other—*or think they can sort each other*—into black, white, and Asian categories. Then consider the odd fact that a third-generation American whose ancestors came from Syria might identify (and be identified) as "white," a Sudanese immigrant might identify (or be identified) as "black," and a Yemeni who migrated to the United States from India, where his family has lived for three generations, might identify (and be identified) as "Asian," yet all can simultaneously and credibly self-identify as "Arab." It is not surprising, given this tremendous variation in phenotype and cultural style, that advocates of Arab nationalism spent most of the twentieth century arguing that Arab identity was

5. One of the best studies of color shifts is Jacobson's *Whiteness of a Different Color* (1998), which traces the historical migration of Jewish, Irish, Italian, and other "ethnic" Americans toward whiteness.

based on a shared language and not, in the final instance, on shared blood or physical resemblance.[6]

The inability of most Americans to "type" Arabs is pronounced even when they use dress as a guide, a fact proven by the regularity with which xenophobes attack and kill Sikhs, who are neither Arab nor Muslim, when they intend to do harm to Arabs. Similarly, a woman wearing a *hijab* (a Muslim headscarf) might be an Arab; she might also be an Indonesian, a Bangladeshi, or a "white" convert from Omaha. Most Arab women in the United States do not wear *hijab*s, and the majority are Christian. The knowledge needed to make such distinctions is rare even among highly educated Americans, who still routinely assume Arabs are Muslims and Muslims are Middle Eastern. In this larger context of gross categorical confusion, Arab Americans become distinguishable as such (become "visible" and subject to special policies) not because they "look" a certain way, but because (1) they openly avow their status, explaining it to others; (2) they belong to specifically Arab voluntary associations (such as mosques, churches, community centers, village clubs, or advocacy groups); (3) they identify themselves as Arab on applications and government forms; or (4) state-issued identity documents specify that they came to the United States from Arab countries.

Almost all government policy pertaining to Arabs in the United States, be it positive, neutral, or negative, is based on identifications rooted in nationality, religion, institutional affiliations, and a set of complex (usually stereotypical and fantastic) assumptions about the political behaviors of people who can be identified in these ways. It would be just as difficult to "profile" Arab Americans phenotypically—that is, "racially"—as it would be pointless for the Highway Patrol to profile African Americans by reference to their countries of origin and religious beliefs. Moreover, the federal government already classifies Arabs officially as "white," which immediately requires that special policies toward Arabs be articulated apart from, and often against, existing racial categories. This is an important distinction, one worth bearing in mind when trying to make sense of "racialization" as it applies to Arabs in the United States. The distinction becomes even more important when the group being marked off for special (mis)treatment is not simply "Arab," but "Arab and Muslim," an identity zone that accounts for well over a billion people and contains most of the available phenotypic variation on the planet.

---

6. Again, the parallels with Latino identities are suggestive.

Despite this impressive diversity, Arabs and Muslims who live in the United States are lumped together and treated as a group with shared characteristics. Such lumping, when carried out by monitoring and disciplinary arms of the state, is based on religion and national origins, not race. The "treatment," however, is based on a politicized, hegemonic assumption that certain ideological "traits" are likely to accumulate among Arabs and Muslims: fanaticism, sexism, anti-Semitism, antidemocratic attitudes, disloyalty, terrorism, and inability to identify sincerely with America and its values. It is easy to liken this assumption to "racism," especially when it involves profiling and collective stigma. Analytical accounts of racialization, however, point to something deeper. They are posed not only as critiques of the Patriot Act and the war on terror, but also as critiques of the identity politics favored by mainstream Arab American advocacy groups. To succeed as collective narratives of identity, new models of racialization must first displace ethnic models of Arab Americanism that seek inclusion in a cultural zone that is clearly associated with "whiteness."

ETHNIC BACKGROUND

It is a commonplace of Arab American studies to note that pan-ethnic Arab identities began to flourish in the United States only after the 1967 Arab-Israeli War, when communities formerly known as "Lebanese" or "Syrian" (and by other regional and national markers) began to embrace an overarching sense of "Arabness" (Terry 1999). This new identification was shaped by U.S. foreign policy in the Middle East, which was unequivocal both in its support for Israel and in its opposition to anti-imperial strains of "Arab nationalism." The enemies of Israel were consistently portrayed in U.S. media as "the Arabs," a designation that accurately captured (and demonized) ideological self-definitions in a region that, through active resistance to Ottoman, European, and Zionist colonial regimes, had reconfigured itself as "the Arab world." Americans who came from Arab countries, or whose ancestors came from places now located in the Arab world, were compelled to rethink their identities in response to U.S. government policies and American media representations. The latter were negative, biased against Arabs and Muslims, and profoundly alienating. The charisma of Gamal Abdel Nasser, the success of the Algerian revolution, and solidarity with the Palestinian struggle became, throughout the 1950s and 1960s, positive forces around which new Arab attachments could form in the United States. The moral example of the civil rights movement also gave early activists a vision of what could be accomplished under a unifying, "Arab American" banner.[7]

The development of Arab American identity as a public alternative to older national, sectarian, and village-based identities gained momentum in the 1970s. Although popular struggles and radical politics in the United States and the Arab world had provided its early inspiration, by the 1990s Arab Americans had created for themselves an agenda that was ethnic, domestic, and tilted decidedly toward themes of integration. To be seen as "an ethnic group like any other ethnic group" was—and, for groups like the Arab American Institute (AAI) and the American Arab Anti-Discrimination Committee (ADC), still is—the goal of this movement.[8] Its points of reference were Italians, Irish, Poles, Jews, and other successfully integrated "white ethnics." Many descendents of the early Syrian/Lebanese immigrants (both Christian and Muslim) had already accepted "whiteness" as their self-image. The embrace of public "ethnicity," and the strategic distance from black identities that often accompanied this embrace, was rooted in an identity politics that tried to blend hegemonic models of Americanization with criticism of U.S. policy in the Arab world. As Asian American, Latino, and other "of color" identities solidified in the 1980s, the appeal of Arab Americanism grew stronger as well. It promised a kind of "civic" acceptance, and it was effective in propagating the idea that Arabs could be "good Americans" (and therefore deserved respect and protection from discrimination), even if pro-Arab politics were seldom tolerated in the American mainstream. By the 1990s, almost all large, influential Arab American organizations, both national and local, endorsed an identity rhetoric akin to the following:

> Arab Americans are a diverse ethnic group. They have been coming to the United States since the late nineteenth century. The early waves of immigrants were mostly Christians from Lebanon and greater Syria, whose success

---

7. For a superb narrative account of these developments, framed as memoir, see Abraham's (2000) essay on being Palestinian, Arab, and American in Detroit in the latter half of the twentieth century.

8. The model of ethnicity preferred by AAI is succinctly described by Maya Berry in an interview with Sally Howell (2000b, 368, 369–70): "I envision a future of ethnic America. As Arab Americans, we are an important ethnic constituency. . . . Our work is like that of any other ethnic constituency, and it doesn't need to be any different. . . . It is very important that we not be defined differently just because of the political climate in the United States."

as entrepreneurs enabled them to assimilate quickly to life in the New World. After the liberalization of U.S. immigration laws in 1965, new waves of immigrants began to arrive from the Arab world, bringing more Muslim Arabs from a broader range of countries. Like other immigrant communities, Arab Americans have overcome many challenges as they have adjusted to life in the U.S. They have made valuable contributions to the larger society, and they cherish their Arab heritage, which is now part of America's diverse, multicultural landscape. If these facts are not well understood today, it is because of anti-Arab prejudice, which is the result of ignorance about Arabs in America and abroad. Ignorance and prejudice facilitate U.S. support for Israel, and negative portrayals of Arabs in American mass media are encouraged and tolerated because they are in line with U.S. foreign policy.[9]

Like other pan-ethnic movements, Arab Americanism is filled with contradictions and silences. It privileges success, especially success that can be measured in economic terms. It is assimilationist, despite all attempts at terminological updating. It glosses over people and positions at odds with pan-ethnic Arab Americanism: Islamists, Maronites, Chaldeans, Assyrians, and other Arabic-speaking groups who do not identify principally as Arabs. It is reluctant to acknowledge the deep anxiety many Arab immigrants experience in dealing with "American culture," which they often find alien, unattractive, or immoral (Shryock 2000a). The advocates of pan-ethnic Arab Americanism rarely mention (or even realize) that large numbers of Arabs have, since the first decades of immigration, chosen not to stay in the United States or have been forced to leave for legal and ideological reasons (Khater 2001). Finally, the centrality of the Arab-Israeli conflict is seen by many Arab Americans as both an indispensable part of their identity and an obstacle to their full inclusion in the politics of multicultural tolerance (Howell 2000a). For Arabs in America, the last point is crucial because it marks the terrain in which foreign and domestic identities collide, variously destabilizing, outing, reinforcing, and stigmatizing each other.

---

9. This text is my own creation, but it varies little from those produced by Arab American organizations. For an example from Detroit, see *Understanding Arab Americans, the Arab World & Islam,* an educational flyer produced by ACCESS (Arab Community Center for Economic and Social Services, 2002) and distributed as part of its post-9/11 educational outreach campaign. For a detailed analysis of these representational templates, see Shryock (2004).

ENTER "RACIALIZATION"

The discourse of Arab American "ethnicity" is unappealing to analysts and activists who are drawn to a politics of "race" and "anti-racism." What makes ethnicity models unattractive is precisely what made them compelling to an earlier cohort of scholars and activists: (1) the success/celebration motifs (rejected now in favor of struggle/alienation motifs); (2) the inclusion/assimilation motifs (rejected in favor of exclusion/marginality motifs); (3) the pan-Arab focus (now seen as parochial and rejected in favor of "coalition of color" motifs); (4) the tendency to identify "American" culture with its upper-middle-class, white, and Christian manifestations (rejected in favor of secularist identifications with workers and people of color); (5) the location of identity within U.S. contexts (rejected in favor of transnational and diasporic identities); and (6) strategic willingness to "mute" criticisms of Israel in exchange for access to public culture venues and inclusion in the political process (rejected in favor of direct, vocal criticism of Zionism). In short, the new rhetoric of "racialization" belongs to a larger field of left/progressive oppositional ideologies. Among Arab American(ist)s, it is marked by a strong attraction to marginality, alterity, and cultural critique, and it is best represented by scholars and academy-oriented writers who have been deeply influenced by feminist thought or cultural studies (e.g., Majaj 1999a; Saliba 1999; Naber 2000; Aidi 2002; Bayoumi 2004; Kadi 1994; Hammad 1996; Hassan 2002b).

In the aftermath of 9/11, the case for Arab American marginality has never been stronger. Racialization discourses cater and respond to this structural position. But when most Arab Americans continue to identify officially as "white," and when an Arab or Muslim "phenotype" is impossible for most Americans to distinguish, why articulate this position in a language of race at all? The intellectual grounds for doing so are not entirely solid. The term "racialization," developed by Omi and Winant in *Racial Formations* in 1986, was broadly conceived, so much so that North American history since Columbus could be interpreted as an unfolding of this process. Racialization, they explain, is "the extension of racial meaning to a previously racially unclassified relationship, social practice, or group" (Omi and Winant 1995, 471). But what makes a meaning "racial" in the first place? In their now famous definition, Omi and Winant describe race as "a concept which signifies and symbolizes social conflicts and interests by referring to different types of human bodies" (1994, 55).[10] The most interesting feature of current thinking on Arabs, Muslims, and race in America is the extent to which it moves even this highly plastic notion of physical difference into noncorporeal terrain.

Reference to "different types of human bodies" is never far from discussion of what makes Asian Americans "Asian," African Americans "black," or white people "white." Popular ideas about Arabs and Muslims in the United States, by contrast, move very quickly beyond the sloppy diagnostics of "Middle Eastern appearance" (if they even start there). The "social conflicts" and "interests" associated with Arabs/Muslims are located not in bodily differences beyond individual control but in a realm of conscious ideology, in specific cultural content, in particular national and religious backgrounds, in precisely the terrain panethnic and racial labels in the United States function to homogenize or obscure. Hence, the slightly jarring effect of passages like the following, drawn from Moustafa Bayoumi's trenchant critique of the Justice Department's "special registration" initiative, which has required

> all visa-holding men from 25 Muslim countries (and North Korea) to undergo an onerous ordeal of fingerprinting, interviewing and photographing upon entry and exit.... The sweeps and programs of the government effected a removal of Muslim men from the US based firstly on the sole fact that they came, at some point in their lives, from Muslim countries. In requiring that "citizens" and "nationals" of those countries suffer its burdens, Special Registration collapsed citizenship, ethnicity and religion into race. (2004, 39)

Rather than suggest that a kind of ideological sloppiness is on display here, I would argue that the claim that Arabs (or Muslims) are being racialized is an attempt to make "moral analogies" that give Arabs and Muslims a more secure place within dominant structures of American identity politics, especially the range of assumptions that link citizenship to racial and ethnic categories. Because Arabs and Muslims are not racialized in consistent ways and are defined

10. Omi and Winant mentioned Arabs only once in *Racial Formations,* and they obviously thought of them, circa 1986 (when the book was first published) as "whites" who were sometimes the victims of "white on white" racism: "Whites can at times be the victims of racism—by others whites or non-whites—as is the case with anti-Jewish and anti-Arab prejudice" (1994, 73).

instead by their association with highly specific (and radically misconstrued) cultural forms, Arabs and Muslims are consistently excluded from these dominant ethnoracial structures of identity, which are the prevailing means by which Others are incorporated into American society.

As a "moral analogy," talk of racialization gives new meanings to processes of stigmatization and mistreatment for which Arabs and Muslims in the United States already have other names: discrimination, persecution, profiling, prejudice, blacklisting, surveillance, intolerance, hate, defamation, Orientalism, harassment, detention, deportation, racism, and so on. The first question that should be asked about "racialization," then, is what does it equip us to say about Arab and Muslim Americans that "ethnicity" does not? Or, when we talk about Arabs and Muslims in the United States, what will we be likely to talk about because we are using the term "racialization" that we would be less likely to talk about if we were discussing "ethnicity"?

There are several answers to these questions, and most arise from taxonomic, experiential, and historical contradictions of which Arab Americans have grown increasingly aware in recent years. These contradictions are signaled in the following tropes, which are well represented in this volume:

1. Reassessments of "whiteness," ambivalence about identifying with or as "white people," and concern over the denial (or the embrace) of "white privilege";

2. Close political and intellectual attention to "of color" identities and movements, which are posed as models to be imitated, causes with which to align, "subject positions" from which to produce and evaluate scholarship, and (just as often) rival positions in contests over access to institutional resources and power;

3. Portrayal of "racialization" as a negative process that is imposed by an external agent, usually the U.S. government, the mainstream, the larger society, or "white people";

4. Portrayal of "racialization" as a reality that must be acknowledged and used (by agents internal to "racialized" groups) to advance movements, shape intellectual agendas, resist state-sponsored discrimination, articulate new identities, and gain access to institutional resources;

5. Reassessments of "blackness," ambivalence about identifying with or as "black people," and concern over appropriations of "blackness" in the pursuit of oppositional, antiracist politics.

The growing rift between "Arab" and "white" identities is the central problem the racialization vocabulary allows us to talk about. This rift is visible in the

DAAS data on race, where "white" and "other" are nearly the only U.S. Census categories Arabs embrace. Arab Americans might identify *with* "people of color," but they very rarely identify *as* Asian or black. Instead, Arabs accept or reject the label "white." This tendency is visible in scholarly and activist literature as well, where Arab identity, both personal and collective, is set against a larger field of "whiteness," which includes and excludes Arabness. The case is succinctly stated by Lisa Majaj in her advice to writers of Arab American literature:

> Our history is not limited to upward mobility on the one hand (the classic American success story favored in our autobiographies) and cultural loss through assimilation on the other. Nor can it be depicted through a straight-forward celebration of community. Rather, our experiences have been at once more complex and more painful. We need to explore experiences not just of ethnic familial warmth and of entry into white middle class America, but of marginalization, poverty and exclusion, not only from American society but from Arab communities as well.
>
> We need more attention to the ways in which we have been racialized in the American context. For too long we have tried to escape into white ethnicity. But our experience has shown us, time and again, that our formal status as white is merely honorary, and is quickly revoked in the wake of political events in the Middle East as well as in the United States. We need more explorations of the implications of this racialization. At the same time, we need to probe links with other groups of color, and to explore the ways in which our racialization can provide new grounds for solidarity and activism. (1999b, 73)

Majaj's call for artful disassociations from "white ethnicity" is based on the assumption that Arab American writing will become better—less escapist—if it engages directly with "other groups of color." This agenda relies heavily on "blackness" for the stock of symbols and cultural forms needed to create alternatives to "white ethnicity." Majaj later mentions "rap"—and only "rap"—as one of the "contemporary American cultural forms" whose effect on Arab American literature should receive more serious attention. The appeal of "blackness" as a cultural style, pronounced among Muslim and Arab American youth and among academics who study public culture, is part of a larger disciplinary politics of color. If "whiteness" is associated with privilege and assimilating forces, "blackness" is associated with the solidarities created by stigma and resistance to power. Hisham Aidi (2003) expands on this theme:

Though Westerners of different social and ethnic backgrounds are gravitating toward Islam, it is mostly the ethnically marginalized of the West—historically, mostly black, but nowadays also Latino, native American, Arab and South Asian minorities—who, often attracted by the purported universalism and colorblindness of Islamic history and theology, are asserting membership in a transnational *umma* and thereby challenging or "exiting" the white West. Even for white converts, like John Walker Lindh, becoming Muslim involves a process of racialization—renouncing their whiteness—because while the West stands for racism and white supremacy on a global scale, Islam is seen to represent tolerance and anti-imperialism. This process of racialization is also occurring in diasporan Muslim communities in the West, which are growing increasingly race-conscious and "black" as anti-Muslim racism increases. To cope, Muslims in the diaspora are absorbing lessons from the African-American freedom movement, including from strains of African-American Islam.

It is easy to exaggerate this "black/diasporan" synergy. In Detroit's rapidly growing Arab and South Asian communities, recent converts to Islam are mostly the "white" spouses of immigrant men (Bagby 2004),[11] and outright identification with African Americans among Arabs, as shown in the DAAS, is virtually nonexistent. Still, "blackness" is doing important ideological work among Arab Americans, just as it does among South Asians (Maira 2002; Prashad 2000), Asians (Prashad 2002), Latinos (Aidi 2003), and other immigrant and ethnic communities of color. Restricted largely to media of popular music, film, and other expressive arts—and kept away from areas of marriage choice, residence, civic association, or church/mosque membership—identifications with "blackness" among Arab Americans resemble those prevalent in the larger society: namely, (1) avid consumption of black entertainment culture, especially its transgressive and oppositional forms, and (2) selective imitation of the models for minority politics black Americans have created over the last century.

Hence, one can easily imagine—and one can actually find—an Arab American hip-hop artist who raps about Palestinian statehood (the Iron Sheik, a.k.a. Will Youmans). One can imagine (and find) a spoken-word performer who denounces anti-Muslim hate crimes and publishes a book of poems entitled *Born Palestinian, Born Black* (Suheir Hammad [1996]). One can imagine (and find)

11. Overall, in the Detroit Mosque Study, 56 percent of converts were African American (mostly men), whereas 42 percent were "European American" (mostly women). See Bagby (2004).

an activist scholar who argues that Arab Americans are rendered invisible by U.S. Census forms that "require" them to check "Caucasian," a classification that marginalizes them within "racial justice movements" (Nadine Naber [2002, 230]). One can imagine (and find) an academic who calls for the establishment of Arab American studies programs and identity-based hiring that replicates "the nationwide initiative to recruit African Americans for African American studies, Jews for Jewish studies, and Asians for Asian and Asian American studies" (Fadwa El Guindi [2003, 631]). Not only are these projects averse to "whiteness" as a kind of Arab identity, they are unintelligible apart from the political agendas and aesthetic forms associated with blackness in America. For Arabs and Muslims, the language of "racialization" is an immediate, powerful link to minoritized models of citizenship.

The link has value, however, because Arab Americans also respond—more eagerly, I would argue, and with greater success—to the disciplines and privileges of "whiteness." This identity zone, like that of "blackness," exists at a remove from most immigrants of color—even Afro-Caribbean immigrants realize that, upon arrival in the United States, they are neither "African American" nor "white" (Waters 1999)—and literal identifications with "whiteness" are not always desirable, even when they are possible (as they are for Arabs, Turks, Iranians, Kurds, and other Middle Eastern populations). For many second- and third-generation Arab Americans, "whiteness" is equated with cultural loss, with a vacant identity space that must be (re)filled with "ethnic" content. For recent immigrants, Arabness is often posed as a moral quality (dependent on cultural upbringing and biological descent) that sets "us" apart from, and makes us superior to, "them," "the Americans" (al-amrikan). In other words, new Arab immigrants tend to enter American identity discourses already prepared to see themselves as a group defined by descent, and defined against a hegemonically "white" population that is unlike them and which they do not want to resemble or become. The collapse of the "melting pot" model of Americanization has made literal identifications with whiteness less appealing and less mandatory.

Still, one can play to and with "whiteness"; one can develop political projects appropriate to it. For instance, the public display of "famous Arab Americans"—wealthy, popular, successful celebrities and politicians, almost all of them assumed to be "whites" of some vaguely ethnic type—is a political project that is not concerned with establishing the "blackness," or even the marginality, of Arab Americans. Its goal is to impress members of the "larger society" (conceived as majority white) with evidence that Arab Americans are already admired by it and therefore already belong to it. Such representational tactics, which are common to all marked groups in the United States, should not be misconstrued as literal bids for "whiteness." The list of "famous African Americans" is equally commonplace. Rather, these celebrations of success and acceptance are addressed to a cultural, political, and economic configuration—partly a "place," partly an "audience"—called "the mainstream."

IN AND OUT OF WHITENESS

If Arab Americans yearn to enter (or alter) an American identity space, it is "the mainstream." Dominated by "white people" but no longer exclusively associated with them, "the mainstream" is territory Arab Americans know well, which makes their persistent exclusion from it all the more unsettling. Arab Americans spend much of their lives in "the mainstream." As demographers have repeatedly shown, Arab Americans are decidedly middle class as a whole; their education levels are higher than the national average, as are their annual incomes (John Zogby 1990; El Badry 1994). Most Arab Americans grow up in majority white communities, speak white-identified dialects of American English, socialize frequently with whites, marry them at high rates, and work with white colleagues. In the Arab communities of Detroit, which are the largest and most highly concentrated in North America, roughly 90 percent of Arabs live outside Detroit in suburbs historically identified as "white" (Baker et al. 2004). It is simplistic (politically and ethnographically) to argue that Arab Americans are "becoming white." There are many contexts—Cainkar's work among Palestinian Muslims in Chicago offers vivid examples (see Cainkar's essay in this volume)[12]—in which "whiteness" is being rejected or withdrawn. It is obvious, however, that a substantial number of Arab Americans are *already* white, while many others are part of an American cultural mainstream whose links to "whiteness" are implicitly recognized by community leaders.

---

12. Cainkar finds minimal identification as "white" among Chicago's Palestinians. The DAAS, by contrast, found the *highest* levels of white identification among its Palestinian respondents, 72 percent of whom chose this category. Muslim Palestinians in the Detroit area identified as white at a rate of 68 percent, which is higher than the average for the entire Arab/Chaldean population.

In an op-ed piece written by Jim Zogby (2001), head of the Arab American Institute, a Washington-based advocacy group, the scrutiny aimed at Arab Americans by journalists after the 9/11 attacks provides an opportunity to reassert the Americanness of Arabs living in the United States. Note what counts here as evidence of "diversity":

> Arab Americans are being discovered, or should I say being rediscovered, by the same papers and networks that have discovered us twice before in just the past decade. As I speak to those assigned to do the story, they discover yet again the diversity of my community. The fact that we are not a new ethnic group in America (we've been here for 120 years). That most Arab Americans are not Muslims (in fact, only 20% are). That most Arab Americans are not recent immigrants (in fact, almost 80% are born in the U.S.). And that many Arab Americans have achieved prominence and acceptance in America (two proud Arab Americans, Spencer Abraham and Mitch Daniels, serve in President Bush's cabinet, and Donna Shalala served in Bill Clinton's cabinet).

The numbers, proportions, and terminology are all debatable, but Zogby's narrative is flawless in its ability to map out the terrain of mainstream acceptance many Arab Americans would like to enter (or already occupy). In directing our attention to the American-born, the Christian, the well-established, the politically influential, Zogby replicates perfectly the characteristics of DAAS respondents most likely to identify as "white." By contrast, the Arab communities Zogby does not speak to (and would encourage his readers not to dwell on) are new, Muslim, born overseas, unknown, accented, culturally peculiar, and politically disaffected. This profile, in the Detroit area, corresponds closely to that of DAAS respondents who were likely to describe themselves as "other."

This paradoxical condition of being "successful" while at the same time being perceived as alien and unappealing is widely shared among upwardly mobile immigrant/ethnic populations of color, who are broadly characterized as "not quite white," "not quite not white," and not "black." Arabs are significantly disadvantaged in relation to these groups—South Asians, Chinese, Koreans, Cubans, and others—insofar as Arabs do not belong to a pan-ethnic/racial identity that is officially marked as alternative to "white" by federal authorities and can serve, in ways sanctioned by law, as a site of compensation for discrimination, protection against civil liberties abuses, and access to special zones of inclusion and representation. Without a label of this sort, mainstreaming is more difficult to achieve because Arab Americans who live in areas of whiteness and embody its styles—the Arabs Jim Zogby describes—must constantly "pay" for their association with Arabs who are stigmatized as Other, without benefit of a label that gives "Other Arabs" access to compensatory programs (which "mainstream Arabs" can also benefit from and are ideally positioned to devise, administer, and control).

The argument that "visibility" (in the form of an official, nonwhite mark) can bring tangible benefits to Arab Americans, whereas "invisibility" as pseudowhites will bring only abuse and insignificance, is compelling. The moral analogy of racialization, seen in these terms, is not simply an argument *against* racism; it is an argument *for* the concessions and inclusions that come with "of color" identity. The message is simple: "Arab Americans are a minority group in the United States. We are defined as white, but this is not our real status. We have more in common with people who are defined as nonwhite, and we should receive the same legal protections (and the same gestures of respect, inclusion, and multicultural tolerance) they receive."

The power of this moral analogy comes not from its oppositional or critical inflection, but from its nearly perfect fit with larger American models of citizenship, community, and personal identity.[13] The dominant institutions of U.S. society, from the Pentagon to the Supreme Court, from General Motors to the University of Michigan, support a model of American belonging in which certain rights should apply to all equally, certain opportunities should be available to everyone, and when that is not the case, the state, major corporate interests, and key institutions of civil society have a compelling interest in seeing that discrimination, underrepresentation, and patterns of exclusion are offset by special policies oriented toward "incorporation" of marked groups whose members cannot fully enjoy "normative" citizenship. To be "marked" on these terms is to be recognized as a group (and as an individual citizen) whose experience of exclusion and discrimination is unjust, authentic, and deserving of correction. To be unmarked, or to be marked as "white," implies that full rights and protections of citizenship are securely possessed by you, that you must be treated as an individual, that your actions do not reflect on the status of others in your group,

---

13. Excellent discussions of these larger models are available in Dresch (1995), Rouse (1995), and, from a more distinctly Arab vantage, Joseph (1999a). I have examined similar terrain in recent essays that focus specifically on Arab Detroit (Shryock 2000b, 2004).

and that the status of your group does not determine how you should be treated as an individual. Of course, all of this is public ideology, but it is a powerful and binding ideology for most Americans, and Arab and Muslim Americans are intensely aware of their vulnerable position outside both the ideology and its binding power. In fact, this combination of "public ideology" and "binding power" is what constitutes "the mainstream" and makes racialization part of its continual (re)formation.

ANALOGIES AND FALSE RESEMBLANCES

I suggested earlier that the development of "Arab-American" identity in the 1960s was successful because it spoke convincingly to communities located on both sides of the hyphen, through the popular discourse of "ethnicity." It played successfully to the assimilating power of whiteness by endorsing a model of "near whiteness" that replicated the successful identity packages developed by Italians, Jews, Poles, Greeks, and other "ethnic" Americans. Attempts to re-define Arabs as "a distinct racial group" have not yet attained the same appeal, largely because of (1) the success of the earlier, ethnic strategy; (2) the ability (and apparent desire) of Arab Americans to locate themselves in zones of white privilege, economically, residentially, educationally, in choice of marriage part-ners, in manner of speech, and professionally; (3) the technical encapsulation of Arabs in the U.S. government's official definition of "whiteness"; and (4) the fact that discrimination and bias against Arab Americans are motivated by specific features of U.S. foreign policy and are not akin to the kinds of racism experi-enced by "historically oppressed people of color," whose position in the Ameri-can racial hierarchy is accounted for, and "remedied," through explicit, often radically oversimplified reference to their "physical appearance."

Here the effectiveness of "racialization" as a moral analogy (of use to Arab Americans and Muslims) begins to erode, even as its location within a larger political morality appears more clearly. Members of officially marked ethnora-cial minorities do not, in American public ideology, *deserve* the discrimination they experience, nor should they be blamed for any negative connotations as-sociated with their mark. Instead, the majority population should recognize marked communities, celebrating those aspects of their "culture" and "heri-tage" that enrich America. The majority population, likewise, should acknowl-edge responsibility for failures to achieve "diversity" and "equal opportunity" and should make amends (one might argue, in a cynical vein, that this is an updated, recalibrated version of "the white man's burden"). Under this protocol, official strategies of ethnic and racial marking can operate very efficiently as a moral shorthand and mass corrective, summarizing complex relations between persons and groups in a simplified, redistributive model of citizenship. What some scholars of pan-ethnic and racialized identities perceive as their "reductive," "culturally flattened," and "ahistorical" quality is actually a measure of their success as managerial constructs that help "incorporate" marked communities into the American mainstream, facilitating access to its institutions and resource flows.

Of course, the model encodes equally efficient corollaries: (1) if you are devoted to beliefs and practices construed as antithetical to "individual rights" and "human freedom"—the sacred stuff of both abstract and racialized citizenship—or (2) if you are associated with enemies of the nation-state and its "majority population," then the protections of citizenship are not available to you. You are not blameless; you do not receive compensation; and you are not a victim. You are an oppressor and must be treated as (morally) unacceptable or a (political) threat. Arabs and Muslims in America are easily placed in this position, given their presumed cultural, political, religious, and financial ties to Arabs and Muslims the U.S. government considers enemies (or enemies of Israel). Arabs in the United States are burdened by popular assumptions that they "reject the liberation of women," "oppose religious freedom," "hate democracy," "deny Israel's right to exist," "do not tolerate the separation of church and state," and so on. These views have been subjected to intense critique for nearly thirty years, by authors ranging from Edward Said (1978) to Melani McAlister (2001), but they remain firmly in place, and they explain why Arabs are "nonwhite whites" who, despite their obvious "taint," will probably not be granted a "color pass" in the near future.

In fact, it is very likely that any official, state-sanctioned *re*marking of Arab and Muslim Americans would entail not a concerted attempt to correct patterns of discrimination based on factors beyond one's control, factors mapped onto bodies, carried in one's blood, or rooted in the language one speaks. Rather, it would involve a systematic attempt to differentiate Arabs and Muslims who consciously and publicly "choose" America and its values from those who publicly (or perhaps privately) do not. Choosing America, for Arabs and Muslims, does not mean identifying as Americans or with America. It means doing both in a very particular way: namely, by denouncing "bad Arabs" and "bad Islam," distancing oneself from them, and cultivating "good Arab" and "good Muslim" identities. One must engage in these corrective, penitential rites of citizenship even (or especially) when one has no connection to "bad" Arabs or "bad" Islam. Only *after* these rites of belonging have been performed does minoritized citizenship (racialized, ethnic, exemplary, provisional, or exceptional) become possible.

MARKING AND ITS CONSEQUENCES

Citizenship granted on these terms involves costly trade-offs and tangible rewards. The costs are typically imposed through policies of depoliticization. In the years since the 9/11 attacks, for instance, Arabs have been encouraged to display their "culture" to America. The music, art, and dance that make Arabs a valuable, entertaining addition to "our vibrant, multicultural society" are vividly arrayed in museum exhibits and concert series across the United States, largely to foster "good will" and "mutual understanding." Arab *political* culture, however, and the political aspects of cultural forms, must be suppressed whenever these entail vigorous criticism of Israel or express solidarity with those who resist U.S. imperial projects in the Middle East. Likewise, Arab Americans are expected to have their own "ethnic economy"—even a "transnational" one, if it facilitates U.S. trade with the Arab world and furthers the business interests of American corporations—but they are not allowed to give financial support to groups, regimes, and movements that threaten U.S. allies or disrupt their trade relations. In simplest terms, domestic recognition as "good Arabs" is granted in exchange for acquiescence in matters of U.S. foreign policy. Since the 9/11 attacks, millions of dollars in grants have poured into the budgets of Arab American business associations and human service organizations across the country (see Cainkar 2002a; Howell and Shryock 2003), much of it earmarked for programs that showcase the community's "heritage" and its market muscle while placing any presumed "anti-systemic politics" under ban.[14]

14. I have been privy to the initial planning for some of these programs at the University of Michigan and in Detroit. Often, the decision to suppress "politics" is explicitly enunciated by event sponsors and organizers. The term "politics" is rarely defined, although everyone knows what it means: criticism of Israel and other "controversial" positions.

In Michigan, where Arabs enjoy considerable political influence, this "carrot and stick" policy has been evolving for decades. Designation as a "special population" by the state government has brought recognition and security to Arab Americans (the number of hate crimes against Arabs in Detroit in the three years following 9/11 was very low compared to other American cities);[15] it has brought the Arab community into close working relations with local print and electronic media (which produce special, mostly positive coverage of Detroit's Arab and Muslim communities),[16] with educational and cultural institutions (like the University of Michigan and the Detroit Institute of Arts), and with arms of the federal government (ranging from the FBI and Homeland Security to the State Department and Americorps).[17] These privileges are part of a structure of "immigrant incorporation" that imposes heavy disciplinary force on the community, yet even progressive, left-leaning activists have found the discipline bearable. In fact, the most prominent Arab American organiza-

15. Speaking to the United Lebanese American Federation in Dearborn in 2004, Robert Ficano, Wayne County Commissioner, reported that the number of hate crimes against Arabs and Muslims in Detroit actually decreased in the three years following the 9/11 attacks. This claim is substantiated by annual reports on anti-Muslim discrimination produced by the Council on American Islamic Relations (Amaney Jamal, personal communication). In the DAAS, 15 percent of respondents said they had personally had a "bad experience" because of their Arab background after 9/11. Over twice as many respondents (33 percent) said that someone "not of Middle Eastern background" had shown them solidarity or support after 9/11.

16. The *Detroit News* and the *Detroit Free Press* provide excellent coverage of the Arab American community. In 2000, the *Free Press* produced a booklet entitled *100 Questions and Answers about Arab Americans*. Ostensibly designed as an in-house educational resource for journalists, the booklet has found its way onto dozens of Arab American Web sites. The *Free Press* displayed the booklet on its own Web site for several weeks following the 9/11 attacks; it received hundreds of thousands of viewings. The booklet can still be accessed at http://www.freep.com/jobspage/arabs.

17. The closeness of these relationships is often difficult for Arab Americans from other cities to understand, and the fact that Dearborn is touted nationally as a model for community cooperation in the war on terror has triggered accusations of "kowtowing" and "cooptation." I recently had to explain to an out-of-town scholar that County Commissioner Robert Ficano was invited to so many Arab American events because Arabs had helped vote him into office, that they were one of his constituencies, and that, as sheriff, he had brought many Arab Americans onto his force. The visitor found it all very strange.

tions in Detroit—ACCESS (the Arab Community Center for Economic and Social Services), ACC (the Arab American and Chaldean Council), and ADC (the American Arab Anti-Discrimination Committee)—whose leadership include individuals who began their careers as socialists and communists in the 1970s, have undergone a dramatic shift toward the political center as a result of their successful immersion in ethnic constituency politics. Since the late 1980s, the annual dinners of these local organizations have been gala events attended by U.S. senators; local mayors and county commissioners; the governor of Michigan; CEOs of Ford, GM, and Daimler-Chrysler; visiting Arab royalty; and celebrity guests of honor, ranging from Jesse Jackson to Colin Powell, from Donna Shalala to Madeline Albright.

Arab Detroit is dominated today by nonprofit ethnic organizations that derive almost all their support from state and federal funds, corporate donations, and grants from private foundations. The largest of these organizations have annual operating budgets of over fourteen million dollars. Their connections to Arabs in other American cities, to Arab diasporas elsewhere in the West, and to the Arab homelands are shaped by the programming agendas and fiscal regulations of their American partners and funding sources. This outcome shows how mainstreaming can be achieved by way of (not in spite of) special identity labels. It also shows how labeling, when carried out by state agencies, can bring even the most stigmatized and politically suspect communities into existing structures of representation and power. Inclusion on these terms has many positive effects. According to the DAAS, over 70 percent of Arabs and Chaldeans in the Detroit area are "very or somewhat satisfied" with the performance of their community organizations, with social service agencies (like ACCESS and ACC) receiving a satisfaction rating of 85 percent.

Scholars and activists who see the racialization of Arabs as a potential site for the construction of genuinely alternative, oppositional, progressive, and transnational political identities should look closely at Arab Detroit. Its leading institutions, now located on a political spectrum that extends from Republican to Democrat, are part of a civic "status quo" that Michigan Arabs can shape and selectively redefine, but only if they discard certain political commitments. Exclusion and profiling are not the only (negative) outcomes of racialization; state-sanctioned marking can also lead to forms of inclusion and empowerment that are far more effective as mechanisms of control. The power of this double-edged sword is reason enough to adopt a wary stance in relation to all attempts, especially those emanating from government agencies, to officialize the minority status of Arabs and Muslims.[18]

CONCLUSION: THE POLITICS OF BEING "OTHER"

To explain what might be gained by "wariness" in relation to racial identity politics, I would like to conclude this chapter with reluctant confessions and a cautious appeal. First, I will admit that when I learned that 64 percent of Arab Americans in the DAAS identified as "white," I was pleased; this finding undermined what I considered exaggerated claims for the "subaltern," "nonwhite" status of Arab Americans then circulating among community activists and scholars. And when I learned that 31 percent of Arab and Chaldean respondents to the DAAS chose "other," I was pleased again, as this finding would serve as a "reality check" for Arab Americans (and non-Arabs) who see "whiteness"—whether technical or ethnocultural—as the inevitable future of Arab populations in the United States.[19] I enjoyed having it both ways, and having it both ways seems to be a tactical stance that is not merely prudent, or careful, but consistent with dominant trends in Arab American history, which has seen Arabs move toward and away from whiteness. It is also consistent with the findings of the DAAS, which show a community structurally divided in its embrace of "whiteness," a term that clearly stands not for a "hue" but for class locations and cultural styles associated with inclusion in the American "mainstream."

I believe there are clear benefits—intellectual, moral, and political—to the taxonomic uncertainty that suspends Arab Americans between zones of white-

---

18. Detroit is now a place where leading Arab community organizations host job fairs for the U.S. Army; where the CIA is an official sponsor of Arab ethnic festivals; where the FBI consults regularly with Arab American community leaders through the offices of antidiscrimination committees; where the U.S. State Department facilitates trade missions and fund-raising junkets in which Arab American leaders and Detroit area politicians plan new economic relations with partners in the Arab Gulf; and where area universities establish official programming relations with sister schools in the Arab world, with funding provided by U.S. presidential initiatives overseen by the State Department. In September 2001, amid fears of violent backlash and internment camps, few predicted that Arab Detroit would be caught up in this elaborate web of disciplinary inclusion.

19. It should also give pause to analysts who claim that Arab Americans, despite strong alienation from whiteness, cannot bring themselves to check the "other" box.

ness, Otherness, and color. Intellectually, the categories associated with these
zones are almost always vacuous and reductive. Edward Said argued passion-
ately against the false comfort of labels:

> No one today is purely *one* thing. Labels like Indian, or woman, or Muslim, or
> American are not more than starting-points, which if followed into actual ex-
> perience for only a moment are quickly left behind. Imperialism consolidated
> the mixture of cultures and identities on a global scale. But its worst and most
> paradoxical gift was to allow people to believe that they were only, mainly,
> exclusively, white, or Black, or Western, or Oriental. (1993, 336)

Politically, the fact that Arabs can credibly identify as "white," "of color," "Asian,"
"black," and "Latino" is a boon to coalition building, insofar as it encourages
solidarity with (and discourages estrangement from) people who accept those
labels. Morally, the inability to fit Arabs into a snug racial straightjacket makes it
more likely that Arab Americans can develop personal identities that operate at
a tactical remove from the racism inherent in all attempts to secure (or improve)
one's place within "the American racial hierarchy." Finally, establishing a place
outside this hierarchy might enable Arab Americans to develop and maintain
links to Arabs (and non-Arabs) in other places, for whom "the American racial
hierarchy" is yet another nationalist discourse that domesticates Arabs, encap-
sulates them in the United States, and severs (or systematically realigns) their
transnational attachments.

I do not want to imply that Arabs are "free agents" in matters of race, or that
racial ambiguity is always desirable. Racial formations are real, and the protections and privileges of racial democracy, American-style, are distributed along
lines that frequently exclude Arabs and Muslims. Over many years of work in
Detroit, I have come to the conclusion that a deep sense of marginality—based
on political opposition to U.S. foreign policy in the Middle East and a heightened sense of religious distinction—is the leitmotif of Arab/Muslim identity
formation there. Detroit's Arab communities are marginal even to the process
of "racialization," which has failed to make them exclusively "white" or "nonwhite" but has convinced them that they are indeed Other.

The American mainstream is racialized. Insofar as Arabs and Muslims are
not part of that mainstream, they will not conform to its politics of color. This
nonconformity is worth preserving, despite its costs. Not only does it protect

Arab Americans from larger political forces that would turn any new, official mark they bear into a medium of discipline and abuse, it also reflects the conviction, pervasive in Detroit and beyond, that American ideologies of "race" distort Arab identities. When DAAS respondents chose "other," many were expressing a desire to be free of coercive labels that say nothing important about them as individuals or as members of a historically and culturally peculiar community. It is a freedom many Americans, frustrated by the limits of our racial thinking and racial projects, would be willing to share.

Civil Liberties and the Otherization of Arab and Muslim Americans

AMANEY JAMAL

THE STATE OF CIVIL LIBERTIES has deteriorated noticeably for all Americans since 9/11. In particular, new legislation passed immediately after 9/11 undermined Muslim and Arab Americans' confidence in their own rights and security. The PATRIOT Acts I and II grant the government significant powers to monitor Americans, even allowing the indefinite detention of "noncitizens," and these new powers have been selectively applied—most noticeably to Muslims. In the interests of national security, nonimmigrant residents are now required to register under the newly implemented NSEER System (National Security Entry and Exit Registry), and noncompliance constitutes a violation punishable by deportation. Although NSEER initially targeted people from countries of origin in the Muslim world, these provisions have now expanded to include most visitors from across the globe. Yet in the weeks and months immediately following 9/11, these policies singled out Muslims and created a wave of fear and anxiety among visitors and immigrants from Muslim-majority countries. U.S. government agents have made thousands of "special interest" arrests, and thousands of people who feared arrest because of visa irregularities sought asylum in Canada (Murray 2004). Despite the antiterrorist rhetoric of this legislation, however, none of those imprisoned was ever directly linked to the September 2001 attacks. The vast majority of individuals arrested were eventually cleared of the crimes alleged to them but many lost months and years of their lives behind bars.

Although the stipulations in the PATRIOT Acts and other Department of Justice decrees ostensibly apply to all Americans, they effectively single out Arab and Muslim Americans. As Louise Cainkar comments, "Ashcroft has already removed more Arabs and Muslims (who were neither terrorists nor criminals) from the United States in the past year than the total number of foreign nationals deported in the infamous Palmer raids of 1919" (Cainkar 2003).[1] Expanded secret evidence procedures are used to keep Muslims under arrest, and other provisions for the intelligence community resulted in FBI interrogations at Muslim and Arab community and religious centers across the United States.

A wave of anti-Muslim popular backlash followed post-9/11 government scrutiny. Passengers refused to board airplanes with apparently Muslim individuals on board and mosques were burned and vandalized. In 2003, the Council on American Islamic Relations (CAIR) reported that hate crimes against Muslim Americans were up by at least 300 percent from 2001. By 2005, hate crimes against Muslim Americans had increased by another 50 percent from 2004 levels. "The violence, discrimination, defamation and intolerance now faced by Arabs [and Muslims] in American society have reached a level unparalleled in their 100-year history in the United States," reports Cainkar (2002). Recent "antiterrorism" legislation has caused high levels of fear and anxiety in the Muslim and Arab American communities. According to a Zogby poll conducted in 2002, 66 percent of all Arab and Muslim Americans worry about their future in this country, and 81 percent feel that their community is being profiled.

Exacerbating the sense of Muslim American vulnerability is mainstream American public opinion. More than ninety-six thousand calls to the FBI were made about "suspicious" Arabs and Muslims in the United States in the week following the 9/11 attacks alone (Murray 2004). In the days immediately after the attacks, the majority of Americans, according to Gallup polls, were in favor of profiling Muslims.

Figure 4.1 summarizes some findings from the Detroit Arab American Study (DAAS) conducted in 2003 (see below for more details on the study). The study finds that comparable numbers of Arab Americans and members of the general mainstream population were willing to support increased surveillance of U.S. citizens in order to ensure security at home. Granting the police more powers to stop and search anyone at random received support from 27 percent of Arab Americans and 31 percent of the general population. When asked a general question about giving up some civil liberties to curb terrorism, 55 percent

---

1. See also Howell and Shryock (2003).

of the general population and 47 percent of Arab Americans expressed support. The general population, however, is much more likely to support civil rights infringements that specifically target Arabs and Muslims. The DAAS found that 49 percent of the general population would support increasing surveillance of Muslim and Arab Americans, while only 17 percent of Arab Americans agreed. Forty-one percent of the general population would uphold the detention of suspicious Arabs and Muslims even without sufficient evidence to prosecute, as compared to only 12 percent of Arab Americans. And 23 percent of the general population would support increased police powers to stop and search Muslim and Arab Americans, while only 8 percent of Arabs supported this infringement on their rights. The Detroit findings are in accord with nationwide polls about attitudes toward Muslims, the purported relation between Islam and violence, and toward Muslim Americans. This backlash granted the U.S. government extended authority and a groundswell of popular support to further promote policies that clash with basic American freedoms and rights.

Why is there so much support for policies that so apparently are anathema to basic American values? Several hypotheses can plausibly explain support for taking away the civil rights and liberties of Muslim and Arab Americans. They range from a general sense of vulnerability to more specific anti-Muslim attitudes and predispositions. While the former can be explained away as general fear and worry in the aftermath of the attacks, the latter, I argue, is far more troubling. For if the American population is willing to support infringements on civil liberties by reason of misperceptions that characterize Arabs and Muslims as "enemy Others," then we must also address the larger phenomenon of the racialization or "otherization" of Arabs and Muslims in mainstream American culture. This racialization process essentially sees Muslims and Arabs as different from and inferior to whites, potentially violent and threatening, and therefore deserving of policies that target them as a distinct group of people and criminalize them without evidence of criminal activity. The binary logic of "us" versus "them," based on a constructed myth of racial difference, permeates U.S. society and provides the lenses through which group differences are organized, imagined, and understood. In the case of the denial of Muslim and Arab American civil liberties, unequal access to civil liberties is justified through a racial logic that is not always based on an association between phenotype and backwardness but still follows various historical patterns of racism in the United States. U.S. history is rife with examples of immigrants being targeted

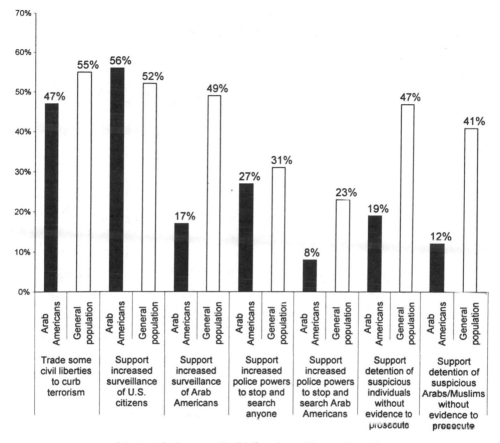

4.1. Restrictions on Civil Liberties to Ensure Security

and denied the benefits of citizenship because of their appearance and cultural backgrounds. Nadine Naber reminds us of this history, arguing that these non-immigrant groups, whether blacks, Asians, or Mexicans, have been denied the benefits of citizenship based on the assumption that they are unassimilable and foreign (2006, 241).

The single most durable explanation of widespread support for ethnic civil liberty infringement, I argue, rests on the racialization of Muslim and Arab Americans as the enemy "Other." Here, I use the term "racialization" to describe the perception and production of an inherent threatening difference between "us" and "them" that provides a scaffold legitimating and supporting the violation of the ethnic minority's civil liberties. Although racialization has its roots

in domestic politics, the findings of this chapter also demonstrate that geopolitical realities shape the ways average Americans construct images of the Arab and
Muslim "Other" in their midst. Both domestic politics and existing geopolitical
realities, especially when the homelands of those "othered" populations are sites
of U.S. military campaigns, combine to justify the domestic subordination of
less-tolerated populations.

THE CIVIL LIBERTIES DEBATE AND ARAB AND MUSLIM AMERICANS

The current civil-liberties debate in the wake of 9/11 has raised vital and exis-
tential questions. The American public's willingness to give up civil liberties
may derive from an intense feeling of individual and collective vulnerability,
ideology, religiosity, racism, or media exposure. For Muslim and Arab Americans, however, the debate on civil liberties after 9/11 is of more instrumental and
immediate concern. If legislation that singles out Muslim Americans continues
to be passed with widespread acceptance, then there may be no end in sight for
discrimination. Therefore, it is crucial to understand the sources of support for
such infringements on civil rights and liberties. Several explanations of support
for these infringements have been advanced both in general and for Muslim
Americans more specifically.

One set of explanations for support on infringements on civil liberties
draws from party identification as "Democrat" or "Republican," and ideological
commitment as "liberal" or "conservative." It has been argued that liberal ideologues tend to hold civil liberties to be inalienable rights for all. Conservative
ideologues, on the other hand, tend to view civil liberties as rescindable because
of the value placed on "security," respect for authority, obedience, and the law
(McClosky and Brill 1983; McClosky 1964).

Perceptions of threat are another crucial factor explaining support for civil
liberties infringements. A wealth of literature demonstrates that those individuals who feel most personally threatened are most likely to protect themselves. As
Davis and Silver indicate, the response to such perceived threats may become
"overwhelmingly intolerant" (Davis 1995; Davis and Silver 2004). Further, others find that those who perceive future threat are more likely to support even
extreme antiterrorism policies domestically (Huddy et al. 2005; Herrmann,
Tetlock, and Visser 1999; Jentleson 1992). This sense of threat not only leads to
an increased toleration for civil-liberties violations, it also increases prejudice

against the suspected group (Bettencourt et al. 2001; Levine and Campbell 1972; Struch and Schwartz 1989). Anxiety and threat are powerful tools in the way the war on terror is fought.

An alternative explanation focuses on racial motivations. According to this logic, Americans in favor of infringing on Muslim and Arab American civil liberties do so because they hold negative views about an entire "people." These negative views are fed by a variety of misperceptions and stereotypes. The Muslim and Arab American had been popularly constructed as an irrational, terror-supporting, and fanatical "enemy Other" long before 9/11. American foreign policy has consistently justified intervention in the Muslim world along similar lines. When U.S. leaders characterize the Arab and Muslim world as inherently undemocratic owing to fundamental value differences between "us" and "them," they promote an environment of intolerance at home. Thus, the racialization of Arab and Muslim Americans, a process decades in the making, also explains the overwhelming support for the infringement of Arab and Muslim civil liberties (Moallem 2005).

In this chapter I move beyond the narrow phenotypical definition of racialization, wherein race relations are strictly structured by biological differences. Rather, I adopt a larger definition of racialization that incorporates the process of "othering." More specifically here, I argue that the racialization of Muslims and Arabs stems from the consistent deployment of an "us" versus "them" mentality, excessively propped up for the justification of military campaigns in the Arab world. The racialization of Arabs and Muslims is not simply contingent on phenotypical differences; rather, this racialization of difference is driven by a perceived clash of values and exacerbated by cultural ethnocentrism. This process of "othering" is based on assumptions about culture and religion instead of phenotype. It is not based on racial divides; instead, it conforms to the process of racialization that has characterized the ways in which the dominant elements in society have interacted with minority ethnic groups more generally. The racialization of Arabs and Muslims stems from two intertwined processes.

First, in a society that is already constructed along racial lines, any perceived difference between the dominant mainstream and a minority "Other" tends to conform to racism's framework. This "othering" process lends itself to the *already existing* paradigm of defining oneself vis-à-vis other groups along the lines of racial categories. This form of racism is not contingent on differences in appearance but on differences in cultural attributes. These differences are exacerbated by popular and government discourses that deem the group an "enemy Other," especially after 9/11.

The loyalties of the Arab and Muslim communities have consistently been questioned since the attacks. Only 38 percent of Americans in the Detroit metro area believe that Arabs and Muslims are doing all that they can to fight the war on terror. Muslims and Arabs across the United States are consistently asked to apologize for 9/11, as if they were behind the attacks. And yet, ironically, the numerous and countless condemnations emanating from mosques and organizations in the United States that emphatically denounce the attacks have received little media attention. Americans remain suspicious of Arabs and Muslims. When asked whether Arabs and Muslims could be trusted, Americans in the Detroit metro area ranked them as the least trustworthy subpopulation. Twenty percent of Americans have little or no trust for whites; 24 percent have little or no trust for blacks, and 30 percent have little or no trust for Muslims and Arabs. Not only are Arabs and Muslims different, they are also a threat treated with great suspicion because they are assumed to originate from the Middle East. They are presumed to be operating "against us."

The binary construction of "us" versus "them" is not new to American social relations in the United States or abroad. Racial relations in the United States have been constructed through the binary lens of the dominant and the subordinate, a legacy of the history of race relations in this country. Likewise, the lens through which America sees the rest of the world is tinted with this dichotomy: "we," whoever and wherever "we" are, enjoy both cultural and moral superiority. Such interactions with "Others" abroad translate into a racial logic in a U.S. context that views ethnic and religious group differences through racial lenses at home. The process of othering, be it based on phenotype or cultural difference, therefore lends itself to racialization, particularly when it involves attributing essentializing characteristics to the *entire* group. The racialization of Arabs and Muslims, however, draws on yet another element of difference. Not only are they different at home, but their difference is exacerbated by geopolitical realities where the United States has utilized the construction of the "Other" as enemy-terrorist to justify its campaigns abroad.

The second process of racialization involves the direct subordination of the minority Other. The very process of rendering the Other inferior to white Americans, or some imagined group of acceptable Americans, is at the heart of racialization. In the case of Muslim and Arab Americans, the way that Otherness is determined is through a process by which the dominant social group claims moral and cultural superiority in the process of producing an essentialized, homogenous image of Muslim and Arab Americans as nonwhites who are naturally, morally, and culturally inferior to real Americans. Terrorism, according to this logic, is not the modus operandi of a few radical individuals, but a by-product of a larger cultural and civilizational heritage: the Arab and Islamic Other.

In Omi and Winant's words, racialization is "a matter of both social structure and cultural representation" (1994, 56). Cultural representations of Muslims and Arabs derive from an American media regime that has vilified this population for decades, and from a social structure that adopts and resorts to the rhetoric of moral superiority to justify its intervention in the Middle East and discrimination against Arab and Muslim Americans.[2] Racialization is not static but is produced, reproduced, and solidified in a variety of forums: family networks, religious institutions, government offices, and even schools (Coates 2004). Since "immigrant America" is a conglomeration of these "subordinate" minority groups, these perceptions of "Other" manifest themselves in the daily interactions that govern the incorporation of minority groups into the mainstream. In this regard, the incorporation of minority groups is not only about the acquisition of necessary language tools and specific, technical labor skills; it is also about confronting one's place in the context of U.S. racial hierarchies.

The racialization of Arabs and Muslims has involved a process of juxtaposing the Other with and separating the Other from dominant mainstream culture. This process did not begin with 9/11, though those events galvanized it. Susan Akram discovers this process in the "deliberate mythmaking" tactics of film and media, in the polemical stereotyping strategies of "experts" on the Middle East, in the selling of foreign policy agendas, and in "a public susceptible to images identifying the unwelcome 'other' in its midst" (Akram 2002). A long history of misrepresentation and the promotion of violent stereotypes mark the popular American media; Arab and Muslim Americans were portrayed as terrorists long before 9/11 (Suleiman 2002; Mandel 2001; Tessler and Corstange 2002; Shaheen 2003; Gerges 2003.) Muslims and Arabs, Akram says, are consistently absent from that desirable group of "ordinary people, families with social interactions, or outstanding members of communities such as scholars

2. According to Rodney Coates, these depictions of "other" entire subgroups is commonplace in American popular culture.

or writers or scientists." This process of demonization, she goes on to say, "has been so complete and so successful that film critics, most Americans and social commentators have barely noticed" (Akram 2002, 4). In fact, since the 1960s large segments of U.S. culture have unofficially classified Arabs and Muslim as terrorists and perceived them as threats to national security (Hassan 2003).

The racialization of Arab and Muslim Americans captures the ways in which the dominant social structure of this country has positioned itself vis-à-vis this subpopulation. Americans have come to know and learn about Islam and Arabs through the prisms of terrorism and barbarism. It is no surprise that 42 percent of Americans in the Detroit metro area believe that 9/11 was a result of a deeply rooted disrespect for democracy, freedom, and the rights of women. A good percentage of Americans clearly believe that there is a fundamental clash of values between "us" and "them." Simply put, the United States was attacked because it is fundamentally "good," while the Other is fundamentally "evil." These perceptions of the Other have shaped post-9/11 discussions and introspective deliberations. Even in our attempts to understand, we still claim moral superiority. Hence we ask the question "Why do they hate us?" Seldom has the question been asked, "Why do *we* hate them?" And "Why have we always considered Arabs and Muslims a threat to our values?" These perceptions of "Other," I argue, are a by-product of the racialization patterns of Muslims and Arabs in the United States. This pattern of racialization explains why large sections of the general American population are willing to do away with the civil liberties of Muslims and Arabs in the United States. Racialization occurs as Arab and Muslim American civil rights are removed; in such infringements, we are witnessing the continual production of the "Arab" and the "Muslim" as a violent race. In what follows, I test this hypothesis on survey data from the Detroit area.

DATA AND TEST

I use data gathered in 2003 as part of the Detroit Arab American Study (DAAS). The DAAS was produced through an intensive collaboration between the University of Michigan, the University of Michigan–Dearborn, and an advisory panel of community representatives from more than twenty secular, religious, and social-service organizations. The DAAS is a representative survey of adults (eighteen years and older) of Arab or Chaldean descent who resided in households in Wayne, Oakland, and Macomb counties during the six-month survey period, July to December 2003. Face-to-face interviews were conducted with 1,016 subjects between July and November 2003. Seventy-three percent of those who were asked to participate in the survey did so. All references to "Arabs and Chaldeans" in this report refer to that population. In addition, 508 members of the general adult population in these three counties were interviewed during roughly the same period through the Detroit Area Study (DAS). This is a representative sample of the Detroit area population, referred to in this study as the "general population." About 85 percent of the questionnaire items are common to both surveys, permitting extensive comparison of the two populations. Analysis performed in this part of the chapter relies on the DAS data.

In order to test my argument, I construct two ordered logit models. The first model examines the factors associated with Americans who support the infringement of civil liberties for members of the *general* population. The dependent variable reflects the answers of respondents to questions about whether they are willing to infringe on the rights of the general population. It is an index variable based on answers to three questions. The first question asks whether the respondent supports an increase of surveillance of the general population by the U.S. government. The second question asks whether the respondent would support giving the police more power to search anyone at random. And the last question asks whether the interviewee supports detaining suspicious individuals even if there is insufficient evidence to prosecute. The second dependent variable asks specifically about the respondent's willingness to infringe on the civil liberties of *Arab and Muslim Americans*. This, too, is an index variable consisting of three questions. The first question asks whether a respondent would support the increased surveillance of Arab and Muslim Americans; the second question, whether he or she would support giving the police more powers to stop and search anyone who looks Arab or Muslim; and the third, whether those surveyed support the detention of suspicious Muslims and Arabs even when there is insufficient evidence to prosecute. The scores were aggregated such that one affirmative response placed the individual in category one, two affirmative responses were assigned to the second category and three affirmative responses placed individuals in the third category. Respondents who disagreed with all three statements were assigned to the zero category.

Several independent variables are included in the equation to test the overall hypotheses I discuss in the previous section. To capture anxiety and perceptions of threat, I include a variable that gauges individual levels of security after the attacks. The question asks: "How much—if any—have the events of 9/11 shaken your own personal sense of safety and security? Have they shaken it a great deal, a good amount, not too much, or not at all?" To capture ideological inclinations, I include measures of party identification: whether a respondent identifies as Democrat or a Republican. I also include a measure of conservative or liberal leanings. The question asks: "Thinking politically and socially, how would you describe your own general outlook—as being very conservative, moderately conservative, middle-of-the-road, moderately liberal, or very liberal?" Finally, I include a set of variables that serve as plausible explanations for the 9/11 attacks. Two of the explanations describe the results as related to either U.S. foreign policy in the region or to the acts of a few extremists. The other two measures address the "clash of civilizations" hypothesis. The first asks whether there is a religious conflict between Islam, on the one side, and Christianity and Judaism, on the other. The second question asks whether respondents believe that the attacks occurred because the United States supports democracy, freedom, and the rights of women. Finally, I also include several demographic variables to gauge whether basic demographic patterns explain support for civil liberties infringements. In the model are controls for religion, education, income, age, and gender. I also include a measure of exposure to the news in the aftermath of 9/11 to gauge whether media consumption is associated with a willingness to infringe on the civil liberties of the general population as well as of Arab and Muslim Americans. Table 4.1 presents the logit coefficients and the chapter appendix provides a complete coding sheet.

The most interesting finding that emerges from the regressions is that the segments of the population supporting civil liberties infringements in general, and those supporting it for Arab and Muslim Americans only, are quite different. Women are more likely than men to support reducing civil liberties of the general population in the hope of achieving greater security. This is a phenomenon well documented after 9/11; the term "security moms" has become part of our cultural jargon (Lawrence 2005). Some have even speculated that George Bush won a significant number of 2004 votes from women who were concerned about security issues. The model also finds that conservatives, as expected, are more likely than liberals to support the civil liberties infringements of the general population. Personal security and whether respondents were shaken by the events of 9/11 are also significant in this model. Those who felt most vulnerable after the attacks were also most likely to express support

Table 4.1

Ordered Logit Regressions on Support for Civil Liberties Infringements for the General Population and for Muslim/Arab Americans

	General population		Arab and Muslim populations	
	Coeff.	*R.S.E.*	*Coeff.*	*R.S.E.*
Demographics				
Gender	**.763****	**(.207)**	.054	(.215)
Education	-.094	(.089)	-.136	(.090)
Income	-.008	(.053)	-.022	(.051)
Age	.281	(.167)	-.023	(.162)
Ideology				
Liberal/conservative	**-.218****	**(.112)**	-.111	(.119)
Republican	**.557****	**(.277)**	-.443	(.300)
Democrat	**-.459****	**(.229)**	-.353	(.228)
Reasons for 9/11				
Religious conflict	.048	(.203)	.199	(.195)
Clash of values	.366	(.202)	**.366****	**(.200)**
U.S. intervention	-.053	(.204)	-.133	(.199)
A few extremists	**.637****	**(.287)**	.296	(.269)
Safety/security				
Personal sense of security shaken	**.454****	**(.233)**	.104	(.269)
Religion and attendance				
Protestant	-.128	(.254)	**.575****	**(.273)**
Catholic	.235	(.261)	.273	(.269)
News exposure				
Follow news	.035	(.049)	-.014	(.051)
N	365		369	

*p<.10

**p<.05

***p<.01

for a reduction in civil liberties. Finally, respondents who believe that the attacks of 9/11 were committed by a few extremists also support a reduction in civil liberties. The clash of civilization indicators (religious conflict and clash of values) are not pertinent here. In sum, gender, ideology and personal safety play an important part in explaining support for civil liberties infringements for all. Further, those who believe that the 9/11 attacks were the actions of a few extremists support civil liberties infringements of the general population. Perhaps they believe that decreased liberties are a good way to guarantee security from those extremist elements.

The characteristics of individuals supporting infringements on the civil liberties of Arab and Muslim Americans are different. Those Americans willing to support reduced rights for Arabs and Muslims are more likely to be Protestant, and they are more likely to attribute 9/11 to an inherent clash of values between the United States and the Muslim world. Ideology, gender, and personal safety are not statistically significant in this model. While the first model supports conventional wisdom—women more likely than men, conservatives more likely than liberals, and Republicans more likely than Democrats are willing to do away with civil liberties—the findings on Arabs and Muslims are more troubling. It appears that those people who believe that the United States was attacked because of a clash of values are more likely to encourage reduced rights for Arab and Muslim Americans. These respondents, who seem most comfortable with constructions of "us" and "them," are willing to do away with the civil liberties of Arabs and Muslims. That Protestants are more likely to be willing to curb Arab and Muslim civil liberties further illustrates that perceived differences based on religious values explain this pattern of support. Religious denomination was not at all significant in the model that gauged support for civil liberties infringements of the general population. Yet when the target group is Arab and Muslim, Protestants (who constitute about 40 percent of the DAS sample) are more willing to reduce their civil liberties.

These worrisome trends raise the most concern among members of the U.S. Arab and Muslim minorities. A Zogby survey (2002) found that 66 percent of Muslim Americans worry about their future in the United States. If the dominant culture sees them not only as different but also as a threat, as adhering to a value system that opposes "American values," then it is all the more acceptable to do away with their civil rights. Since the attacks of 9/11, hate crimes against Arabs and Muslims in the United States have consistently been on the rise year after year. The racialization of Arabs and Muslims by the mainstream, decades in the making, has manifested itself after 9/11 in support for discriminatory legislation and law enforcement. The media has long portrayed this minority as a population to guard against. The general population, these results show, is following suit.

THE DEBATE ON TOLERANCE

The disturbing reality reflected in the findings above has also paved the way for an opportunity. While worrying about the presence of the "Other" in their midst, Americans are also attempting to learn more about this population. Since 9/11, copies of the Quran have been selling briskly at bookstores across the country. Interfaith dialogue and mosque open houses, which strive to educate Americans about Islam, became more common features after the attacks. In fact, a third of the DAAS respondents reported that they had received an act of solidarity or kindness from a member of the general population. Although many Americans remain wary, they also seek tolerance for the Arab and Muslim "Other."

Yet tolerance and the discourse on tolerance are not void of the context in which tolerance is either granted or withdrawn. The very fact that Muslims and Arabs are rallying Americans to be more tolerant illustrates a conundrum surrounding the issue of toleration itself. Some Arabs and Muslims who have accepted racial profiling claim to understand lengthy interrogations as their children stand by at airports, and apologize over and over for 9/11 because they feel this self-subjugation will win tolerance from the mainstream. However, tolerance assumes equality and good faith in interactions. It also assumes that dominant forces—media, religion, government, and so on—are not operating to espouse intolerance against a certain population. In the end, tolerance is granted by elite members of a dominant mainstream that is united in its culture and values toward a subordinate Other. In the words of Herbert Marcuse, tolerance is "determined and defined by the institutionalized inequality (which is certainly compatible with constitutional equality). . . . In such a society, tolerance is de facto limited on the dual ground of legalized violence or suppression (police, armed forces, guards of all sorts) and of the privileged position held by the predominant interest and their connections" (Marcuse 1965). He goes on to say, "In the United States, this tendency goes hand in hand with the monopolistic or oligopolistic concentration of capital in the formation of public opinion, i.e., the majority." Essentially, tolerance is a tool of racialization.

Whether tolerated or rejected, the construction of the Other is similar. We can take great pride in our toleration of those who do not share our values. Or we can take great pride in resisting accommodation because others don't share our values. In the end, the construction of the Other is the same. Whether tolerated or resisted, the Other is, for the general population, always that which is different. This element of difference—and the ways it is constructed and manifested—define how tolerant we are. The process of racialization is inherent to our toleration of the Other. Rather than look for the commonalities that unite all humankind, we erect differences, and applaud our tolerance, or justify our intolerance. Thus, the debate on whether Arabs and Muslims are worthy of civil liberties protections is the wrong one to have. The racialized symptomatology of constructing Arabs and Muslims as "enemy Others" itself needs to be scrutinized and fixed. Unfortunately, Arabs and Muslims possess neither the resources nor the power nor the media necessary to alter mainstream public opinion. The tides of public opinion continue to operate against them.

APPENDIX

1. *Gender:* Male or Female
   Coding: 1: Male; 2: Female
2. *Education:*
   Coding: 1: Less than High School; 2: High School; 3: Some College; 4: BA;
   5: Professional Degree
3. *Age:*
   Coding: 1: 18–24; 2:25–57; 3: 58+
4. *Household Income:*
   Coding: 1: less than $19,999; 2: $20,000–49,999; 3: $50,000–74,999; 4:
   $75,000+
5. *Republican:* Generally, speaking, do you usually think of yourself as a Republican, Democrat, Independent or what?
   Coding: 1: Republican; 0: All Else
6. *Democrat:* Generally, speaking, do you usually think of yourself as a Republican, Democrat, Independent or what?
   Coding: 1: Democrat; 0: All Else
7. *Liberal/Conservative:* Thinking *politically and socially,* how would you describe your own general outlook—are you very conservative, moderately conservative, middle-of-the-road, moderately liberal, or very liberal?

Coding: 1: Very Conservative; 2: Moderately Conservative; 3: Middle of Road; 4: Moderately Liberal; 5: Very Liberal

8. *Protestant:* Are you Protestant, Catholic, or Orthodox Christian?

Coding: 1: Protestant; 0: Other

9. *Catholic:* Are you Protestant, Catholic, or Orthodox Christian

Coding: 1: Catholic; 0: Other

10. *Follow 9/11 Events/Media:* Since 9/11, how closely have you been following the news about the "war on terrorism"—very closely, closely, a little, or not much at all?

Coding: 1: Very Closely; 2: Somewhat Closely; 3: A Little; 4: Not Much at All

11. *Explanations for 9/11:* Now I'll read you some possible explanations for the terrorist attacks on 9/11. For each one, please tell me whether you think this is a possible explanation or not. Just answer yes or no.

a. *U.S. Intervention:* It's because of the U.S. intervention in the Persian Gulf.

b. *Extremist Beliefs:* It's because of the extremist beliefs of a few terrorists.

c. *Religious Conflict:* It's because of the conflict between Christianity and Judaism on one side and Islam on the other.

d. *Clash of Values:* It's because the U.S. believes in democracy, freedom, and equal rights for women.

Coding: 1: Yes; 0: No

12. *Personal Security Shaken by Events of 9/11:* How much—if any—have the events of 9/11 shaken your own personal sense of safety and security? Have they shaken it a great deal, a good amount, not too much, or not at all?

Coding: 1: A Great Deal; 2: A Good Amount; 3: Not too Much; 4: Not at All

13. *Civil Liberties:* General Population

a. Do you support increasing surveillance of U.S. citizens by the government? [Response Options: Yes or No]

b. Do you support giving the police powers to stop and search anyone at random? [Response Options: Yes or No]

c. Do you support detaining some suspicious individuals even if there is not sufficient evidence to prosecute them in the courts? [Response Options: Yes or No]

14. *Willingness to Give up Civil Liberties of Arab Americans:* Index variable consisting of the following three questions:

a. Do you support increasing surveillance of Arab Americans by the government? [Response Options: Yes or No]

b. Do you support giving the police powers to stop and search anyone who appears to be Arab or Muslim, at random? [Response Options: Yes or No]

c. Do you support detaining some suspicious Arabs and/or Muslims even if there is not sufficient evidence to prosecute them in the courts? [Response Options: Yes or No]

FIVE

"Whiteness" and the Arab Immigrant Experience

SAWSAN ABDULRAHIM

MOST OF THE LITERATURE on Arab Americans weaves a relatively consistent narrative—one that celebrates the "assimilation" of an early wave of immigrants and bemoans the current "racialization" of the group. This narrative recounts that, while Arabic-speaking immigrants at the turn of the twentieth century faced prejudice, they overcame hardship and eventually joined the "American mainstream."[1] At the same time, they became incorporated into the United States' system of racial categorization as white. However, a number of political forces and events taking place over the past few decades brought this process to a halt. The Arab world and Islam presently embody the marked "Other" against which an American identity is constructed. By virtue of their historical, cultural, and transnational connections to a perceived foreign enemy, Arab Americans are pushed outside the national consensus and marked as the "enemy within."[2] As nation and race in the United States have historically entwined,[3] it has been argued that members of the group feel the white racial designation no longer reflects their experience (Samhan 1999; Majaj 2000; Naber 2000).

---

1. The term "Arabic-speaking" has been used in other writings in reference to immigrants at the turn of the twentieth century because, while they spoke Arabic, not all necessarily identified as Arab.

2. For writings on the impact of September 11 on this process, see Cainkar (2004b) and Hagopian (2004).

3. See Omi and Winant (1994).

Although the narrative sketched above has become dominant in Arab American writings, its assumptions and omissions remain largely unexamined.[4] On the one hand, the narrative on the early experience, in its focus on assimilation, overlooks the highly racialized process through which some immigrant groups in the United States "became white." On the other hand, many of the recent writings on the racialization of Arab Americans, especially in a post–September 11 environment, operate from the presumption that racialization occurs only through moving away from "whiteness," in a predictable trajectory, and through engaging in nonwhite racial formation.[5] In most of this literature, white racial formation is rarely critically examined. Instead, matters pertaining to "whiteness," and its relationship to power, remain obscured in favor of advocating for what is believed to be a slightly more comfortable position for Arab Americans vis-à-vis an unexamined "white center."

The current essay utilizes a "critical whiteness" framework to examine this white center looking in from the discursive and marginal position Arab Americans occupy on the racial hierarchy. This discursive position, often associated in Arab American writings with invisibility and erasure,[6] can serve as a location for the marking and critical evaluation of "whiteness." Given that the main objective is to place "whiteness" at the forefront of the analysis, the essay does not address the question of whether Arab Americans are, or should be categorized as, white or nonwhite. Instead, it asks the following question: In what ways can an examination of Arab immigrants' interactions with race in the United States describe and shed a new light on "whiteness?" In other words, when Arab Americans identify as nonwhite, why do they do so? *And,* when they assert a white identity, in what sense do they do so, for what benefits, and at what costs?[7]

This chapter starts with a review of "whiteness" and Arab American literatures. It explores how—presently and in the local contexts of Detroit and Dearborn—Arab immigrants describe, relate to, reinforce, or undermine "whiteness" through narratives of their own identities. This examination re-

4. Exceptions to this are writings by Sarah Gualtieri (2001), Lisa Suhair Majaj (2000), and Helen Samhan (1999).

5. Omi and Winant define racial formation as "the sociohistorical process by which racial categories are created, inhabited, transformed, and destroyed" (1994, 55).

6. On Arab American invisibility, see Nadine Naber (2000) and Lisa Suhair Majaj (2000).

7. These questions are adapted from the afterword to *Are Italians White?* by Roediger (2003).

quires both abandoning race-neutral language of assimilation and Americanization and resisting the tendency to situate Arab Americans solely as racialized victims. The arguments put forth derive from a qualitative study that set out to examine how Arab immigrants interact with the census race question and represent themselves within the confines of that official system of categorization.[8] The study examines Arab immigrants' racial formation in a highly segregated context, not only in relationship to the white racial category, but also in relationship to what Toni Morrison refers to as a "black presence."[9] In other words, it explores how immigrants relate to "blackness"—"whiteness's Other"—in the process of organizing their relationship to "whiteness." The discussion in this chapter focuses on deconstructing the narratives of two Arab immigrants who express divergent views of their racial identity.

WHITENESS AND IMMIGRATION IN THE UNITED STATES

Most writings on race in the United States have focused on nonwhites treating the white racial category as invisible, normative, and natural. In recent years, however, there has been a proliferation of a new genre of race writings specifically concerned with white racial identity formation. This work, referred to as "whiteness studies" or "critical studies of whiteness," argues that, like other racial categories, "whiteness" is constructed, dynamic, and context-specific; it is negotiated by individuals and collectives as both an identity and a social position (Doane and Bonilla-Silva 2003; Rasmussen et al. 2001). "Whiteness" is a structuring system that operates through "unknowing" and "unseeing" racial subjects.[10] In return, it offers its subjects a location of structural advantage.[11] Historically in the United States, "whiteness" has been a category that immigrant groups were included in or excluded from, and an ideology embraced and given new meanings by those allowed entry into it (Roediger 2002).

An integral component of "whiteness" studies has been to document the historical processes through which different European immigrant groups at the

---

8. The analysis presented in the essay is part of the author's dissertation research in the School of Public Health at the University of Michigan, Ann Arbor.

9. The term "black presence" is adapted from Tony Morrison's *Playing in the Dark* (1993).

10. In addition to Rasmussen et al. (2001), see Ware (2002).

11. See Frankenberg (2001).

turn of the twentieth century gained white racial status.[12] This work demonstrates that white racial consciousness was constructed through a highly contested process with the participation of immigrants who were deemed to be "in-between" or "not-yet-white." In an era when fitness for citizenship was being hotly debated, immigrants allied themselves with African Americans at times, while at other times they sought to assert their claims to citizenship and upward social mobility by distancing themselves from them.[13] They fought against nativism not for the promise of a more equal society but for one divided by a reformulated "whiteness" that has come to incorporate them (Jacobson 1998; Ignatiev 1995). In his study on how the Irish became white, Ignatiev argues that, through seeking white racial status, immigrants contributed to the consolidation of an unreachable color line.

In their efforts to deconstruct "whiteness," scholars in the field have turned many of their critiques inward. Almost every collection of essays on "whiteness" starts with an acknowledgment that the earliest—and most articulate—writings on "whiteness" are by black authors who wrote on how white ideologies operate to maintain inequality and oppression.[14] As such, "whiteness" studies existed long before the term itself came into common usage, even though contributions of nonwhite subjects to the field have only recently begun to be acknowledged as valid. Relatedly, the dominant view that "whiteness is invisible" has come under critique.[15] As writings by authors of color indicate, while "whiteness" may be invisible to those who benefit from it, it is certainly visible to those who suffer its consequences.[16] Furthermore, an important critique of "whiteness" studies addresses the risk that, in the process of deconstructing the category, one can easily fall back into conceptualizations that reify race as opposed to challenging it (Ware 2002). While one of the goals of "whiteness" studies is to extend critical race theory by destabilizing socially constructed racial categories, the field continues to operate from a black-white dualism model and pays little attention to identities that are neither white nor black.

12. See Roediger (1991, 2002), Brodkin (1998), Jacobson (1998), Haney-López (1996), and Ignatiev (1995).

13. Roediger (2002) demonstrates how this process unfolded in *Colored White*.

14. The most frequently cited black authors on "whiteness" are Du Bois (1903), Fanon (1967), and Morrison (1993).

15. On "whiteness as invisible," see Peggy MacIntosh (1990).

16. For a critique of "whiteness as invisible," see Ruth Frankenberg (2001).

Two important questions remain ripe for exploration from a critical "whiteness" perspective. The first inquires into what happened to those who "became white" but who did not profit from their "whiteness."[17] The second invites exploration of why groups or individuals who are subordinated and racialized as "not quite white" continue to assert a white identity.[18] Although these two questions are interrelated, the former has come to dominate in Arab American writings while the latter remains almost completely overlooked. One of the most prevailing themes in Arab American writings is that they are a group who "became white" but who currently do not reap the benefits of "whiteness." While a claim is never made that there is a consensus on how Arab Americans identify, the increasing emphasis on their invisibility in the white category and engagement in nonwhite racial formation has preempted a critical exploration of how members of the group have engaged in white racial formation in the past and how they may continue to do so in the present.

The main narrative on Arab Americans describes the racism and exclusion early immigrants faced, and how they overcame the odds through hard work and perseverance. The economic achievements of members of the group are often explained by the cultural values they brought with them such as dedication, strong family ties, and independence. This narrative recounts that, by World War II, Arabic-speaking immigrants had "followed the middle-class path up the economic and social ladder" (Naff 1994, 31), and "moved from the central city . . . into the suburbs" (Aswad 1974, 10). In other words, they have "assimilated" (Suleiman 1999). Beyond mention of a few court cases in which the racial position of "Arabs-as-white" was questioned in the U.S. legal system,[19] how immigrants responded to the racism they encountered and the arguments they employed to gain citizenship rights remain largely absent in these accounts. Instead, the story of the Arab American early wave is often narrated in race-neutral language—the language of assimilation.

A few writings, however, have critically explored how Arabic-speaking immigrants interacted with a racialized structure through a process at the end of which they "became white." In looking at some historical documents, authors

17. This question was posed in the introduction in Rasmussen et al. (2001).

18. This question permeates the historical analysis of "whiteness" presented by Roediger (2002).

19. On a review of citizenship court cases, see Massad (1993) and Suleiman (1999).

Lisa Suhair Majaj (2000) and Helen Samhan (1999) argue that when Arabic-speaking immigrants were faced with the threat of losing citizenship rights, they battled for white racial status within the context of white supremacy. In courts and in the media, immigrants asserted that they were not "Asiatic" or "Negro" but "civilized whites." Relying on similar documents, Sarah Gualtieri (2001) further suggests that immigrants' active and organized participation played an important role in their inclusion in the racial hierarchy as whites, *and*, more important, in the shaping of the meanings of "whiteness" at that time.

WHITENESS AND ARAB IMMIGRANTS IN DETROIT AND DEARBORN

An examination of how Arab immigrants in Detroit and Dearborn, Michigan, presently engage in discourses on race and "whiteness" rests on two premises. The first is that, even in a post–September 11 political climate, Arab Americans continue to exercise individual and collective agency in organizing their relationship to "whiteness." They are active subjects and not merely objects of a hostile political discourse that sees them as terrorists and foreign, or a sympathetic discourse that sees them solely as racialized victims. The second premise is that Arab Americans' current interactions with race and "whiteness" are neither monolithic nor homogeneous, but are varied and contingent. Arab immigrants in Detroit and Dearborn engage in different, even contradictory, racial identity formations; there are those who identify as white and those who identify as non-white, and each identity choice is driven by its own set of arguments. It is exactly this divergence and tension that makes the study of "whiteness" from the point of view of the Arab immigrant experience both provocative and pressing.

The discussion presented in this section draws on qualitative research carried out among Arab immigrant owners of small businesses in Detroit and Dearborn. The business owners occupy a distinct location in the local economic structure and constitute a social class whose members share economic interests. As previously indicated, the discussion will focus on the narratives of two Arab immigrants who position themselves differently in relation to "whiteness" and "blackness." Moreover, while I do not negate the value of research and writings on Arab Americans that address the effects of national- or global-level forces, I argue that it is important to pay close attention to the effects of the local context. Specifically, making overarching generalizations about Arab Americans may obscure local historical and economic factors that shape racial identity formation. This is especially important in Detroit, a place that has come to be seen by insiders and outsiders alike as a "black space" (Hartigan 1999), and Dearborn, a suburb whose history is entwined with the maintenance of racial segregation (Georgakas and Surkin 1998; Sugrue 1996; Good 1989).

Because of Detroit's racial history and current racial context, it constitutes an ideal location for a study of "whiteness." Moreover, because the city's metropolitan area is home to the oldest and most highly concentrated Arab American community in the United States (Shryock and Abraham 2000), it offers a unique opportunity to examine "whiteness" from the discursive and marginal racial position of Arab Americans. Although Detroit and Dearborn border each other, they constitute two spaces that have had conflicting histories and continue to have very little in common today. Therefore, in this chapter, Detroit refers to the city of Detroit *only* and not to the metropolitan area that encompasses Dearborn and other suburbs. A quick summary of the recent history of Detroit and Dearborn may shed light on the rationale behind this distinction and place in context how Arab Americans became integrated into the racial hierarchy and the economic structure in the two spaces the way they are today.

Detroit is one of the most racially and economically segregated cities in the United States (Massey and Denton 1993), a quintessential representation of what has been termed the "urban crisis."[20] Throughout the twentieth century, Detroit's history has been one of institutionalized forms of racial segregation and racial conflict. The city's population in the year 2000 was 81.6 percent African American and 12.3 percent white. In contrast, Dearborn—which borders Detroit's west side—was 86.9 percent white and less than 1.3 percent African American in the year 2000.[21]

Although employment with the automobile industry was one of the main pull factors originally, a large number of immigrants from Arab countries arrived in the Detroit metropolitan area following the Immigration and Naturalization Act of 1965 and after the forces of deindustrialization and economic restructuring had been set in motion.[22] A convergence of factors opened the

20. On the racial history of Detroit, see Sugrue (1996).
21. These data are obtained from the U.S. Census Bureau Web site: http://www.census.gov.
22. See Shryock and Abraham (2000).

door for Arab immigrants to buy businesses in Detroit that had been previously owned by members of European immigrant groups.[23] Currently, Arab Americans in the metropolitan area engage in a multitude of economic spheres, one of which is small business enterprise. As entrepreneurs, they are represented as a "middleman minority" in the predominantly African American city of Detroit,[24] and as business owners in a thriving ethnic enclave in Dearborn, where a large number of Arab immigrants live and work.[25]

Based on the 2000 census, almost 30 percent of Dearborn's residents claim an Arab ancestry, while less than 1 percent of Detroit's do so.[26] These estimates are obtained from the census ancestry question, which is included only on the long census form. Because the census defines people who trace their origins to the Middle East and North Africa as white, information on how persons of Arab ancestry respond to the race question are nonexistent. Persons who check the "some other race" category and write Arab are automatically entered as white; their agency to identify as nonwhite is undermined by the census. Moreover, though the census flags certain situations that involve reassignment during the data-entry phase, this situation—reassigning an "other race—Arab" to "white"—does not receive an allocation flag.[27] Consequently, data on the percentages of Arab Americans who identify as "white" and those who identify as "other race—Arab" are lost. More important, differences between the two groups—on socioeconomic and a host of other variables available through the census—remain masked.

The census race categories are highly problematic, as they reflect the history of how race was manufactured in the United States to justify colonialism and slavery (Shohat 1998; Wright 1994). Nonetheless, race continues to play a fundamental role in structuring social relations, and data obtained from the census race question, albeit imperfect, provides a means of exploring the racial structure. How Arab immigrants interact with the census race question and

23. On the 1967 Detroit racial uprising and white flight, see Sugrue (1996).

24. On the "middleman minority" theory, see Bonacich (1973, 1980).

25. On the ethnic enclave economy, see Portes (1987).

26. See de la Cruz and Brittingham (2003).

27. This information is based on a phone conversation with Angela Brittingham of the U.S. Census Bureau and coauthor of *The Arab Population Report: 2000*, as well as on feedback provided by staff at the Government Publications Office at the University of Michigan's Graduate Library.

choose to locate themselves within historically constructed categories can shed light on how racial ideologies become embodied and given meaning through new agents. The question as to how Arab immigrants answer the census race question and, more important from a "critical whiteness" perspective, why they answer it the way they do, promises to contribute to critical race theory and to the burgeoning field of "whiteness studies."

There is a range of responses Arab immigrants offer to the census race question.[28] Naturally, some Arab immigrants indicate that they avoid identifying their race on official forms whenever possible. They express concern that when someone asks about their race, it is with the intention to discriminate against them. Others say that they find it difficult to answer the question because the response categories do not make sense to them. They avoid answering the question by projecting what Mary Waters terms a "raceless persona" (1999); while they don't know what they are, they at least know that they are neither white, nor black, nor American Indian.

The two Arab immigrants whose narratives are analyzed in the remainder of this section did provide answers to the race question. The first participant checked the "other race" category; the second checked "white." These two participants were selected from a larger qualitative sample *specifically* because their divergent views of their own racial identities offer a unique opportunity for examining how "whiteness" can be constructed, or undermined, through racial subjects. The comparison is made more relevant by the fact that the two participants share many background characteristics. They are both males who immigrated to the United States from the same Arab country at about the same age and have been living in Dearborn for almost the same number of years. Both arrived with less than a high school education but quickly became embedded in social networks that provided them with referrals to job opportunities. They entered the secondary labor market in unskilled low-wage jobs shortly after their arrival.[29] With support from extended family members, they were both able to move out of the secondary labor market and to purchase the businesses they currently own.

28. The information presented in this section is based on an analysis of forty-six interviews with Arab immigrant business owners in Detroit and Dearborn.

29. For a discussion on the primary and secondary labor markets, see Portes (1983).

The first participant owns a business in Detroit whose customer base is 80–90 percent African American. He indicated that he always checks the "other race" category on the census and other official forms and writes in "Arab." While he knows that some Arab Americans check "white," he himself insists on writing in the word "Arab." For this participant, September 11 was by no means a wake-up call. When asked about whether and how his life was affected by the event, he replied that it just proved what he has always thought: "I always thought that we are not liked here. I always thought we are hated. I always thought that we are looked down on, because of the movies mainly. And it [September 11] just proved it." But September 11 is not the only factor affecting how this immigrant views his position in the United States. He was asked about what he likes and dislikes about the neighborhood where his business is located in Detroit:

> *Participant 1:* Things I like . . . we've been here for a while, the neighbors know us, they like us. And things I don't like . . . when somebody comes from outside the neighborhood, and they don't know us, they have pre-set notions about Arabs.
> *Interviewer:* What pre-set notions do they have about Arabs?
> *Participant 1:* Like we are trying to steal from them, trying to cheat them of their money, trying to think that they are thieves, this kind of mentality.

This participant's racial identity forms not only in relation to the rhetoric of Arabs and Muslims as terrorists, but also in relation to a localized image of the Arab as an "outsider" in Detroit—a merchant making money in a disenfranchised, predominantly African American neighborhood. He, however, subverts this image by identifying himself as an "insider" and those who level criticism against his existence in Detroit as "from outside the neighborhood." In identifying as an "other race," he is asserting a nonwhite racial identity and disassociating himself from "whiteness." He further expresses ambivalence about a hyphenated Arab American identity, which he believes assumes a relationship between "becoming American" and "becoming white":

> *Interviewer:* What does the term Arab American mean to you?
> *Participant 1:* Arab American!
> *Interviewer:* . . . for example, who do you think is an Arab American?

Participant 1: I don't believe in the phrase itself, Arab American . . .

Interviewer: You don't think that the term captures . . .

Participant 1: The term! No. Is it like I am not pure American! Is that what it is? [No one is a] pure American except the American Indians. And, unfortunately, normally . . . the term American is used for the White race.

Interviewer: White!

Participant 1: Which is not fair either.

This immigrant's insistence on representing himself racially as "nonwhite" agrees with his ambivalence about identifying as an ethnic American in the United States. "America" is for the "white race," and because he does not identify as white, it follows that he cannot identify as an American. On the other hand, his inability to identify as an ethnic American may be the price he has to pay for rejecting "whiteness" in a system that is structured around white privilege, "the term American is used for the White race."

The second participant, on the other hand, identifies as an Arab American and expresses pride in his hyphenated identity. When asked whether he identifies as an Arab American, he replied: "I am Arab American, I am . . . I want to be Arab American. . . . I am not saying I am Arabic and I want to be American. I always say that *I am* Arab American." Throughout the interview, he expressed affections for the United States, his "second home," in statements such as "I love this country" or "I [would] die for this country." This participant owns a business in the heart of the ethnic enclave in Dearborn and his success depends on providing excellent service to Arab customers in the face of stiff competition. In the aftermath of September 11, he expressed appreciation that he and his business were protected in the ethnic enclave, as he heard numerous stories about other Arabs who owned businesses "among American people" who were harassed after the event.

Unlike the first participant, who insisted on answering "other race" to the census race question, the second participant quickly answered that he always checks "white." He was asked why:

Participant 2: See, first of all, this country belongs to White Americans . . . it does not belong to, say, Black Africans, or Indians, or let's say . . .

Interviewer: You think the U.S. belongs to Whites?

Participant 2: Whites, yes.

Interviewer: Not to African Americans?
Participant 2: No.
Interviewer: Yes, so you think [America] belongs to Whites?
Participant 2: Yes.

On the surface, this participant's identification with the white racial category may seem counterintuitive, given his statements about feeling protected in the ethnic enclave at a time when Arabs living and working outside the enclave were being harassed. Placing his statements in historical perspective, however, it may seem "logical" for him to want to "be white" given his belief that "whiteness" in the United States is a prerequisite for "becoming American." He is subjectively identifying with "whiteness" for "rational" reasons: America belongs to whites and one has to become white in order to become American. Eager to become American and have access to all the opportunities America offers, this immigrant is required to interact with a structure that rewards "whiteness." And he does. He internalizes "whiteness" in his quest for being accepted as an American. This participant's narrative recalls Roediger's view that the United States continues to be a place where new immigrants are attracted to "whiteness" and to all its material and psychological benefits (2002). Arab immigrants are not immune to this attraction.

Although the two immigrants provide ostensibly divergent answers to the census race question—one embraces the white category and one rejects it—both expose the "hidden" racial character of the assimilation discourse. That is to say, they challenge the notion that Arab immigrants' interactions with "America" take place along a line between "Americanization" and "resistance to Americanization" (Shryock and Abraham 2000). Issues of race and "whiteness" permeate the American immigrant experience, and the Arab immigrant case should not be seen as an exception. While some may engage in nonwhite racial formation, others may seek to rectify their precarious sense of belonging in America by embracing "whiteness." Historical evidence suggests that exclusion from "whiteness" may at times lead to stronger attachment to it (Roediger 2002; Haney-López 1996).

Even though the question of how Arab Americans identify on the census in relation to the white category is particularly salient, "whiteness" is not the only, and may not be the most important, frame of reference for immigrants' racial formation. In the United States, new immigrants develop racialized identities in a context shaped by what has been termed the historical burden of a white-black relation of domination and oppression (Alba and Nee 2003). Moreover, identities are formed not only through imagining shared characteristics with other members of a group, but also through the fabrication of an "Other."[30] Thus, it is pertinent to explore how Arab immigrants themselves relate to "whiteness" not only as its object others, but as its subjects. This is particularly salient in the highly racialized context of Detroit and Dearborn—namely, the "whiteness" of Dearborn and the "blackness" of Detroit.

Therefore, in addition to how the two aforementioned Arab immigrants interact with the census race question, how they position themselves in relation to both "whiteness" and "blackness" was examined. The two participants were presented with a series of linear diagrams, each with two constituted categories on opposite ends of a line: Arab and white, Arab and black, and white and black. They were asked to mark on each linear diagram where they would position themselves in relation to the two categories and then asked to explain why they chose to position themselves the way they did. The remainder of this section focuses on how the two Arab immigrants interact with "whiteness," not in isolation, but in the presence of "blackness."

Not surprisingly, when the diagram included a category for Arab opposite one of the two other constituted categories, both participants positioned themselves as close as possible to Arab and as far away as possible from both white and black. However, when the diagram showed the constituted category "black" on one end of the line and "white" on the other, the two immigrants positioned themselves differently. The first participant, who identified as "other race" on the census race question, positioned himself in the middle between "white" and "black." Conversely, the second participant, who identified as "white" on the census race question, positioned himself as far away as possible from "black" and as close as possible to "white" on the line.

The first immigrant, who positioned himself in the middle between "white" and "black," explained why:

> *Participant 1:* Because I see no difference between Black and White. There is no difference between the two.

30. See Said (1978), Morrison (1993), and Hall (1996).

Interviewer: There is no difference?
Participant 1: In my evaluation.

The participant is well aware that, in Detroit, there *is* a difference between black and white. In fact, the structural position he occupies—an Arab business owner in a segregated African American neighborhood—is a constant reminder of this reality. In spite of this contradiction, he distances himself from "whiteness" and disturbs the process through which it comes to be embodied by immigrants as an unexamined center of American life. His unwillingness to adopt white identity de-centers "whiteness" and allows him to articulate a position that is not necessarily constituted through a distancing from "blackness." He carves out a new location that renounces "whiteness," not only on the census form, but, more important, as an ideology created and given life through a fabricated and distant "black Other." While this participant may continue to be "invisible," as far as not being counted in the census is concerned, his invisibility has the potential of disrupting the process through which "whiteness" is made.

The second immigrant, who positions himself as "white" and as far away as possible from "blackness," argues for a different location. Rarely interacting with blacks given the location of his business, an ethnic enclave surrounded by a white space, he makes the following statement about blacks:

Participant 2: . . . a lot of times, they rob a gas station, they kill the guy, they take the money, they rob the liquor store. You hear and see what is going on, people get killed for the money. And, then, they find out, they get the guy, they catch him, and he is Black.

Clearly, the notion that "whiteness" in the United States is constructed through distancing from "blackness" is neither a historical phenomenon nor one that members of a racialized and beleaguered group shy away from. While racism is by no means an American invention, the negative stereotypes voiced by this immigrant resonate with racial ideologies that are pervasive in American culture, those of "blacks as criminal." This process of articulating one's "whiteness" through the fabrication of a racialized, distant "black presence" is intriguing for its reflexive character.[31] The black in the eyes of the "white" Arab *is* the Arab in

---

31. On the reflexive nature of the "black presence," see Toni Morrison (1993).

the eyes of "white" America. In order for a racialized Arab to become "white" in a white racial space—Dearborn—he would need to project his "Otherness" on to a secondary "Other."

The old models of assimilation—which posit a linear evolution from an immigrant identity to an American ethnic identity—have increasingly come under scrutiny. Even the most eager supporters of the assimilation model acknowledge that the process has been made possible to European immigrants and denied to African Americans and other immigrant groups (Alba and Nee 1997, 2003). Thus, the assimilation narrative has contributed to producing a biased immigration history that takes into account neither the effects of racism and racialization in the United States nor the dynamic process through which "whiteness" was constructed and shaped (Roediger 2002). Although some writings on the Arab American experience adopt a race-neutral assimilation paradigm, other writings have contextualized that experience within the history of race and "whiteness" in the United States.

In this chapter, I argued that the process through which Arab immigrants form racial identities is highly subjective and that even the racial marking of Arabs and Muslims in a post–September 11 environment may not lead to a uniform and complete disillusionment with "whiteness." "Whiteness" is an ideology that continues to be molded against a black "other," often by members of groups who hold a precarious position on the racial hierarchy. Therefore, the possibility that Arab Americans may not be naturally transforming to nonwhite racial subjects, even in the current political climate, should be left open for exploration.

The objective of this exploration was not to argue for a position in terms of where Arab Americans fit on the racial hierarchy, supporting or opposing the standpoint that they are not treated the way whites are treated so their experience is naturally that of racial minorities and they need to be categorized as such. Thus, it is neither intended to back nor counter lobbying efforts for extracting Arabs from the "white" race category.[32] I propose that any resolution to the precarious location Arab Americans occupy in the racial hierarchy ought to

---

32. This is in reference to some efforts by Arab American national organizations in response to the escalating demonization of Arabs and Muslims in the United States; see Samhan (1999).

be engaged through a framework that is intended to challenge racial hierarchies, not reinforce them. Nonetheless, the demonizing of Arabs and Muslims, which began well before September 11, 2001, is part of a dynamic process of racialization that ought to be understood in the context of the race history of the United States and, what is more important, challenged.

SIX

Strange Fruit?

Syrian Immigrants, Extralegal Violence,
and Racial Formation in the United States

SARAH M. A. GUALTIERI

MOB IN FLORIDA LYNCHES WHITE MAN; WIFE SLAIN announced the bold-type headline of the *New York Evening World* newspaper on May 17, 1929.[1] The accompanying article described briefly the circumstances surrounding the killing of "N. G. Romey, white, a grocer," by a mob after a dispute with the local chief of police. Other reports in the English and Arabic-language papers in the United States revealed that the dead man was Nola Romey, who, with his wife, Fannie, and their children, was a member of one of two Syrian families living in Lake City, Florida.[2] Early in the morning of May 17, 1929, he became the victim

An earlier version of this article appeared in *Arab Studies Quarterly* 26, no. 3 (Summer 2004):63–85. It was first presented at the Conference on the Lebanese Diaspora, held in Beirut in 2001 and organized by Paul Tabar. This text has authority. I thank Michelle Hartman, Melani McAlister, María Elena Martínez, Theresa Mah, and Nadine Naber for their careful reading and suggestions on how to improve the argument.

1. The article appears in the papers of the NAACP, Part 7, The Anti-Lynching Campaign, 1912–1955, series A, "Anti-Lynching Investigative Files, 1912–1953," reel 10, University Publications of America, 1987. See also "Florida Mob Lynches White Storekeeper," *Chicago Defender,* May 25, 1929, 1.

2. Although the *Lake City Reporter* erroneously described them as "native born Assyrians," May 24, 1929, 1; *Miami Herald,* May 18, 1929, 1; *Florida Union Times,* May 19, 1929, 19; *New York Times,* May 18, 1929, 18; *Meraat ul-gharb* (Mirror of the West), May 23, 1929. "Syrian" refers to persons originating from the late-Ottoman provinces of *bilad al-Sham,* or geographical Syria. This area included the present states of Syria, Lebanon, Israel/Palestine, and Jordan. Although

of the state's well-established tradition of extralegal violence, more commonly referred to as lynching, and his death became part of a larger story of the frequency with which Americans brutally inflicted what they called justice on the bodies of the powerless.[3]

But what did it mean that Romey, an immigrant from Syria in southwest Asia, was described as a "white man"?[4] Was this simply the *New York Evening World*'s way of distinguishing him from the scores of black men who were more typically the victims of "Judge Lynch"? Or, was there something more complicated about Romey's racial status that rendered the designation "white" as much a problem as a description? This chapter seeks to answer these questions by interrogating the idea, and implications, of Syrian-Arab whiteness at a particular historical moment. In doing so, it suggests how a reexamination of this lynching can help frame the agenda of Arab American activism at the beginning of a new century when the possibility of violence, verbal and physical, legal and extralegal, seems to threaten the lives of so many Arabs in the United States and abroad.

ARAB "WHITENESS": A CRITICAL REAPPRAISAL

Recent scholarship on the racialization of Arabs in the United States points to the paradoxes of their categorization as white in American classificatory schemes.[5] This designation, many argue, is at odds with the lived experience of

---

the majority of emigrants from *bilad al-Sham* to the United States were from what became the Republic of Lebanon, they described themselves as "Syrian" and were referred to as such in the sources used for this essay. As for Romey's name, it is most probably an anglicized version of the Arabic "Rumi" or "Rumia," while his first name, Nola, is anglicized from Niqula (Nicholas). His wife, Fannie (who was Syrian) may have changed her name from the Arabic "Famia."

3. *Syrian World* 3, no. 12 (June 1929):46; *Miami Herald*, May 18, 1929; *New York Times*, May 18, 1929.

4. I use the term "Asia" to be consistent with the census terminology of the day. Syrian immigrants were listed as "foreign-born white" under the broad category of Asia. See figures for 1910–40 in U.S. Bureau of the Census (1943, 33).

5. By "racialization" I mean, following Thomas C. Holt's succinct definition, the processes by which groups were "made into races" (2000, 53), and Howard Winant's argument that "the concept of racialization signifies the extension of racial meaning to a previously racially unclassified relationship, social practice, or group" (1994, 59). A historical example would be the extension of the term "black" to Africans whose specific identities were Mande, Ibo, and Akan. In the United

Arab immigrants and their children, who do not benefit from the privileges that whiteness ostensibly confers nor identify with the white majority.[6] Rather, they face discrimination in the workplace; endure degradation by the media, film, and television; and suffer the psychological and physical terror of bombings, vandalism, incarceration and hate speech.[7] Despite their official status as white, Arabs are a minority without minority status, the "most invisible of the invisibles" (Kadi 1994, xix). According to Therese Saliba, "Arabs and Arab Americans remain victims of racist policies, even as they are rendered invisible by the standards of current racialized discourses" (1999, 305).[8] Other scholars argue that Arab subjection to a combination of political intimidation, violence, and the racialization of Islam in the United States have made them "not quite white" or "honorary white."[9] Because of the way that race and fitness for citizenship have historically been inter-

---

States, these processes typically included land expropriation, exploitation of labor, and popular and official debate over racial classification. "Race" is thus a historically contingent category that acquires meaning within specific relations of power. See also Barot and Bird (2001). A related concept is that of racial formation, which Omi and Winant define "as the sociohistorical process by which racial categories are created, inhabited, transformed, and destroyed" (1994, 55).

6. Among the recent interventions in the field dealing with race and racialization of Arabs are Therese Saliba, "Resisting Invisibility," Helen Hatab Samhan, "Not Quite White," and Lisa Suhair Majaj, "Arab-American Ethnicity: Locations, Coalitions, and Cultural Negotiations," all in *Arabs in America*, edited by Michael W. Suleiman (1999a); Joseph Massad, "Palestinians and the Limits of Racialized Discourse," (1993); Nadine Naber, "Ambiguous Insiders: An Investigation of Arab American Invisibility" (2000); and Sarah Gualtieri, "Becoming 'White': Race, Religion and the Foundations of Syrian/Lebanese Ethnicity in the United States" (2001).

7. There is quite an extensive literature documenting the emergence and circulation of Arab stereotypes in television, film, and textbooks, as well as politically motivated violence and intimidation. Among the pioneering and more comprehensive studies are: Janice Terry, *Mistaken Identity* (1985); Jack Shaheen, *The TV Arab* (1984); Michael Suleiman, *The Arabs in the Mind of America* (1988); Nabeel Abraham "Anti-Arab Racism and Violence in the United States" (1997); and Susan Akram, "The Aftermath of September 11, 2001: The Targeting of Arabs and Muslims in America" (2002).

8. On this point see also, Salah D. Hassan, "Arabs, Race and the Post-September 11 National Security State" (2002b, 21).

9. This literature is influenced by critical approaches to race, which stress its social construction, and is also a reply to earlier scholarship that stressed the benefits of assimilation, including (although implicitly) within whiteness. See, for example, Soheir A. Morsy (1994) and the works cited in note 5 above.

twined in the United States, this not-quite-white status renders Arabs suspect in the American polity. They are in fact considered a threat to it on the grounds that they originate in countries that are perceived as fanatical and backward. By this logic, not only are Arabs not quite white, they are not quite free also. They are subject to "the hyphen that never ends" (Joseph 1999a, 268; Moore 2002, 33).

The body of scholarship on questions of race in the Arab American experience is extensive, but it must be supplemented. Two areas that warrant more thorough and specific attention are the history of ideas about Arabs as a "race" in the pre–World War II period and the social practices that helped situate them within specific racial hierarchies. Although we have quite a substantial literature on how Arabs have been racialized in relation to foreign policy crises and in the mainstream media in the post–World War II era, we do not have an adequate understanding of their racialization in earlier periods. This lack is not just an issue of a gap in the literature related to chronology. There is also a great deal of conceptual and empirical work to be done on the question of how Arab racialization has related historically to that of other groups. We need more studies like that of Ronald Stockton, whose analysis of American images of Arabs found them to be primarily derivative, that is rooted in older "hostile archetypes" that targeted blacks and Jews (1994, 138). He demonstrates how themes of sexual depravity, physiological and psychological inferiority, conspiracy, and "secret powers" were familiar in the repertoire of American racism and anti-Semitism and were transferred to Arabs, particularly during moments of crisis, such as the oil embargo of the early 1970s. In 1989, for example, at the height of the Palestinian uprising against the Israeli military occupation of the West Bank and Gaza Strip, a national monthly on Middle East affairs published a cartoon entitled "Reading the Arab Mind" that was strikingly similar to one published ninety years earlier depicting "the Jewish mind." The cartoon shows the "Arab mind" compartmentalized into categories like "vengeance," "fanaticism," "double talk," and "blackmail," while the "Jewish mind" is divided into images depicting the "worship of money," "cowardice," and "theft." Both depictions focus on the group's hostile orientations to the world and assume rigid thought processes that are different, and threatening (138). Like all stereotypes, these images impose a set of negative, unchanging traits upon an entire group, effectively taking it out of history.

Studies that demonstrate the linkages among racist imagery of Arabs, Jews, and blacks help move the discussion to a new level, where the focus on discrimination is coupled with an examination of how patterns of exclusion build upon those of the past. Toward this goal, scholars of Arab racialization could examine how the epithets and images used to discredit Syrians as "trash" and unworthy voters in the 1920s owed much to an evolved ideology about Asian alienness and black unworthiness for full participation in the American polity (Conklin and Faires 1987). As historian Thomas Holt argues, "from the poison tree of these 'original sins' as it were flowed much of the ideological justifications, discursive formulations, as well as the asymmetries of power *that made subsequent racialization projects possible*" (1997, 7).

Efforts to trace similarities in racialization projects should also account for their differences. What, for example, were the ramifications on both the Arab American community and other communities of the Syrian struggle to be recognized as white in the early part of the twentieth century? How did Syrian participation in their racialization affect social relations at different times and in different places?[10] This process of stock-taking will encourage debate not only on the history of discrimination against Arabs in the United States, but also on the ways in which they have sought to position themselves within and benefit from racial hierarchies that perpetuate racist discourse, most frequently and detrimentally directed at African Americans. By better understanding the history of the *production* of racist attitudes, including within their own communities, Arab Americans will be in a better position to build coalitions that seek to dismantle them. Over time, this endeavor will reveal that when there has been collaboration with white supremacy, there has also been resistance forged through partnership and dialogue with people of color.[11]

RACE AND LYNCHING IN THE JIM CROW SOUTH

The practice of lynching, in which mobs of varying sizes seized persons, often while they were in police custody, and killed them, had been on the rise since the

10. A brief discussion of how Syrian and Greek whiteness facilitated their move into the niches of groceries and restaurants in the Carolinas can be found in Stathakis (1996). Soheir Morsy and Kathleen Moore have hinted at the problems associated with claiming whiteness, namely that it has promoted racialist, even eugenicist criteria to construct identity and affiliation with the dominant social group, but more thorough investigations on the implications of these choices are needed. See Morsy (1994) and Moore (1995, 43).

11. A good example is the outreach by the Association of Arab American University Graduates to members of the progressive black community in the 1980s. See for example Odell (1980).

late nineteenth century, when the "New South" began to adopt its infamous Jim Crow laws.[12] These laws erected a stringent policy of racial segregation, disenfranchised blacks, and encouraged the exercise of frequent and horrific violence against those who allegedly violated community standards.

Although historians and sociologists have noted the varying types of lynchings (depending on region and time period, for example), the underlying intent of the vast majority of lynchings in the post–Civil War era was the same: to enforce a system of white supremacy. They occurred in the North, Midwest, and Far West, but the highest numbers were in the South, where lynch mobs killed an estimated 3,943 persons between 1880 and 1930 (Brundage 1993, 8).[13] The state of Florida was especially prone to lynching. Between 1921 and 1946, Florida was the site of sixty-one recorded lynchings, more than twice the number in Alabama and Louisiana, and only slightly fewer than Georgia. Mississippi had the highest number at eighty-eight.[14]

In the Jim Crow South, it was overwhelmingly black men who were subjected to lynching's gruesome violence.[15] They were the "strange fruit" of which Billie Holiday later sang in her haunting song, hanging from the poplar trees, their bodies tortured and defiled, left for public display and, increasingly, public entertainment in the form of commodified spectacle and dismemberment. Thousands came, for example, to be spectators at Sam Hose's lynching in Newman, Georgia, in 1899—many in specially chartered trains. A crowd of men, "souvenir seekers," rushed to cut off pieces of his body, parts of which were sold at "inflated prices" in the market that developed for such things. Sam Hose's knuckles were later displayed in a grocery store window, an event that became seared on the mind of scholar W. E. B. Du Bois, and undoubtedly thousands of other African Americans (Holt 1995, 3; Hale 1998, 214).

Although the circumstances surrounding the 1929 Romey lynching in Florida are not entirely clear, it is known that his killers preferred to riddle his body

12. James R. McGovern notes that what distinguishes lynching from murder is community approval, "either explicit, in the form of general participation by the local citizenry, or implicit, in the form of acquittal of the killers with or without trial" (1982, x).

13. For statistics outside the South (and a superb analysis of how race and gender came together in the practice of lynching) see Hall (1979, 134).

14. See U.S. Congress (1948, 100). On racial violence in Florida see also Ortiz (2005).

15. Between 1880 and 1930, 3,220 of those lynched in the South were black, and 723 were white (Brundage 1993, 8).

with bullets, rather than torture him slowly and end his life with a hangman's noose. They left his body in a ditch where it could be detected, but it did not become a public spectacle around which crowds gathered in unabashed celebrations of white supremacy. In this and other regards, the Romey lynching did not seem to "fit" the prevailing pattern of extralegal violence in the Jim Crow South. No one suspected him of raping a white woman or of committing murder (the two most common, and often false, accusations made against black lynching victims), and he was officially classified as white. The Syrians had, after all, emerged victorious from a hard-fought battle to claim their whiteness in federal naturalization courts, and their community leaders initially used this victory to argue that Romey's murder was a terrible injustice.[16]

They could not argue that the lynching of a purported white man was a total aberration because the South did have a long history of lynching whites. In the antebellum period, the *majority* of persons lynched were white, not so much because blacks escaped condemnation for alleged criminal activity, but because lynching them would have involved destruction of slave property—something planters were unlikely to condone (Brundage 1993, 5; Hall 1979, 131). The lynching of whites continued in the post-Reconstruction era, but in much smaller numbers.[17] Of these, historians have focused on a few highly publicized cases: Leo Frank (Atlanta, Georgia, 1915), a Northern Jew accused on weak circumstantial evidence of raping and murdering a young female in his employ; John Hodaz (Plant City, Florida, 1930), a Hungarian immigrant accused of dynamiting the home of a Florida farm family; and Joseph Shoemaker (Tampa, Florida, 1935), a labor activist who was tortured and killed for his socialist views.[18] According to historian Fitzhugh Brundage, these cases involved whites who were perceived to have "merited" lynching because they had "deviated from community standards of behavior, whether by abusing their spouses and children or by holding un-

16. On the history of the Syrian racial prerequisite cases, see Gualtieri (2001).

17. E. M. Beck and Stewart E. Tolnay argue that the decline in white lynching was linked to the development of the South and the establishment of more formal avenues of punishment. The lynchings of blacks, however, were "so intimately intertwined in the broader race conflict and competition that extended far into the new century" that they continued to be tolerated by legal authorities (1997, 150–51).

18. Frank was lynched after his sentence was commuted. For an especially interesting analysis of the Leo Frank case (which includes a critique of the literature), see MacLean (1991). On Shoemaker and Hodaz see Howard (1995).

orthodox moral, social, or political beliefs" (1993, 87). The lynching of whites, in his estimation, "had nothing to do with race," but was about punishing violators of southern codes of honor, deference, and respectability (Brundage 1993, 86). Did, then, the killing of Romey fit *this* pattern of extralegal violence? Was it, to use Christopher Waldrep's term, a "nonracial lynching?" (2002, 125).

I argue that the answer to these questions is "no." In the story of Nola Romey's lynching, race and ethnicity came together in the mob's decision to kill him. Legally Syrians were white, but to view Romey's death as just one of those rare occurrences when mobs lynched white men to enforce "community standards" would be to miss the more complex work of race at this particular time and this particular place. More specifically, Romey's death at the hands of a lynch mob stands as an important episode in the history of the racialization of Syrian Arabs as "inbetween" peoples, that is, neither fully white nor black, in the Southern racial scheme.[19] The lynching of Romey *did*, then, have much to do with race, and the work that race as ideology could do in the era of Jim Crow.

My contention that the Romey lynching was about race is not merely an argument that Syrian Arabs were the victims of white racism more commonly directed at blacks. Nor does this essay intend to claim a separate history of Arab racialization in the United States, situated outside of the black-white paradigm that has until recently dominated the field of race studies. Rather, I am suggesting, first, that this lynching urges us to examine the instability of Arab whiteness within a particular social formation, that is, all the interrelated structures of economic, political, and social power, as well as the cultural systems that both produce and reflect those structures (Holt 2000, 22). The social formation in which Nola Romey was lynched and his wife killed was characterized at the national level by antiforeign sentiment, immigration restriction, and concerns over the success of Americanization programs. In Florida, there were additional tensions produced by the white establishment's desire to control the black labor force; and in Lake City the practice of lynching coexisted with, and was perhaps made possible by, a tradition of police corruption. The use of extralegal violence to silence the Romeys reflected the tensions around who could, and could not, be incorporated as full and equal members of the Lake City community at that particular moment in time.

Thus, although the *New York Evening Herald* described Romey as a "white" man, the events surrounding his lynching and other instances of violence reveal

---

19. On the concept of "inbetween-ness" see Barrett and Roediger (1997).

that the whiteness of Syrians is best conceived as being probationary, its credibility periodically called into question by government authorities and public
opinion.[20] In this regard, Romey's lynching echoed some of the complicated racial
dynamics of the Leo Frank case, which revealed him to be "inconclusively white"
(1998, 65). Complicating the matter is the fact that Syrians often chose a strategy
of resistance to racism that reinforced exclusionary ideologies and practices. The
Romey lynching provides insight into this process, for it engaged the Syrian immigrant community around questions of racial violence and the proper response
to it. Not only does the case provide evidence as to how Syrians were racialized
(and in this case brutalized) by dominant white society, it also reveals a history
of conscious race-making on the part of Syrians, a history of defining their status
as white in opposition to African and Asian Americans. The second argument I
wish to make, then, is that the racialization of Syrians was *relational* and their investment in whiteness took place in a context in which they attempted to distance
themselves from groups marked as the ultimate Others.

THE CIRCUMSTANCES OF THE LYNCHING

The obvious question that begs to be answered is: Why? Why was Nola Romey
in police custody in the first place and what could have been so egregious about
his alleged offense that it prompted a private mob to snatch him from jail, cir-
cumvent state authority, and lynch him? If we follow Brundage's argument that
whites were lynched for holding "unorthodox moral, social, or political beliefs,"
then we are still left puzzled. While, for example, Leo Frank was accused of
rape and murder, John Hodaz of attempted murder, and Joseph Shoemaker of
harboring radical political beliefs, Romey faced none of these charges. He was
guilty simply of challenging white authority, of talking back when his killers
expected him to remain silent. John F. Baker, Lake City's chief of police, embodied this authority, and the challenge began with an argument over a display of
vegetables outside the Romey store.[21]

20. I borrow this term "probationary" from Jacobson (1998, 8).

21. A colleague suggested that John Baker could in fact be Syrian, his last name being the anglicized version of the Arabic "Bakar." None of the documents suggest this. He and his father were
born in Florida, and his mother was born in Kentucky. See entry for John F. Baker, line 56, Enumeration District 12, Lake City, Columbia County, Florida (U.S. Bureau of the Census 1930).

By the 1920s, Syrians in the South had begun to transition out of peddling into ownership of grocery and dry-goods stores. Their success in this particular economic niche was the result of years of thrift and savings that they channeled into the purchase of stores in urbanizing areas. In addition, Syrians were often able to secure a foothold in local economies because they could function, but blacks could not (Stathakis 1996, 100). Their arrival in many market towns, where they established restaurants, confectionaries, and dry-goods stores was in fact viewed by native middle- and upper-class whites as a way to deprive blacks of potential economic opportunity. Syrians were not, in the words of a South Carolina senator, "our kind of people," but they nonetheless contributed to a culture of segregation in which their economic success did not greatly threaten the livelihood of native whites (Stathakis 1996, 57).

The Romeys, like so many of their compatriots, operated a grocery store, outside of which they displayed produce for sale—a practice that may have been contrary to Lake City ordinances.[22] In the second week of May 1929, John F. Baker appeared at their store and ordered Fannie Romey to remove her vegetables from the sidewalk. At this point, the reports of what followed begin to vary widely. The local paper, the *Lake City Reporter,* indicated that the chief of police had had "trouble with Mrs. Romey" over her use of the sidewalk.[23] According to the *Miami Herald,* which carried the story of the lynching on the front page, Fannie Romey "resented the order" to remove her produce and warned Baker: "We're going to kill you before Sunday."[24] The *Syrian World,* which based its report on the investigation conducted by a Syrian lawyer, F. S. Risk, provided a substantially different account. According to its report, Fannie Romey had protested the order but her defiance was met with swift action on the part of Baker and his men, who began to drag her across the street toward the patrol car. However, the arrest was stopped by the intervention of some of the town's "leading citizens."[25] The

22. On the history of how Syrian immigrants occupied this particular economic niche, see Naff (1985) and Truzzi (1997). On the ordinance see the transcript of the testimony by Arthur Hall (police sergeant) in the *Lake City Reporter,* May 24, 1929.

23. *Lake City Reporter,* May 23, 1929.

24. *Miami Herald,* May 18, 1929. It was most likely this report that was translated and printed in the popular New York Arabic-language newspaper *Meraat ul-gharb* [sic] (Mirror of the West). See *Meraat ul-gharb,* May 23, 1929.

25. *Syrian World* 3, no. 12 (June 1929):46.

Syrian World's report contained additional information on events leading up to the vegetable dispute, which shed light on why Baker had gone to the store in the first place. One week before Fannie Romey's altercation with the chief of police, the eldest Romey child (Icer)[26] had taken his three siblings out for a drive in the family car around the local lake. They were struck by a speeding car, which later turned out to have been stolen. The police arrested the occupants of the stolen vehicle, absolved Icer Romey of all blame, and promised him that the reckless driver would be responsible for covering the cost of repairs to the damaged car. This last piece of information is crucial, for it led to the dispute between Baker and Fannie Romey that ultimately ended in tragedy.

His car fixed, Icer called on Baker to honor his promise, but the police chief denied having made it and refused to settle the claim. Fannie Romey then challenged what must have appeared to her as blatant unfairness and abuse of power, confronted Baker, and called him a liar. The chief of police did not take lightly this charge from a Syrian woman, and he quickly decided on a course of action to assert his authority and, it would seem, his masculinity. He headed for the Romey store and asked to see either Nola or Icer. Finding neither, he began arguing with Fannie Romey and demanded that the offending vegetables be taken inside, a strange request because other grocers also had outdoor displays and thus a special punishment for her outspoken behavior.

Several reports related that the chief of police's altercation with Fannie Romey, and the attempted arrest, infuriated her husband. Perhaps feeling that his own honor was at stake, Nola phoned Baker to convey his anger and informed him that he wished to keep his vegetables displayed outside on the sidewalk. This conversation resulted in a second and more deadly visit from the chief of police. Again reports differ, particularly over the question of who fired the first shot. The *Syrian World* claimed that Baker and his men began firing in the store "without the least provocation, but presumably for purposes of intimidation only."[27] When Romey attempted to hide behind the counter, one of the policemen struck him in the head with a gun, causing him to fall to the floor. Fannie Romey rushed to the front of the store and, seeing her husband lying in a pool of blood, shot at the chief

---

26. *Syrian World* listed his name as Esau, a transliteration most likely of the Arabic name 'Isa. He is enumerated in the 1920 census as Icer, and this name was used in several of the English language reports.

27. *Syrian World* 3, no. 12 (June 1929):47.

of police, who returned fire, mortally wounding her. While she lay on the floor admonishing her son Icer not to intervene, one of the policeman shot at her several more times "with a curse and the exclamation 'Aren't you dead yet?'"[28]

The Florida newspaper reports and the testimony given by the police officers and a witness claimed that Fannie Romey had fired at Baker first, when he attempted to remove her husband from the store. In response, as the *Florida Times Union* put it, "Baker was said to have fired five times, several of the shots taking effect in the woman's body."[29] Nola Romey was taken to the local jail, where he was "reported to have made threats to get even for the shooting of his wife."[30] Later that night, a mob removed him from his cell and lynched him. The fact that Fannie Romey had already been gunned down was apparently not retribution enough for the killers, and they directed their rage over her defiant behavior at Nola. The headline in the *Lake City Reporter* called attention to the causal relation between their deaths: "Woman Killed in Pistol Battle With Police Chief; Husband Taken from Jail, Lynched."

According to the *Miami Herald,* "An examination of Romeo's [sic] cell in the city jail failed to show any marks of an instrument having been used to pry off the lock," although the *Lake City Reporter* reported that the sheriff (who lived in the jail) had found a "heavy iron pipe," and a "twisted and bent lock."[31] Typical of so many lynchings at this time, both the sheriff and the chief of police claimed to have no clues as to the identity or size of the murderous mob.[32] Members of the coroner's jury impaneled to hear the investigation of his lynching determined that "Romey came to his death at the hands of persons unknown to us."[33]

THE SIGNIFICANCE OF RACE AND ETHNICITY
IN THE ROMEY LYNCHING

The literature on whiteness has consistently underscored its invented quality by examining how immigrant groups claimed, appropriated, and ultimately

28. *Syrian World* 3, no. 12 (June 1929):47.

29. *Florida Times Union* (Jacksonville), May 17, 1929, 5.

30. *Lake City Reporter,* May 24, 1929.

31. *Miami Herald,* May 18, 1929, p. 22; *Lake City Reporter,* May 24, 1929.

32. *Miami Herald,* May 18, 1929, 22, and *Florida Times Union,* May 19, 1929, 19.

33. *Lake City Reporter,* May 24, 1929.

defended the status of being white.[34] A central goal of this literature has been to render whiteness visible, to recognize it as a racial construct, to have "it speak its name" (Lipsitz 1998, 1). Most important, critical studies of whiteness reveal it to be a "site where power and privilege converged and conspired to sabotage ideals of justice, equality, and democracy" (Fishkin 1995, 430). Understanding this process of "becoming white" has helped historians of ethnicity address the complexities of race in America, but it has also revealed that it is not always easy to distinguish between the two. As Stuart Hall argues, race and ethnicity play hide-and-seek with each other (cited in Sollors 1996, xxxv). How, then, were race and ethnicity at work in this story?

Like other north Florida towns, Lake City had a large black population. According to the 1930 census, the majority of the population (954 out of 1,682, or 57 percent) was black (U.S. Bureau of the Census 1933, 437). In this context, any challenge to white authority in Lake City could be interpreted as a threat to the system of privilege and domination over a more populous nonwhite segment of the community. Lynching was a way to preserve this domination and perpetuate "the ascendancy of an entrenched group" (Ingalls 1987, 615). In Lake City, where there were only twenty persons of foreign birth, native whites were concerned primarily with maintaining their ascendancy over blacks, and they had already demonstrated a willingness to use intimidation and violence in order to do so. In 1900, Spencer Williams, described in the press as a "negro gambler," was literally shot to pieces when a posse tracked him down and killed him. He had allegedly wounded a city marshal who had tried to arrest him. His body, filled with approximately two hundred bullet holes, was brought into town and displayed in front of the Court House, where it was surrounded by a crowd.[35] Extralegal violence continued into the new decade when, in 1911, six black men were lynched after a mob gained entry to the Lake City jail where they were being held, removed them to the outskirts of town, and shot them (NAACP 1969 [1919], 18; *Los Angeles Times* May 22, 1911, 15). According to a press report, the shooting lasted an hour, and at daybreak citizens from Lake City found the men

34. This literature is very extensive. Among the works I have found most useful for this project are Roediger (1991), Ignatiev (1995), Jacobson (1998), Brodkin (1998), Fishkin (1995), and Lipsitz (1998).

35. "Negro Shot to Pieces by Mob," *New York Times*, Nov. 28, 1900, 6.

"mutilated beyond recognition."[36] In 1920, B. J. Jones, the black chairman of the Columbia County Republican Club of Lake City, barely escaped with his life when he challenged the political status quo. Jones had angered the white citizens of Lake City and Jacksonville with his efforts to encourage blacks, particularly black women, to vote. He was reported to have visited churches, lodges, and night schools and to have threatened to have black women expelled if they failed to exercise the franchise. In an effort to silence him, a mob took him from his home at night and carried him several miles from Jacksonville. They put a noose around his neck, but "after being allowed to think he would be lynched, [he] was allowed to escape."[37] It is not clear why in this instance the mob decided against lynching, although by the early 1920s some Florida government officials openly discouraged lynching and insisted on the use of the criminal justice system to try persons accused of alleged offenses. Still, several months before the killing of Nola and Fannie Romey, Lake City was by no means committed to eradicating lynching and the white supremacy that supported it. As the November 1928 election approached, the local paper cited Southern newspapers that decried the possibility of a victory by the Republican Party and "its anti-lynching plank." The *Atlanta Constitution* combined gendered and racist rhetoric to sound the alarm: "In the pending national campaign, the question of white supremacy is paramount and supercedes every controversial issue—it strikes at the very hearthstone of every white man's home in the South."[38] The Republican Party did win the election, an event that no doubt angered many white Floridians. Two weeks later, perhaps to soften the blow and reassert racist imagery, the Elks Club of Lake City hosted a blackface minstrel show and urged attendees to "lay aside your worries, and enjoy the occasion."[39]

At this time of native white anxiety over political and economic power, Romey's killers drew on a familiar white supremacist script that advocated the punishment of blacks who challenged the southern caste system by talking back—the same "offense" that Romey committed. The killing of Romey not only connected him to black disempowerment, but also sent a message to the black inhabitants of Lake City, and the few foreigners there, that attempts to

---

36. "Six Negroes Are Lynched by Fake Florida Officials," *Los Angeles Times*, May 22, 1911, 15.
37. *New York Times*, Oct. 7, 1920, 2.
38. Cited in the *Lake City Reporter*, Aug. 3, 1928.
39. *Lake City Reporter*, Nov. 9, 1928.

combat injustice, or any challenge to white authority, could be, and in this case were, met with terror. The lynching of Nola Romey sat squarely within a tradition of extralegal violence aimed at preserving white power in a city in which blacks formed the majority.

In this regard, it is significant that the two incarcerated black men who might have served as witnesses to Romey's abduction from jail claimed that they had seen and heard nothing. The point is that for blacks—those who had the most to fear in the Jim Crow South and on whose bodies lynching had acquired its terrifying significance—the lynching of Romey must have reminded them of their own precarious position in Lake City. Like Romey, they were also outside the protection of the law.

Black outsiderness in the South was linked to the systematic exclusion of African Americans from white-controlled spaces and institutions. In contrast, Romey was an outsider because of his foreignness, because he lacked roots in the community and belonged to a "suspect" immigrant group. The suspicion that Syrians were unfit to become American citizens because they were "aliens other than white," had led to the series of racial prerequisite cases between 1909 and 1915.[40] After numerous appeals and intense intervention by the Syrian immigrant elite, government officials declared Syrians to be white for the purposes of naturalization, a legal decision that Nola Romey benefited from in 1916 when he and his wife were naturalized.[41] The racial prerequisite cases helped save Syrians from the restrictive immigration policies imposed on other Asian groups in 1917 and 1924. The Immigration Act of 1917, for example, not only excluded certain classes of Asians from immigrating into the United States, it also underpinned the 1923 Supreme Court decision in *United States v. Thind*, which denied the right to naturalize to Indians.[42]

Syrians, in contrast, won the legal battle for their whiteness, but it nonetheless remained provisional. They continued to be targeted by a reinvigorated nativism and reminded of their precarious status in the American racial hierarchy. In 1920, a candidate for a political campaign in Birmingham, Alabama, circulated a

40. See Gualtieri (2001).

41. See entry for Nola Romey, line 32, Enumeration District 129, Valdosta City, Lowndes County, Georgia, U.S. Bureau of the Census (1920).

42. *United States v. Thind*, 261 U.S. 204 (1923). For more detailed discussions of the shared racial logic of immigration and naturalization law see Lesser (1985–86) and Ngai (1999).

handbill that read: "They have disqualified the negro, an American citizen, from voting in the white primary. The Greek and Syrian should also be disqualified. I don't want their vote. If I can't be elected by white men, I don't want the office" (cited in Conklin and Faires 1987, 77). A few years later, terrorists (allegedly from the Ku Klux Klan) dynamited the home of a Syrian family in Marietta, Georgia (Jusserand 1923), and only a few weeks before the Romey lynching, Syrians were outraged when Senator Reed of Pennsylvania described them as "the trash of the Mediterranean, all that Levantine stock that churns around through there and does not know what its own ancestry is" (U.S. Congress 1929).[43] The bombing and the derogatory comments were representative of a wider anti-immigrant feeling in the nation. It is possible that in a town like Lake City, with a white minority unaccustomed to seeing immigrants, let alone non-European ones, Romey's Syrianness, his "cultural distance" from the town's inhabitants, made him a "not quite white" outsider, vulnerable to extralegal violence.[44] As if to confirm their outsiderness, relatives arranged for the burial of Nola and Fannie in Valdosta, Georgia, where they had lived several years before moving to Lake City, and which had an established Syrian population.[45] A resident of Valdosta, George Lahood,

43. Senator Reed included other groups in addition to the Syrians in his description of the "trash," which "came here in large numbers from Syria and the Turkish Provinces and from different countries of the Balkan peninsula and from all that part of southeastern Europe." He did, however, single out "Arabs" when he linked fitness for immigration to self-government. "How can anyone expect an Arab, who has lived under some patriarchal government where he did not even dare whisper his views, to come here and participate intelligently in the American processes of democracy?"

44. Ingalls, for example, noted the connection between outsiderness and vulnerability to mob violence in his study of lynching in Tampa, Florida. At the time of the lynching, Romey had been in Lake City for four years, having moved there from High Springs, Florida. Roberta Senechal de la Roche argues that "lynching varies directly with cultural difference" expressed in symbolic aspects of social life such as language, religion, cuisine, clothing and entertainment (1997, 58).

45. *Miami Herald*, May 18, 1929; *Florida Times Union*, May 19, 1929, 19. The four children were taken in by a relative (and father of the other Syrian family in Lake City), Ellis Moses, and moved to Birmingham, Alabama. Entry for Ellis Moses and family, line 33, Enumeration District 37-77, Birmingham City, Jefferson County, Alabama, U.S. Census 1930. Nola Romey is listed in the 1920 census as a "retail merchant" with a fruit stand in Valdosta City. His wife, Fannie, son, Icer, and daughter, Emmaline are also listed. See entry for Nicholas Romey, line 32, Enumeration District 129, Valdosta City, Lowndes County, Georgia, U.S. Bureau of the Census (1920).

"representing [a] number of Syrian citizens," had sent an anguished telegram to Florida governor Doyle Carlton urging that he intervene to ensure the safety of the eldest Romey child, Icer.[46] "We ask that you have Esau Romey removed from jail Lake City to jail Tallahassee for protection," the telegram requested. "We do not uphold wrong but simply ask this young boy, who is innocent, be removed as to be protected from probable mob violence" (Carlton 1929–32).[47] The Syrians in Valdosta had good reason to be afraid for the life of Icer. Not only had the police taken him to the county jail, but three men "whom he knew" came to tell him that they were going to lynch his father.[48] Governor Carlton responded to the telegram of George Lahood by ordering Sheriff Douglass to conduct an investigation into the killings.[49] One day later, Douglass responded to the governor with a telegram informing him that Icer Romey had been released from his jail. "If I think or see that there will be any more trouble, about the boy," he wrote, "I will see that he is protected as far as I can."[50] Less than six months into his term, Governor Carlton was tackling the economic problems of the State of Florida, including those brought about by the invasion of citrus groves by the Mediterranean fruit fly (Tebeau 1971, 395). He believed that lynching sullied the reputation of the state and would later speak out forcefully against it. At the time of the Romey lynching, however, his priorities lay elsewhere.

George Lahood's appeal to the governor was part of an effort by Syrians in the South to demand an inquiry into the lynching. Members of the Syrian community in Jacksonville attempted to organize a committee to bring the case to trial, but it soon folded owing to a lack of "public support."[51] Syrian leaders in New York City, home of the largest Syrian community in the nation, quickly mobilized to investigate the lynching. Naoum Mokarzel, veteran defender of Syrian rights and owner and editor of the popular Arabic-language paper *al-Hoda* (The guidance), hired a lawyer to investigate but cautioned his readers against a rush to judgment, especially in a case that involved police officers. His

46. *Miami Herald*, May 18, 1929, 22.

47. The telegram was reprinted with slight changes in the *Miami Herald*, May 19, 1929, 22.

48. *Valdosta Daily Times*, May 18, 1929, 2.

49. Telegram to Sheriff W. B. Douglass, May 17, 1929 (Carlton 1929–32).

50. Telegram to Governor Carlton from Sheriff W. B. Douglass, May 18, 1929 (Carlton 1929–32).

51. *Syrian World* 4, no. 1 (Sept. 1929):53.

brother, Salloum (editor of another paper, the *Syrian World*) was also reserved and wrote in an editorial, "A certain feeling of prejudice undeniably exists against the Syrians in some parts of the South and any rash action on their part might tend to aggravate matters unnecessarily."[52] Perhaps Syrians hoped that the incident would fade from memory, and they were thus unwilling to confront the established power that had reminded them that the path toward assimilation in America would be replete with obstacles. They may have been consoled by the fact that three Lake City clubs, the Rotary, Kiwanis, and Woman's, condemned the lynching publicly in the *Lake City Reporter*. The Rotary Club regretted that "the peace and dignity of our community have been shamefully and grievously violated"; the Woman's Club announced that "such disregard for law is repulsive to all right thinking people and brings great reproach upon our community."[53] None of the denunciations mentioned Nola Romey by name, but referred to him as "the prisoner" and "a citizen . . . killed before he had been brought before any court for hearing."[54] Indeed, these responses suggest that it was the specter of lawlessness that provoked the white establishment of Lake City to express concern over the lynching and not the extinguished life of two immigrant members of the community. Other citizens of Lake City expressed their objection to the shooting of Fannie Romey and the lynching of Nola in unsigned letters sent to Governor Carlton. All of them implicated the chief of police and his fellow officers in their deaths. One letter from "the People of Lake City" asked the governor "to look in the way things are going on here, it is a shame for the officers of this town to take people out and Shoot them. We are suposed [*sic*] to live up to the Law and they are to pertect [*sic*] us and it is a plain case they killed Romie for nothing."[55]

The reaction of members of the Syrian community to the Romey lynching revealed what had been an important development during the naturalization controversy of 1909–15: a Syrian discourse about, and affirmation of, whiteness. The reasons for this development are obvious enough—whiteness meant access to citizenship and the privileges it afforded, while nonwhiteness could render persons vulnerable to disenfranchisement and degradation. Anxious to avoid

52. *Lake City Reporter,* May 24, 1929.

53. *Lake City Reporter,* May 24, 1929.

54. *Syrian World* 3, no. 12 (June 1929):48.

55. Unsigned, undated letter to Governor Carlton (Carlton 1929–32).

that vulnerability, Syrian elites reacted defensively to any act that called their racial status into question. In a telling response to Romey's death, the Syrian newspaper *al-Shaab* exclaimed, "The Syrian is not a negro whom Southerners feel they are justified in lynching when he is suspected of an attack on a white woman. The Syrian is a civilized white man who has excellent traditions and a glorious historical background and should be treated as among the best elements of the American nation."[56] The commentator in *al-Shaab* was arguing that Romey had been the victim of racial misidentification and that his lynchers had not understood what he believed to be true: that Syrians were *fully* white. His use of the adjective "civilized" was significant and harked back to the arguments made by candidates for naturalization in the racial prerequisite cases that asserted Syria's place as the birthplace of Western civilization. But the main purpose of the article was to argue that the Syrian was "not a negro." By doing so, the writer appeared unconcerned that black persons were regularly the victims of extralegal violence.

In a broader sense, the lynching of Nola Romey underscores how the racialization of Syrians made sense, or acquired meaning, in relation to a racialized Other, namely African Americans. Romey's "whiteness" mattered to Syrians because his lynching summoned fears among them that they had become, in that instant, surrogate blacks. Understanding the link between the racialization of Syrians and blacks helps explain why a common pattern among Syrians was to reaffirm and invest in their whiteness. They did so in letters, court cases, newspapers, interviews, and, although it is much harder to document, in social relations. Like other immigrant groups (the Irish, Italians, and Jews), Syrians "grasped for the whiteness at the margins of their experiences" (Roediger 1994, 190) rather than challenge the *premise* that whiteness was a legitimate prerequisite for social, economic, and political privilege. When confronted with violence and discrimination in the period of Jim Crow, the response of community leaders often reinforced racist and even eugenicist discourses instead of challenging them. All this confirms what is unfortunately obfuscated in everyday discussion of race in the United States: that whiteness is not a biological fact, but a result of long-standing social structures *and* of choices made within a particular historical context (Ignatiev 1995, 2). In the aftermath of the Romey lynching, Syrians in the South increasingly supported and reinscribed their position on the

56. Cited in *Syrian World* 3, no. 12 (June 1929):42.

white side of the color line. There is evidence, for example, that they participated in one of the major processes of white confirmation, movement into neighborhoods that excluded nonwhites in the post–World War II period.[57]

A great deal of work still needs to be done on the kind of choices made by Syrians and the implications of these choices for their relationships with other racialized groups. Why, for example, did influential Syrians get involved in assisting the naturalization of a South Asian immigrant, but not lend help to the NAACP antilynching campaigns?[58] The simple answer is that Syrians were a small immigrant community, lacking in power and trying to make a difficult life better by defending their right to naturalize as citizens and to earn a decent living. As a marginal group in the segregated South, they had to "know their place" and not risk losing the security of their whiteness by voicing opinions that were contrary to the prevailing views held by native whites. But what would rejecting whiteness have implied for Syrians and for other groups at this time and at other historical moments? These are the types of questions that investigations of other cases of Arab engagements with race would help to answer.

In conclusion, I have used the Romey lynching to probe larger questions about race and ethnicity in the United States, and to analyze the ways in which Syrians positioned themselves within, and understood, racial classification in the first half of the twentieth century. The lynching reveals the racially ambiguous status of first-wave Arab immigrants in the United States, but it also demonstrates how immigrants strove to resolve that ambiguity by affirming their whiteness. It is yet another instance that proves that whiteness is not an ahistorical, self-evident category, but one that was historically construed and contested, and which has had different implications for different groups (including those that were not allowed to claim it). One of the legacies of the Syrian success in claiming whiteness is the racial classification of Arabs as "white" in federal statistics, including the census. Arab Americans are, however, increasingly dissatisfied with this classification because they have been victims of discrimination

57. This subject merits more thorough investigation. Preliminary evidence can be found in Stathakis (1996, 213–17).

58. Syrians in New York helped Bhicaji Franyi Balsara become naturalized in 1910. His petition for naturalization had originally been turned down on the grounds that he was an "alien other than white." See *United States v. Balsara,* 180 Fed. 696 (1910). On the NAACP campaign, see Zangrando (1980).

based on the perception that they are "not quite white," and foreign. Unlike Italians and Jews, with whom they shared earlier experiences of racialization, the whiteness of Arabs in the United States has proved to be profoundly unstable in the post–World War II period.

Arab Americans have addressed the problem of their racial classification in a number of ways. Encouraged by the ethnic revival of the 1960s, and dismayed by their vilification after the 1967 Arab-Israeli war, they formed pan-ethnic organizations that asserted their Arab identity as a political strategy for countering racism and claiming rights (Naber 2000, 41).[59] Two of these organizations, the Arab American Institute and the American Arab Anti-Discrimination Committee, lobbied Congress to change the classification of Arabs as "Caucasian" on the 2000 census to either a separate "Middle Eastern" or "Arab American" category (Suleiman 1999, 15; Saliba 1999, 309; and Samhan 1999, 222–23).[60] Their arguments for doing so were multifaceted, ranging from the desire to have a more accurate count of the Arab population in the United States to more strategic implications of a new category, namely, that minority status would render Arabs eligible for federally funded programs and provide greater protection under antidiscrimination laws. The Office of Management and Budget decided not to introduce a new category, citing a lack of consensus and the relatively small size of the community as two important reasons (Samhan 1999, 223; and Arab American Institute 1993).[61] It is worth noting that since September 11, 2001, Arab American activists have become less convinced of the utility of an official minority category, as it could lead to a greater convergence of ethnic classification and racial profiling (Hassan 2002b, 21).

Arab American feminists, more than any other segment within the community, advocate identification with people of color with whom they share a history of marginalization and objectification by white, middle-class Americans.[62] This position has also been the springboard for coalition building across the lines of

59. For an individual profile of this "conversion" to an Arab identity, see Don Unis's story in Shryock (2000a, 601).

60. For an interesting discussion of how the debate on racial classification points to a split within the Arab American community between those in favor of maintaining formal classification as "whites" and those wishing to ally with people of color, see Majaj (1999a, 322).

61. My thanks to Helen Samhan for providing me a copy of her statement.

62. See, for example, the collection edited by Joanna Kadi, *Food for Our Grandmothers* (1994) and the interesting analysis of it by Michelle Hartman in this volume.

ethnicity, as when Japanese Americans, Jewish Americans, and Arab Americans joined forces to oppose the infringement on the civil rights of Arab Americans during the 1991 Gulf War. "Such coalitions," Lisa Majaj notes, "make clear that it is possible to bridge the insularity of identity politics without diminishing the specificity of ethnic concerns" (1999a, 323).

A third area in which Arabs in America reject whiteness is in literary and cultural production. Nowhere is this position framed more bluntly and provocatively than in Lawrence Joseph's poetic manifesto "Sand Nigger," which stresses the links between Arab American and black marginalization and resistance.[63] This position builds on the radical politics of the 1960s, when African American and Third World leaders, including Malcolm X and Gamal Abdel Nasser, connected the histories of peoples of African and Arab descent in a common anti-imperialist, anti-white supremacist struggle. More recently, identification with blackness is manifested in the appropriation of hip-hop style and not in a politics of affiliation per se. It is also possible for this trend to work in reverse in what is being called "the other September 11 effect." The rise in conversions to Islam in Europe, Latin America, and the United States represent a new movement of protest against the hegemonic white West, but the interest in things Arab and Muslim can take odd turns. The wildly popular Brazilian telenovela *El Clon,* for example, offered a "profusion of Orientalist imagery," as did the coupling of a burqa-like veil and lingerie in a photo shoot of rapper Li'l Kim (Aidi 2003, 42–52).

I have argued elsewhere that the disavowal of whiteness by Arab Americans cannot be productive in itself and therefore should not be done without consideration of the history of how and why Arabs "became white" in the first place (Gualtieri 2001, 52). The idea of Arab whiteness in the United Sates is mainly a legacy of Syrians' encounter with naturalization law, and of their continued conscious and strategic decisions during the first half of the twentieth century to separate themselves from nonwhites, notably Asian and African Americans. These decisions facilitated access to certain privileges, such as citizenship and the right to purchase property and to participate on the white side of the color line where this meant advantages over nonwhites in housing, schools, politics, and jobs. That the affirmation of whiteness could follow in the wake of the lynching of a member of the Syrian community reveals the power of racial violence to

---

63. Excerpted in Abraham and Shryock (2000, 24).

silence opposition and dissent. As Brundage observes, "there are many linger-
ing questions about how generations of blacks and whites repressed, forgot, and
reshaped their memories of lynching" (1997, 15).

The current disassociation from whiteness among some Arab Americans
is a powerful response to race and class inequalities in the United States. It is a
position forged in dialogue with other communities of color whose fight against
racism has been instructive to Arabs who, in turn, have focused attention on
the specificity of anti-Arab racism and its global implications. Attention to the
history of the production of racist attitudes within and across communities will
ensure that these alliances continue to grow. These efforts may also serve to
uncover the submerged stories of Syrians like Nola and Fannie Romey, whose
untimely deaths form part of the sediment on which later racialization projects
were, and are, being built.

SEVEN

Grandmothers, Grape Leaves, and Kahlil Gibran

Writing Race in Anthologies of Arab American Literature

MICHELLE HARTMAN

ARAB AMERICAN LITERATURE began to be increasingly anthologized start-ing in the late 1980s and into the 1990s. Three major anthologies appeared be-tween 1988 and 1999, making a broader range of Arab American literary works available than ever before. *Grape Leaves: A Century of Arab-American Poetry* (Orfalea and Elmusa 2000 [1988]), *Food for Our Grandmothers: Writings by Arab-American and Arab-Canadian Feminists* Kadi 1994), and *Post Gibran: An-thology of New Arab American Writing* (Akash and Mattawa 1999) are all easily accessible books, published by relatively mainstream publishers. Each of these three works embraces a significantly different focus, showing the breadth of Arab American literary production: the first focuses on poetry spanning a cen-tury; the second on different genres of writing by contemporary feminists, both U.S. and Canadian; and the third on new writers of different genres, men and women, with an emphasis on experimentation.

I would like to acknowledge the editors of this volume, Amaney Jamal and in particular Nadine Naber, for their patience in working with this piece. I would also like to thank Sarah Gualtieri and other colleagues for reading and commenting on this paper: Jenny Burman, Anne McKnight, Yumna Siddiqi, and especially Alia Al-Saji and Stephen Sheehi. Thanks also to the students in my diaspora literature seminar at McGill: Amer El-Balaa, Sheema Hosain, and Heather McCafferty, and my research assistants Collyn Echo Ahart and Dima Ayoub. And the final thanks are due to my best and most demanding reader, Alessandro Olsaretti.

Although with the advent of the twenty-first century more and more an-thologies are being prepared and published, these three remain the best-known collections of Arab American writing and will be the focus of the analyses in this chapter. Other anthologies have been excluded from discussion here; some have appeared after the completion of this chapter (Kaldas and Mattawa 2004; Muaddi Darraj 2004), others were excluded on the basis of the more narrow definition of their scope and project (Dahab 2002; Handal 2001).[1] Since their appearance, the three works under consideration here have been reviewed and distributed in a range of academic and nonacademic locations throughout North America.[2] They are used in university courses and appear as recommended reading in a variety of locations.

With this level of visibility and availability, these three anthologies have all also come to be important locations for the self-representation of Arab Ameri-cans in the articulation of their identity. Like all anthologies, these three works invoke emblems of the community they represent. This serves as a gesture to the community and is also important in the symbolic representation of the group

---

1. Because of constraints of space and to keep the definitions precise, I did not consider Eliz-abeth Dahab's *Writing in the Desert* which treats only Arab Canadian women writers of French or Nathalie Handal's *Arab Women Poets*, which deals with both Arab and Arab American poets. Salma Khadra Jayyusi has also published a number of important anthologies, many of which contain contributions by Arab American authors, but all of which primarily focus on literature written in Arabic. In a study in progress, I deal with *Writing in the Desert* in conjunction with *Food for Our Grandmothers* to explore some of the complementary, but different, processes involved in the Canadian context specifically. During the revision period of this article, another relevant anthology has been published: *Dinarzad's Children: An Anthology of Contemporary Arab Ameri-can Fiction* (Kaldas and Mattawa 2004). A recent collection of essays by Arab and Arab American women about writing fiction and poetry also is interesting to consider in this concept because of its use of familiar tropes, *Scheherazad's Legacy: Arab and Arab Amercian Women on Writing* (Muaddi Darraj 2004).

2. See, for example, *A Celebration* (1995); Abu-Jaber (1995); Allen (2000); Boullata (1990); Cichy (1994); Civantos (1996); Daher (1995); Douglas (1995); Fischbach (1996); Gabriel (2001); Ghazoul (2000); Hasan (2003); Hembold (1998); Houissa (2000); Katz (1995); Maksoud (1994); Metres (2001); Peters (2001); Shadroui (1991); Vandrick (1995); Yadegar (1995); Zoghby (1988). Here my focus is largely on the United States and to a certain extent Canada, because of *Food for Our Grandmothers*'s attention to Arab Canadian feminists. No doubt these works have also trav-eled outside these confines, though to my knowledge the books are not widely distributed outside North America, and to explore this issue falls outside the scope of the present study.

to the "outsider" or "mainstream" audience. Three important emblems of the community in these anthologies, which also recur in Arab American literature more generally, are grandmothers, grape leaves, and Kahlil Gibran. They embody familiar themes in Arab American self-identification: an emphasis on family and community, shared food and other cultural customs, and a history of cultural and literary contributions to both the Arab world and the United States. In order to understand how these three anthologies construct community identity in the United States, I will analyze the interaction of these emblems and symbols of the Arab American community in relation to race. As interest in the Arab American community and its literature grows in the United States, it is crucial to explore the terms by which Arab American identity is constructed racially. Literary anthologies are a particularly productive site of analysis of these issues, as they explicitly define and delimit the identity that they claim to represent and use race and the racialization of Arab Americans strategically in these constructions.

Literary studies generally, and anthologies specifically, are important and urgent locations for the study of Arab American engagements with race and racialization. Anthologies, by definition, delimit an identity because they are collections—they can collect nineteenth-century poetry, plays written by Egyptian women, or American literature broadly defined, to give just three examples. Thus, literary anthologies are particularly potent locations to challenge, establish and enshrine national, ethnic and/or racial identities (Christian 1995). Because anthologies necessarily categorize literature, as Karen Kilcup points out, "Composing an anthology creates a miniature canon no matter how resistant the editor is to the vexed notions of goodness and importance" (Kilcup 2000, 37). The works analyzed in this study illustrate some of the ways in which anthologies reinforce community identification with specific prize qualities, often identified as inherent qualities. Very often these essential characteristics are drawn upon to firm up and solidify community identity, such as poetry being in the "Arab blood" or the closeness of family and kinship ties. Because they are often deemed inherent and essential, such notions then contribute to the process of racialization of Arab Americans in the United States.

Particularly in the United States, where anthologies serve as the main location of texts for literary study in schools and universities, moreover, a link between economics, canon formation, and the solidifying of a community identity is crucial (Graff and Di Leo 2000; Kilcup 2000, 42–43; Banta 1993; Fliegelman 1993; Lauter 1993; Warren 1993). Because the exigencies of publication and marketing control the production of anthologies, the market thus also has a say in how students consume literary information (Wu 1997; Kilcup 2000, 40–45; Schrift 2000, 168–69, 173). These factors thus intersect with the contested racial and identity politics of the United States. Most studies of Arab Americans and race focus on historical, social, and political constructions of these identities rather than on how they are constructed through literature and literary institutions.[3] In this chapter I analyze not only anthology production and consumption, but also how canon formation and its relation to group identity is informed by race. Therefore I am concerned in both with how Arab American anthologies ally themselves with various canons and also with how they draw on discourses of racial identity. I will focus on two main themes: the conscious development of anthologies for identity and community building and how Arab American racialization is strategically employed in this context. In addition, these readings will probe the role of literary institutions (like anthologies and canons) in the articulation of an Arab American identity in the United States.

In order to contextualize how racial discourses are employed in Arab American anthologies, it is crucial to understand the complex, contradictory, and contested history of Arab American racialization in the United States.[4] To understand how Arab Americans have been inconsistently racialized in the United States, scholars of Arab America have undertaken a serious investigation of the formation of a "white" (and "not quite white") Arab American identity through the racial prerequisite laws (Gualtieri 2001; Majaj 2000; Massad 1993; Morsy 1994; Samhan 1999).[5] This investigation includes tracing the history of how Arab Americans were categorized as nonwhites, how they fought the categorization legally, and how their legal status changed and developed over time,

---

3. The important exceptions to this are the important studies of Lisa Suhair Majaj, which investigate race, ethnicity, and identity formation in Arab American literature in some detail. I am particularly indebted here to her work that reads literary texts in relation to race and the historical and legal ramifications of Arab American "whiteness," "inbetween-ness," and "racialization" in the United States (1999a, 1999b, 2000).

4. Arab American literary critics have been calling for a greater investigation of race and racialization of Arab Americans in relation to literary studies. See in particular Majaj (1999b, especially pages 72–74), and Salaita (2000). For more detail, see the discussion of these issues in Majaj (1999a, especially pages 321–22).

5. On the related issue of religious racialization see Naber (2000); on political racism see Samhan (1987).

particularly after they achieved "white" status through this litigation. There is a general consensus among scholars that although the identity of Arab Americans as "white" has been variously embraced and contested, the experiences of Arab Americans—individually and as a group—have very often not matched their official legal status (Gualtieri 2001; Joseph 1999a; Majaj 1999a; Naff 1985, Saliba 1999; Samhan 1999; Suleiman 1987, 1999). Therefore, many works use terminology like "honorary," "probationary" or "inbetween" whiteness to examine Arab American identity in the United States.[6] Some scholars have treated the question of how Arabs "became white," how they have and have not benefited from this status over time, in a comparative context with other groups, and by investigating in detail their relationship to laws in the United States that established, preserved, and maintained racial hierarchies in all areas of social life.[7]

I seek to situate the study of race and Arab American identity and belonging in the literary field. Like other racialized/ethnic groups, Arab American literary identities are crucial to claiming an acknowledged position in the United States. The theoretical underpinnings of my analysis here draw upon the critical work of Henry Louis Gates, Jr., who has pointed out how race has also played a central role in the way in which literature is produced, read, and taught in the United States. In particular, he has argued that canon formation in the United States is bound up in issues of race and racialization and that this matter must be addressed in U.S. literary studies, and not only those focused on African American literature (Gates 1991, 23–32, 1985, 1992). In "The Master's Pieces: On Canon Formation and Afro-American Tradition," for example, Gates places particular importance on the role of the anthology to shape and change literary traditions and canons in the United States. His study details how African American literature has been crucial to literary realities in the United States since slavery and elaborates on how African American slave narratives were identified in 1846 as the only "authentically American" literature, in distinguishing this new tradition from British literature

6. A number of studies of the indeterminate status of European immigrant groups and their tenuous relationship to whiteness are particularly useful in thinking through these issues in the Arab American context: Brodkin (1998); di Leonardo (1994); Jacobson (1998); Ignatiev (1995); and Roediger (1994).

7. Some of the studies upon which these scholars draw include Delgado and Stefancic (2001) and Haney-López (1996); for an analysis of how "whiteness" was used to develop U.S. national identity, see Hale (1998); Jacobson (1998), Lipsitz (1998); and Roediger (1994).

(1991, 21–22). He also draws links to the historical context of building anthologies of black literature since the mid–nineteenth century, while also analyzing his
own experience as editor of the *Norton Anthology of African American Literature*
(28–32). Gates's work is so useful here because of his attention to the dynamic
interactions and relationships between canon formation, racial thinking, and the
power relations between white and racialized groups in the United States.

My approach here differs from that of Gates in that I will neither draw out
a history of Arab American literature nor argue for its importance and centrality within the traditions of U.S. literary canons. Here, rather, I employ Gates's
analysis to emphasize the importance of the structural relationships between
building anthologies, its connection to establishing canons, and the need to
question both of these processes in relation to how they are informed by race,
even as they are taking place.[8]

The increased interest in Arab American literature from the 1990s on, and
again in the period after September 11, 2001, is no doubt linked to the increased
visibility of Arab America more generally. Increased visibility and interest makes
this study increasingly urgent[9] and partly answers the call of the critic Lisa Suhair
Majaj, for example, for more investigation into Arab American racialization and
the importance of building links with communities of color:

8. In this line of argument, I also hope to avoid some of the problems that would arise in
submitting Arab American and African American literature to a comparison. African Americans
have been considered the "prototypical" minority group; other groups have used comparisons
with them to attain minority status and advantages, which has often led to the disenfranchisement of blacks. This is part of the problem with the "black-white" binary into which the U.S.
racial system is divided. For a detailed discussion see chapter 5 of Delgado and Stefanic (2001,
67–83). What I hope to do here is not reproduce a problematic discourse in order to prove that
Arab Americans are similar to African Americans, but rather to draw on some of the most important and sophisticated studies of these issues that have been developed by African American
critics like Henry Louis Gates, Jr., and in conjunction with African American literature.

9. Majaj has articulated "new directions" for Arab American literature and criticism in her
essay by the same name (1999b, 72–76). See also Salaita (2000, 26–27). Some of the issues they
insist upon include: a move from nostalgia about the community to confrontation; more of an
emphasis on Arab Americans' multiple experiences; a more nuanced and less defensive feminism;
increased attention to social criticism; more complex understandings of who is included and who
excluded in definitions of Arab American identity; embracing new cultural forms; keeping new
audiences in mind without being stymied by them; playing an activist role; producing children's
literature and more novels and plays in addition to poetry.

For too long we have tried to escape into white ethnicity. But our experience has shown us, time and again, that our formal status as white is merely honorary, and is quickly revoked in the wake of political events in the Middle East as well as in the U.S. We need more explorations of the implications of this racialization. At the same time, we need to probe links with other groups of color, and to explore the ways in which our racialization can provide new grounds for solidarity and activism. (Majaj 1999b, 73)

Majaj suggests that literature and literary studies are an appropriate location for such a project. This chapter's attention to the discourse around race and its strategic employment in anthologies will provide a step toward questioning the formation of an Arab American literary canon, which is currently in progress. That in turn will lead to increased engagement in the production and analysis of literature that critically investigates these issues.

As interest in Arab American literature grows, the continued formation and revision of the canon of Arab American literature is taking place—in these three anthologies and elsewhere—which has an impact on how Arab American identity is shaped and reshaped. Indeed, all three anthologies take the responsibility of articulating notions of Arab American identity and community seriously. Precisely because they offer so much to Arab American identity formation and community building in addition to the dissemination of literary works, it is productive to engage them in a rigorous critique of how race informs their projects. The critical readings of the introductions of each text, linked to an analysis of its overall project, show that Arab American identity formation in the texts employs racial discourses in different ways, with different strategic goals and effects. Questioning these discourses and holding them up to scrutiny can help better to achieve the working bases for solidarity and activism with other groups of color, as suggested by Majaj, and such an examination can lead to determining which are best suited for continued deployment in the articulation of Arab American identities in this context.

To accomplish this analysis, my first area of inquiry in each anthology is its stated project and, in particular, how it articulates its mission. Second, I investigate how each defines "Arab American" implicitly and explicitly, and the connection of this definition to race. In conjunction with these readings, the analyses of the texts treat how Arab American anthologies are carving spaces for themselves within literary canons in the United States, while negotiating not only an Arab American identity, which is informed by Arab racializa-tion, but this identity in conjunction with and opposed to other groups in the United States—particularly but not exclusively those that are also racialized. My readings below show how these anthologies use three interrelated strategies of racialization: framing their projects, locating themselves in relation to other groups, and choosing emblems.

In relation to the first category, I will identify how each anthology frames itself in relation to its identity as Arab American and the figures, emblems, and canons it engages. I will also analyze in detail how the introduction to each work employs racial discourses strategically, influenced by structuralist approaches to literature (Genette 1972, 1982). Second, I will examine more specifically how each of these works explicitly or implicitly locates itself in relation to one of three canons: the "mainstream American canon", largely white to this day, consist-ing of figures like Whitman, Longfellow, and Frost;[10] other racialized or "eth-nic" literatures such as African American, Latino, and Native American; and the Arabic literary canon, including such celebrated figures as Mahmoud Darwish, Taha Hussein, and Nazik al-Mala'ika. Finally, I will explore how the emblems invoked in the anthologies are used to reinforce, undermine, or otherwise engage with the strategies of identity building implicit or explicit in their introductions. These analyses will show that all of the anthologies use race and the racialization of Arab Americans strategically in their articulation of Arab American identity, but that they do so in very different ways. The strategy for invoking race in each anthology is closely linked to that anthology's political and social project and therefore is also linked to how this work is able to function institutionally in the building of an Arab American literary canon as well as identity more generally.

GRAPE LEAVES: A CENTURY OF ARAB-AMERICAN POETRY

The seventeen-page introduction to *Grape Leaves: A Century of Arab-American Poetry* explicitly justifies the existence of the anthology itself, its value and as well

---

10. Despite many scholars and critics engaged in a revision of the U.S. literary canon and its assumptions, scholars seem to agree that a white, male-dominated canon of works is still very much the predominant paradigm (Fetterley and Schulz 1982; Kafka 1989; and also the essays on the *Heath Anthology* published in *American Literature* by Banta [1993]; Fliegelman [1993]; Lauter [1993]; and Warren [1993]).

as that of its individual contributions. On its first page, the introduction firmly claims a space within "ethnic" American literature. It employs the "equal time" principle in its self-validation: Arab Americans deserve a poetic "anthology of their own" because other similarly marginalized ethnic and racial groups have them. The introduction states boldly, "There exist poetry anthologies for virtually every American ethnic group: black, Hispanic, Jewish, Indian, Chinese, Armenian, and so on" (Orfalea and Elmusa 2000, xiii). Although careful to include the words "and so on," certain groups presented in a specific order define the multiethnic space that is claimed for Arab Americans here.

It is not a surprise that the first group mentioned is labeled "black." African Americans are consistently located as the most visible, prominent, and disenfranchised "minority" group in the United States, upon which all other groups traditionally build their case for claiming minority status (Delgado and Stefancic 2001, 67). Mentioning this group first in the list, therefore, powerfully claims both an affiliation and a justification for the anthology.[11] "Hispanics" follow—a group that is often specifically linked to black Americans as a similarly oppressed minority. The next group, "Jews," occupies a significantly different space in the U.S. public imagination as a group with a history of discrimination, but which has been successful in the United States. Locating this group immediately after African Americans and Latinos emphasizes the range of different experiences of groups considered minorities. In particular, Jews have been granted white status in the United States, thereby shifting the attention from Arab American racialization to their "white ethnic" belonging (Brodkin 1998). Furthermore, Jews are also the specific group to which Arabs/Arab Americans are often required to compare and/or contrast themselves in order to gain status or "equal time" for their concerns (Massad 1993; Saliba 1999). The list then continues with Indians and Chinese—two Asian groups geographically near the Arab world—and then Armenians follow. Placed last, they are another "model minority" group, like the previous three, and one with which Arabs share historical, cultural, and geographical ties.

---

11. The use of a lower case "b", undoubtedly an editor's choice, also stands out in such a list of groups, all the rest of which are capitalized. Though some writers consciously use the lower case "b" in order to invoke parity with the lower case "w" in white, others have done the opposite and use a "W" and "b" to designate these terms in order to draw more attention to the whiteness. This debate serves as a reminder of how the continued lower status of African Americans within the United States is debated in rhetorical as well as practical ways.

Much like the complicated "racial" hierarchies that govern official United States policies and institutions, the chosen groups represent different types of categorization—linguistic, racial, religious/ethnic and national. This list demonstrates another problematic notion in identity formation in the United States—here identities are understood as exclusive; one is "black" or "Hispanic," not both. Not only is the United States' official confusion about categorizations reflected in this list, but it also reproduces an implied hierarchy of which groups are the most oppressed and therefore perhaps the most deserving of attention. This strategy of locating Arab Americans within the complex fabric of U.S. society relies on a general and vague notion of their place within it. Rather than clarifying or defining a specific, discrete location for Arab Americans, it juxtaposes them with a number of other groups. All of these groups are considered to be ethnic and/or racial minorities in the United States. As a strategy, therefore, this list locates Arab Americans generally within a context of other so-called minority groups, but resists assigning them a more specific space. This strategy has the advantage of leaving options open for identity building but at the same time risks being so vague that it does not advance any proposal for the consolidation of an identity or how to promote specific affiliations and alliances.

The use of race as part of the strategy for justifying the publication of this anthology is not limited to this list. African Americans, for example, are invoked in an earlier location in a specific claim to the importance of anthologies of "minority" literatures, "When a teacher wants to imbue her black students with a sense of pride, she might read Langston Hughes, Gwendolyn Brooks, or Sterling Brown" (Orfalea and Elmusa 2000, xiii). This statement implies that anthologies are useful teaching tools in the formation of positive identities and that students deserve literary role models from their own backgrounds in order to achieve that. Black students will be proud if they read works of prominent African American authors. The choice of African American figures here is not accidental; the names Langston Hughes, Gwendolyn Brooks, and Sterling Brown have become a part of a U.S. canon, though an African American one.[12]

---

12. Gates discusses the separate development of the African American canon from the mainstream one, as early as the mid-1800s and certainly by the 1920s, with the publication of a number of anthologies of "American Negro" Literature (1991, 24–25) and also traces the challenges to this and ambiguities that arose from them (27–29).

The parallel here implies that Arab Americans, like African Americans, deserve to instill pride in their community through literature in anthologies. Invoking the names of African American figures in particular draws upon the capital of black oppression and also their recognized literary achievements. The introduction claims that Arab Americans deserve to have an anthology because of their parallel experiences of oppression and that the anthology will act as a corrective showing their literary achievements. The invocation of African Americans as a group against which to measure one's oppression and belonging is a strategy highlighted above. This introduction underlines the justification for the volume's publication, specifically by positing that turn-of-the-century Syrians were considered, next to Chinese, the "most foreign of all foreigners" and citing the claim of a U.S. journalist that Arabs "are the last ethnic group in America safe to hate" (Orfalea and Elmusa 2000, xiv).[13] At least one reviewer of the anthology seizes upon this notion when he refers to this line in his positive assessment of the volume, pronouncing it a "worthy project" in the face of this prejudice (Shadroui 1991, 73a).

The third justification for the volume employs a shift in strategy, deploying the notion of Arab/Arab American exceptionalism. Here, the introduction distances itself from the other "minority," "ethnic," and/or racialized groups with which it was affiliating itself in the previous examples and rather claims exceptional, inherent qualities of Arab Americans in order to position itself in relation to canonical "white" authors. The first of the examples given in the text is the Arabs' "natural" love of poetry. This strategy of claiming an exceptional quality can be understood as a way in which to counter the discrimination identified above: Arab Americans have inherited an innate appreciation for poetry and thus are cultured and refined. The notion that poetry is "in the Arab blood" is reiterated several times. The introduction defines them as "a group whose love of poetry is native and deep: the two million Arab Americans" (Orfalea and Elmusa 2000, xiii) and proclaims that "the great Arab love of poetry had not been drained from new world veins" (xv).[14]

13. The quote about Syrians being the most foreign of all foreigners is repeated in the section introducing Kahlil Gibran (Orfalea and Elmusa 2000, 19) and is the only such quotation repeated in the anthology. It is interesting to note that the same quotation appears in Shakir (1983).

14. See Majaj's critique of this element of *Grape Leaves* in her discussion of the politics of memory (1996).

These three justifications for publishing an anthology of Arab American poetry follow a familiar argument about why and how ethnic or minority literatures are important in the United States: oppressed/minority groups can create great art, these groups have an inborn love of art/poetry, and so on, and that if one group can show its pride in these creations, others should be deemed similarly deserving of such an opportunity. These lines of argumentation have been employed frequently in anthologies to prove their importance and can be located in relation to the same arguments that Gates identifies in tracing the history of African American canon formation. Gates's use of the words of James Weldon Johnson shows this logic in play,

> The final measure of the greatness of all peoples is the amount and standard of the literature and art that they have produced. The world does not know that a people is great until that people produces great literature and art. No people that has produced great literature and art has ever been looked upon by the world as distinctly inferior. (Johnson, cited in Gates 1991, 25).

The logic of *Grape Leaves*'s introduction, therefore, echoes a central sentiment in African American literary development and justification. Its strategy for claiming the rightful and respected place for Arab Americans in the United States is to prove their humanity through literary production. To further demonstrate how this point is argued in the introduction to *Grape Leaves,* I will analyze two specific arguments: the definition of literary quality and the discourse around family, particularly as it is linked to gender.

Notions of literary quality and excellence often inform the discourse around anthology compilation and are intimately linked to the question of canon building. As Gates, among others, has shown about the United States, from its inception race has informed the process of assigning literary value and has been central to shaping anthology projects. This is particularly evident in U.S. "ethnic literature" and how it is considered distinct from "American Literature" and circumscribed by this terminology (Kafka 1989, 31). Valorizing an unproblematized notion of "quality" is a particularly difficult question in this context (Morris 1995). How is quality defined, and by whom? *Grape Leaves* states openly that in selecting pieces, "quality was our touchstone above all" (Orfalea and Elmusa 2000, xviii). Although in a literary context that may sound perfectly reasonable, it is far from a neutral statement. The discourse around "quality" is loaded with racial (and other) meanings, particularly when it is linked to the validation of a group's or an individual's humanity. That quality will vindicate the importance of Arab Americans recalls Gates's discussion of the case of Phillis Wheatley, the African slave deemed by a distinguished panel of white American men in 1772 to be qualified to be a poet. He reminds us that Wheatley was granted her "human status" through her production of poems that mimic the accepted canon of poetry in the United States at the time.[15] Wheatley's case draws upon the notion that equality and humanity in society should somehow be linked to "parity" with the dominant group. Another statement by Johnson underlines this message, "And nothing will do more to change that mental attitude [racism vs. blacks] and raise his status than a demonstration of intellectual parity by the Negro through the production of literature and art" (Johnson, cited in Gates 1991, 25).[16]

Grape Leaves echoes this notion of parity in many locations; one example is in descriptions of Arab American poets and poems. The quality of Arab American literary production is almost exclusively asserted, and thus validated here, through comparisons to canonical U.S. male poetic figures, all but one of whom are white. Examples include stating that "Walt Whitman would have approved" of Doris Safie's poetry (Orfalea and Elmusa 2000, xxiii), that Joseph Awad and Samuel Hazo are "Frostian," that Elmaz Abinader uses imagery like Ezra Pound, and that the Beat and Black Mountain poets can help to explain Etel Adnan (xxvi). The lack of one name of an African American writer, save Sterling Brown in the introduction after the initial opening lines, is striking. This absence is more notable because of the number of names mentioned and even more important in the contrast between white poets representing "quality" and black poets representing "pride." Brown, for example, is not listed as an example of a "great poet" but rather one who sung the "trials of his people" (xxiii).

---

15. Gates also underlines that writing, for Wheatley as for other slaves who gained their freedom through proving their humanity in this way, "was not an activity of mind; rather it was a commodity which they were force to trade for their humanity" (1985, 9). The discussion of Wheatley specifically is found in Gates (1985, 7–9; pages 9–11 treat how people deemed as "others" write themselves into humanity).

16. Gates locates such statements as an answer to statements by the likes of renowned U.S. figures such as Ralph Waldo Emerson, "If the black man is feeble and not important to the existing races, not on a parity with the best race, the black man must serve and be exterminated" (Gates 1991, 23).

The introduction to *Grape Leaves* employs not only the notion of equality through parity but also uses other exceptional features of Arab/Arab American culture to define Arab Americans through certain purportedly essential characteristics. It then strategically employs these essential and exceptional traits to prove literary quality. For example, the introduction cites the British Orientalist and translator of Arabic verse A. J. Arberry, in order to prove that some traces of the Arabic language and thus a sort of "Arab essence," "remain" in Arab American poetry. In order to demonstrate this, the introduction itself quotes Arberry as saying, "Rhythm is the most outstanding characteristic of Arabic poetry" (Orfalea and Elmusa 2000, xxvi). Here the introduction relies on the authorization of a British Orientalist to support the notion that the attention to the rhythm of the text is somehow "authentically Arab." Just as Frost, Pound, and Whitman serve as models to which Arab American poetry is compared positively, Arberry also speaks with the authority of "disinterested scholarship" to show that Arab American attention to rhythm in poetry is somehow authentically "Arab." The introduction then goes on to underline examples of how rhythm is "endemic" to Arab American poetry, stating that: "from Naimy's dancing leaves to Nasser's 'Ooof!' Even the Xerox machine is seductively swaying" (xxvi). Within the U.S. context in which this volume clearly locates itself, it is notable that rhythm in particular is fetishized here as an "identifiably Arab characteristic" of Arab American poetry, particularly because it is one of the most frequent tropes employed in relation to what separates "whites" from "people of color"—by all groups (Roediger 1994). Black Americans, in particular, but also Latinos and others, are meant "naturally" to have rhythm, whereas whites are not.

All of these examples show how the introduction to *Grape Leaves* defines "quality," which it insists is its most important guiding principle for the selection of pieces included in the anthology. Quality is also defined explicitly here as the previous publication by the author of his/her poetry in books and journals; merit is not defined in any other way: "[contributors] had to have published in at least three literary magazines, or at least one book, with work of merit" (Orfalea and Elmusa 2000, xviii). Drawing on Gates's work, we know that marginalized groups often predicate a claim to humanity and civilization on the production of "high quality" literature and poetry. How quality is defined therefore is a particularly urgent question. Moreover, it is important to recognize that proposing literary excellence as a universal category, which somehow transcends cultural moments and definitions, specific cultures and ethnic/racial labels, is patently false. Social, political, and cultural factors all contribute to the definition of what the "literary" is; what is "universal" is then already representative of a particular, dominant group. In the United States, where race is a central organizing concept in society, what is "universal" is generally associated with white America and thus often seems invisible; this is one of the arguments advanced by critical race theorists to call for more detailed investigations into the meanings of whiteness (Delgado and Stefancic 2001; Crenshaw et al. 1995; Haney-López 1996). If poetry is categorized by race or ethnic group—as it is in an anthology of Arab American poetry—to use "universal" standards for its quality is necessarily contradictory. That is to say, when we categorize literature by ethnic, cultural, or racial categories, we recognize and emphasize its difference from other groups. Logically, therefore, its content, perhaps form, and other features theoretically may be different than that of these other groups. Claims to "universality" and "universal value" therefore should be eliminated from the discussion, as these difference show their irrelevance.

Grape Leaves, however, does not reject universality or quality but rather operates within this set of contradictory assumptions. It claims a separate and distinct space for Arab American poetry while comparing Arab Americans favorably with canonical U.S. poetry, employing the terms set by the canon. In our critical reading practices, therefore, it is important to question to what extent this project aims to reproduce the "master's voice" (as Gates would have it) and publish poetry acceptable to mainstream U.S. society. In building a canon of Arab American literature through an anthology, how are Arab Americans positioned? Does the strategy of linking Arab American projects to African American ones valorize, deny, or seek to transcend these experiences? Does the ambiguous Arab American position strengthen the identity formation and pride of the community or simply leave it vague and undefined?

These questions recur in relation to how *Grape Leaves* treats the question of the Arab American family: it makes the dramatic claim that for Arab Americans, "family *is* self" (Orfalea and Elmusa 2000, xix; italics in the original). This broad statement can be understood in a number of contexts including U.S. stereotypes about ethnic/racialized families, critically inherited notions about families from Arab countries of origin, and how these ideas are connected to what scholars like Suad Joseph have called the "relational self" (Joseph 1994, 1999b). The idea here is that Arab American families somehow overshadow the individual and that one's self is always determined by one's relationship to the group. This putatively warm, loving, and unified family also evokes the gendered stereotypes about the woman of color (mother/grandmother) who nurtures the large racialized family because she is the product of her passions, emotions, and affections (di Leonardo 1994, 177–89). Furthermore, communities of color have often marked women as bearers of reproduction of the community, particularly as a reaction to white supremacy. Thus, whereas the notion of family as self is one that can be used strategically to emphasize shared cultural values and group solidarity, it is also loaded with additional meaning that can be unpacked to understand further implications.

For example, the notion that the family *is* self is highly problematic when read in relation to the emblematic figure identified by *Grape Leaves* as representative of Arab Americans—Kahlil Gibran. Indeed, he must be seriously rehabilitated in order to be squeezed into this definition. As his writings are staunchly opposed to the subjugation of the individual to the group, the introduction wrestles with how to make sense of this contradiction.[17] Furthermore, other individual authors in the collection also challenge this simple notion, such as D. H. Melhem's *Rest in Love*. A tribute to her mother, this poem explores many issues, including the labor that accompanies being a woman in a traditional Arab American family. It is not surprising that publications working to build and celebrate community would underline the family, which can be understood and claimed as a positive value. This insistence on family can become reactive, however, when it becomes a prescriptive notion, especially when family and gender intersect and collide, particularly in relation to race. This is a problematic stance when it contradicts the writings of authors whom it is meant to stand for and represent, like Gibran and Melhem. For example, *Grape Leaves* activates stereotyped notions of the family of color, drawing on racialized and cultural nationalist tropes of women that mark the community (Williams 1996). The introduction's use of these notions conveys the message to Arab Americans that their identity not only is tied to their families, but that it should be, as the anthology does lay a claim to defining Arab American identity prescriptively.

Another example of this collision between the family, race, and gender is even more pronounced where *Grape Leaves* conflates the Arab American relationship to poetry—identified throughout as "in the blood"—with family relations and

---

17. Indeed, in this difficult negotiation it ends up in contradictory statements like, "The exception to this love of family (at least nuclear and conjugal) was Gibran himself" and "It is the human family that is important to Gibran" (Orfalea and Elmusa 2000, xx).

the women's roles within them. In another attempt to show the importance of poetry to Arabs, and therefore Arab Americans, the introduction cites a quotation attributed to Ibn Rashiq, "The ancient Arabs wish one another joy but for three things—the birth of a boy, the coming to light of a poet, and the foaling of a noble mare" (Orfalea and Elmusa 2000, xv). Here, the Arab connection to poetry is proposed as natural and innate, made obvious although the metaphor used is that poetry is "still flowing in new world veins." I argue that the notion of an innate connection between Arabs and poetry is one part of the symbolic economy of how this anthology uses strategies drawing on racial logic and cultural essentialism in order to present a positive Arab American identity.

This particular example is problematic not only because it exceptionalizes Arab Americans in relation to allegedly "inborn qualities"; it also couples this "inherent" love of poetry with an explicitly misogynistic message. The qualities that the introduction proposes to be innately connected to being an Arab are the importance of family and poetry. The putatively "Arab" focus on the family is used here to emphasize the celebration of male children only. For an anthology that partly bases its claim for existence on trying to counter stereotypes about Arab Americans, this focus seems to undermine the book's goals.[18] The glorification of an "authentically" Arab proverb that neglects Arab girls, while conflating the favoring of boys with the appreciation of poetry, reinforces the "mainstream" pathologization of Arab men as misogynistic. Understanding the alleged misogyny of Arab men as an inherent feature in Arab (and also Muslim) culture holds much currency in mainstream discourse in the United States.[19] Hence, by connecting a laudable characteristic, the love of poetry, with one that reinforces mainstream U.S. stereotypes about Arabs, that only boys are appreciated and celebrated, contributes to a logic that posits the Arab American as not only racially Other but also inferior to whites.

18. This point is used to underline the Arab love of poetry by at least one reviewer, who interestingly chooses to omit the bit about the love of male children in her review in *MELUS* (Zoghby 1988, 91).

19. The literature on how Arab men are represented in mainstream U.S. culture as pathologically misogynistic is large and growing. For some examples see Salem Manganaro (1988) and Kadi (1994, especially pages 125–32 and 150–59). The collection of Hollywood movie plots involving Arab and Muslim characters *Reel Bad Arabs: How Hollywood Vilifies a People* bears out this assertion in relation to cinema (Shaheen 2001).

Clearly, it is not the intention of *Grape Leaves* to denigrate Arab American culture by identifying it as misogynistic. However, the strategies it uses to define Arab American identity activate accepted racialized ideas about Arabs and Arab Americans, particularly in conjunction with ideas about gender and the family. The critical close reading of some salient elements of *Grape Leaves*'s introduction shows how racial discourses in the United States deeply inform the logic of this anthology. Within even the most "literary" justifications for the inclusion of certain works in the anthology, racialized discourses about mainstream and other groups and essentializing qualities they share can be located. Critical analyses of the community and canon building being done through this anthology, like the other two discussed below, demonstrate the importance of unpacking the discourses of race, essentialism, and exceptionalism within them.

POST GIBRAN: ANTHOLOGY OF NEW ARAB AMERICAN WRITING

Post Gibran rejects *Grape Leaves*'s varied strategies that draw on racialized tropes to prove American equality and to define literary quality in terms of the white American canon. Similarly, whereas *Grape Leaves* is a celebration of Kahlil Gibran and his generation of poets, *Post Gibran,* true to its title, attempts to move past this circumscription and to place an explicit emphasis on publishing works that are new and experimental. The rhetoric of comparison to the great names of the canon becomes irrelevant in this context; there is not one in its three-page introduction. Even more important to this study, *Post Gibran* employs different strategies than *Grape Leaves* to engage with issues around race and ethnicity.

This does not mean that the discourses of race, strategic essentialism, and cultural exceptionalism are totally absent here. On the contrary, *Post Gibran*'s introduction relies heavily on the notion that Arab Americans are genuinely and truly "Arabs," which is purposely defined broadly. Rather than elaborate on how Arabs are unique or draw comparisons to other so-called minority groups in the United States, *Post Gibran* deploys an even broader concept when it speaks of a generalized Arab "spirit." This appealing definition of Arabs/Arab Americans seeks to offer alternative ways to think about the question of self-definition and identity and to transcend the problems of essentialism and "Arab blood" as well as comparisons with other groups, to understand where Arab Americans might belong in the United States. The strategies used by *Post Gibran* to define this "spirit" in which Arab identity is located are multiple, therefore, and will be discussed in more detail below.

Post Gibran begins by defining the Arab spirit as Gilgameshian (this word occurs four times in three pages), civilized, and multicultural: "Besides, the definition of Arabness itself is open, as it always has been, since the core of our civilization has spawned countless variations over time and space from the earliest millenniums onward" (Akash and Mattawa 1999, xii). From this point on, like *Grape Leaves,* the introduction to *Post Gibran* emphasizes the need for this anthology in order to combat discrimination against and media distortions of Arabs and Arab Americans. This anthology is being compiled to "set the record straight" and is a chance for the community to define itself and once again its "spirit." *Post Gibran* claims that it will correct the distorted images of Arab Americans prevalent in the United States: "If the image of us is truly being created by the American imagination, the time has come to invalidate that image and render it unrecognizable both to ourselves and to the world. That false image of ourselves has power over us only if we choose to accept an alien design for our destiny" (xi). Words like "unrecognizable," "false," and "alien" highlight the way in which the "American imagination" has misunderstood who the Arabs are and insist that now is the time to reclaim a true or authentic "Arabness." In this sentence therefore, the "American imagination" is contrasted to "us"—presumably Arabs/Arab Americans. This anthology is therefore conceived in order to counter stereotypes and correct existing misconceptions about Arabs/Arab Americans.

The strategy of defining who is an Arab/Arab American by a general spirit, then, runs up against the more specific delimitations of terminology implied in a binary opposition between "Americans" and "us." "Arabness" is allegedly open to everything, but how the "American imagination" perceives it is alien and false. Here the "American" is rigidly and specifically defined, closing the door on a broader definition of American multiculturalism that accepts "Arabness" and an Arabness that can also encompass America. Of course, the introduction here is speaking in general terms of a clearly recognizable trend in mainstream U.S. perceptions of Arabs and Arab Americans. But the strategy of defining identities as broad and encompassing also gets trapped in this very logic if at the same time static oppositions between groups are drawn.

In a related way and in contrast to *Grape Leaves*'s approach of employing both racialization and humanization through parity with other groups, *Post*

Gibran marginalizes connections to American literary traditions and invokes the bond between Arab Americans and "authentically Arab" literature. Rather than the emphasis on Whitman, Pound, and Frost, therefore, *Post Gibran* delineates the poetic tradition of Arab Americans as follows: "From Gilgamish [*sic*] to Mahmoud Darwish and from Innana to Nazik al-Mala'ika, we continue to carry the traditions of our civilization which forged the very humanness of our humanity" (Akash and Mattawa 1999, xi). The obvious parallel here is that like *Grape Leaves, Post Gibran* seeks to underline Arab American humanity through its publication. In a somewhat opposite way to *Grape Leaves, Post Gibran* uses the strategy of Arab American cultural exceptionalism to combat racism. Rather than seek to find an equal place in the U.S. mainstream, white, male canon, however, *Post Gibran* draws links to ancient Near-Eastern mythical figures and contemporary Arab poets. This is a creative challenge to the logic of *Grape Leaves* and redefines humanity and civilization within a racist United States as being Arab. It does, however, also run the risk of emphasizing a parochial message about Arab American identity.

A brief analysis of the specific figures invoked here reveal some of the important nuances in how this strategy operates. Mahmoud Darwish and Nazik al-Mala'ika both are modern poets, a man and a woman, who hail from Palestine and Iraq respectively. These two Arab countries have had a specifically contentious and difficult relationship with the United States in the 1990s, and even before. Moreover, though in some ways these poets may seem different and seem to represent different things owing to gender, country of origin, and generation—and in some ways they do—they both are major canonical names in the mainstream, standard Arabic literary tradition. Both write conventional poetry that is among the most accepted as representative of their eras and poetic movements—Darwish as a contemporary resistance poet and Mala'ika as a pioneer of the free-verse movement in the 1950s. Gilgamesh and Innana are both ancient Near-Eastern mythical figures who represent the cultural and literary heritage attributed here to the Arabs and passed down to all humanity. I would argue that their use proposes a mythical prenational, nonsectarian past that all Arabs could presumably feel connected to, allowing diverse groups to identify with them. Read together with Mala'ika and Darwish therefore, these four characters all offer a representation of the Arab culture that is uncontroversial and culturally sanctioned within mainstream definitions of "Arab." Using ancient figures who can be invoked beyond any modern notions of identity and linking them to modern canonical Arab literary figures and historical contexts suggests a seamless continuity—at least of "spirit"—between them. Moreover, within the context of seeming neutrality and "humanity," two specific modern figures are chosen as representative, reinforcing a particular notion of what modern Arab identity is—a celebrated and lionized male Palestinian resistance poet and a noncontroversial female Iraqi free-verse poet whose works are not known for questioning gender norms or the role of women.

Moreover, while the proposed pan-Arab identification with Gilgamesh is a strategy that advances a message of multicultural openness, it can work in a counterproductive way as it is employed in relation to the definition of the "Arab spirit." This problem can be seen in the uneasy coexistence between the open, multicultural Arabness proposed by *Post Gibran* and its contrast with closed and rigid American ideas or "imagination" about Arabs, as presented in the example above. This perception is reinforced, for example, in the statement, "We feel it is the duty of *Jusoor* [the journal with which this volume is associated] to present to American readers not secondhand versions of their own works, but to expand aspects of that creativity of our native Gelgamishian [*sic*] spirit in conformity with a world view that is our own" (Akash and Mattawa 1999, xi–xii). Here once again, there is a contrast between us (Arabs) and them (Americans) that shows the dilemma of Arab Americans. Can Arab Americans be "Americans" when "American readers" are defined as "them"? Who are these undifferentiated Americans—white Americans, African Americans, Armenian Americans, and so on? The key phrases here are, "*their* own works," which are opposed to "a world view that is *our* own" (my italics). The American readers here are understood to be "mainstream" American readers whose worldviews are necessarily opposed to one that is "ours"—or Arab. Arab American readers/writers—the authors, subjects, and presumably also one of the implied readerships of the anthology—are thereby located firmly on one side of their compound identity. While on the one hand *Post Gibran* allows Arab American readers/writers to define an open identity in many ways, on the other hand it calls into question if this identity can be somehow thus "American" by defining "American" identity as fixed and not explicitly recognizing or valorizing its potential for multicultural openness, rather relying on a closed definition that is defined by the racism of the mainstream.

In the context of combating stereotypical media images of Arabs, this rhetoric about correcting stereotypes and misunderstandings about Arabs is certainly understandable. And by highlighting this use of language, I by no means wish to imply that the introduction espouses some sort of "clash of civilizations" theory. Moreover, I do not intend here to overemphasize a point, by extrapolating from one sentence in the introduction alone. What is problematic in this introduction, however, is that its notion of "Arabness," appealing in its vagueness, is perhaps so broadly defined as to render it almost necessarily essentialist, though it does not directly employ the language of race (Akash and Mattawa 1999, xii).[20] At the same time that this "Arab spirit" is meant to be open and multicultural, it must necessarily be different than what is defined as "American" so as to be original and not "secondhand." The strategy here is clearly a contrast and perhaps even a response to the logic of parity employed in *Grape Leaves*. However, the result is that though little else is clear about the definition of "Arabness" that informs the self-identity of this anthology of Arab American literature, it is consistently shown as different than "Americanness." Although the anthology's explicit strategy is to embrace multiculturalism, it also relies on a logic that contrasts "us" and "them"—which marginalizes U.S. multiculturalism at the same that it promotes Arab openness—and presents them as oppositional.

Although *Post Gibran* does attempt to move beyond race as a category in employing the concept of "spirit," it maintains a focus and insistence on "Arabness" that suggests that there is an essence that defines people and culture. The way in which this informs *Post Gibran* can further be identified in the shift away from *Grape Leaves*'s focus on literary excellence and "quality" to its own project of identifying new writers and forms of literary experimentation. One way in which this is expressed is the explicit solicitation of pieces in genres that have been underrepresented in Arab American literary production, such as fiction and drama—one of the steps called for by Majaj in her contribution to this very

20. The inclusion of a short story by Penny Johnson, not of Arab heritage, represents the inclusion of people who embody the Arab spirit though are not of Arab heritage. It is notable that she is married to a Palestinian and lives and works in Palestine, and that her story is about a Palestinian girl. Thus the legitimacy on which she is granted an "Arabness" in an Arab American anthology is in conjunction with a focus on a political and human reality of the Arab world, and not at all on a connection to Arab Americans or the U.S. context. This recalls the submission policy of *Mizna*, the Arab American literary magazine, "*Mizna* is always seeking original writing and visual art for our upcoming publications. We welcome submissions on Arab-American themes that explore the diversity of our community. Contributors do not have to be of Arab descent provided their work is of relevance to the Arab-American community."

anthology. In connection to this strategy, the introduction to *Post Gibran* also explicitly articulates a specific interest in and call for pieces that embrace the Arabic language and what it refers to as "Arab concerns." By prescribing not only genres but also defining identity as Arab American as connected to language and the vaguely termed "concerns," the anthology prescribes two ways in which the identity they seek to define can be expressed. Therefore, at the same time that *Post Gibran* insists that its contributors embrace an "Arabness" defined as multicultural—and presumably at least vaguely cosmopolitan—an identity that is like a "bouquet of mixed flowers," there is an explicit insistence on texts that literally manifest a quite concretely defined Arabness, identified as "concerns" (topics and themes?) and language (Akash and Mattawa 1999, xii). This interest betrays the fact that the anthology does define a prescriptive notion of what it means to be an Arab in this anthology—one must show an attention to politics, culture, language, and so on.

This prescriptive notion is reinforced by one of the somewhat odd elements of the structure of the anthology—the inclusion of translated pieces from Arabic by authors who are not generally considered Arab Americans, have never made claims to be, and who are not particularly "new" authors, as are most of the other authors. Indeed, these contributions are all by well-established and even canonical figures within the Arabic literary traditions: Mahmoud Darwish, Tawfiq al-Hakim, Yusuf Habashi al-Ashqar, translations of *zajal* by Adnan Haydar, a piece by George Tarabishi on Taha Hussein, and a discussion of Mona Saudi's sculpture. These contributions are grouped in a separate section, which is labeled "fragrance from the garden." (Akash and Mattawa 1999, 386–445).[21] A possible interpretation of its inclusion within such an anthology is that these writers are meant to represent the original "garden" or source from which the Arab American writers are meant to spring. This controversial notion reinforces an essential and essentialized Arab identity for which Arab Americans should strive and underlines the importance of paying homage to Arab literary figures, much in a parallel—if opposite—way to the focus on the white U.S. canon in *Grape Leaves*.

Therefore, though *Post Gibran*'s strategies for defining Arab American identity are complex, they draw on multiple techniques that can be contradictory.

---

21. Other critics and reviewers have also questioned and commented upon the inclusion of this incongruous section (Peters 2001, 187; Ghazoul 2000, 3–4).

At the same time that it defines "Arabness" as multicultural and claims that it can encompass everyone, it nonetheless also draws on two essentialist notions that undermine this claim. First, though "Arabness" is meant to be an open and all-embracing category, it is contrasted to "Americanness," which is defined as oppositional to Arabs. This contrast leads to a necessary contradiction and difficulty for Arab Americans. *Post Gibran* suggests that Arab Americans should produce "new literature," but it is best if it somehow shows that they are "truly Arabs" in contrast to Americans (read: mainstream white Americans), by showing their "spirit" and drawing on their "origins" and language without being "secondhand" copies of American literature. Second, writers who show a connection to the Arabic language and Arab "concerns" are valorized as somehow more worthy of inclusion and part of this "spirit" than others. This can be read as encouraging Arab Americans to embrace the history and culture of their heritage, which no doubt it is. But by allowing for slippage between the Arabic language, the mainstream Arabic literary tradition, Arab concerns, and the Arab spirit—all in contrast to "Americanness" (which theoretically could participate in all of the above)—a problematic logic based in essentialist notions shows through.

The strategy of employing implicitly essentialist definitions of Arabness here, in conjunction with an explicitly open multicultural definition of Arabness, has both advantages and disadvantages in such an anthology. For example it allows many individual contributions to question, challenge, and refute ideas that are inscribed in this introduction. I have already given the example of Lisa Suhair Majaj's piece, which I cite above, and there are many others, including Saladin Ahmed's "Poem for Countee Cullen," Naomi Shihab Nye's "Long Overdue," and Nathalie Handal's "Poetry as Homeland." Moreover, it decenters such notions as that the United States somehow "invented" diversity, and it valorizes cultural and linguistic connections to the Arab world that are often devalued in the United States. Because the introduction is very short and less explicit, it is also vaguer than the much longer introduction to *Grape Leaves*. Leaving more to the reader's imagination and interpretation allows the anthology and the ideas it embraces to be used more flexibly in some ways. In other ways, however, it can be seen that this strategy does not entirely free *Post Gibran* from activating some of the ideas embedded in the racialization of Arab Americans. The contradictions and problems that arise because of this strategy, for example, raise crucial questions about its usefulness in defining an Arab American identity through the process of anthology building and canon formation in Arab American literature. Vagueness of definition does not relieve the problematics of essentialism and thus, despite its openness, *Post Gibran* does also employ strategies of racializing Arab Americans, albeit in a significantly different way from *Grape Leaves*.

FOOD FOR OUR GRANDMOTHERS: WRITINGS BY ARAB-AMERICAN AND ARAB-CANADIAN FEMINISTS

Food for Our Grandmothers: Writings by Arab-American and Arab-Canadian Feminists has much in common with *Post Gibran* in its shift in focus away from Kahlil Gibran as the main emblematic figure of Arab American literature and toward new writers and approaches. This anthology's very existence is ignored, however, within the text of *Post Gibran*'s introduction, "Since *Grape Leaves: A Century of Arab American Poetry,* no anthology of our literature, even partial, has come out" (Akash and Mattawa 1999, xii).[22] Lack of awareness of this volume seems ironic indeed, as *Food for Our Grandmothers* received considerable critical attention and many more reviews than *Post Gibran* and *Grape Leaves* combined.[23] Several plausible reasons for this exclusion point to features that set this work apart from the other two anthologies. The first is located in its subtitle, which identifies its specific contributors—Arab American and Arab Canadian feminists. The feminist focus and its publication by a small, nonprofit, collectively run publisher perhaps might limit its reception and/or its audience; though it received more attention than the other works, this may be limited mainly to feminist groups.[24] Linked to its feminist project is the volume's inclusion of many memoirs, essays, and personal narrations rather than poetry or generically experimental works

22. It should be noted that *Post Gibran* was published in 1999, five years after the publication date of *Food for Our Grandmothers* (Kadi 1994), presumably leaving enough time for it to be noticed. Moreover, Lisa Suhair Majaj's contribution in *Post Gibran* mentions *Food for Our Grandmothers,* to which she also contributed.

23. I base this assertion on my reading of over two dozen printed and on-line reviews of these works in journals and newspapers.

24. *Food for Our Grandmothers* was reviewed in locations where I did not locate reviews for the others, including but not limited to publications devoted to women's/feminist and/or lesbian issues: *Ms.* (Maksoud 1994); *off our backs* (Douglas 1995); *Lambda Book Report* (Katz 1995); *Women's Review of Books* (Helmbold 1998); *Middle East Women's Studies Review* (Naber 1996); *Feminist Teacher* (Vandrick 1995); and *Sojourner: The Women's Forum* (Yadegar 1995).

like plays, once again raising the question of the definition of "literature." Would the pieces included in *Food for Our Grandmothers* meet the standards of "literary quality" outlined in *Grape Leaves,* for example? Like the works of other marginalized groups, feminist writers are often challenged on the basis of their works not manifesting the allegedly "universal" values of literature. Moreover, feminist voices, like others, often challenge accepted notions of community, which can contribute to their isolation.

Related to its feminist focus, the question of race is treated explicitly from the very beginning of the *Food for Our Grandmothers* eight-page introduction; many of the individual contributions also draw and expand on this focus.[25] There is also a strong emphasis on class and the complex interconnections of race, gender, and class. The introduction asserts the dilemma faced by Arab Americans and Arab Canadians: "As Arabs, like other people of color in this racist society, our race is simultaneously emphasized and ignored" (Kadi 1994, xvi). This theme of being both racialized and ignored is central to the Arab American experience, and has been explored by a number of scholars. Helen Hatab Samhan, for example, has argued that Arab American belonging in U.S. society is often tolerated as long as it is not deemed political, at which point the mechanism of racialization is mobilized and Arab Americans lose their rights (Samhan 1987, 1999; also Morsy 1994; Naber 2000). Being "inbetween," or insecure within racial hierarchies because of a provisional white status, is articulated here in relation to the binary oppositions of black and white in the United States and Canada, "Not Black. Not white. Never quite fitting in. Always on the edge" (Kadi 1994, xvi). How race is dealt with in *Food for Our Grandmothers* is particularly important in three areas: the insistence on experience, naming and defining the terms of the project, and the treatment of family and community.

Food for Our Grandmothers differs from *Grape Leaves* and *Post Gibran* not only in its foregrounding of race, but also in its focus on Arab American writings and experience rather than on literary form. Whereas *Post Gibran* chooses works based on generic or other experimentations and *Grape Leaves* insists on "quality

---

25. Most of the narrative pieces treat this issue in some way. For some that deal very explicitly with race, see Boudakian, "Crossing Over to the Other Side"; Haddad, "In Search of Home"; Mahoul, "Battling Nationalisms to Salvage Her History"; Majaj, "Boudaries Arab/American"; Mamary, "Mint Tomatoes and the Grapevine"; Rashid "What's Not in a Name"; Saliba, "Sittee"; and Salome, "Wherever I Am."

above all," *Food for Our Grandmothers* privileges the notion of representing the diversity of experiences of Arab American and Arab Canadian feminists, pointing out that even with this span there are still missing experiences. The contributors are defined, for example, as "writers, activists, artists, poets, teachers, and mother and daughter team, and two (blood) sisters. We are lesbians, bisexuals, and heterosexuals; of different generations; working class, middle class, upper-middle class; women born in the Arab world and women born here" (Kadi 1994, xvii). It is within this context of experience, then, that *Food for Our Grandmothers* locates its project of community building and alliance formation.

It is from within this emphasis on the contributors' multiple social roles and their feminist identification that this anthology establishes links and bonds with other groups of color, "I hope this collection of essays and poems offers landmarks, signposts, names and directions not only for Arab-American and Arab-Canadian communities but for other communities of color and our allies" (Kadi 1994, xvii). The very next sentence is a list of other anthologies with which *Food for Our Grandmothers* explicitly identifies itself:

> I am thinking of *This Bridge Called My Back: Writings by Radical Women of Color,* edited by Gloria Anzaldúa and Cherríe Moraga; *Home Girls: A Black Feminist Anthology,* edited by Barbara Smith; *Making Waves: An Anthology of Writings By and About Asian American Women,* edited by Asian Women United of California; *A Gathering of Spirit: A Collection by North American Indian Women,* edited by Beth Brant. (Kadi 1994, xvii)

As in *Grape Leaves* a list of groups is named, asserting a connection to them partly based on shared experiences of racialization. The notion of parity identified above—other groups have anthologies and therefore so should Arab Americans and Arab Canadians—is activated once again here. But *Food for Our Grandmothers* employs a somewhat different strategy: its introduction pushes these bonds further by asserting this anthology's own usefulness to these other groups. *Grape Leaves* concentrates on the positive contributions the volume will make to the Arab American community as well as invoking a universal notion of "great literature," embodied in canonical, white, U.S. male authors. *Food for Our Grandmothers,* on the other hand, sees its role as promoting and furthering work being done by feminists of color for other feminists of color. In this it takes a thoughtful stance in how it locates Arab Americans as a racialized group that can be an active partner in working with other communities of color and also benefit from these affiliations.

Within this context, naming the anthology and defining Arab American and Arab Canadian feminists is a process discussed in great detail, acknowledging considerable difficulties (Kadi 1994, xv–xix). The introduction debates three different terms and settles on Arab American/Arab Canadian (rather than either "people of Middle Eastern/North African descent" or "West Asian/North African") in part because "It allows us to reclaim the word Arab, to force people to hear and say a word that has become synonymous with 'crazy Muslim terrorists.' It affirms our identity and links us to our brothers and sisters in other Arab countries" (xviii).[26] This usage allows *Food for Our Grandmothers* to reclaim a name, history, and culture and discuss some of the issues and problems related to them. Within the complex and nuanced contemplation of terms in the introduction and its specific treatment of race, however, it is striking that locating Arab Americans and Arab Canadians as people of color is taken for granted.[27] The introduction proposes that there is a link between experiences of discrimination by Arabs and other groups in North America. And certainly the calls for solidarity between people of color are well-informed appeals for positive community affiliations.

Not problematizing or contextualizing the racialization of Arab Americans as people of color, though, also erases elements of this history and can complicate such unity between groups. For example, the introduction claims, "In the United States and Canada, it is not only white people who refuse to see us, it is other people of color—Latinos, Africans, Asians, Natives—who do not acknowledge our existence" (Kadi 1994, xix–xx). In addition to the general

26. Though Kadi insists on this reclaiming of the term "Arab" for political reasons, she does not ever explicitly discuss that some of the women whose works are included in this anthology may not identify with the label Arab, whereas they might more readily with West Asian/North African or Middle Eastern descent. This includes writers who are Armenian, Iranian, and Jewish, for example. Kadi does not assert that "Arab" is a political label that can incorporate all of these other groups as well. There is not space here to discuss the larger implications of this issue and naming, but it would be a fruitful subject for further analysis.

27. It is also notable that there is not a more complex and problematized discussion of feminism and what it might or might not mean to this group, particularly as many "sisters" (identified in Kadi 1994, xviii) to these Arab American women are suspicious of this terminology and have challenged it.

invisibility of Arab Americans in North America, which affects the perceptions of all groups, their invisibility to other people of color is perhaps at least
partly related to the ambiguity of the Arab American racial status, at least in
the United States. As almost all writers on race and the Arab American experience have underlined, being "inbetween" black and white is both an ambiguous
and an ambivalent position. Indeed a number of contributors to *Food for Our
Grandmothers* explicitly treat this issue, including women who discuss ben-
efiting from white skin privilege and those who are ambivalent about how to
affiliate themselves, because they often "pass" in the United States as white.[28]
The complexity of this problem is compounded by the fact that not all Arab
American women do "pass" as white and that women who feel and are labeled
as "inbetween" may be viewed and treated in different and contradictory ways
as well. For many Arab American women who identify as women of color, this
stance is one of conscious political solidarity in order to challenge racial hierarchies in multiple ways.

The label "women of color" therefore has provided a space for many Arab
Americans to assert, and also politicize, their identity and solidarity with others. For many it is a way in which to validate their experiences and lived reality,
which do not match their legal classification as "white." A detailed exploration
of how racialized identities are formed, however, must not ignore the history of
Arab American whiteness in the United States and the requisite privileges that
this granted them over time in contrast to other communities who were marked
as nonwhite. Whether or not individual or groups of Arab Americans benefit
from white skin privilege in a racist U.S. society, feel connected to this racial
classification, or indeed have been oppressed by U.S. racism, it is important
to acknowledge this complex community history. Not all individuals do benefit, of course, but as a collectivity, Arab Americans have fought for, claimed,
and benefited from their legal definition as white.[29] This is, of course, not a

28. Some examples are: Boudakian "Crossing Over to the Other Side," Haddad "In Search
of Home," Halaby "Browner Shades of White," Mamary "Mint Tomatoes and the Grapevine,"
Mahoul "Battling Nationalisms to Salvage Her History," Majaj "Boudaries Arab/American" and
Sharif, "Global Sisterhood: Where Do We Fit In?" (all in Kadi 1994).

29. For some of the legal benefits accrued through the attainment of "whiteness," especially as
it is legally construed, see Lipsitz (1998) and Haney-López (1996) on citizenship, immigration, and
land ownership in particular. See also Delgado and Stefancic (2001) and Crenshaw et al. (1995).

straightforward history. For example, the "white" identity of Arab Americans has been unsettled at numerous moments for groups as well as individuals, and research has shown how it has often been revoked and has not prevented discrimination against Arab Americans (Joseph 1999a; Majaj 1999a, 2000; Morsy 1994; Saliba 1999; Samhan 1987, 1999). Moreover, as many Arab Americans have also argued, white status often obstructs Arab American opportunities to claim rights and benefits of citizenship in the face of discrimination and has reinforced their invisibility in the United States. On the other hand, a historical perspective shows, for example, that unlike blacks in the Jim Crow South, the legal status of Arab Americans as white provided them with privileges—such as land ownership—at the expense of blacks and "others" who did not share this legal status. This is by no means a prescription that Arab Americans and Arab Canadians should or should not identify as white or as people of color. Nor is the fact that Arab Americans have been classified historically as white necessarily something absolutely positive or negative. Rather here I would suggest that a more complex and contextual understanding of Arab American racialization might promote deeper links with other communities based on recognition of shared and different histories.

Calling for these links once again recalls notions of universal literary value, which *Food for Our Grandmothers* effectively marginalizes along with the shadow of Kahlil Gibran. Similarly, it avoids the kind of racialized discourse that *Grape Leaves* inscribes and also the explicit rejection of these notions of value and racialized discourse in *Post Gibran*. In this way, *Food for Our Grandmothers* is able to grapple directly with the issue of race and racialization in relation to Arab Americans. Another related way in which this anthology shifts its focus away from employing vague and contradictory strategies of identity building in relation to race is in its self-definition through embracing the two other emblems framing this study—grandmothers and grape leaves. This focus is reflected in the book's very title: *Food for Our Grandmothers*. Here, these emblems emphasize both family/community and food as a specific cultural production. The introduction states that this title was easy to choose because it represents well the "incredible number of contributions" treating these themes and issues. The introduction and also individual contributions celebrate grandmothers—particularly as links to homeland and identity. This anthology is conceived explicitly as giving something back to these women, and the contributions are arranged in sections that are organized around different Arabic foods. The theme of food is not merely touched upon in a superficial way but is interwoven into the structure of the book, whose sections include: olives, bread, thyme, *laban,* grapeleaves, and mint. Not only idealized and simplified understandings of family are represented, though; many pieces draw out negative as well as positive sides to the traditional family structure, challenge patriarchal values, and critique the marginalization of gays and lesbians. Moreover, alternative community solidarities are highlighted—women's groups, for example.

Moreover, *Food for Our Grandmothers* is also aware of issues such as the unpaid labor involved in food preparation and the painstaking work many women have devoted in this field at the expense of others. As discussed above, the stereotype of ethnic women/women of color who hold the family together with food—the Arab women "stuck in the kitchen"—is an issue that recurs. This emphasis on food risks naturalizing these women's unpaid labor and locating it as something only to celebrate. As I have shown above in relation to *Grape Leaves,* such ideas indeed can be tied to the process of racialization of Arab women, like other women of color, and showing them as naturally tied to these activities, unable to "advance" like white women, and victims of an endemically oppressive and misogynistic Arab society. In her own contribution to the volume, its editor, Joanna Kadi, takes this issue on directly by identifying the labor of these grandmothers as "cultural work" and explicitly locating it as a parallel to her own cultural work, manifested in one way in the compilation of the anthology (Kadi 1994, 231–37).

By locating grandmothers' food preparation as cultural work that can be passed down and appreciated through generations, this anthology rejects a racial explanation for poetry and creative production (it is in the blood), or one vaguely linked to a spirit. It is still worthwhile to question if its emphasis on "grape leaves" and grandmothers reinscribes the very notions that they seek to dismantle—keeping women figuratively, if not literally, in the kitchen. The framing and title of the work, though, is conceived of as a positive message, reinforcing that this anthology should be seen in some way as giving "food" back to these grandmothers who nurtured the anthology's contributors. Thus, this volume proposes that there is value in literary work that is connected to Arab American and Arab Canadian culture and heritage, and the work of Arab American and Arab Canadian grandmothers is thus also valorized by equating it with the seemingly more "intellectual" cultural work of writing and producing an anthology. In addition, Kadi's individual contribution to the volume presents a compelling argument for understanding the continuity of Arab American and Arab Canadian women's experiences as cultural work.

What sets how *Food for Our Grandmothers* treats the issue of race and the racialization of Arab Americans apart from the other two anthologies discussed in this chapter is its shift in emphasis. Here, the introduction places an emphasis on culture and specific cultural production and couples it with an explicit discussion of race and positionality of Arabs in North America. This discussion moves the definition of Arab American/ Arab Canadian identity away from essentializing categories. It does not, however, ignore the question of race totally, because of its centrality to the United States and systems of identity and community affiliation there. It therefore strategically uses Arab American racialization as a tool in alliance building with other groups of color, while calling racial discourses into question at the same time. In these ways, *Food for Our Grandmothers* engages with race and the racialization of Arab Americans and Arab Canadians in ways that can lead toward potentially more productive conceptualizations of Arab American identities.

CONCLUSIONS

As the analyses above reveal, the explicit and implicit strategies of the racialization of Arab Americans that these three anthologies use vary widely—some are sophisticated and linked to investigations of gender and class, others reproduce old paradigms and hierarchies, and others draw on deeply problematic essentialist notions to define the community. Particularly within the feminist framework of *Food for Our Grandmothers*, intersections of race, class, and gender are explored both in the overall project and in the introduction specifically. When such discussions are explicit, of course, they are easier to engage. Here I have shown that much of the discourse around race in Arab American literature and literary study, however, is implicit. Ideas bound up in essentialized and essentializing notions, such as that "poetry is in the Arab blood," are an integral part of the strategy of building community identity in *Grape Leaves*, for example. *Post Gibran* rejects this strategy on the surface, but nonetheless proposes that there is an Arab spirit that itself can be defined, at least partly, as somehow essentially "Arab," though this itself is defined as open and multicultural. Such strategies of essentialization inform the identity-building projects of *Grape Leaves* and *Post Gibran* and are employed in many different and often contradictory ways to claim legitimacy, authenticity, and value in a racist U.S. system. *Food for Our Grandmothers* provides both the most specific discussion of race and the positionality of Arab Americans and Arab Canadians; it also employs the most concrete and creative strategies in defining a group identity that is based in culture rather than essence and complicates the positionality of Arab Americans while working toward useful conceptualizations of it.

In the study of these Arab American literary anthologies it is crucial to recall that they help to build the literary canons that themselves can be central to the definition of communities and identities. Literary canons, however, do shift and change over time and can be influenced, as Elise Salem has argued in relation to Arabic literature: "If one recognizes that canons are forever pliable and not fixed, and that they are ideologically determined and not pure, then they are a most useful commodity" (Salem 2000–2001, 96). Because canons are bound up in delimitations, definitions, and identity formation, it is thus important continually to develop more detailed understandings of how racial ideologies and racialization are implicated in this process for Arab Americans. I propose that in order to make use of these canons productively in our critical reading and teaching practices, their underlying principles can be analyzed in connection to these questions. Arab American literary canons can be helpful in defining and building community identity and solidarity, so as Lisa Suhair Majaj has advocated, "we need not stronger and more definitive boundaries of identity, but rather an expansion and a transformation of these boundaries" (Majaj 1999b, 77).

As critics, scholars, readers, teachers, and activists, it is vital for us to deepen our knowledge about how Arab American literature relates to and engages with the history of race and racism in the United States, and the specific, complex, and contradictory places that Arab Americans have held in it over time. One way of working with this relationship in literary terms, for example, is to explore literary links between Arab Americans and other groups, such as African Americans, in more specific detail. This is not in order simply to advocate or point out a parity or equality of experience, but to build on both shared and different experiences better to understand the complexities and diversity of the literary production of these communities. In teaching and writing about Arab American literature, it is important to ask difficult questions about the impact of race and racial thinking on it—including whiteness, blackness, and being "inbetween." Arab American literary publications, like these anthologies, expand the reach of Arab American voices and can be used effectively to probe these issues. Journals like *Al-Jadid* and *Mizna* regularly publish pieces that investigate these questions (Debis 2001; Shamieh 2001; Wade 2001; West 2000). In addition, it is essential to follow the lead of literary scholars and activists like Joanna Kadi, Lisa Suhair Majaj, Steven Salaita, and others in pushing for gender and class to be included in these discussions and to expose the links between them in complex ways. This period of canon formation and interest in Arab American literature can be productively used to investigate the process of Arab American racialization in relation to literary studies and to complicate simple notions of what the community and its literary production are and can be.

EIGHT

The Prime-Time Plight of the Arab Muslim American after 9/11

Configurations of Race and Nation in TV Dramas

EVELYN ALSULTANY

FROM CELEBRATING THEIR MURDER

TO SYMPATHIZING WITH THEIR PLIGHT

TWO SIGNIFICANT SHIFTS occurred after September 11, 2001, in the representation of Arab and Muslim Americans in the U.S. media: an increase in representation and, in conjunction, an increase in sympathetic portrayals. Although there have been abundant stereotypical representations of Arabs in the U.S. media and most notably in Hollywood cinema, portrayals of Arab Americans have been scant.[1] Thus the first notable shift we witness is an increase in Arab *American* characters in U.S. mainstream television. As Jack G. Shaheen has tirelessly documented in *The TV Arab* (1984) and *Reel Bad Arabs: How Hollywood Vilifies a People* (2001), before 9/11 Arabs had predominantly

---

I would like to thank Ella Shohat, Ebony Coletu, Akhil Gupta, David Palumbo-Liu, and Jack G. Shaheen for comments on earlier versions of this piece.

1. Jamie Farr on *M.A.S.H.* (1972–83) and Hans Conreid on *The Danny Thomas Show* (1953–71) are the only consistent Arab American characters in the history of U.S. television. A few films have also featured Arab American characters that are not the embodiment of evil, such as Tony Shalhoub's character in *The Siege* and David Suchet in *A Perfect Murder*. Otherwise, Arab American actors have played stereotypical Arab roles or portray persons of other ethnicities (Italians, whites, etc.). See Shaheen (2002, 191–212).

been represented variously as villains, oppressed veiled women, exotic belly dancers, rich sheikhs with harems, and most remarkably as terrorists. While representations of Arabs and Muslims as terrorists continue with increased dedication after 9/11, the second significant shift is that sympathetic portrayals that humanize Arab and Muslim Americans have entered the mainstream. Prime-time TV dramas—such as *The Guardian, The Education of Max Bickford,* and *7th Heaven*—have explicitly sought to counter representations of Arabs and Muslims as terrorists and fundamentalists, backward and uncivilized. Instead they present Arab and Muslim Americans as unfair targets of hate and discrimination. Through prime-time TV dramas, stories of Arab and Muslim Americans being misunderstood, detained, harassed, attacked, and murdered have entered U.S. living rooms, reaching millions of viewers.[2]

This shift toward representing Arab and Muslim Americans and portraying them sympathetically is particularly significant when considering how audiences have been positioned throughout the history of representations vis-à-vis Arabs and Muslims in the U.S. media.[3] Over the past four or five decades,[4] the majority of television and film representations of Arabs and Muslims have been as terrorists, seeking to elicit a celebration from the audience upon their murder (e.g., *True Lies, The Siege,* and *Executive Decision*). Within this historical framework, contemporary prime-time TV dramas evoking sympathy

2. For example, an estimated 25.2 million people in the United States tuned into *The West Wing*'s post-9/11 special episode, according to Nielsen ratings.

3. Granted, how various audiences read and interpret media is not passive, but complex and varied. As Jose Esteban Muñoz (1999), Ien Ang (1991, 1995), Purnima Mankekar (1999), and others have demonstrated, audiences have agency; audiences accept, reject, resist, critique, identify, disidentify, and interpret the media with which they come into contact. Hence an insistence has arisen within cultural studies to examine not only the site of the production of an image, but also various sites for its reception. A thorough examination of reception is beyond the scope of this chapter, which seeks to examine dramatic televisual narratives produced for public consumption.

4. The inauguration of the state of Israel in 1948 and particularly the Arab-Israeli War of 1967 are turning points in representations of Arabs in the U.S. media. Before 1967, reflective of a Eurocentric colonial ideology (see Shohat and Stam 1994), Arab men were largely represented as rich and exotic, living in the desert outside of civilization with harems of women. Some were good and some evil. The good Arabs often required help from white men to defeat the evil Arabs. After 1967, Arab men came to be predominantly represented as terrorists, and Arab women became absent from representations (see Shohat 2006, 17–69; Naber 2000).

from viewers are a noteworthy development. Sympathy is a device used to gain audience identification and is usually associated with a "good" character as opposed to an "evil" one. In portraying Arab and Muslim Americans as victims of injustice, sympathy is sought from viewers, and an attempt is made to rework the hegemonic racial configuration that marks Arabs and Muslims as fanatical terrorists who threaten U.S. national security. Instead of presenting Arabs and Muslims as justifiable targets of hate, violence, and discrimination, some TV dramas represent Arab and Muslim Americans as unfair targets of misdirected fear and anger.

As the events of September 11 had the effect of confirming the stereotype of the Arab terrorist, some writers and producers of prime-time television programs created a new type of character and story line in an attempt to avert the dangerous potential of the stereotype. Characters that humanize Arab Americans were introduced along with story lines reflecting Arab and Muslim Americans in a post-9/11 predicament, caught between being associated with the terrorist attacks by virtue of ethnicity or religion and being American. Such TV episodes told the tale of the unjust backlash against Arab and Muslim Americans, seeking to garner audience sympathy as opposed to blame and hatred. Thus within some mainstream representations of Arabs and Muslims, there has been a shift from celebrating the murder of Arab terrorist characters to sympathizing with the plight of Arab Americans after 9/11.

This chapter examines a selection of TV dramas that represent the plight of Arab and Muslim Americans post-9/11. The central questions I pose are: How are Arab and Muslim Americans represented in TV dramas since 9/11? How are race, religion, citizenship, and nationalism configured in these representations? What kinds of explanations are offered about the current historical moment and alleged crisis in national security? What stories are being narrated to the U.S. public about Arab/Muslim Americans through the media? What is the relationship between media viewership and citizenship? I argue that the TV dramas examined here, even when seeking to resist hegemonic racist configurations of the monolithic Arab Muslim terrorist, participate in reworking U.S. sovereignty through narrating ambivalence about racism in the case of Arab and Muslim Americans. I conclude by considering how media viewership is a form of virtual citizenship through which viewer-citizens are interpellated into national discourses through the virtual courtroom in TV dramas.

AMBIVALENT RACISM, MOMENTARY MULTICULTURALISM,
AND ARAB/MUSLIM RACIALIZATION

According to Giorgio Agamben, ambivalence is central to modern democratic sovereign power. By ambivalence, Agamben means regarding the same act as concurrently unjustifiable and necessary. Such a breach in logic comes to be reasoned through "exceptional" moments of crisis, which the state uses to call for a suspension of established codes and procedures to legitimize government abuses of power. Agamben claims that what characterizes modern democratic Western politics is that the exceptions have become the rule. The state of exception, he writes, becomes "the hidden foundation on which the entire political system rest[s]" (Agamben 1998, 9). Thus the United States is not necessarily in an exceptional state of crisis during this "war on terror," but rather operates through a perpetual "state of exception" to justify and enable exercising unilateral power, such as detaining, deporting, and denying due process to Arabs and Muslims, and waging wars in Afghanistan and Iraq.

By ambivalence in the case of Arab and Muslim Americans post-9/11, I am referring to an undecidedness about racism. Given that racism cannot be both good and bad and has been established as unjust over the past few decades since the civil rights movement, in order for this ambivalence to justify U.S. sovereign power, it would be necessary to reconfigure racism as bad in general but legitimate in the case of Arabs and Muslims after 9/11. News and talk shows often featured politicians and civil rights lawyers debating whether or not racial profiling is good or bad, right or wrong. Racism came to be articulated as wrong and indefensible and also reasoned as necessary for a short period of time (as if racialization and racism can be contained) because the United States is in an exceptional state of national security.

In order for this illogical ambivalence to acquire weight, race and racism had to be reconfigured after 9/11. This adjustment was accomplished through momentary diversity and simultaneous racialization and criminalization of Arabs and Islam. By momentary diversity, I am referring to a process by which the American citizen came to be ideologically redefined as diverse instead of white and united in the "war on terror," defined in opposition to Arabs and Islam, signified as terrorist and anti-American. Thus non-Arab, non-Muslim racialized groups became temporarily incorporated into the notion of American identity, while Arabs and Muslims were racialized as terrorist threats to the nation. By racialization, I am referring to the process of assigning derogatory meaning to particular bodies distinguished by ethnicity, nationality, biology, or geography, as well as legitimizing discourses, in this case the process by which the categories "Arab" and "terrorist" came to be conflated, consolidated, and interchangeable. Thus racism toward Arabs and Muslims is configured as legitimate and racism toward other groups illegitimate. Rachad Antonius (2002) refers to this process of justifying racism specifically towards Arabs and Muslims as producing "respectable racism." By defining racism toward Arabs and Muslims as legitimate or respectable, even necessary, not only are individual acts such as hate crimes or employment discrimination condoned, but government practices of detaining and deporting Arabs and Muslims without due process are enabled. By racializing Arabs and Islam, producing momentary diversity as the paradigm of U.S. citizenry, and articulating ambivalent racism, the Constitution and principles of democracy come to be suspended based on the logic of the state of exception, and thus, according to Agambem (1998), furthers U.S. imperial power.

The TV dramas examined in this chapter on the surface appear to contest the dominant positioning of Arabs as terrorists, Islam as a violent extremist ideology, and Arabs and Islam as antithetical to U.S. citizenship and the U.S. nation. These TV programs are regarded as "liberal" or socially conscious as they take the stance that racism toward Arab and Muslim Americans post-9/11 is wrong, while other TV dramas do not (e.g., many TV dramas, such as *Threat Matrix,* *JAG, The Agency,* narrate that U.S. national security is at risk because of Arab Muslims). Nonetheless, despite somewhat sympathetic portrayals of Arab and Muslim Americans, they narrate the logic of ambivalence—that racism is wrong but essential—and thus participate in serving the U.S. government narratives.

I argue that, ultimately, discourses of the nation in crisis not only trump the Arab American plight, but also inadvertently support U.S. government initiatives in the "war on terror." I further claim that these prime-time stories seek to bring viewers into various national debates to participate in a form of virtual citizenship and serve as a racial project to redefine U.S. borders, U.S. citizens, and the position of Arabs and Muslims vis-à-vis the U.S. nation. This chapter specifically examines two episodes from the prime-time dramatic series *The Practice.*[5]

---

5. This study is part of a larger project that examines representations of Arab and Muslim Americans in the mainstream U.S. media after 9/11, including TV dramas, news reporting, and nonprofit advertising.

TV DRAMAS AS RACIAL PROJECTS

The programs examined are a sampling of the prime-time TV drama genre. Prime-time television, the 8–11 P.M. time slot, is the most sought-after time slot for television program producers because it lends itself to the largest viewing audience, targeting people at home after a standard nine-to-five workday. Nielsen ratings indicate that eighteen to thirty million viewers tune in to any given program during these prime-time hours on a major television network station (ABC, CBS, NBC, FOX). The majority of programs in this time slot are comedies (sitcoms), "reality" television programs, and dramas. Of these three prime-time genres, dramatic series are considered to be "quality television" because most address serious and realistic issues reflecting news stories.[6] They also tend to represent institutions of authority: a government agency, the police, or the legal system. *The Practice* is about the legal system. Broadcast on ABC from 1997 to 2004, it tells the story of lawyers and their cases and culminates with courtroom verdicts. It is part of a genre that includes *Law and Order, NYPD Blue,* and others that represent institutions of authority, and individuals seeking to pursue justice while confronting ethical and moral dilemmas. After 9/11, such prime-time dramas became forums to articulate and work through the events of 9/11.

TV dramas are critical sites for post-9/11 racial projects. Omi and Winant define a racial project as "simultaneously an interpretation, representation, or explanation of racial dynamics, and an effort to reorganize and redistribute resources along particular racial lines" (1994, 56). TV dramas interpret, represent, and explain the current racial dynamics in which Arabs, Arab Americans, Muslims, and Muslim Americans have come to be signified as terrorists, anti-American, and a threat to the United States and its citizens. TV dramas operate alongside a variety of other post-9/11 racial projects, such as the PATRIOT Act and government measures to detain, deport, and monitor Arabs, Arab Americans, Muslims, and Muslim Americans, that mark Arab bodies as dangerous and undeserving of citizenship rights. In other words, racialization is not only promoted on the state

---

6. While reality television programs have gained a large prime-time audience, they do not carry the same reputation for quality as dramas that seek to reflect and engage with real-life issues facing individuals and the nation. Similarly, while some sitcoms do take on issues such as racism (most notably *The George Lopez Show* and *Whoopie*), most focus on interpersonal relationships.

level, but operates through a complex web that includes media discourses, institutional measures, and individual citizenship acts (e.g., hate crimes).[7] TV dramas sometimes collaborate and at other times resist collaborating with government discourses. Either way, they explain these racial projects and the controversies surrounding them to the public and offer viewers subject or citizenship positions in relation to such national debates.

As TV dramas narrate, explain, and debate government-initiated racial projects, they also operate as racial projects themselves. Through performing ideological work, rationalizing or contesting government measures that redistribute resources along racial lines (such as who gets a lawyer, who is eligible for citizenship, who gets a visa, a job, etc.), and articulating momentary diversity, they participate in defining and redefining racial dynamics (which bodies are threatening, deviant, suspect, criminal, terrorist, and un-American and therefore merit and justify denying rights). The connection between media and government is particularly palpable when examining these TV dramas that not only respond to and represent post-9/11 national debates, but also represent government agencies such as the police and court system. The story lines within the programs examined revolve around these institutions and therefore, I later argue, have a particular significance in positioning the audience as a virtual citizen. While other programs might encourage viewers to imagine themselves in relation to fashion or sexuality trends (MTV), or family (sitcoms), for example, these prime-time TV dramas encourage viewers to think about national issues and debates and their own relative position as citizens.

DEBATING ARAB AMERICAN CIVIL RIGHTS
IN THE VIRTUAL COURTROOM

The Practice takes viewers into the courtroom and after 9/11 into debates about the rights of Arab and Muslim Americans. On an episode entitled "Bad to Worse" (initially aired on December 1, 2002, and rebroadcast several times since), an airline seeks to bar Arabs from being passengers on their airplanes in the name of safety and security after 9/11. An Arab American man is suing the airline for discrimination, and the preliminary case goes to court. It is clear that the Arab American man, who is a university professor, is innocent and the unfair target

---

7. See Volpp (2003).

of discrimination, but the case is heard to determine whether or not the racial profiling of Arabs and Muslims after 9/11 can be reasoned to be justifiable. Ms. Dole, a young white woman lawyer, is hired to defend the airline, whose slogan is "We Don't Fly Arabs," and it seeks to advertise and publicize itself as "the most security conscious airline in the new world." Ms. Dole is conflicted about defending the airline, aware of the racism and injustice inherent in the case, but takes it on to further her career. A debate ensues in the courtroom over whether racial profiling is justified and whether certain biases can be considered reasonable or whether there are legitimate forms of racism.

This particular episode and others correlate with actual events, as they represent specific occurrences. After 9/11, for example, there were instances of non-Arab passengers on airlines complaining about and refusing to fly with Arabs, Muslims, and South Asians who were mistaken for Arab, leading to their removal from flights. A Muslim man was escorted off his America West flight in New Jersey because other passengers were uncomfortable with his presence and therefore the pilot had *the right* to exclude him.[8] An Arab American Secret Service agent on his way from Washington D.C. to President Bush's ranch in Texas was barred from an American Airlines flight because the pilot found him to be suspicious.[9] Dozens of Arab, Muslim, and South Asian Americans filed suits for being barred from flying, and many submitted complaints for the extra searches, extra security, and racial profiling. In Lincoln, Nebraska, a Muslim woman was asked to remove her *hijab* in public before boarding an American Airlines flight.[10] Meanwhile, news programs featured debates on whether or not it was just to profile Arab and Muslim Americans racially to ensure safety. Republican writer Ann Coulter, best known for her comment that the United States should invade Muslim countries, "kill their leaders and convert them to Christianity,"[11] furthered the national debate on racial profiling when she publicly expressed the opinion that airlines ought to advertise the number of civil

8. See the Council on American-Islamic Relations' 2002 Civil Rights Report at http://www
.cair-net.org/civilrights2002/.

9. "Inquiry into Secret Service Agent Barred from Flight." CNN.com. http://www.cnn
.com/2001/US/12/28/rec.agent.airline.

10. Council on American-Islamic Relations' 2002 Civil Rights Report. http://www.cair-net
.org/civilrights2002/.

11. See http://www.anncoulter.com (Sept. 13, 2001).

rights lawsuits filed against them by Arabs in order to boost business. When asked how Arabs should fly if discriminated against, she replied that they should use flying carpets.[12] Through the "Bad to Worse" episode of *The Practice,* the viewing audience participates in this debate as jurors in a virtual courtroom.

According to the debate within the virtual courtroom of *The Practice* about discrimination against Arab Americans, citizens have one of two options: political correctness or safety. The choice becomes clear, as there are grave consequences. If political correctness is chosen to avoid being racist, then safety is forfeited. As for electing safety over discrimination, not all racisms are alike in keeping with how the debate is framed: some are reasonable, others are not. Racism is reduced to political correctness and political correctness reduced to useless pleasant etiquette. Here is where we see the construction of the discourse of exceptionalism: racism is wrong except in certain cases and only during *exceptional* times of crisis. The CEO of Seaboard Airlines, the fictional airline represented in the episode, claims it would not be reasonable to discriminate against African Americans, but it would be and is reasonable to discriminate against Arabs, Arab Americans, Muslims, and Muslim Americans. As is often the case, "Arab," "Arab American," "Muslim," and "Muslim American" are conflated and used interchangeably as if they denote the same identity.[13] The attorney for the Arab American client, Mr. Furst, and the airline CEO debate the issue of political correctness versus safety in court:

> *Mr. Furst:* What if research showed that blacks were more likely to commit mayhem on a plane?

12. "An Appalling Magic," The Guardian Unlimited, May 17, 2003. http://www.guardian.co.uk/usa/story/0,12271,957670,00.html.

13. Omi and Winant have referred to this type of conflation as the consolidation of oppositional consciousness and attribute the erasure of difference and diversity within communities to being a common phenomenon of racism (1994, 66). To clarify, "Arab" refers to persons from a collective of countries in North Africa and West Asia. There are approximately 300 million Arabs in the Middle East. "Arab American" refers to persons who are citizens or permanent residents of the United States and who trace their ancestry to North Africa or West Asia. There are approximately 3 million Arab Americans in the United States. "Muslim" refers to persons who practice the religion of Islam. It is estimated that there are 1.2 billion Muslims worldwide. "Muslim American" refers to persons who practice the religion of Islam and who are citizens or permanent residents of the United States; estimates are at 7 million.

Airline CEO: I would never exclude against blacks because I would consider that bias to be unreasonable. This prejudice isn't.

Mr. Furst: There are 1.6 billion Muslims in the world. So you're discriminating against all of them because of the actions of 19? That's reasonable?

Airline CEO: Start your own company and run it the way you'd like. I should get the same courtesy.

Mr. Furst: We don't give people the right to be a bigot in this country.

Airline CEO: How about the right to be safe?

The CEO's assumption is that Arabs and Muslims are a threat to flight security and in order to make passengers safe, airlines should have "the right" to bar Arabs from their flights. Moreover, as a CEO, he has "the right" to run his company as he desires. What "rights" will be protected? Do people have the "right" to be racist? The "right" to run their business as they wish? The "right" to be safe? Do Arab Americans have citizenship "rights"? According to the terms of this debate, safety trumps all other rights during times of crisis. Safety requires racism, and eliminating racism compromises safety. Ultimately, it is more important to be safe than it is not to discriminate; times are too urgent to be concerned with being politically correct. Furthermore, other racialized groups, in this case African Americans, are momentarily incorporated into the dominant conceptualization of American national identity during this "crisis" in order to consolidate the new racialized enemy. The inclusion of African Americans is necessary to the logic of exceptionalism. If we can simultaneously be racist against all racialized groups, then these are no longer exceptional times. It becomes necessary to consolidate groups that have been historically discriminated against into a coherent whole (U.S. citizens of all backgrounds united against the war on terror) in order for the logic of ambivalence within the argument to hold: that racism is both wrong and necessary against Arabs and Muslims at this time. Thus, momentary multiculturalism is used to racialize Arabs and Muslims and to create respectable or legitimate forms of racism. This debate surrounding the right to be racist and the right to be safe is elaborated in the closing arguments through defining the U.S. nation in crisis.

Mr. Furst and Ms. Dole each give heartfelt closing arguments invoking their children for additional emotional gravity. Mr. Furst says that his nine-year-old daughter recently told him that she was surprised to learn that African Americans used to be required by law to sit at the back of the bus, and he appeals to the court not to repeat a similar mistake with Arab Americans. Ms. Dole states that she cries for her son who is growing up in a world where planes are used as bombs, and therefore in order to create safety, it is unfortunately necessary to racially profile Arabs and Muslims.

The closing arguments center on defining the U.S. nation and its borders. Mr. Furst concedes that it is in fact reasonable to be suspicious of "Muslims" ("They blew up the World Trade Center for God's sake!"), but encourages people to put those feelings aside and to consider larger and more important issues, namely "our civil rights," "our freedom," and how we define this country. In so doing, he sets up an "us"/"them" dichotomy: "they" blew up the World Trade Center, but "we" need to think about who "we" are as a people and whether or not "we" stand for equal rights; and although "they" violated "us," "we" cannot in turn violate "our" freedom. On the one hand, he defends his client's rights but at the same time he fails to acknowledge that his client is American, too, and also has the right to be safe. Importantly, Mr. Furst draws a parallel between barring Arabs from flying on airplanes and segregating African Americans from the white population to sit at the back of the bus. Through drawing this historical and comparative parallel, viewers are asked if perhaps presumed-reasonable racisms come to haunt "us" later. Do "we" agree that having blacks sit at the back of the bus is regrettable and shameful, and do "we" want to repeat this history by barring Arabs/Arab Americans from airplanes? He asks, haven't "we" learned the importance of judging people by their character and not by the color of their skin? Mr. Furst makes an important case against repeating a racist past and for defining the nation according to moral principles. His case, however, rests on acknowledging the public's right to be racist. Although he advocates not to act upon feelings of violation, Arab bodies are reinscribed as outside of American citizenship through appealing to "real" Americans not to be racist because greater moral principles are at stake.

In contrast, Ms. Dole argues that American citizens are entitled to security, and though racial profiling is "a terrible thing . . . it has become necessary." She states that although people want justice and revenge, what is most important is safety—and the desire for safety is not "paranoia" or unreasonable because the government tells us every day that we are still at risk. Not only is the courtroom, a site of national authority, represented, but government authority is also asserted when viewers are confronted with the discourse from the daily news about the crisis in national security. She continues that "we" are faced with an enemy and that enemy has clear features: they are Arab. Contributing to a broader histori-cal mythology of the United States as a land of open borders, and neglecting a history of racist immigration restrictions, Dole says that America used to be a land with open borders, a place for any immigrant to fulfill the American dream, but that it is no longer possible so long as planes can be used as weapons. While Mr. Furst seeks to define the nation according to principles of freedom, civil rights, and equality, Ms. Dole instead shifts the discourse to defining the nation's borders: the borders should be closed and Arab Americans should be profiled in order to make U.S. citizens safe. Ms. Dole defines a nation in crisis and uses the very language from the Bill of Rights ("we the people") to argue for the suspension of its application in specific racialized configurations—vis-à-vis Arab and Muslim Americans.

The main question that is posed by this program is: Can we as a nation justify discriminating against Arabs, Arab Americans, Muslims, and Muslim Americans when we have been taught that discrimination is wrong? The answer, according to *The Practice*, comes in the form of the judge's verdict in which he states that he finds it "almost unimaginable" that whether or not it is legally per-missible to discriminate based on ethnicity is even being debated in court. He addresses Mr. Furst and Ms. Dole's closing arguments. To Mr. Furst, he says that he is being asked to waive legal and moral principles in the face of potentially boundless terrorism. To Ms. Dole, he says that he too loves being an American and became a judge to protect the freedoms provided by the Constitution. He concludes his verdict in the following way:

> The reality is that we make exceptions to our constitutional rights all the time. . . . none of them is absolute. The legal test for doing something so pa-tently unconstitutional is basically: you better have a damn good reason. There has been one other long-standing reality in this country: If not safe, one can never be free. With great personal disgust, I am denying the plaintiff's motion for a TRO.

Although this episode seeks to demonstrate sympathy for Arab and Muslim Americans after 9/11 and repeatedly states that discrimination is unjust, rep-resenting what is considered to be a "liberal," "progressive," or "left" position, the ultimate message is that these times are unlike others and therefore normal rules do not apply. The judge recalls an article that he read in the *New York Times* written by Thomas L. Friedman in which he described the events of 9/11 as "beyond unimaginable." The writings of Friedman are used to justify an assault on Arab American civil liberties. Friedman, Foreign Affairs columnist for the *New York Times* and author of numerous books based on his many years of reporting in the Middle East, has gained mainstream status with his interpretations of 9/11 and other crises. He has won numerous Pulitzer Prizes for his reporting on the Sabra and Shatila massacre, the first Palestinian Intifada, and 9/11. He is considered a "liberal," however, he supported the U.S. invasion of Iraq in 2003 and his post-9/11 writings included encouraging the government to create a blacklist of those who critique the U.S. government for contributing to terrorism as opposed to counterterrorism. Friedman wrote in one of his *New York Times* columns that those who point to imperialism, Zionism, and colonialism as causes for terrorism are hatemongers who are in league with the terrorists (Friedman 2005). It is quite fitting that the mainstream, presumably liberal, writings of Friedman are used in the mainstream, presumably liberal story line of *The Practice* to articulate that the Constitution can be violated if there is a good reason. And, alas, there is a good reason, thus practicing discrimination against Arab and Muslim Americans is necessary and justifiable.

This is the formation of ambivalence Agamben identifies as necessary to the state of exception and sovereign rule. Ambivalence lies in defining racism as simultaneously wrong and necessary. Arab and Muslim Americans are unfairly victimized, but the real unfair victim in all of this is the U.S. nation and its citizens, who fear for their safety. By the show stating that what happened on 9/11 was unimaginable, the United States assumes a position of innocence, and the audience is not encouraged to imagine another perspective. The judge's words, "If not safe, one can never be free" evokes the president's rhetoric of freedom—"they hate us because we are free," and thus "we must discriminate in order to be free." Ultimately, despite representative sympathy, which comes in the form of deep regret and remorse surrounding the verdict, racism is legitimized: sacrifices to Arab and Muslim American civil rights must be made in the interim. This is not a verdict to celebrate: Dole is not proud; the judge is filled with disgust; and the Arab American man holds his wife as she cries. Within this apologetic moment, hatred toward Arabs is rendered "understandable," but the roots of terrorism are "beyond our imaginations."

This plight is indeed represented: it is established that Arab Americans are the unfair targets of discrimination after 9/11. Yet sympathy for the Arab

American in the episode is compromised through discourses that hold more weight: namely, the right to be racist and national security threats. Discriminating against Arab Americans is reasonable at this time because, first, "they" committed a terrorist act, and, second, the government tells us everyday that we are still at risk of another terrorist attack. What comes to be represented is less the "plight" of the Arab Muslim after 9/11 and more the staging of the national debate on racial profiling and the national anxiety about flying with Arabs and Muslims. The Arab American man remains silent and unable to represent himself to the audience, sitting in the background not uttering one word, while his lawyer, a white man, speaks for him. Thus, the Arab American man remains a foreigner in the minds of American viewers. Furthermore, what America is "supposed to be" is debated in relation to Arab and Muslim Americans. Dole's closing remarks make a larger statement about how America has changed. She suggests that the United States should no longer be open to immigrants because "they" ruin America by making "us" unsafe. Through arguing for security, not only is racial profiling justified, but so are closed borders and new INS measures to detain and deport Arabs and Muslims.

Apparent here is the important function of racialization in creating the moment of exception so necessary to the abuse of government power. First, the nation in crisis needs to be established. Given the events of September 11, it is not difficult to make this point: we do not want terrorists, who are likely to be Arab and Muslim and who hate our freedom, to attack and kill again. Second, the necessity of exceptionalism needs to be established. In order to do that, a norm of democracy and freedom for all peoples regardless of race needs to be affirmed. Thus, it can be stated that it was wrong to discriminate against African Americans and gestures are made to bring disenfranchised racialized groups temporarily into the dominant designation of "American." Then, Arabs and Muslims need to undergo a process of racialization in which their potential threat to the nation becomes intertwined with their ethnic/racial background and religious beliefs. And lastly, it can be stated that racism is wrong but compulsory against this potentially threatening population at this particular exceptional time of crisis. Thus the logic is in place for the U.S. government to exercise power without constraint and use national crisis to justify acting outside of democratic legal conventions: implement the USA PATRIOT Act, invade Iraq, wage war in Afghanistan, hold prisoners in Guantanamo without legal recourse, and initiate mass deportations of Arabs and Muslims from the

United States. This very logic comes to be articulated in TV dramas through portraying a sympathetic Arab American character, and while it seems that the audience might be encouraged to sympathize with the Arab American's post-9/11 plight, as opposed to celebrating the murder of Arab terrorists, viewers are presented with the very logic that supports U.S. imperial projects at home and abroad.

"IN WAR, LAW IS SILENT"

Another episode of *The Practice,* entitled "Inter Arma Silent Leges"[14] (initially aired December 9, 2001), which translates from the Latin to "in war, law is silent," again represents the plight of Arab/Muslim Americans after 9/11. Similar to the episode examined above, it also appears to sympathize with Arab Americans while simultaneously narrating the U.S. nation in crisis, the logic of exceptionalism and ambivalence, the regretful need for security over liberty, and thus the logic to support government abuses of power. The story begins with the information that the U.S. government is unfairly detaining an Arab American man. As the plot develops, viewers learn that he has refused to speak to his wife and children and is apologetic to them for what he has done. What he has done remains a mystery to viewers, who are left to assume that he was involved with terrorism. It is ultimately revealed that the man is innocent and so intent on proving his loyalty to the United States that he has voluntarily given up his rights and agreed to be held prisoner in order to assist with the government's terrorism investigation.

Ms. Washington, an African American woman attorney, is hired by Dr. Ford, a white woman, to find and represent her husband, Bill Ford, the Arab American man being detained by the government. She admits that her husband's "real name" is Bill Habib but they both use her maiden name, "Ford," signaling that white names are "safer" or more acceptable than Arab ones. Dr. Ford has been

---

14. "Inter Arma Silent Leges" is not in the Constitution, but it has become common wartime ideology for the courts to become deferential. The phrase came from Cicero's writings in B.C. Rome and has appeared time and again in U.S. legal documents during times of war. For example in the *Korematsu v. United States* case (323 U.S. 214, 219–20, 1994): "We uphold the exclusion order [of Japanese Americans from the West Coast] . . . hardships are part of war, and war is an aggregation of hardship."

unable to get any information on her husband, and Ms. Washington quickly learns that the information is classified, requiring security clearance and that Mr. Habib is being detained without representation, which violates his rights as a U.S. citizen. Ms. Washington appears before a judge in court to argue against an FBI representative that she has a right to see her client. When she asks the FBI representative what Mr. Habib is being charged with, she is informed that he is not being charged with anything, but is being held as a material witness to something classified by the Foreign Intelligence Surveillance Act. The judge orders that Mr. Habib be permitted to see his lawyer and wife, stating that he will protect what is left of the Constitution. The FBI representative begins to challenge the judge's orders, but the judge warns him not to test his authority. The notion that courts have reduced power during times of war is set forth here, but the judge seeks to resist the complete suspension of the Constitution and uses his authority to allow Ms. Washington to see her client, Mr. Habib.

In addition to raising the issue of suspending the Constitution during war, this episode focuses on the government's practice of detention and their "voluntary interview program," both initiated after 9/11. It questions the possible injustice in detaining Arabs, Muslims, and South Asians and also the government's practice of not releasing information about the detainees. After 9/11, the Justice Department initiated a "voluntary interview program" through which they sought to interview thousands of Arab and Muslim immigrant men between the ages of eighteen and thirty-three, also referred to as those who "fit the criteria of people who might have information regarding terrorism."[15] The point of the "voluntary interview program" was to obtain assistance on the "war on terror." Many Arab and Muslim Americans feared that if they did not comply with being "voluntarily" interviewed, it would be perceived as unpatriotic and might jeopardize their citizenship and lead to detention or deportation. Also after 9/11, over a thousand Arabs, Muslims, and South Asians were rounded up and detained. The Justice Department refused to release information on the people detained—how many, their names, or what they were charged with.[16]

15. "Ashcroft Announces 'Voluntary Interviews' with 3,000 U.S. Visitors." IslamOnline.net . http://www.islamonline.net/english/news/2002-03/21/article04.shtml.

16. "Hundreds of Arabs Still Detained." Mar. 13, 2002. CBS News. http://www.cbsnews .com/stories/2002/03/13/terror/main503649.shtml.

As Leti Volpp has written, "while the government refused to release the most basic information about these individuals—their names, where they were held, and the immigration or criminal charges filed against them—the public did know that the vast majority of those detained appeared to be Middle Eastern, Muslim, or South Asian. We knew, too, that the majority were identified to the government through suspicions and tips based solely on perceptions of their racial, religious, or ethnic identity" (2003, 148). Volpp's point is that the information released and concealed functioned to appease part of the population that could find comfort in the knowledge that the government was being proactive in fighting terrorism—knowledge and comfort based on the racialization of Arabs, Muslims, and South Asians. Detaining these particular racialized bodies comforted some and alarmed proponents of civil rights who demanded information and due process. In this episode of *The Practice,* the government's practice of detention and voluntary interviews of Arabs and Muslims is questioned. The judge acknowledges that the Constitution is put at risk by keeping Mr. Habib from speaking to his wife and children and demands that he be brought to the courtroom for his full citizenship rights.

Mr. Habib is first brought to the court conference room before being led into the courtroom. He is shackled, and his wife is instructed by a government official not to speak to him in case she is perceived to be giving him code. We learn that Mr. Habib has "voluntarily" turned himself in as an act of patriotism. Ms. Washington introduces herself to Mr. Habib as his lawyer and informs him that he is about to have a hearing. Mr. Habib objects: he did not request a lawyer or a hearing (his wife had hired her). Mr. Habib worries about his family and their safety. His wife assures him that they are fine. Once in the courtroom for the hearing, Mr. Habib takes the stand:

> *Ms. Washington:* Do you know why you're in custody?
> *Mr. Habib:* The government believes I may have information about someone. . . . I don't really know. He didn't do anything, but he may have known some people with ties to others who are wanted for questioning.
> *Ms. Washington:* What information? What do they think you know?
> *FBI Representative:* Objection.
> *Judge:* Sustained. You can't know that Ms. Washington.
> *Ms. Washington:* You haven't talked to your family in weeks. Why did they keep you from speaking to your family?
> *Mr. Habib:* They didn't. I chose not to call my family.

Ms. Washington: Why?

Mr. Habib: I was told anyone I spoke with would be subject to investigation. I do not want to bring my family into this. My wife and children were born here. They have no connection to any Arab, other than me.

Ms. Washington: Have you been interviewed?

Mr. Habib: Many times.

Ms. Washington: Did you know you had the right to have an attorney present?

Mr. Habib: I waived my rights.

Ms. Washington: You waived them? Voluntarily?

Mr. Habib: I talked to them on my own. They didn't force me. Not in any way.

Ms. Washington: Did they make you afraid?

Mr. Habib: Am I fearful, I guess I would say yes. But I have made all my decisions voluntarily.

Ms. Washington again questions Mr. Habib about his decision not to speak to his family, and he reiterates that he did not want to risk involving them in any way. The judge asks why Mr. Habib needs to be held in custody when he is clearly cooperating. The FBI representative says that Mr. Habib is helping through wiretaps and overseas contacts and that it is necessary to hold him as they are constantly learning new information.

FBI Representative: We can't risk losing him. Look. We're trying to get the information we need to stop the potential murder of thousands of Americans. That means depriving some Americans of their civil rights. I don't like it, but that's how it is.

Ms. Washington: You're imprisoning an innocent man.

Mr. Habib: Ms. Washington, enough. If my country thinks I should be here, I will stay here.

Ms. Washington: Your country?

Mr. Habib: Yes, I am an American. I am serving my country.

Ms. Washington, in disbelief, asks Mr. Habib if he has been tortured or mistreated. The judge asks him whether or not he objects to being held further. Mr. Habib clearly states that he has not been mistreated and that he is being held voluntarily. The judge concludes that Mr. Habib will remain in custody because "In war, law is silent."

Much like in the episode discussed above, viewers are presented with the plight of Arab/Muslim Americans after 9/11. In the prior episode, an Arab American man is barred from flying, and in this case, an Arab American man is detained by the government. Both men are innocent, but guilty by association. In this case, Bill Habib is helping the government because he might know someone who knows something about someone involved in terrorism. Mr. Habib accepts that he is guilty by association. He proclaims that he is American and that he wants to protect his family from interrogation because they are truly innocent, having no ties to any Arabs (all of whom are presumed terrorist suspects) except for him. Meanwhile, he is of Arab descent, has ties to the Arab world, and therefore accepts a degree of guilt and responsibility. A line is drawn between innocent Americans, Arabs involved with terrorism, and helpful Arab Americans who can assist the U.S. government and prove their loyalty and patriotism. Although he is being unfairly detained with no rights or representation, it is justifiable to hold him and deprive his family of him and any information on him because it is a matter of national security. A similar message is repeated from the aforementioned episode: it is justifiable to suspend civil rights for the greater good and safety of the American citizenry because it is a time of crisis. Although unfair, it is both "voluntary" and necessary.

Accusations that the U.S. government is treating detainees unfairly are countered with Mr. Habib's insistence that he is not being held against his will. The fact that he has not contacted his family because he wants to protect them demonstrates that the U.S. government is being thorough in their questioning of all Arabs/Arab Americans and anyone associated with Arabs/Arab Americans in order to prevent another attack during this "war on terror." Nonetheless, "voluntarism" operates to excuse the government from abusing their power. If Mr. Habib and presumably other Arab, Muslim, and South Asian Americans detainees agree to being held, and voluntarily refuse legal representation, it excuses the government from wrongdoing and from abusing its power. If voluntary, then citizen-patriots are collaborating with the government in the "war on terror." Suspending civil rights comes to be rescripted: it is not a sovereign, totalitarian, or dictatorial endeavor, but a cooperative and well-intentioned one. Even if it is unfair to be in prison while assisting the government, not only is it an exceptional time of crisis and therefore necessary and justifiable now as opposed to during normal times, but it is voluntary: no one is being explicitly forced by the government.

Mr. Habib is very clear that he has made his own choices. Nonetheless, the question remains: what if he made different choices? What if he had chosen to have a lawyer, to call his family, to be released? He states that such choices come with consequences and thus he chose the options with fewer consequences. Within the terms of this discourse of crisis and exceptionalism, had Mr. Habib or the many men he represents refused, he would be a traitor-terrorist. As Judith Butler has written regarding September 11:

> Dissent is quelled, in part, through threatening the speaking subject with an uninhabitable identification. Because it would be heinous to identify as trea-sonous, as a collaborator, one fails to speak, or one speaks in throttled ways, in order to sidestep the terrorizing identification that threatens to take hold. This strategy of quelling dissent and limiting the reach of critical debate happens not only through a series of shaming tactics which have a certain psychological terrorization as their effect, but they work as well by producing what will and will not count as a viable speaking subject and a reasonable opinion within the public domain. (2004, xix)

If Mr. Habib had chosen a different path, not only would his family undergo in-vestigation, but also he would inhabit the position of traitor. During times of war, the terms are binary and clear: good or evil, "with us or against us." This strategy of quelling dissent and limiting debate that Butler describes also operates through producing exceptionalism as an acceptable logic and thus justifies the suspension of Arab, Arab American, Muslim, and Muslim American civil rights. Thus the stories that the media tells and viewers receive are also restricted by the dominant discourse of national security. Critical debates, such as story lines that render ter-rorist acts as within our imaginations and comprehension, do not surface because such discourses are not permissible within the dominant available rhetorical spaces. For example, when the country music trio The Dixie Chicks voiced their disapproval of the U.S. war on Iraq during a concert in London, country music stations in the United States refused to play their albums, branding them as unpa-triotic.[17] Similarly, when Linda Ronstadt, during a concert in Las Vegas, dedicated a song to filmmaker Michael Moore in honor of his controversial film *Fahrenheit*

---

17. "Dixie Chicks Pulled from Air after Bashing Bush." Mar. 14, 2002. http://www.cnn.com/2003/SHOWBIZ/Music/03/14/dixie.chicks.reut/.

9/11, which criticizes the Bush administration's response to 9/11, hundreds of fans booed, left the theater immediately, and defaced posters of her.[18] If these speaking subjects become attacked, shamed, and terrorized in public spaces, what can pass through the mainstream media is also discursively restricted.

After 9/11, there were pressing debates over the treatment of Arab and Muslim Americans, and particularly over "voluntary interviews," detentions, deportations, and civil rights afforded to Arabs and Muslims—both American and not. The "Inter Arma Silent Leges" episode ends on the note that we are back to the times of interning people and unfairly suspecting people because of their racial/ethnic/religious identity. We have not learned from our mistakes and are engaged in repeating history—committing injustice and practicing racism. Ms. Dole, the defense attorney from the previous episode, interjects that the public is afraid and thus it is reasonable *though* unjust. Like the other episode of *The Practice,* this one, too, seeks to draw a parallel to injustices committed toward other racialized groups—in this case Japanese Americans during World War II. Japanese internment represents another exceptional time of crisis in which overt discrimination came to be seen as legitimate and necessary. A case is presented against the detention of Arabs and the violation of civil rights in light of a history of racism repeating itself. Regardless, the nation is constructed as being at risk and Arabs as threats to the nation, therefore such arguments for civil rights cannot be sustained when the nation is in crisis. Thus, like the aforementioned episode, this one also ends on a morose and apologetic note despite representing Arab Americans sympathetically through their post-9/11 plight: there is nothing to celebrate about this moment, but in crisis, injustice is justifiable and "in war, law is silent." Detention, discrimination, and racism are both wrong *and* essential. This ambivalence, justified through the politics of fear and rule of exception, enables the U.S. government to exercise sovereign power both within and outside its borders. This logic, articulated through TV dramas, is the same logic articulated by the U.S. government to the citizens about the current state of national crisis.

NATIONAL CRISIS AND VIRTUAL CITIZENSHIP

Representations of Arabs and Muslims have indeed shifted since 9/11. While representations of them as terrorists persist, some writers and producers of TV

18. http://www.abc.net.au/news/newsitems/200407/s1158278.htm.

dramas have sought to make a difference through representing the plight of Arab and Muslim Americans post-9/11 to evoke sympathy from the viewing public. While such efforts should be commended, they need to be examined more closely to reveal whether they succeed in making prime-time mainstream interventions or further the official nationalist discourse that disavows racist views on the one hand while supporting racist policies and practices on the other, signifying newer and more complex forms of racism. Stuart Hall has claimed that even liberal writers and producers of media with the best of intentions who seek to subvert racial hierarchies inadvertently participate in inferential racism. Hall defines inferential racism as "apparently naturalized representations of events and situations relating to race, whether 'factual' or 'fictional,' which have racist premises and propositions inscribed in them as a set of unquestioned assumptions" (2000, 273). The writers and producers of the programs examined here are seeking to make an intervention and have good intentions, but they inadvertently support the government's discourse on the state of affairs and reinscribe the notion that the nation is in a state of crisis and that Arabs are a threat to the nation by naturalizing the government's discourse that we are in an exceptional state of crisis that merits U.S. sovereign measures.

Audience sympathy is evoked for the plight of the Arab American after 9/11, but the right to be racist and suspicious of Arab and Muslim Americans is affirmed, and government practices to profile racially, detain, deport, and terrorize Arabs and Muslims are accepted. Although Arab Americans are represented as victims and guilty only by their association to Arabs (non-Americans), the government's discourse about the continued Arab and Muslim threat to national security is narrated, and viewers are interpellated as citizens virtually participating in these national debates.[19] Viewers virtually sit in the courtroom, hear the various perspectives, and receive more information than offered in newspapers or the news media. Viewers' fears and biases are privileged over the Arab and Muslim American plight, and consoled and affirmed as reasonable during unreasonable times.

Mass media is an essential means through which meaning is produced and exchanged between citizens of a nation. As Stuart Hall, Toby Miller, David Morley, and other theorists of the media have demonstrated, representations perform ideological work, that is, they do not simply reflect reality but actively

19. I borrow the term "interpellation" from Althusser (2001).

produce meaning that affects and shapes racial categories and national identity. TV dramas after 9/11 came to function as national narratives, as stories broadcast nationwide (and often even beyond the borders of the United States) with versions of what happened, why it happened, who is responsible, how it is being dealt with by the government, and how best to deal with it as citizens. News stories became the subjects of TV dramas and participated in a field of meaning about the place of Arabs and Muslims in the United States, and one site for the articulation of explanations, bringing the U.S. public into current debates about Arabs, Muslims, racial profiling, discrimination, and national security. TV dramas interpret, represent, and explain racial dynamics post-9/11 and in doing so, redefine U.S. borders, U.S. citizenship, and forms of patriotism. They offer a way to think about the current crisis and support the actions of the government.

Although how viewers will relate to and interpret these TV dramas is variable, the media is a powerful tool used to interpellate viewer-citizens into supporting the rule of exception—that is, into internalizing that the U.S. is a democratic government and that the suspension of due process, civil rights, and democratic principles is justifiable because of the exceptional state of crisis. The TV dramas examined here participate in the narrative that we are in a state of exception. They convey a message that U.S. residents are at risk and must give up some things now for the greater good later. The United States is figured as a good democratic country trying to spread peace in the world and therefore that the ends will justify the means. Perhaps it would be more accurate to state, as Agamben does, "means without ends."

The national discourse on Arab and Muslim threats to national security and the need to profile racially in order to attain safety can be considered a "technology" in the production of truth. Toby Miller defines a "technology" as a "popularly held logic" and truth as "an accepted fact" (1998, 4). True statements, according to Miller, are "contingent on the space, time, and language in which they are made and heard" (5). In other words, truth is produced through the ideological work performed by the media, such as prime-time television programs or government policies, and becomes part of our "common sense." Miller continues: "When these technologies congeal to forge loyalty to the sovereign state through custom or art, they do so through the cultural citizen" (4). The cultural citizen is interpellated into these logics and becomes a subject for their enactment. Truth is produced and attained not only at the juncture in which media representations and government hegemonic projects congeal and cooperate, but also more importantly through the interpellation of the viewer into citizenship. I argue that for some viewer-citizens, such interpellation takes place in the virtual courtroom. The stakes of the nation are defined in court—even virtual court: debates are enacted; racial projects are reasoned; ideological work to produce common sense is performed. As Miller has stated, "The audience participates in the most uniformly global (but national), collective (yet private), and individually time consuming practice of meaning making in the history of the world . . . the concept and occasion of being an audience provide a textual link between society and person. . . . So viewing television involves solitary interpretation as well as collective behavior" (24). In other words, it involves imagining the self as part of a greater collective, in this case citizen of the United States. Not only is race formed and reformed at different historical moments to define borders, citizens, and enemies, but the public is also "formed and reformed on a routine basis through technologies of truth—popular logics for establishing fact" (5).

According to Hartley, we are all "citizens of media"; in other words, "participation in public-decision making is primarily conducted through media" (1999, 157). He writes, "It seems to me that what has in fact been occurring over the fifty-odd years that television has become established as the world's number-one entertainment resource and leisure-time pursuit is that a new form of citizenship has overlain the older, existing forms" (158). This new form of citizenship is one in which viewers-citizens are part of democratainment, "The means by which popular participation in public issues is conducted in the mediasphere" (209). In other words, "Audiences are understood as 'citizens of media' in the sense that it is through the symbolic, virtualized and mediated context of watching television, listening to radio and reading print media that publics participate in the democratic process on a day to day basis" (206–7).

Above all, what is defined through these TV dramas representing the plight of the Arab Muslim American is a nation in danger. The emphasis on the enduring threat Arabs and Muslims pose to U.S. national security operates to support national racial projects. As McAlister has written, "the continuing sense of threat provides support for the power of the state, but it also provides the groundwork for securing 'the nation' as a cultural and social entity. The 'imagined community' of the nation finds continuing rearticulation in the rhetoric of danger" (2001, 6). The rhetoric of the nation in danger, through the news media and TV dramas, has become accepted as truth and common sense. Discourses on safety and risk are a form of governmentality. In this case, "crisis" is used to justify racist views and practices; to racialize Arabs, Arab Americans, Muslims, and Muslim Americans as threats to the nation; and hence to use them as the contemporary racialized enemy through which the nation defines its identity and legitimizes its abuse of power.

NINE

Arab Americans and Muslim Americans in the *New York Times,* Before and After 9/11

SUAD JOSEPH *and* BENJAMIN D'HARLINGUE,
with ALVIN KA HIN WONG

SINCE THE FALL OF THE SOVIET UNION, Arabs and Muslims in general and Arab American and Muslim American citizens by association and by direct action have become increasingly targeted for discriminatory policies and practices in the United States, fueled by the "war on terrorism" media frenzy. We live in dangerous times, the media and public authorities drum daily. No threat is more imminent than that of Islam, no site more at risk than the American homeland, and no enemy more fearful than the enemy within, we are told.

The media mantra of the urgent threat of Islam and of the Arabs and Muslims who transport it travels through numerous pathways. Of interest to this project is the manner in which respected print news media increasingly reflect and reproduce racialization of Arab Americans and Muslim Americans. This paper examines how the *New York Times (NYT)*, arguably the most influential U.S. newspaper and one of the most influential newspapers in the world, narrates Arab Americans and Muslim Americans in ways that result from and enable racial policing by associating them with terrorism and a demonized, globalized Islam. That the *NYT* is widely considered a "liberal" newspaper, known for advocacy of civil and human rights, makes it a critical site for examining the representation of Arab Americans and Muslim Americans in print news media.

Following September 11, 2001, contradictions in the ideals and practices of citizenship in the United States increasingly came to the fore, with Arab

Americans and Muslim Americans becoming the most visible site of these contradictions. Tensions in the constitution of the body politic were projected onto the U.S. citizenship of Arab Americans and Muslim Americans, as the war on terrorism took the appearance of a war on "Muslim terrorism." While the trope of the "violent Muslim" has a long history, rooted in imperialist and orientalist representations, it has appeared with greater force and persistence since 9/11.

Since the attacks, Arabs and Muslims have been frequently represented in the United States media as "other." The subtext of such depictions appears to be that one cannot be Arab or Muslim and American at the same time; that being both, one is neither and therefore not quite a citizen; that the hyphen between Arab or Muslim and American is not quite attached (Joseph 1999a). The print news media have increasingly represented Muslim Americans and Arab Americans as if they are not true members of the body politic, not quite part of the national community. The marginalization of Arab Americans and Muslim Americans prompted the Council on American-Islamic Relations to place numerous ads in the *NYT* in the aftermath of 9/11 with photographs of Muslims of all ethnicities and colors, declaring them to be "American."

We argue in this chapter that while the rhetorical maneuvers we discovered in the *NYT* are at times explicitly racial in their grammar, their organization of racial investments through other categories, such as religion, ethnicity, and nation, have the effect of racializing religion, ethnicity, and nation. Our understandings of race, racialization, and racism are informed by the work of Michael Omi, Howard Winant, and Etienne Balibar. In *Racial Formation,* Omi and Winant state:

> We define racial formation as the social historical process by which racial categories are created, inhabited, transformed, and destroyed. . . . First, we argue that racial formation is a process of historically situated projects in which human bodies and social structures are represented and organized. Next we link racial formation to the evolution of hegemony, the way in which society is organized and ruled. (Omi and Winant 1994, 55–56)

The concept of racial formation focuses attention on the constructed, shifting, and contingent character of race, racial identification, and ascriptions. Racial categories are continually reconstituted, materially, and discursively, through structure and representation. Race is made and remade through polyvalent circuits that organize meaning, power, and resources. For Omi and Winant, racial projects, the activities through which race and racialization function, operate at the intersection of cultural representation and socioeconomic structure and are the building blocks of racial formation. Conglomerations of racial projects, sets of racialized meanings, structures, identifications and disidentifications, can be understood as racial formations.[1]

We argue that the *NYT,* taken as a representational apparatus, has contributed significantly to the project of racializing Arab Americans and Muslim Americans. We do not mean to argue that the *NYT* dictates how its readers view race. Rather, it is one representational apparatus that contributes to racialization and takes on the effect of a racial project. It is situated within larger, constantly reconstituted arrays of racial projects and formations. In critically reading race in *NYT* articles, it is important to bear in mind that

> [t]he effort must be made to understand race as an unstable and "decentered" complex of social meanings constantly being transformed by political struggle. With this in mind, let us propose a definition: race is a concept which signifies and symbolizes social conflicts and interests by referring to different types of human bodies. (Omi and Winant 1994, 55)

In *NYT* articles, the social conflicts, meanings, and interests are staged and encoded through the language and imagery of racial embodiment.

We refine Omi and Winant's analysis to argue that it is not merely different types of human bodies that are signified. Omi and Winant do not consider the international character of racial formation. Because national categories are racialized in U.S. discourse, race may signify categories other than, but related to the order of, human bodies. Race may refer to or be referenced through the categories of nation, sexuality, gender, class, religion, ethnicity, or language.

---

1. Omi and Winant argue that: "An alternative approach is to think of racial formation processes as occurring through a linkage between structure and representation. Racial *projects* do the ideological "work" of making these links. *A racial project is simultaneously an interpretation, representation, or explanation of racial dynamics, and an effort to reorganize and redistribute resources along particular lines.* Racial projects connect what race *means* in a particular discursive practice and the ways in which both social structures and everyday experiences are racially *organized,* based upon that meaning" (Omi and Winant 1994, 56).

Here, Etienne Balibar's theorizing of race offers some important amend-
ments to Omi and Winant. Balibar considers race a "transnational phenomenon" (1991, 17). Like Omi and Winant, he sees race as both a matter of cultural
representation and a material structure.[2] For Balibar, as it is for Omi and Winant, racism has to do with essentialism and hierarchy, stereotypes and the construction of Otherness. Balibar's reflections on racism add to Omi and Winant's
by addressing how racialization and racism may operate through categories not
specifically named as race, such as immigration and religion: "The functioning
of the category of immigration as a substitute for the notion of race and a solvent
of 'class consciousness' provides us with a first clue" (20). Placing immigration
at the center of his account of race, Balibar treats race as a transnational phenomenon having to do with colonial genealogies. Drawing on P. A. Taguieff,
Balibar analyzes differentialist racism—a new racism from the era of decolonization that focuses on cultural rather than biological differences.[3]

Theorizing differentialist racism, which operates through the tools of essentialism, allows us to analyze race beyond discourses of phenotype, while
not disregarding moments in which discourses of phenotype still operate. Cul-

2. Balibar argues that: "Racism—a true 'total social phenomenon'—inscribes itself in practices (forms of violence, contempt, intolerance, humiliation and exploitation), in discourses and
representations which are so many intellectual elaborations of the phantasm of prophylaxis or
segregation (the need to purify the social body, to preserve 'one's own' or 'our' identity from all
forms of mixing, interbreeding or invasion) and which are articulated around stigmata or otherness (name, skin colour, religious practices). It therefore organizes affects . . . by conferring upon
them a stereotyped form, as regards both their 'objects' and their 'subjects'. It is this combination
of practices, discourses and representations in a network of affective stereotypes which enables us
to give an account of the formation of a racist community" (1991, 17–18).

3. Balibar describes the new differentialist racism: "The new racism is a racism of the era of
'decolonization,' of the reversal of population movements between the old colonies and the old
metropolises, and the division of humanity within a single political space. Ideologically, current
racism, which France centres upon the immigration complex, fits into a framework of 'racism
without races' which is already widely developed in other countries, particularly the Anglo-Saxon
ones. It is a racism whose dominant theme is not biological or heredity but the insurmountability
of cultural differences, a racism which, at first sight, does not postulate the superiority of certain
groups or peoples in relation to others but 'only' the harmfulness of abolishing frontiers, the
incompatibility of life-styles and traditions; in short, it is what P. A. Taguieff has rightly called a
differentialist racism." (Balibar 1991, 21).

ture bears the marks of natural essentialism in ways that allow it to do work imagined in the discourse of phenotype.[4] The work of differentialist racism is to construct essential cultural difference; to mark cultural distinctness as homogenous, static, and embedded; to install boundaries between cultures; and to reproduce and represent a hierarchy of cultures based on the essentialization of cultural difference.[5] The *NYT* articles that we examined often contribute to a racial project through their essentializing of Arab Americans and Muslim Americans as culturally distinct from the "rest" of America, their direct and indirect assertions of impenetrable difference, and their implied judgment that the "culture" of Arab Americans and Muslim Americans is not only incongruent with "American" culture, but also suspect.[6] In many instances, the modes of racialization discursively enacted enhance the social space from which further racializing processes and racial projects beyond *NYT* may be enabled. The articles highlighted below, we argue, are complicit in building racial hegemony.

This chapter documents discursive processes by which religion, immigration, ethnicity, language, space, gender, and sexuality become racialized and constitute racialized subjects. Our research investigates word choices, rhetorical moves, and thematic patterns that, by racializing Arab Americans and Muslim Americans, make them problematic to the U.S. nation-state. It closely examines the *New York Times*'s representations of Arab Americans and Muslim Americans in the aftermath of September 11, 2001, and the racializing effects of those representations. Given the national and international platforms on which the *New York Times* operates, how it represents a subject is of tremendous impor-

4. Balibar suggests that, "culture can also function like a nature, *and it can in particular function as a way of locking individuals and groups a priori into a genealogy, into a determination that is immutable and intangible in origin*" (1991, 22).

5. According to Balibar, differentialist ideology presents itself as an explanatory framework for racism: "In fact, what we see is a general displacement of the problematic. We now move from the theory of races or the struggle between the races in human history, whether based on biological or psychological principles, to a theory of 'race relations' within society, *which naturalizes not racial belonging but racist conduct*." (1991, 22–23).

6. Omi and Winant relate racism to essentializing processes: "A racial project can be defined as *racist* if and only if it *creates or reproduces structures of domination based on essentialist categories of race*. . . . Our definition therefore focuses instead on the 'work' essentialism does for domination, and the 'need' domination displays to essentialize the subordinated" (1994, 71).

tance to the subject and to the public discourse related to the subject—nation-wide and worldwide.

We argue first that the *NYT* represents Arab Americans and Muslim Americans in a manner that mostly operates to differentiate them from other Americans. The ordinariness of and internal differences among Arab Americans and Muslim Americans is at times subtly and at times crassly subverted through a series of direct and indirect associations and representations, the effects of which are to essentialize and racialize Arab Americans and Muslim Americans and represent them in their "collective," essentialized identities, rather than their individualities or differences. Arab Americans and Muslim Americans are portrayed largely as Muslim, even though the overwhelming majority of Arab Americans were Christian until the 1970s and many experts say that Christians are still the majority among Arab Americans (Arab American Institute [AAI] 2006; Samhan 2005). And Muslim Americans are represented as largely Arab, even though Arabs are a minority of the Muslims in America—and in the world. The largest group of Muslim Americans is African American and the largest group of Muslims globally is South Asian.

Second, Arab Americans and Muslim Americans are represented as intimately tied to their countries of origin, more so than other immigrants and more tied to their countries of origin than they are to the United States. Third, Arab Americans and Muslim Americans are represented as highly religious, and more religious than most Americans. Arab Americans and Muslim Americans are represented as religiously devout Muslims. Fourth, devout Muslims are represented as devoted to Islam and other Muslims before they are devoted to the United States and other Americans. Fifth, through a series of associations, Arab Americans and Muslim Americans are portrayed as linked to international Muslims and Muslim movements, which are themselves racialized as dark and dangerous. Sixth, Muslims around the world are represented primarily in terms of their religious devoutness. That devoutness is represented as being thinly differentiated from religious fanaticism. Fanaticism is discussed as the character of people who are trained primarily for collective identity rather than for individuality. Seventh, the "irrational religious rage" of Islamic fanaticism against the United States emerges as a thin veil separating the hearts and heartbeats of Arab Americans and Muslim Americans from globalized Islamic fanaticism and terrorism. Arab Americans and Muslim Americans, in this rhetorical maneuver, are transformed into high-risk citizens, subtly justifying indiscriminate violation of the civil rights of, as well as possible violence against, a vibrant part of the body politic.

The *NYT* articles that we analyzed for this paper were selected from the period 2000 through 2004. We constructed our article pool using the database ProQuest Current Newspaper, which contains full-text articles from the *New York Times*. Using the ProQuest Current Newspaper database, we searched for the following keywords: "Arab American," "Arab," "Muslims," "Muslim American," "Middle East American," and "Islam." Additionally, we searched for specific Arab American identity categories that referenced predominantly Arab countries. For example: "Egyptian American," "Yemeni American," "Moroccan American," "Libyan American," and so on. Of all the Arab American subgroups, only "Egyptian American," "Yemeni American," "Jordanian American," "Syrian American," "Lebanese American," and "Saudi American" yielded articles. Of the articles generated from the Proquest search, we selected those that were specifically about Arab Americans and Muslim Americans rather than articles about the Middle East or articles in which Arab Americans and Muslim Americans are only peripherally referenced. We obtained a pool of articles that can be divided into two categories. The first category consists of 279 articles about Arab Americans, Arabs in the United States, Muslim Americans, and/or Muslims in the United States. As we proceeded with the downloading, we discovered the important rhetorical linkage between Arab Americans and Muslim Americans and the coverage of Muslims globally. We began to select those articles that focused on Muslims outside the United States, calling this category, "Islam Globally." In this second category, we examined 90 articles. These 90 articles do not exhaust the articles printed in the *NYT* during this period on Muslims outside the United States. However, the articles downloaded and considered here appear to capture a range of discursive representations in the *NYT* that critically link Arab Americans and Muslim Americans to Muslims internationally.

We selected articles ranging from September 2001 to May 2004 to explicate the representational patterns we found in *New York Times* articles spanning January 2000 to December 2004. Through close textual readings of individual *NYT* articles, we document the discursive processes by which *NYT* representations essentialize and differentiate Arab Americans and Muslim Americans from other Americans. Although it is not possible to exhibit the full range of representations that appear in the *NYT*, we demonstrate how several important patterns organize *NYT* representations of Arab Americans and Muslim Americans and the racializing strategies that structure those representations.[7]

ESSENTIALIZING ARAB/MUSLIM AMERICANS

Racialization processes create racial categories by constructing distinct racial groups (based on phenotype, culture, or religion), within which difference is homogenized and between which difference is emphasized. Inasmuch as the *New York Times* presents Arab Americans and Muslim Americans in their "collective identity" rather than their individualities, Arab American and Muslim American identities are essentialized, facilitating the racializing project. Internal differences among Arab Americans and Muslim Americans are further glossed by the depiction of all Arab Americans as Muslims and all Muslim Americans as Arab. Indeed, in the *NYT* rhetoric the operative category appears to be "Arab/Muslim" Americans, as if "Arab" and "Muslim" were one and the same.

The *New York Times* often titles articles to suggest they are about Arab Americans when the text concerns non-Arab peoples. An article by Matthew Purdy provides an example. The title of Purdy's September 14, 2001, article, "For Arab-Americans, Flag-Flying and Fear," suggests a story about Arab Americans, but the story that follows is about Pakistani Americans. It discusses Muslims generally, but not the "Arab-Americans" mentioned in the title. At no point in the article does Purdy clarify that Pakistanis are not Arabs. Describing events post-9/11, Purdy quotes a concerned mosque president speaking about the plane assaults: "I hoped it's not someone from the Muslim community." Purdy does not make clear why all Arab Americans would necessarily be concerned about the Muslim community, a point that needs to be interrogated, given that scholars generally agree that the majority of Arab Americans are Christian. The "Muslim community" and "Arab Americans" are assumed to be one, in Purdy's article. Purdy describes another man whose brother was harassed while wearing "Pakistani

---

7. It is beyond the scope of this chapter to analyze the frequency with which articles appear that exhibit the patterns we examine. In order to demonstrate that *New York Times* articles are most often fixated on the particular themes we suggest recur, we compiled quantitative data, to show which words or types of words are used most frequently to construct *NYT* articles. As part of a future paper, we intend to publish the quantitative data we compiled on the *NYT*.

clothes." Purdy does not explain whether this second man is Pakistani, an Arab American wearing "Pakistani clothes," a mixed-heritage person of Pakistani and Arab descent, or none of the above. The connection between the harassment of a man dressed in Pakistani clothes and the Arab Americans alluded to in the title appears not to merit explanation for Purdy, eliding the differences between Arab Americans and Muslim Americans.

A similar conflation is evidenced in Laurie Goodstein and Gustav Niebuhr's September 14, 2001, piece, "Attacks and Harassment of Arab Americans Increase." Goodstein and Niebuhr's article discusses people of Middle Eastern and South Asian descent, while placing Sikhs, Pakistanis, and Afghans, under the sign "Arab." The article's title enables audiences, who may be unaware of religious, ethnic, national, and geographic distinctions, to conflate these diverse peoples into a homogenized and inaccurately conceived Arab American identity. Goodstein and Niebuhr's conflation of groups under the heading "Arab American" seems to rest upon the belief that the groups in question look alike: "People of Middle Eastern and South Asian descent—or even those who appear to be— are increasingly becoming targets of harassment and violence by civilians and of intense scrutiny by police officers under pressure to track down suspects in the terrorist attacks." While people of Middle Eastern and South Asian descent have faced and do face harassment, the title of the article leads the reader to assume they can all be glossed as Arab Americans. One of the article's informants, a chief of police in Providence, states that four "Arabic males" are being searched out as suspects in relation to 9/11. Naming a suspect group "Arabic males" discursively genders and racializes a category for police practice.[8] We are not told how the search for "Arabic males" casts suspicion upon all people of Middle Eastern (who are not all Arab) and South Asian (who are not Arab) descent. This elision does more than normalize the conflation of diverse communities. It works to instruct and prepare them collectively for policing.

Appearing on September 14, 2003, Marjorie Connelly's article, "There's Still a Chill in New York for Arab-Americans, Poll Says," reports the "singling out"

---

8. Clearly the article's authors and informants evidence some confusion as to which group or groups they are discussing. In any case, it is improper to speak of "Arabic males"; to refer to men whose heritage is Arab, one would say "Arab males," not "Arabic males," for people are Arab, not Arabic.

of "Arab-Americans, Muslims, and immigrants from the Middle East."[9] The story's text seems to render Muslim, Arab, and Pakistani identities as the same:

> Typical of those who think Arabs are targets for discrimination is Shirley Haq, who came to the United States from Pakistan as a child. "As soon as people hear you are a Muslim," Ms. Haq, a 38-year-old real estate agent who lives in Manor Heights, Staten Island, said in a follow-up interview, "you hear comments about who Muslims are and what they do."

Connelly translates Ms. Haq's comments about Muslims into comments about Arabs, eschewing the identities of Muslims of Pakistani and other non-Arab descent. A racialized regime of seeing, evinced in Connelly's article, posits an essentialized phenotype on the bodies of all people of Arab and/or Muslim descent.

> "A friend of mine feels under pressure because he is a Muslim," said Renzo Balducci, a computer scientist who lives in Carroll Gardens, Brooklyn. "When meeting people, he looks obviously like a Middle Eastern man and feels a bit of coldness." But Mr. Balducci regards such singling out as unavoidable these days. "It's quite natural," he said. "In the news, Muslims are seen daily as being connected with acts of violence in all the current events in Iraq, Afghanistan, Israel and so on."

Mr. Balducci's statement seems to imply that Muslimness and Middle Easternness appear on bodies. The article presumes that there is a discernable "Muslim look" or "Middle Eastern look." The assumption that Middle Easternness and Muslimness are bodily manifestations which can be readily observed accompanies a discourse in which "singling out" is banalized, called "quite natural" and "unavoidable." Here, it is clear that an imagined Muslim/Middle Eastern

9. The crux and context of Connelly's story is a poll that "found New Yorkers divided on the question of whether Arab Americans look upon terrorists with understanding. About a third of New Yorkers said Arab Americans were more sympathetic to terrorism than other American citizens; 44 percent said they were not. A citywide poll taken a month after the September 11 attacks found virtually the same result" (Connelly 2003). Reporting on the sentiments of "New Yorkers" toward "Arab Americans," Connelly's article proposes these as distinct categories, appearing unaware of the fact that quite a few New Yorkers are Arab Americans.

appearance or look and the contempt for persons so imagined is enabled by and creates the terms of legibility for a link between Muslims and violence.

Even when attempting to specifically portray the diversity of Arab Americans, *NYT* writers often stumble. In a February 17, 2004, article entitled "Arabs in U.S. Raising Money to Back Bush," Leslie Wayne writes: "Arab-Americans are not a monolithic group. The term is used generally to refer to people from Arab countries, but they may have diverse religious, ethnic and cultural backgrounds, like Lebanese and other Arab Christians or Muslims from Egypt and Pakistan." Wayne's definition of Arabs not only erroneously includes Pakistanis but also Iranians: "The fund-raisers are people like Mori Hosseini, the Iranian-born chief executive of ICI Homes, a home builder in Daytona Beach, Fla." Wayne continues, "Mr. Hosseini's enthusiasm runs counter to what some polls say is a drop in Mr. Bush's popularity among Arab-Americans"—implying that this Iranian-born chief executive is an Arab American.

Muslim Americans are, again, collapsed as Arab Americans in a blithe definition of the American Muslim Alliance, found in an article by Francis X. Clines (Oct. 3, 2001). Clines characterized the American Muslim Alliance as "the main organization devoted to the political assimilation of the nation's seven million Arab-Americans." The seven million figure is the high-end figure usually given for all Muslim Americans, including African Americans (the largest single group of Muslim Americans), and people from India, Indonesia, Eastern Europe, China, Malaysia, and other countries. By asserting the category "Arab" to signify all "Muslim Americans," Clines deploys Arabness as a primary racialization tool. Arabness becomes the sign of racial Otherness organizing the identity "Muslim."

Just as Muslim identity is marked as Arab, Arab identity is assumed to be Muslim. In "Islam Attracts Converts by the Thousands, Drawn Before and After Attacks," from October 22, 2001, Jodi Wilgoren narrates:

> Nine years ago, Jim Hacking was in training to be a Jesuit priest. Now, he is an admiralty lawyer in St. Louis who has spent much of the last month explaining Islam at interfaith gatherings. Mr. Hacking's search began in the 12-step program Overeaters Anonymous and intensified when he befriended an Egyptian-born woman, Amany Ragab, at the law review at St. Louis University. He made the Shahadah on June 6, 1998, and proposed marriage to her the next day. This summer, the couple traveled to Mecca.

Wilgoren appears content to conclude that Amany Ragab is Muslim simply by asserting that she is "Egyptian-born." This narrative effaces the identity of the over 15 percent of Egyptians who are Coptic Christian. Additionally, it seems to assume that his "befriending" an Egyptian-born woman is an adequate explanation of why he would convert to Islam. It implies a sexual seduction of white men by racialized Muslim women. This motif is a particularly effective racializing maneuver in the American context given the dominant narratives of U.S. race relations within which white men are frequently represented as seduced by black women.[10] The creation of the category, the seductive Muslim woman, is a homogenizing move that imagines Muslims and Arabs as the same. By conjuring the image of Arab women spreading Islam through sexual relations, it evokes the sexualized and racialized hierarchy of American cultural politics.

THE DANGER OF DIVIDED LOYALTIES

The second pattern we found was that Arab Americans and Muslim Americans are represented in many *NYT* articles as intimately tied to their countries of origin, perhaps more so than they are to the United States—and more tied to their countries of origin than are other American immigrant groups. Indeed, there is the implication that Arab Americans and Muslim Americans are more closely affiliated with Arab or Muslim countries in general, regardless of their specific ancestry, than they are to the United States. Laurie Goodstein's September 12, 2001, article, "In U.S. Echoes of Rift of Muslims and Jews," connected the 9/11 attacks to Muslims and Arab Americans, while it linked the events' significance to Israel and Palestine.

> Even though there was no definitive information yet about who was behind the terrorist attacks that struck New York City and Washington yesterday,

10. Under American slavery, racist and sexist ideology attempted to justify the rape of black women by white men through the myth of the aggressive and corrupting sexual character of black women. According to Hazel V. Carby, "Confronted by the black woman, the white man behaved in a manner that was considered to be entirely untempered by any virtuous qualities; the white male, in fact, was represented as being merely prey to the rampant sexuality of his female slaves" (1987, 27). See also Aptheker (1982); Collins (1991); Davis (1981); hooks (1981); and White (1985).

Muslims and Arab-Americans in the New York region and across the country immediately braced for the backlash with the grim panic of students rehearsing a duck-and-cover air-raid drill.

A terrorist attack on the United States detonates particular repercussions here among both Muslims and Jews, whose kin in the Middle East are locked in a bitter battle that many people immediately assume has now arrived like an unwelcome immigrant on American shores.

In the face of suspicion and discrimination, Muslims struggled to assert their identities as loyal American citizens and to say that their religion does not approve of violence against innocents. Jews, meanwhile, could not help linking the victimization of Americans to that of Jews in Israel.

Goodstein's narrative figures Muslims and Arab Americans as having anticipated blame for "who was behind the terrorist attacks"—as if they knew already. Her choice of words approximates violence as she asserts that the attack "detonates particular repercussions." The effect is to spread rhetorically the affective link to physical detonation. Next she glosses all American Muslims and Jews as being Middle Eastern by claiming that "[B]oth Muslims and Jews" have "kin in the Middle East." Doing this, she misrepresents the reality that most U.S. Muslims and Jews are not Middle Eastern and do not have relatives in the Middle East. Stating that the "bitter battle that many people immediately assume has now arrived like an unwelcome immigrant on American shores," she immediately makes clear in the next sentence that it is the Muslims who have to prove that they are worthy, "loyal" American citizens. Thus they must be the unwelcome immigrants. Jews, she implies, are like "us," identifying the "victimization of Americans to that of Jews in Israel." This maneuver also homogenizes Jews, but does so by folding them into the U.S. cultural "us."

The article positions Muslim Americans as needing to defend Islam and their claims to Americanness; they "struggle" to assert their loyalty as Americans. Jewish Americans, on the other hand, are portrayed sympathetically, revictimized by terrorism that is defined as Arab and Muslim. Whereas the American national statuses of Arab Americans and Muslim Americans (the narrative slips between the two groups) are called into question by events of September 11, the "Americanness" of Jews is affirmed by those same events. Muslims are discursively routed and rooted to the Middle East, destabilizing their U.S. citizenship claims; Jews are linked with the Middle East in a way that articulates their community with the U.S. nation. Thus U.S. Arab Muslims are linked to "bad" Palestinians and white Americans to "good" Jews.

Representations of Arab Americans often question Arab Americans' loyalty to the United States by questioning their stances on U.S. foreign policy. Patricia Cohen's September 29, 2001, article, "Response to Attacks Splits Arabs in the West," approaches the question of loyalty by taking issue with opinions of "Arab intellectuals in the West" vis-à-vis the causes of so-called "virulent radicalism" and "murderous attack."

> Since the end of the First World War when the French and British willy-nilly carved up the decaying Ottoman Empire, people have been divided over who is to blame for the veil of misery that shrouds millions of people across the Arab world.
>
> Are outsiders or insiders, Westerners or Arabs primarily responsible for the persistent poverty, corruption and repression? The question has been bubbling up since Sept. 11, as people grope to explain the virulent radicalism that has been growing across the region. For while a single madman can be dismissed as an evil aberration, what intelligence reports describe as a sprawling army of nearly 11,000 cannot.
>
> Among Arab intellectuals educated and living in the West, who are at once both outsiders and insiders, the question is particularly pointed. Revulsion at the murderous attack has brought a moment of unity here. (In the Arab world it is not hard to hear voices calling the attack justified retribution.) Across continents Arab writers and scholars have been e-mailing one another vehement condemnations.

By labeling "Arab intellectuals in the West" as "both outsiders and insiders," who are split on whether to bláme U.S. policies or Arab governments, Cohen implies one cannot be both Arab and Western. That Arab intellectuals must "choose sides" amidst "suspicion over loyalties and motives" implies that there is uncertainty about the trustworthiness of Arabs as U.S. citizens. "Virulent radicalism," outside the U.S. body politic, she says has a "sprawling army," which apparently emanates from the "veil of misery that shrouds millions of people across the Arab world." It is a world that seeks "retribution" against the United States. By invoking a "veil of misery that shrouds," the "Arab world" is constructed in terms of feminine difference marked by subordination. The veil comes to signify mysteriousness and oppression that may be the fault of Arabs.

Cohen's narrative segues into a domestic narrative of infantile sibling rivalry over geographic loyalties.

> But the attack has also created new pressures to choose sides within a group that is at times wrung with suspicion over loyalties and motives. Now, like feuding brothers who etch a chalk line across their bedroom floor Arab intellectuals in the West are split over how to respond to the attack. All are horrified at the senseless deaths. But on one side are those who argue that it is essential to understand how United States policies helped create the conditions that produced such monstrous fanatics. On the other are those who insist that any attempts to link the attacks to grievances against the West play into terrorist hands.

In using the familial metaphor and citing the feud among the brothers in the domestic space of the bedroom, Cohen reinstates the frequently used trope of the dysfunctional Arab family. These brothers are given a choice—side with the U.S. government, be a part of the U.S. state household, or side with "an evil aberration," "a sprawling army of nearly 11,000." To side with evil is to rebel against the patriarchal law of the state's house. To defer to the state is to be loyal to the patriarchal law. In Cohen's scenario, the feuding brothers, Arab intellectuals in the West, represent racialized dysfunctionality. They are thus figures to be corrected, disciplined, and punished as naughty children.

As Jasbir Puar and Amit Rai point out, the figure of the terrorist is a rearticulation and rejuvenation of the monster trope, a trope that co-evolved with colonialism and has long been established in the Western imagination. As a technology of governmentality, the monster-figure constructs both the subject to be punished and the subject to be corrected (Puar and Rai 2002). The imagined monster figure is the evildoer, the racialized and sexualized enemy that cannot possibly be the citizen. Racialization of subjects through the monster frame enacts a disciplining, whereby patriotism to the U.S. imperial racial state is required of subjects if they are to dissociate themselves from the monster image. In the above quote from Cohen, failed adult status, linked to a split group psyche, is produced and managed through the construction of a binary between those who align with U.S. state interests and those who do not.

Familial division reoccurs as a theme describing divided loyalties. In an October 29, 2001, article entitled "A Family, Both Arab and Arab-American, Divided by a War," Susan Sachs and Blaine Harden note "a perceptual chasm that is widening between Arabs and Americans . . . the pressure under which many Arab-Americans, torn between old family and new flag, must now live." The idea of a chasm between Arabs and Americans questions the citizenship of Arab Americans by juxtaposing family and flag. The new flag represents the new, modern United States.[11] The Arab family is presented as old, before entry into modern (U.S. national) time. This binary of family/old versus flag/new nation not only rehearses the modernization discourse of family loyalty as primordial/primitive and national loyalty as modern/progressive but also implies that those who continue to embrace familial loyalty are suspect citizens. The presence of the flag enacts both a pedagogical and a disciplining action.

Deploying flags in a spatial and temporal framing that raises the question of loyalty, Matthew Purdy's April 7, 2002, article, "On Arab-America's Main Street, New Flags and Old Loyalties," focuses primarily on "a fund-raiser for a congressman organized by Arab-American professionals." The theme of split loyalties is prevalent in this story about one Mr. El Filali, who engages in pro-Palestinian activities by day and support for U.S. congressional representatives by night. The article points out how U.S. flags get trumped by larger Palestinian flags. Waving Palestinian flags is called a form of "abandon," implying irrationality, possibly fanaticism. Purdy calls such activities "contradictory . . . after Sept. 11." Another Arab American's "bond with America," Purdy says, "grew hideously stronger after Sept. 11." What might be hideous about an Arab American's bond with the United States? The man in question, Mr. Merhi, had lost a godson in the September 11 attacks. After 9/11, mainstream media discourse often proclaimed the bond between U.S. nation and citizen as one of pride, continuity, and internal cohesion in the face of an external threat. Mr. Merhi's bond to the U.S. nation is, however, considered troubling to the point of hideousness, likening him to the monster, the enemy within that disfigures the body politic. The deployment of the word "hideous" positions Arab Americans' loyalties to the United States as disturbing aberrations. Purdy suggests there may be underlying

11. According to Anne McClintock, flags are types of national fetish objects, deployed as liminal markers to manage racial, gender, class, sexual, and national contradictions. For McClintock, fetishistic spectacles serve as an organizing mechanism for nationalist projects. Fetishism facilitates the teleology of the nation by providing a conduit to invoke, frame, transfer, and/or disavow difference and power relations. In this instance, the flag serves as a modern(izing) symbol held against the backdrop of atavistic, familial, antinational forms (1995).

"tension within the hyphenated identities." When, at the end of the article, an aide to Congressman Pascall is quoted as saying Mr. Merhi made comments that were "over the line" regarding Palestine and Israel, the narrative of hideousness, hyphenation, and temporally/spatially distant loyalties merge to situate Arab Americans as marginal American citizen.

The representation of Arab Americans as tied to their countries of origin takes on a specific spatial component that racializes and links subjects' bodies and cultural geographies. Appearing on November 4, 2001, "Struggling to Be Both Arab and American," by Jodi Wilgoren, discussing Arab Americans in Dearborn, Michigan, exhibits a profound anxiety about space. Arab Americans' in-between or hyphenated identity status is inscribed with the space of transnational migration: "Yet even as Arab Americans claim their place, the alienation is obvious. In dozens of conversations, with new 'boaters' who have been here a few months and those whose families have stayed for generations, people here inadvertently but consistently refer to non-Arabs as 'Americans'" (Wilgoren 2001a). In this racializing anti-immigrant discourse, the term "boaters" implies illegality, usually referring to Central American, Caribbean, and other adjacent migrants to the United States. Present-day Arab immigrants do not travel to the United States by boat. "Boaters" places Arab Americans in a genealogy of racializing discourse aimed at illegal immigrants. Labeling Arab American immigrants "boaters," Wilgoren fixes migration as a permanent status, disallowing for a grounded identity in the nation. Even Arab Americans who are long-term citizens are articulated within the same frame as boaters. "Middle Eastern people outside the Middle East" constructs Arab Americans as anchored to the Middle East, foreclosing the possibility for them to fully inhabit citizen space within the American polity.

Wilgoren continues to mark Dearborn as a cultural, political, and sexual space apart from America: "As their culture permeates street and social life, Arabs are also organizing to influence local politics, starting with the schools, where they make up nearly two-thirds of the ballooning enrollment. At Stout Middle School, like other schools here, Muslim girls in head scarves jump rope in sex-segregated gym classes." Wilgoren seems to posit "their culture" against an implicit culture in the rest of us. By highlighting "girls in head scarves" in "sex-segregated gym classes," Wilgoren contributes to the construction of difference delineated through clothing. And while sex segregation is typical in U.S. gym classes, Wilgoren's linking of sex-segregated gym classes with "Muslim girls in head scarves" appears to make the sex segregation an aberration of Islam that colors Dearborn schools.

Conflicts around schools are frequently linked to residential segregation. "Arab Americans long ago spilled over from the South End, near Ford's Rouge Plant, to dominate Dearborn's East End, and are increasingly buying houses—whose values keep rising despite warnings of immigrants ruining the neighborhood—in the West End and even in nearby Dearborn Heights." Using the phrase "spilling over," Wilgoren evokes the imagery of a toxic spill. The specter of failure of containment of an "alien" population is rearticulated as contamination and domination. Reifying cultural and religious difference, Wilgoren blames Arab Americans for failure to assimilate into the nation: "Considering the community's longevity and upward mobility, many question why it has not moved further into the mainstream. New waves of immigrants reinforce old-world ways. Religious differences and disagreements of America's place in the world exacerbate feelings of isolation." Wilgoren's article's discursive deployments of culture, religion, sex, and nationality not only spatially map race onto Arab Americans' bodies, but also reinscribe the precariousness of Arab American citizenship by suggesting its shaky grounding upon "divided loyalties."

MUSLIMS AS DISTINCTIVELY DEVOUT

When the *NYT* is reporting on Muslim Americans engaged in activities that are shared by non-Muslim Americans, the distinctive religious devoutness of Muslims is a centrally figured representation. Religiosity is marked as that which makes Muslim Americans different, that which makes their quotidian activities not so normal or everyday. Muslim Youth Day at Six Flags Great Adventure is the topic of "Stalled Since 9/11, a Gathering Resumes with High Security," by Jill P. Capuzzo, which appeared on September 18, 2004. The article focuses on the prayer practices, religious dress, food, and religious beliefs of the Muslim attendees. Islamic religious practice is particularly emphasized in this article and made to seem like a priority before American roller coaster fun, and possibly even inhibitory to normal theme park experience.

> It may have been Aqsa Khan's first visit to Six Flags Great Adventure, but she knew enough to hustle over to the park's largest roller coast as soon as the midday prayer ended. . . .

After waiting two hours to get in, Yasser Abraham and his family headed straight to the picnic area, where halal dishes like samosas, biryani and buttered chicken replaced the usual burgers and fries.

Before racing off to their favorite rides, most gathered for the midday prayer. Giant blue plastic tarps were spread across the pavement in front of Fort Independence, where men knelt facing east during the hourlong sermon. Behind them, women lined more blue tarps on the ground beside Bluebeard's Lost Treasure Train. Three other less formal prayer sessions were scheduled throughout the day.

Although Six Flags and other amusement parks cater to group events on a regular basis, the *New York Times* does not usually make such events objects of news. Overall, the article's narrative can give the reader the impression that Six Flags' usual amusement routine was disrupted by Muslim difference and religiosity. The theme park's temporal order was thrown out of joint—Halloween decorations had to be put up late. "Six Flags would usually have had its Halloween decoration up by now, but the park honored the sponsor's request to hold off hanging skeletons, witches and ghosts, which Mr. Farrukh said were viewed as idols by some Muslims." Prayer times took priority over the rush to rides. That halal food is noted to have replaced the usual menu of burgers and fries reminds good citizens that "American" food is being displaced by foreign food. We were made quite aware of the political significance of food in national symbolism in the call by many "patriots" to change french fries to freedom fries (France had not backed the U.S. war on terror to the satisfaction of many U.S. nationalists). The article singles out differential dress as a cause of bias against Muslims.

> Most of those who came to Friday's event—while highly sensitive to the bias against Muslims, often brought on by their style of dress—were unaware of this week's controversy.... While most of the women at the event complied with some version of the dress code, or hijab, fully covering their bodies and heads, standards were somewhat loosened for the men, many of whom were admitted in shorts and T-shirts.

In declaring that "bias against Muslims" is "often brought on by their style of dress," Capuzzo implies that it is Muslim dress, not racism, that causes violence against Muslims. This racializing discourse, which projects intolerable difference onto Muslims, is gendered insofar as Capuzzo scrutinizes women's so-called "dress code" and invests the hijab as the cause of curiosity, conflict, and bias.

Clothing is but one of many cultural cues that signal difference in this piece. The article also discusses "threats and racial epithets" leveled at the event and its participants. Although such sentiment is described as discriminatory by a Six Flags spokesperson, Six Flags still runs extra FBI checks on the sponsoring group.

> Ms. Siebeneicher [Six Flags spokeswoman] said that the most disturbing thing about the questions she fielded about the event was the implication that Six Flags was playing host to a terrorist-friendly organization.
>
> She said one talk show host asked if the company would rent the park to Nazis. The park's guest services phone lines and the company's corporate offices in Oklahoma were flooded by callers asking Six Flags to reverse its decision and threatening to boycott or sue the park.
>
> "It's truly sad and very unfortunate that people feel that way," she said. "This is America. Six Flags doesn't discriminate against race, religion or sexual orientation. We're not about politics."
>
> Nevertheless, Six Flags did run an additional F.B.I. check on the sponsoring group, despite the fact that they had rented the park to the group twice before.

This passage occasions a comparison between Nazis and Muslims. There is a general denunciation of discrimination, but Six Flags still invites FBI investigation of Muslims. Thus, Muslims are made to seem worthy of suspicion. A distinction is made between prejudicial statements and police scrutiny, where the former is considered discriminatory and not the latter. Capuzzo, Six Flags, and the FBI seem to share the view that the threat of terrorism looms behind Muslim religiosity.

Representations of Islam as the primary factor determining the life practices and identities of Muslims enact a process of othering. "Stitch by Stitch, a Daughter of Islam Takes on Taboos," an article by Hilarie M. Sheets, printed November 25, 2001, is about an artist, Ghada Amer, whose primary subject matter is not limited to Islam. From the article, we can gather that Amer's work treats an array of subject matter across cultures, including but not limited to Islamic cultures. Yet the article's title categorizes the artist, Ghada Amer, as "a Daughter of Islam," as if Islam were itself a distinct kinship structure, one united and all-defining family.

"What is going on now politically is like a mirror of what has always gone on in myself, because I am a hybrid of the West and the East," says Ghada Amer, a 38-year-old Egyptian-born artist who lived in France from the age of 11 and moved to Manhattan four years ago. "It's a clash between civilizations that of course don't understand each other. I've lived with these contradictions all my life."

It's no surprise, then, that Ms. Amer talks about making art as both therapeutic and biographical. Her subject is women, always, and in both her paintings and her sculptures, in which embroidery is her main tool, she beautifully and subtly investigates the place of women in the history of all cultures.

"I don't want viewers to see my work as the work of 'the other,'" she says. "That's the most insulting thing that could happen."

Sheets's title contradicts Amer's moment of self-definition. Amer describes herself as "a hybrid," but Sheets describes her as "a daughter of Islam." While Amer does not want her work to be seen as Other, Sheets's title sums up Amer's identity through Islam. The treatment of Islam as the driving identity for any Muslim reduces not only the historical, cultural, and theological diversity of Islam, but also the complexity of all Muslims. Colonialist strategy, Trinh Minh-ha has noted, homogenizes the "Other" as a way of creating an oppositional binary, which defines the other as enemy (1989). When news representations contain the identities of Muslims by making Islam the key thing to understanding all there is to know about Muslims individually or as a group, Muslims are made to seem distinct and homogenous, unique and different by means of religious identification. Although Sheets's article does not mark Amer as an "enemy," it constructs an "Otherness" to which discourses about enemies may attach.

Discourses of Arab Muslim Otherness parallel representations of racialized groups of Muslims that are not Arab. The December 17, 2001, article "A New Minority Makes Itself Known: Hispanic Muslims," by Evelyn Nieves, attempts to explain why Latinos might convert to or be attracted to Islam. Devoutness comes to the fore as a determining factor in some Latinos' conversion to Islam.

Religion scholars say that Islam also attracts those who prefer a more rigorous way to worship than what they find here in the Roman Catholic Church.

"There are those in the Roman Catholic tradition who are somewhat discontent with the modernizing trends of the Catholic Church," said Wade Clark Roof, chairman of the religious studies department at the University of California at Santa Barbara. "To those people," Mr. Roof said, "a religious tradition such as Islam, that attempts to maintain a fairly strict set of patterns and practices, becomes attractive."

Conversion is explained through marking Islam as holding off the modernizing processes. Islamic practices are said to be more "rigorous," "strict," or devout, than the supposedly more modern Catholic Church. Converts are represented as those who are already particularly prone to devout religiosity:

"I loved religion," said Ms. Ballivian, who converted to Islam eight years ago in Virginia and now practices in Los Angeles. "I was very religious in Catholic high school. I told myself that I would study philosophy and religion. I remember getting in trouble in Catholic school for debating things like the concept of original sin at a really young age. When I actually studied Islam, it made it all simple."

Nieves's representation of Islam and its converts not only portrays Islam as a less modern and more religious religion than Catholicism, but portrays Latinos as more devoutly Catholic than non-Latino, white Catholics, a common move in the racialization of Latinos. In turn, the figure of the religious Latino who converts to Islam to act out devoutness reinscribes representations of the racialized extreme religiosity of Muslims.

Muslim Americans are frequently represented as uniformly devout, and Muslims' everyday activities are represented with relation to prayer. Daniel Wakin's May 28, 2004 article, "Even Muslims on the Move Stop at Prayer Time," details Muslim taxi drivers' prayer practices and represents prayer as imperative to all Muslims. The title uses the word "even," implying that it is beyond what one would expect, or out of the ordinary, that people on the move would stop to pray, and also suggesting that every Muslim, no matter what that person is doing, stops to pray at particular times. Muslims are portrayed as having no choice, feeling compelled to pray:

You drive a cab, wafted across the city on the whims of your fares. But you are Muslim, and must pray five times a day—which involves ablutions, facing east and a series of prostrations in submission to God.

What to do? . . .

The drivers congregate in South Asian restaurants that provide prayer space in basements or back rooms. They have an imprint of the city's mosques

in their brains, at the ready wherever a fare may take them as prayer time closes
in. Using a small carpet kept in the trunk, they pray in the back seat, or even
on the side of the road.

The article depicts Muslims' brains as hardwired for religiosity: mosque sites
organize their psyches. In this representation, the compulsion to pray mani-
fests in Muslims very bodily schema. In Wakin's article, the racialization of
religion produces a racial body. This is an example of "how the return of the
biological theme is permitted and with it the elaboration of new variants of the
biological 'myth' within the framework of cultural racism" (Balibar 1991, 26).
Wakin's article moves into a more explicit staging of worship focused on the
Muslim body.

> A large cheap rug lay over a bed of ornamental mulch. Then men first washed
> in a restroom at the arrivals terminal. They then unrolled tiny carpets over the
> rug, took off their shoes and faced east toward Mecca to pray as planes roared
> overhead and traffic whooshed by. A tuft of pine trees hid them from the road.
> In front of their bending bodies was a chain link fence and then a sea of yellow
> cabs waiting their turn to approach the taxi stand. The cabbies prayed quickly
> so they could reach their taxis before it was their time to move ahead in line.
>
> The cabbie prayer strategies are a prime example of how outsiders trace
> new religious pathways in a city burbling with the world's faiths, sociologists
> of religion say.

Marked as "outsiders," here Muslims appear to bring prayer practices into
the space of the city, paving religious pathways that become the outside within
the city. The ultimate contradiction and outside to the capitalist city is represented by a decision for religion over money: "Sometimes it boils down to a
choice between prayers or fares. Mr. Abdemula said if he is near a mosque where
parking is difficult, he will put on his off-duty sign and forsake business well
before the hour of midday prayer."

Some *NYT* representations make Islamic religious devotion seem so determining, so much the overriding force in identity formation, that it turns against
its own practitioners, causing internalized conflicts and self-contempt. "Gay
Muslims Face a Growing Challenge Reconciling Their Two Identities," written
by Robert Worth, published January 13, 2002, represents Islamic religiosity as
homophobic, and suggests that gay Muslims have split identities.

Although reconciling their sexual and spiritual life has always been difficult, several gay Muslims said the Sept. 11 attacks and their aftermath have driven them more deeply than ever into a double life. . . .

Some are resigned to the belief that their impulses are evil, and regard the holy month of Ramadan as an opportunity to redeem themselves, several gay Muslims said.

While many *NYT* representations of Muslim Americans repeat the theme of split identity, it is usually a split between Muslim and American identity. Here, the split is represented as gay identity versus Muslim identity, while all the responsibility for homophobia and the psychic trauma it produces is projected onto Islam. Gay Muslim identity is made abject, constructed as that which is unliveable, evil even for gay Muslims themselves.

At the same time, Worth implies that non-Muslim religions and countries are relatively accepting of gay identities. Against Christian or Jewish gay identities, gay Muslim American identity in particular is made to seem problematic:

Yet to be both Muslim and gay may be particularly challenging, because unlike Christianity and Judaism, Islam is still inseparable from culture and politics in many countries where it is practiced. . . .

That perceived threat is reflected in harsh penalties in many Arab and Islamic countries. Under the Taliban, people found to have engaged in homosexual behavior had a brick wall collapsed onto them. This was done several times in the last several years, according to international news reports and Taliban radio and newspaper sources. Other countries are similarly severe.

By denying that Christianity and Judaism infuse, and are imbued with, culture and politics, Worth's piece portrays the United States as a fairly free and safe haven from homophobic violence, in contrast to predominantly Muslim countries, which are portrayed as far more oppressive. Interestingly, Worth's article clearly describes instances in which U.S. Islamophobic discourse intersects with homophobic discourse:

Yet if the United States represents freedom and safety to gay Muslims, many of them also say they have been shocked and upset, since Sept. 11, by their fellow Americans' ignorance and disrespect toward Islam, even among other gays. . . .

> Several said they had been offended by articles in the gay and mainstream press suggesting that Mohamed Atta and other hijackers may have been motivated by repressed homosexual rage.

In much U.S. press, then, Islam is blamed for causing homophobia, even while Islamophobic news articles ascribe violent (repressed) homosexuality to Muslims. Projecting a dysfunctional sexuality onto Mohamed Atta calls to mind Jasbir Puar and Amit Rai's argument that representations of terrorists construct them as racially and sexually monstrous and perverse. This coincidence between racist, Islamophobic, and homophobic discourses is missed when Worth glosses these as "disrespect toward Islam." Indeed, in the instances that the article describes, homophobia is central to assaults on Islam. Worth's fantasy of a less homophobic United States is further contradicted by the depiction, in this same article, of homophobic violence in U.S. civil society and the state.

> Muslim clerics are far from the only people who are hostile toward homosexuality. In October, an Associated Press photograph that appeared in newspapers showed a Navy crewman on an aircraft carrier standing next to a bomb on which the words "Hijack this" and a crude antigay slur had been scrawled.

In their essay "Monster, Terrorist, Fag," Puar and Rai contextualize the "Hijack this" incident within a larger problematic, in which nationalism and the war on terrorism are constituted and executed through racialized and sexualized discourses. By linking gays to terrorism, the bomb's inscription ascribes a sexual identity to its targets. Because U.S. bombs in the war on terror have been aimed overwhelmingly at Muslims, the bomb nominates Muslims as queers. Enacting a racialized heteronormative violence that proposes to eradicate a terrorist imagined as queer and Muslim, the Navy's homophobia articulates the fantasies of imperial aggression in the war on terror.

If Worth's article can carry a narrative suggesting a more tolerant United States, more amenable than Muslim countries are toward gays, it is only by gingerly passing over the centrality of homophobia in a U.S. nationalism that violently excludes and attacks Muslims. Worth is able simultaneously to represent the United States as tolerant of gay citizens and as violently homophobic toward Muslims, precisely because Muslims do not count as full citizens or members of the nation-state who deserve respect. The U.S. government has used the discourse of tolerance as a justification for waging war against Muslim countries. Calling itself tolerant and predominantly Muslim countries intolerant, the United States claims to usher in freedom from gender and sexual oppression, while it enacts massive military aggression that is both racist and homophobic. In sum, Worth's piece articulates a problematic in which Islam is blamed for the disavowed homophobia of U.S. nationalism, while gay Muslims are invested as the epitome of the pathology of Muslim religious devotion.

DEVOTION TO ISLAM AS AN OBSTACLE TO PARTICIPATION IN THE NATION

Muslim Americans are often portrayed as more devoted to Islam than to the United States. Representational devices that collapse diversity into homogeneity may serve to present all Arab Americans and Muslim Americans as conforming to one congregate anti-American ideological positioning. From March 8, 2002, "Muslims Return from Mecca with Joy, yet Concern," by Chris Hedges, portrays Muslim religious devotion in close affinity with anti-American sentiment. As the backdrop for this story about Muslims, Hedges begins with a scene in an Arab American community:

> Despite gray skies and freezing winds, the mood is festive in this heavily Arab-American community.
>
> People have been returning from the hajj, the pilgrimage to Mecca that all Muslims are expected to make at least once in their lives. The pilgrims have come home to white banners offering congratulations in Arabic, strings of lights flashing outside their homes and restaurants booked for homecoming parties.
>
> They have also come home with a sense of uncertainty. While many of those who made the pilgrimage this year left Islam's holiest sites feeling renewed in their faith, many also left disturbed by the growing gap between the Muslim world and the American world.
>
> The distance between the two cultures was felt keenly, pilgrims said, when Muslims from other countries chanted "Death to Israel" and "Death to America" during a ritual stoning of the devil that is part of the pilgrimage.

In this representation, loyalty to Islam conflicts with loyalty to the United States. The article locates the Arab American community as the site of people who have intimate contact with "anti-American" feeling. Although the article's opening scene is apparently festive, it quickly turns to negativity, as Hedges posits a "gap" between "Muslim" and "American" worlds, as if the two must be oppositional and anyone living both must be in a position of "uncertainty."

The article by Hedges portrays a massive crowd at Mecca, and calls it "a mirage," or "a vast wave." Muslim Americans are represented as "caught up," overtaken, suggesting that Muslim group identity envelops individual Arab and Muslim American identities. Muslim religious devoutness is represented as close to religious fanaticism, and fanaticism is represented as the character of a race of people who are trained primarily for collective identity rather than for individuality. Tensions from the conglomeration of Muslims at Mecca—labeled a "pressure cooker" of "anti-American sentiment"—are transferred to the moment of return from Mecca to the predominantly Arab American community. Implied conflicts of interest manifest as confusion, or vacillation across a fissure that supposedly increasingly separates "the Muslim world and the American world," as Muslim Americans are represented as "disturbed," and "hoping to reconcile . . . Islam . . . with the religion espoused by militants." The article poses Muslim Americans as "troubled by the alienation . . . from other Americans." Alienation appears to emanate from Mecca, moving through the circuit of Islam, and landing in Arab America, where anti-American sentiment is transported as uncertainty and is consolidated as withdrawal from identification with the nation.

Numerous *NYT* articles depict Muslim Americans as identifying more closely with other Muslims and Islam than with other Americans. John Leland's article from May 5, 2004, "Tension in a Michigan City over Muslims' Call to Prayer," portrays an Islamic center in Hamtramck, Michigan, as a public disruption: "To hear people in this blue-collar city tell it, things were fine until the al-Islah Islamic Center petitioned to broadcast its call to prayer, or azan, over an outdoor loudspeaker." While giving little space to quotes from supporters of the Islamic center, Leland quotes its critics at length.

> Jackie Rutherford, a librarian and youth-care worker, sat on her front stoop watching three men in Islamic shirt-dresses and tupi caps at the house across the street. "I don't know what's going to happen to our little town," said Ms. Rutherford, 39.
>
> "I used to say I wasn't prejudiced against anyone, but then I realized I had a problem with them putting Allah above everyone else," she said, of the plan

to amplify the call to prayer, which mosques announce five times a day. "It's throwing salt in a wound. I feel they've come to our country, infiltrated it, and they sit there looking at us, laughing, calling us fools."

The language of wounding implies harm to the physical well-being of an otherwise healthy, or "fine" body politic. Muslim Americans are portrayed as foreign invaders who are loyal to Islam to the point of total disregard for other Americans, who are portrayed as displaced and imposed upon. Leland points out, "Three mosques have opened in the last few years, increasing in size while the congregations at neighboring Roman Catholic churches dwindle," and quotes a born-again Christian, Joanne Golen, as saying, "'I don't want to be told that Allah is the true and only God five times a day, 365 days a year. It's against my constitutional rights to have to listen to another religion evangelize in my ear.'" Leland's article creates a spectacle of Muslim religiosity and generously quotes non-Muslims who act as if they are being marginalized by Muslims: "'Everyone talks about their rights,' Mr. Schultz said. 'The rights of Christians have been stripped from them. Last week there were Muslims praying downstairs, in a public building. If Christians tried to do that, the A.C.L.U. would shut us down.'"

Not only does Leland's piece portray Muslims as trampling on public space and private rights, Leland suggests that Muslims intentionally distance themselves from other Americans:

> Like others in his mosque, Mr. Musad said, he was drawn to the Muslim community here not for its engagement with the rest of America, but for its distance.
>
> "What attracted me was seeing school girls with veils and burkhas," he said. "It's more authentic here than in New York, more roots. There's village life."

Leland construes one mosque participant's preference for seeing veils and burqas as un-American. Veils and burqas are signified as central organizers of social life and markers of separateness from Americans society. Leland points up difference by projecting it onto the clothing of Muslim American women and men. While the dress of non-Muslims does not receive comment, Leland offers a description of "men in Islamic shirt-dresses and tupi caps."

Because Muslims are positioned at odds with other Americans, relationships between Muslims and non-Muslims are marked as disruptive aberrations. When irreducible difference is projected onto Muslim Americans, they are marked as deviant, and relationships with them become deviant. Judith Matl-off's October 28, 2001, piece is entitled "When a Spouse Is Muslim, New Bonds, New Rifts." By attaching the descriptor "Muslim" to one spouse and leaving the other unmarked, social relations of "bonds" and "rifts" appear to be determined by Muslimness. The partner who is not Muslim needs no marking; they are the presumed norm. "These are trying times for couples in which one partner is Muslim." It appears that a radical reorganization of social relations occurs around a Muslim partner: "Sometimes there is a staunch closing of ranks, as is the case with Ms. Plapinger and Mr. Ahmed. Sometimes couples are torn apart." Marriage, the space of the domestic, is inscribed by the national, even as it re-produces the limits of national membership. Because Muslim Americans are marked as more tied to Islam than to the United States, a non-Muslim spouse of a Muslim is forced into a choice between devotion to a Muslim spouse or devotion to the United States. The thrust of the article is that the pull of Islam is so great it can tear apart couples. Inasmuch as the heterosexual couple figures centrally as a building block of the nation and a source of national reproductiv-ity, anxiety arises over the threat interreligious dating with Muslims poses to the harmony of the nation's family.

Devotion to Islam is represented as posing a problem for participation in the U.S. national order. William Glaberson's October 21, 2001, article, "Interpreting Islamic Law for American Muslims," contrasts Islamic law with U.S. jurispru-dence. Treating Islam as atavistic and incongruous with modernity, he implies that Muslim Americans are incompatible with the U.S. polity. Glaberson states: "For millions of American Muslims, the centuries-old body of Islamic law ex-plains how they should live their lives in this country." The article implies that it is difficult for Muslim Americans to live under U.S. jurisprudence, insofar as it differs from Islamic law: "One complication for many Muslims has been that, unlike the courts of some Muslim counties, American courts have refused to defer to Islamic law in some important areas. American courts, for example, have consistently declined to accept a divorce procedure acceptable under Is-lamic law, which permits a husband to divorce his wife simply by announcing the divorce three times." By highlighting divorce as an example, difference is produced through the frame of gender relations. Difference is not a relation of equivalence here: Islam is marked as in need of change. That Christianity and Judaism are both older than Islam does not faze Glaberson, who asserts that for Muslim Americans the issue is "the challenge of interpreting an ancient religion for a modern society." Marking Muslims as incompatible with law opens up the space for legal exceptionalism, the subtext of which can justify the use of extralegal measures by the state to deal with people it constitutes as outside the frame of law. As law professors Susan Akram and Kevin Johnson have observed, "the current treatment of Arabs and Muslims is more extralegal than the internment" of Japanese during World War II.

> No Executive Order authorizes the treatment of Arabs and Muslims; nor has there been a formal declaration of war. Moreover, nationality which is more objective and easier to apply than religious and racial classifications, is not used as the exclusive basis for the measures. Rather, the scope of the investigation is broad and amorphous enough to potentially include all Arabs and Muslims, who may be natives of countries from around the world. (2002, 337)

As Arab Americans and Muslim Americans are subsumed under the racialized logic of exceptionalism, they are increasingly marginalized from citizenship. Giorgio Agamben argues that exception has been paradigmatic of sovereignty in political modernity. It is by the enactment of modes of rule not constrained by prescriptions of law that law gains its force. Exception arises from law and applies to law inasmuch as law is suspended in the state of exception. Law's power to exceed itself is precisely what consolidates its normative force. Agamben argues that "bare life in the political realm constitutes the original—if concealed—nucleus of sovereign power" (1998, 6). The distinction between bare life and political life is, according to Agamben, central to the founding of sovereignty. Bare life is that which is excluded from political life; yet the political takes bare life as its object upon which to act. This contradiction is revealed in modern democracies by their constitutional valorizations of rights to life, which accompany the utter failure to secure the well-being of bare life, most evidenced by the always-looming presence or threat of the concentration camp. Because the camp has been reintroduced for the internment of Muslims and Arabs, it is crucial that we consider how discourses of difference—such as the implication of Muslim incompatibility with U.S. law—can set the grounds for mobilizing technologies of governance capable of stripping Arab Americans and Muslim Americans of their status as subjects of the body politic. U.S. nationalism unleashes its sovereign power through ongoing renewals of the idea or the practice of the camp. This mode of state violence will continue, so long as the state recognizes some people as citizens worthy of rights, while relegating others to abject positions, such as noncitizen, alien, enemy, fanatic, or terrorist.

LINKING ARAB AMERICANS AND MUSLIM AMERICANS TO INTERNATIONAL MUSLIMS AND MUSLIM MOVEMENTS

Dated April 6, 2002, Susan Saulny's piece "Demonstrations Highlight Deep Divisions over Growing Conflict in Middle East," evidences the tendency to explain Arab American and Muslim American politics in terms of religiosity, drawing a link between Arab Americans and Muslim Americans and international Muslims and Muslim movements. Discussing demonstrations in Brooklyn in support of Israel as well as demonstrations in support of Palestine, the article overwhelmingly covers the arguments of supporters of Israel, while it ties Arab American support for Palestine to religious devotion.

> Outside the Palestinian Mission, meanwhile, Mr. Pataki, Mr. McCall and other elected officials condemned the Palestinian political leadership and supported what they called Israel's right to defend itself against suicide bombers. Buffeted by a wave of suicide attacks, Israel embarked on a military assault a week ago that it said was aimed at dismantling a terrorist infrastructure controlled by Mr. Arafat.
>
> The City Council speaker, Gifford Miller, said New Yorkers should have a special understanding of the reaction to the bombings, given what happened on Sept. 11. "This is our fight as well," he said. "This is our battle for freedom from terrorism." . . .
>
> [State Controller, H. Carl] McCall, who visited Israel four weeks ago, said: "As Americans, our hearts go out to the terror victims and their families. And as Americans, we need to keep sending the message to Washington—the president must remain steadfast in his support for Israel."
>
> Another speaker, Jose Luis Pacanowski, who teaches social studies at a high school in Midwood, Brooklyn, denounced the cost of round-the-clock police protection at the Palestinian Mission. "As a Jew living in New York City, I feel the P.L.O. have no right to be here, in New York City, being subsidized by the government," he said. "Yasir Arafat has made this very personal, and I feel threatened."
>
> He added, "Would we want an organization representing Osama bin Laden having a headquarters here and being protected by our police department?"

Although Saulny is mostly quoting these views, they are disproportionately given voice in Saulny's piece, in comparison to the mere two relatively brief quotes from individual Palestinian supporters. While accusing the PLO of terrorism and comparing Yasser Arafat to Osama bin Laden, these quotes portray Americans and Israelis as comparably victims of terror. Because the Palestinian mission is regarded as nothing more than the representative of the PLO, it is supposedly not deserving of police protection, and perhaps should not even exist, because the PLO should not be here, or so the argument goes. If the PLO has no right to be in the United States, and the Palestinian mission is seen as merely an extension of the PLO, the implication is that any body representing Palestinians should not be allowed either. If one follows this logic, Arab American protesters, by association, may not be welcome either, for their rallying represents Palestinian interests. Further, if the fight for Israel is considered a fight for American freedom from terrorism, then Arab Americans who support Palestinians—equated here with the PLO and Yasser Arafat, who is himself compared to Osama bin Laden—suddenly seem like supporters of terrorism. Thus they are not really Americans because Americans are those who can empathize with Israel as having been victimized by terrorism. In sum, this article contains a subtle discursive thread that ties together Palestinians, Arab Americans, and Osama bin Laden. Once bin Laden is invoked—in any of these twenty-eight *New York Times* articles or in other U.S. news articles—a whole signifying chain of association is raised that calls to mind so-called Islamic fanaticism and draws links between Muslims everywhere, portraying them as a looming, threatening network.

The specter of Muslim religiosity is precisely the imagery this article deploys in its depiction of a scene of Arab American supporters of Palestinians, thus buttressing the possibility for linking Arab Americans to the much fantasized "Islamic terrorism" (even if Saulny does not explicitly say that there is in fact such a link): "In Patterson, a city with a large Arab-American population, about 200 supporters of the Palestinians gathered in a parking lot opposite the Robert A. Roe Federal Building. The hourlong rally followed a Muslim prayer service in which about 50 men and boys knelt on rugs laid over the pavement with the bronze dome of the Passaic County Courthouse looming overhead." Because Muslim religiosity is centralized in the representation of Arab American protestors, there is a glossing of religious difference amongst Arab Americans. Furthermore the specifically Muslim religious devoutness of Arab Americans is demonstrated through its manifestation in politics. From such a portrayal, the message is sent that it is devotion to Islam that seals Arab Americans to Palestinians, and both groups to Osama bin Laden.

INTERNATIONAL MUSLIMS—DEVOUTNESS AND FANATICISM

A September 29, 2001, article by Peter Steinfels expresses a skepticism as to whether there are Muslims whose politics seriously diverge from those of Osama bin Laden. In the article, "Amid Islam's Complexity, Scholars Are Challenged to Influence Change Without Compromising," Steinfels questions whether Muslim American organizations are communicating calls for peace and condemnations of terrorism to Muslim audiences.

> Authentic Islam, the world has been told repeatedly in recent days, condemns terrorism, rejects violence against innocent civilians and advocates peace. The message has come from many of the highest Muslim religious authorities, from American Muslim organizations, from the pope, from the president and from many others. . . .
>
> But without in any way questioning the value or sincerity of such statements, many people want to know whether these condemnations, voiced to non-Muslim audiences at a moment of crisis, are consistently and systematically communicated to primarily Muslim populations.

Muslims may not necessarily be a constitutive part of Steinfels operative "world." That is, if "the world" has been instructed, "Islam . . . condemns terrorism," then why the concern over whether this information has been communicated to "Muslim populations," unless the latter fall out of the world in question? Refusal to recognize that Muslims occupy the same time and space as non-Muslims enables Steinfels's line of inquiry. Alternatively, his query could be read as allowing for one world that is split into "primarily Muslim populations" and "non-Muslim audiences" but still encompasses both groups. The question, then, becomes: when Muslim leaders are talking to "primarily Muslim populations," do they perhaps talk to part of the world or to people outside the world? Either of these two spatial renderings could serve as the basis upon which Steinfels constructs an argument about the inconsistency of Muslim leadership. The possibility for failure to "consistently and systematically" relay "the message" is dependent upon Muslim movement in another space, outside or fractured inside the normative world to which Muslim communication is unknowable. The implication is that Muslims do not fully participate in the quotidian space of the body politic, and Steinfels demands that Muslims disclose their other activities.

If there is some ambiguity about whom Steinfels counts as members of a world community, his invocation of "modern civilization" begs questions of group membership and implies the backwardness of Muslims, installing Muslims outside the world community of modern civilization. "Are there significant networks of Muslim scholars and intellectuals striving to articulate a genuinely Islamic vision that would embrace individual freedom, political democracy, pluralism, equal rights for minorities and women and other values that have emerged as the better part of modern civilization?" Steinfels interrogates the very compatibility of "a genuinely Islamic vision" with "modern civilization," implying that Muslims are either not in modern civilization or at least do not compose its "better part." Steinfels marks the "West" as the exemplary manifestation of "modern civilization." For Steinfels, "if Osama bin Laden's network is only a tiny group at the end of a spectrum, at many other points on that spectrum there are Muslims closer to his worldview than to the West's." Ideological adherence to the set of values, "individual freedom, political democracy, pluralism, equal rights for minorities and women," or "the better part of modern civilization" is what qualifies one for membership in Steinfels's "West." Moreover, Steinfels imagines that these are the actual attributes proper to the "West," its specific possessions. Against these, Steinfels posits "the official class of religious teachers in many parts of the Muslim world," who are "intellectually calcified"—one might say caught in static, timeless, backward thought—and promote "anti-Western, antiliberal" theories. Liberal and West are articulated as equivalents that oppose bin Laden, the West's opposite. Though Steinfels says that there is a spectrum between bin Laden and the West, the construction is evidently quite Manichaean:

> Meanwhile, are there counterparts to those extremist ideologues? Are there Muslim thinkers and scholars immersed in their faith, sensitive to the frustrations and resentments of the Muslim world, and yet appreciative of Western liberties not as an affront but as a stimulus to re-examine the riches of Islam and determine what can and cannot be affirmed with full religious integrity?

In asking if there are Muslim "counterparts to those extremist ideologues," Steinfels exposes his suspicion about the very possibility of liberal Muslims. The ideologies Steinfels prescribes for Muslims enact closures around the discursive parameters of "world." When discussing the ideological space Muslims supposedly occupy, using the phrase "Muslim world," a religious identity, "Muslim," precedes and modifies "world." In another deployment, "world" remains unmarked, suggesting a presumed self with whom Steinfels identifies, in contradistinction to a differently remarked upon (Muslim) Other. Where "Muslim" does not explicitly precede "world," "world" is articulated as compatible with modern civilization, West, and liberalism. The notion of "the Muslim world" differentiates "Muslims" from all the rest. The (normative, unmarked) "world" witnesses one performance by Muslim leaders, while Muslim populations, framed in "the Muslim world," partake in the ideological space of bin Laden.

Reference to "the Muslim World" assumes a homogenized conglomerate group that listens with one set of ears and speaks with one voice; it does not partake in "individual freedom." This homogenizing is an example of what Etienne Balibar calls "differentialist" or "culturalist" racism, whereby racialization is achieved through reference to "a deep psychology," "since it carries with it an image of Islam as a 'conception of the world' which is incompatible with Europeanness and an enterprise of universal ideological domination." Balibar notes that this discourse often organizes "contemporary Arabophobia, especially in France," where it entails "a systematic confusion of 'Arabness' and 'Islamicism'" (1991, 24). Although Steinfels does not mention Arabs or Arab Americans in his article, Balibar's observations about Arabophobia can be extended to the U.S. context as well, as examples we provide in other sections make clear.

Steinfels charges Muslim American organizations with the responsibility to "influence change without compromising." In a paternalistic tone, Steinfels advises how to support "Western liberties":

> What can be done to encourage a network of Muslim thinkers—without compromising them? American Muslim organizations might play an important role, as might private foundations and academic centers.
>
> An enterprise like this, although it cannot be directly part of a struggle against terrorism, is surely not irrelevant to the outcome.

Listed in juxtaposition, "American Muslim organizations" and "private foundations and academic centers" appear separate. The latter groupings, presumably non-Muslim, must "encourage" Muslim intellectual activity. As Muslim

American organizations are guided by non-Muslims, full agency in the struggle against terrorism still lies elsewhere from Muslims' partial effort. In sum, colonialist discourse echoes throughout Steinfels's narrative: Muslims occupy a place not fully part of the civilized time-space of the world, and non-Muslims must discipline Muslim leaders into more consistent accountability toward Western liberal ideology.

Steinfels implies that "equal rights for minorities and women" are grounded in Western values but are without assurance in Muslim ideology. The colonialist civilizing imperative that accompanies such a suggestion has been aptly summed up by Gayatri Chakravorty Spivak as: "white men, seeking to save brown women from brown men" (1999, 303). In this case, non-Muslim white men are posited as saviors, not only of women generally, but of "minorities," as both are held to suffer under backward Muslim ideology. The United States, then, is constructed as a site of equality for minorities—sexual, religious, racial, and so forth—thus disavowing the processes of exclusion so integral to the U.S. national formation, contemporarily and historically.

NYT authors often liken all Muslims to terrorists, to the point of practically disallowing for any discussion of Islam or Muslims that does not address terrorism to some degree. "A Portrait of the Prophet Behind Islam," Alessandra Stanley's December 18, 2002, piece, criticizes the documentary film *Muhammad: Legacy of a Prophet*. Stanley labels the film "hypersensitive" because it offers "heartwarming depictions" of Muslim communities, rather than discussing Muslims with relation to terrorism. Stanley suggests that the film's angle is due to Muslim sponsorship.

> Perhaps understandably, given the climate after Sept. 11, the film also seeks over and over to reassure viewers who fear a link between the Koran and the rise of Islamic fundamentalism. Steering viewers away from considering terrorism, the filmmakers illustrate Muhammad's teachings by focusing on a cozy, comforting portrait of Muslim communities in America. Heartwarming depictions of a Muslim New York City firefighter, a hijab-wearing nurse in Dearborn, Mich., and a black Muslim Capitol Hill staff member in Washington, packaged around glowing testimonials by clerics and academics, turn the Muhammad story into a lengthy infomercial for Islam.
>
> That is partly because most of the sponsors (they include Arabian Bulk Trade, Sabadia Family Foundation, Irfan Kathwari Foundation, El-Hibri Foundation,

and Qureishi Family Trust) are Muslim-American business and community organizations eager to have the story told in the most favorable light possible.

Stanley insinuates that Muslim funding creates a distorted representation of Islam. Within Stanley's reasoning, one must conclude that any positive media depiction of Islam is hiding something behind its portrayal, that something has been "packaged" for marketing purposes. Stanley is saying that information cannot be trusted from a film that presents a "cozy, comforting portrait of Muslim communities in America." For Stanley, any discussion of Islam that does not represent Islam as linked to terrorism must be a distorted infomercial, not a serious, objective documentary.

> Some of the academics recruited to help narrate the story are so eager to banish stereotypes about Islam that they sound like missionaries, not historians. Karen Armstrong, a former nun who wrote a biography of Muhammad, is perhaps the most colorful partisan, dismissing critiques of Muslim practices like polygamy or the veil in a plumy, authoritative British accent that makes her sound like Margaret Thatcher defending free enterprise.

By comparing academics to missionaries, Stanley attributes sympathetic observations about Islam to religiosity. Denouncing academics for their supposed failure to criticize Muslim practices, while not elaborating, historicizing, or contextualizing debates around Muslim practices, Stanley's own rendering gives a selective, biased, slanted history. Stanley's quick criticism reconsolidates the dominant terms on which Muslim cultural and religious practices are discussed as always already wrong and problematic. In Islamophobic discourse, Islam is construed as needing condemnation from the privileged viewpoint of those outside Islam. Finding little merit in the film, Stanley criticizes its depictions of historical and contemporary Islam.

> To their credit, the filmmakers did not airbrush one of the more infamous incidents in Muhammad's path to power: the execution of the men of Bani Quraizah, a Jewish tribe in Medina, the community that Muhammad ruled after he fled persecution in Mecca. A narrator cautiously states that according to Muslim sources, the Jewish tribesmen sided with Muhammad's enemies at the siege of Medina.

The filmmakers can only be credited with not "airbrush[ing] one of the more infamous incidents," however, simultaneously implying that there are other "infamous incidents" neglected by this film. Stating that the narration proceeds "cautiously," Stanley suggests that history is not being presented forthrightly. "For all its tiptoeing through history, however, the documentary is well worth watching both as the first serious attempt to tell the story of Muhammed [sic] on television and also as a testimony to the hypersensitivity of our times." It seems that for Stanley, only negative events can constitute an authentic historical construction of Islam. The "infamous incidents" Stanley alleges of the past relate to the "terrorism" Stanley emphasizes in the present. In this representation, what Muslims as a group do today is determined by the entire history of the religion. The history Stanley constructs is projected back from the point of the racializing project through which Stanley understands and portrays Islam today.

ARAB AMERICANS AND MUSLIM AMERICANS
AS HIGH-RISK CITIZENS

The title of David Halbfinger's September 24, 2001, article, "A Request for Patience If the Law Overreaches," is phrased as a plea to accept legal authorities' illegal activities. It is a call for Arab Americans to submit to and tolerate discrimination at the hands of the state because, it is implied, Arab Americans are high-risk citizens. The title, however is unclear regarding whether the request for patience comes from the *NYT* or from the state. Although the issue of racial profiling is explicitly raised, the very coordinators of law enforcement profiling practices are made to seem benevolent.

> New Jersey's attorney general today called on the state's many Arab-Americans to help the authorities investigating the terrorist attack on America, but also warned of widespread "ignorance" and urged people to report any abusive treatment by law-enforcement agents.
>
> The attorney general, John J. Farmer Jr., whose greatest challenge before Sept. 11 was rooting out another kind of racial profiling, said that with nearly 200 people being sought by federal investigators in connection with the attacks, "It's inevitable that the net is going to sweep too widely."

The structure of the police investigation identifies Arab Americans as a group to be policed. The attorney general warns of "ignorance," to which "abuse" may be attributed. Yet the very idea of "abuse" assumes a right to rule and domination because it implies that surveillance and other police activities are legitimate and normal, so long as they are not taken to a certain extreme (Mills 1997, 26). The systemic problem of racial profiling is never itself called into question. The violence of the discriminatory practice is projected onto individual attitudes and made to seem aberrant to rather than normative of the regulatory apparatus of the state. In the same instance in which police violence is characterized as perpetrated by some misinformed people—implicitly not including the attorney general, who orders police operations—the systemic character of profiling is dismissed as "inevitable," as if the state can do nothing but subject Arab Americans to its repressive scrutiny.

Simultaneously posed as protector of Arab Americans and as helplessly in need of Arab American connections, the attorney general is said to have "pleaded for help in the investigation into the attack on America, asking anyone with information—or anyone being sought for questioning—'to please come forward, if only through an intermediary.'" Arab Americans are asked to accept racial injustice in the name of national justice. But why should Arab Americans be asked—before any other Americans—for information on a "terrorist attack"? The implication is that Arab Americans are privy to information on terrorism by virtue of their ancestry. Are all American Jews of Israeli descent suspect when some American Jews of Israeli descent are caught spying on the American government?

NYT writers often fail to keep a critical distance from the explanatory gestures of the state, making it difficult to distinguish between what the state says and what *NYT* authors say. The effect of this elision facilitates the justification of state surveillance over Arab Americans and Muslim Americans. "Longer Waits for Arabs; Stir over U.S. Eavesdropping," by Neil A. Lewis and Christopher Marquis, appeared on November 10, 2001, and it extensively cites and quotes the U.S. government's justifications for policies restricting visas and authorizing eavesdropping on "young men from Arab and Muslim nations in an effort to prevent terrorist attacks." The authors' narrative voice treats government policies as actual prevention measures, rather than as actions the state labels as such. Lewis and Marquis reinforce the legitimacy of government policy insofar as they accept as exhaustively explanatory the government's assertion about what lies behind the policy. "The changes in visa procedures and the new authorized eavesdropping represented what government officials said was a fundamental shift in antiterror policy to emphasizing prevention." Objectives, means, and ends are represented narrowly, aligned with how the state narrates them. Other ways of understanding eavesdropping and visa regulations—for example as practices of a racializing project—are foreclosed. "The new State and Justice policies on visas and the monitoring of communications between suspected terrorists and their lawyers highlighted the problem of trying to reconcile growing national security concerns with traditional civil liberties issues." Rather than reporting the government's view, the authors seem to adopt the government's view that when civil liberties need to be reconciled with security, security must be prioritized. The loss of the reporters' autonomous positionality transforms the government's view into objective imperative—justifying the targeting of "risky" racialized communities.

Neil A. Lewis's January 9, 2002, piece, "I.N.S. to Focus on Muslims Who Evade Deportation," discusses government efforts to track and deport men from "Muslim and Middle Eastern countries that have Al Qaeda presences." Lewis offers quotes from both advocates and critics of profiling practices. At a key moment, in which one of Lewis's sources defends profiling, Lewis suggests that profiling cannot be condemned across the board:

> Before Sept. 11, the merest hint of using profiles to screen for potential wrongdoers was widely regarded as a violation of some elementary American value. But the debate has become more complex.
>
> "Profiling is not a four-letter word," said Victoria Toensing, a lawyer in Washington and a former senior Justice Department official.
>
> Ms. Toensing said in an interview that it was naïve to think that the national or ethnic characteristics of Al Qaeda terrorists should not be taken into account in some fashion.
>
> "It's Al Qaeda that has profiled by choosing principally radical Muslims, mostly from Middle Eastern countries," she said. "Prioritizing by looking at males who come from countries where there is support for Al Qaeda is common-sensical."

By suggesting that profiling "has become more complex," that it may not contradict any American values, Lewis undermines anti-profiling arguments framed in patriotic rhetoric. Lewis posits a pre–September 11/post–September 11 temporal dichotomy, whereby profiling is marked as more condemned prior to

September 11, 2001, but too "complex" to be flatly criticized after then. Deploying September 11, 2001, as a temporal marker, marking that date as an event, Lewis insinuates that there is and should be changes in profiling practices and in attitudes toward those practices. Indicating the necessity of a shift effaces the genealogy of profiling. Before September 11, police engaged widely in racial, religious, and national profiling. These practices went unnoticed or uncontested by large segments of the U.S. population, while many people from profiled communities and their allies waged an ongoing struggle against police profiling, violence, and harassment. By ignoring the history of profiling and protest against profiling, while implying that profiling was generally condemned in the U.S. before September 11, 2001, Lewis imagines a pre–September 11, 2001, consensus grounding a post–September 11, 2001 consensus. This notion exemplifies the differentialist moment Etienne Balibar describes, in which antiracism is marked as an abstraction that must be analyzed and transcended (1991, 22–23). By proposing that everyone agreed racial profiling was bad before, but now it is "more complex," Lewis gives the impression that lessons from racial conflict have allowed for a moment in which good and necessary religious and racial profiling can be distinguished from bad religious and racial profiling.

Ira Berkow's February 21, 2003, article, "Rower with Muslim Name Is an All-American Suspect," argues for a necessary type of profiling. It implicitly criminalizes Arab Americans by casting them against African Americans with Muslim names. Newark Port Authority stopped Aquil Abdullah, a Catholic African American rower, whose father is a convert to Islam. "Abdullah was on a no-fly list. 'What this means,' Andrew Kurpat, a police officer with the Port Authority in Newark, explained yesterday, 'is that anyone with a common Muslim name has to be checked out, to see if it's an alias, to see if he's on a terrorist list.'" Berkow states, "He was no terrorist." Berkow carefully distinguishes Abdullah from others whom authorities might profile:

> There are a few things that set Abdullah apart from someone with another common Muslim name like Muhammad or Hussein. One is that he is the only black man to win either a national single sculls rowing championship or a race at the prestigious Henley Royal Regatta in England. . . . Another difference is that Abdullah was not even his name at birth. He was born in Washington with the name Aquilibn Michael X. Shumate. When his father, Michael Shumate, converted to Islam when Aquil was 6, he changed his and his son's last

name to Abdullah. . . . "Here's a guy representing his country in athletics and he's as American as you can get."

We are further told that Abdullah is "not a member of any mosque," but is "Catholic, actually." Abdullah's racial identity, professional athleticism on behalf of the United States, birth name, and Catholic faith qualify him as "All-American" and set him apart from other people with Muslim names. What might be the characteristics of those Muslims we are to think more worthy of policing? Berkow begs this question, and Abdullah opines:

> And if he were on an airplane with someone with Arab characteristics, how would [Abdullah] feel? "I would raise an eyebrow and get a good look at who he was, and check out what he was doing," he said. "But I know I'd feel a sense of shame, too, because I know the feeling of being followed by a detective in a department store because of assumptions he made because I was black. The issue is terribly conflicting for me."

Even as he is himself profiled, Abdullah subscribes to a regime of surveillance that positions Arab Americans as suspect through the construction of an imagined Arab phenotype. (It is important to ask the question: what is an "Arab characteristic"? Is it possible to even speak of such a thing, given the range of embodied subjects that get designated under the sign "Arab"?) Moreover, Abdullah accepts the legitimacy of the policing apparatus that interpellates him as a subject in need of policing, and he even goes as far as to call for an increase in the efficiency with which profiling is executed: "'I can understand the concern,' Abdullah said recently with a graceful, disarming demeanor and an easy smile. 'It's legitimate, of course, and some of my friends are angrier about the name profiling than I am, but I do wish the authorities could be quicker about the check.'"

Abdullah is positioned precariously between Arab Muslim Americans and Americans not of Muslim or Arab descent. As an African American, a member of a non-Arab group that has dealt with police profiling for years, and as a person with a Muslim name who faces religious profiling, Abdullah's rendition of events can function as a go-ahead for profiling. That is, Berkow's article constructs a discourse that speaks a subject—Abdullah—that gives consent to, justifies, and forgives discriminatory police practices. Berkow offers a quote from Abdullah himself excusing harassment, making racialized citizenship seem acceptable—especially if a racially black man approves. Complicity with disciplinary technologies marks Abdullah as a model subject, one who accepts racial and religious policing, even if he is targeted by it. This racialized citizen monitors Arabs, who may be subordinated even to racialized citizens. While it may appear that Abdullah's status as a member of the national community is confirmed as "all-American," it is only awkwardly so, for he has been and can be subjected to profiling; he is comparable to Arabs and Muslims, but not quite them.

Although media representations portray them as high-risk citizens, Arab Americans and Muslim Americans are not only increasingly targeted by police violence but face ongoing vigilante violence as well. Blaine Harden's September 14, 2001, piece, "For Many, Sorrow Turns to Anger and Talk of Vengeance," re-hearsing racist speech directed at Muslims and people of Arab descent in the immediate wake of September 11, 2001, aggressively mobilizes the category "American" to back a discourse of revenge:

> More than a few Americans are beginning to obsess about how to get even.
>
> Phil Beckwith, a retired truck driver, announced his modest proposal for avenging the attacks on New York and Washington. . . . "I know just what to do with these Arab people," . . . "We have to find them, kill them, wrap them in a pigskin and bury them. That way they will never go to heaven."

Here, the proposal to murder "Arab people" predicates the generic invocation of the word "American." If "more than a few Americans" constitutes the group of people considering acts of vengeance, and the group of people against whom revenge is sought is named as "Arab," then the two categories appear to stand at odds. Racialization inscribes the logic of this call for violent revenge through a religious trope. The demand that Arabs be "wrap[ped] in a pigskin" no doubt attempts to reference the Islamic injunction to Muslims not to eat pork. This is a particularly pertinent example of a racial project, inasmuch as it relies on modes of racial knowing that signify the body and culture, in order to propose specific acts of physical and psychological violence.

While Blaine Harden's piece gives extensive space to racist articulations such as that, it contains five sentences that describe or cite antiwar sentiments, and it offers no critiques of racism. With no counterbalance, the article presents graphically violent language that is overwhelmingly racially inflected. The excitement of a drive to violence is articulated within the frame of patriotism: "Eager to do something, anything, to relieve their frustration, Americans today bought guns and ammunition, inquired about military service, planned patriotic celebrations for the weekend and let their anger run loose in conversation." If Americans are those who are buying weapons, flocking to the military, expressing an angry nationalism, we must ask who falls outside the nation, who is not allowed in this category, and how this economy of violent Americanness is racially inscribed. Harden's description of Americans as ready "to relieve their frustration" suggests that people committing or preparing to commit racist acts in the name of the nation are suffering and deserve sympathy; they are the ones that count as true Americans. The feelings of those who experience racist violence are not taken into consideration. Indeed, Harden's article replicates the ideology of the violence it reports. Although Harden is quoting others who are not affiliated with *NYT*, the article carries and distributes the violent impact of the words it quotes. The article actively organizes the national community around a racialized discourse of violent vengeance. Insofar as the article, as representational text, actually makes an impact structurally through wording, it evidences what Etienne Balibar refers to as "an essential dissymmetry within the racist complex, which confers upon its acts and 'actings out' undeniable primacy over its doctrines, naturally including within the category of actions not only physical violence and discrimination, but words themselves, the violence of words in so far as they are acts of contempt and aggression" (Balibar 1991, 18). In this sense, the article itself, though there is no direct evidence of the author's intention, is a racial project through and through; it represents, explains, and interprets, and the force of its discourse has the capacity to reproduce and alter social structural relations.

As might be said of all racial discourse, Harden's text is sexualized; it bears the imprint of racial violence and meaning production at the center of U.S. history, in that it calls forth a racialized imagery of rape and mob violence:

"Attempting to parse this situation with the sort of legality you might find during a rape trial is not appropriate here," said Paul D. Danish, a county commissioner in Boulder, Colo. The United States, Mr. Danish said, should order a handful of Arab nations—including Afghanistan and Iraq—to hand over responsible parties. "If they do not comply, we should declare war," he said. "My interest is only in seeing them change their behavior or in seeing their destruction."

The trope "rape" is deployed here to make an argument for extralegal action. The explanatory logic of the "rape" trope proposes a course of action based on experiences of gendered racial conflict in U.S. history. In the post-reconstruction United States, white mobs lynched thousands of black men, who they claimed had raped white women. Lynch mobs acted extralegally, but with the tacit and active support of law. The calling forth of this imagery in the article positions the nation-state parallel to white women in the earlier discourse, and the avengers, all men (racially unmarked, but presumably white), occupy the same position as they did in the earlier discourse, only here Arab and Muslim peoples and states are subjected to vigilante and military force working in conjunction.

Harden's article relays a discourse of revenge that constitutes its targets through a discursive slippage between Osama bin Laden, predominantly Arab and Muslim nations, and people of Arab or South Asian descent. Descriptions of actual and possible violence begin with brutal bodily assault and segue to military warfare on a massively destructive scale to premeditated and anxious public violence within the U.S. against racialized citizens:

> "If I could get my hands on bin Laden, I'd skin him alive and pour salt on him," said Bruce Cristina, 45, a worker at Ogden Metalworking. "Nothing would be cruel enough." . . . "Level the country that's harboring them," he said. "The whole country." . . . "I'll be honest with you," said Burnie Stokes, the shop's owner. "I'll see somebody that's Arabic, Pakistani or Indian, I'm looking at him like, 'What the hell do you have under your coat?'"

Brutal descriptions of imagined bodily mutilation are accompanied and reinforced by incitements to fight for the armed forces of the state, as Harden narrates:

> So far, at least, the attacks on Tuesday have had "minimal impact" on the number of people volunteering for the armed forces, said Douglas Smith, spokesman for the Army Recruiting Command in Fort Knox, Ky.
>
> But Mr. Smith said that recruiting stations around the country had received a higher than usual number of calls from veterans who wanted to know if they can do anything.

Using the operative words "so far," Harden prophesies future military growth and mobilization. Harden's sympathies are revealed when he gives the space to quote "one of the few young people to respond to recent events by trying to join the Army": "'Everybody was talking about Pearl Harbor, and that made me think of my grandfather,' said Mr. Stuart, who is unemployed. 'The very day after, he told his family he wanted to go into the military. I couldn't get that out of my mind.'" Calling forth the memory of Pearl Harbor, a sequence of events is brought to mind that might suggest a course of action for contemporary events, making mob violence, internment, and bombing campaigns feasible possibilities.

Finally, these actions are celebrated and affirmed within the boundaries of the national space:

In Riverton, Wyo., the town where Mr. Beckwith made his proposal about Arabs and pigskins this week, most of the town was expected to turn out on Friday night for homecoming ceremony before the high school football game.

During the national anthem, everyone at the game will be expected to stand and hold up a version of the American flag that was printed in the local newspaper.

The spectacle of national unity with violence against people of Arab descent caps the article and suggests future actions in the name of the nation. A caption to a photograph accompanying Harden's article evidences the results: "A masked man fired 21 shots at Hassan Awdah on Wednesday as Mr. Awdah, a Yemeni American, stood behind a bulletproof-glass window at his gasoline station in Gary, Ind."

CONCLUSION

As African American poet June Jordan wrote, following her visit to Lebanon in April 1996 after Israel invaded and killed more than 100 civilians in the United Nations camp at Qana, "Arab peoples and Arab Americans occupy the lowest, the most reviled spot in the racist mind of America. . . . I believe that to be Muslim and to be Arab is to be a people subject to the most uninhibited, lethal bullying possible" (1996, 13). Major U.S. print news media, it appears from our research, have contributed to the uninhibited bullying of Arab Americans and Muslim Americans through misrepresentations that are hard to explain away coming from such leading respected liberal newspapers as the *New York Times*. It is not necessary for us to argue intentionality on the part of individual reporters or the

NYT as a representational apparatus to make the argument of the damage that such misrepresentation does to the civil liberties, rights, and active citizenship of Arab Americans and Muslim Americans. Nor is it necessary to cull the assertions about Arab and Muslim noncitizens living in the U.S. from statements made specifically about Arab Americans and Muslim Americans. Indeed, the argument of this chapter is precisely that these misrepresentations question the possibility that persons could be Arab and American, Muslim and American. Thus the conflation of citizen and noncitizen Arabs and Muslims and the insidious linking of Arab Americans and Muslim Americans to a demonized Islam and Muslims globally has the concerted effect of casting doubt on the Americanness of Arab Americans and Muslim Americans. This elision between Arab Americans and Muslim Americans and what is represented as "fanatical," "violent," "terrorist," U.S.-hating Muslims around the world, has set the stage for surveillance, policing, harassment, and incarceration. Although we do not suggest that such state-deployed disciplinary practices will be eliminated by more accurate representations of Arab Americans and Muslim Americans, we argue that legitimate, respected newspapers must be accountable for their contributions to the larger array of racializing projects. The results of this survey call for a reckoning by print news media that pride themselves on standing up against racism.

T   E   N

"Look, Mohammed the Terrorist Is Coming!"

Cultural Racism, Nation-Based Racism,
and the Intersectionality of Oppressions after 9/11

NADINE NABER

IN AN OCTOBER 2006 SPEECH to the National Endowment for Democracy, George Bush used the phrase "Islamo-fascism" in defining "the enemy of the nation" in "the war on terror." He argued that "These extremists distort the idea of jihad into a call for terrorist murder against Christians and Jews and Hindus—and also against Muslims from other traditions, who they regard as heretics. The murderous ideology of the Islamic radicals is the great challenge of our new century. These militants are not just the enemies of America, or the enemies of Iraq, they are the enemies of Islam and the enemies of humanity" (Bush 2005). Bush's spokesman, Tony Snow, explained that Bush uses the term "Islamo-fascists" in order to clarify that the war on terror does not apply to all or most Muslims, but to tiny factions (Nir 2006). Since the attacks of September

Parts of this chapter originally appeared in *Cultural Dynamics* 18:235–67. Reproduced with permission from Nadine Naber, "The Rules of Forced Engagement: Race, Gender and the Culture of Fear among Arab Immigrants in San Francisco Post-9/11, Copyright (© Sage Publications, 2006), by permission of Sage Publications Ltd. This research was funded by the Russell Sage Foundation. I am grateful to each and every person who participated in this project. I am indebted to my research assistant Eman Desouky and to the following people for their invaluable feedback and support: Sarita See, Matt Stiffler, Jessi Gan, Lee Ann Wang, Maylei Blackwell, Frances Hasso, and Paola Bachetta.

11, 2001, Bush has repeatedly claimed that "this is not a war against Islam" and that the "war on terror" is a confrontation with a particularly militant Islamic ideology. Yet federal government discourses coupled with the local and global implementation of the "war on terror" tell a different story—a story of an open-ended arbitrary war against a wide range of individuals and communities.

This chapter provides a historically situated, ethnographic account of the ways in which "the war on terror" took on local form within the particular "anthropological location" of Arab immigrant communities in the San Francisco Bay Area of California within the first two years following September 11, 2001.[1] In part 1, I will explore the ways in which dominant United States discourses on "terrorism" and "Islamic fundamentalism" were reproduced within 9/11-related immigration policies in California.[2]

I argue that official federal government policies such as special registration, detentions, and deportations have constituted particular subjects as potential enemies within the nation—specifically working-class nonresident Muslim immigrant men from Muslim majority countries. In this sense, a set of solid and fixed signifiers have come to demarcate the "Muslim Other/enemy within" (e.g., masculinity, foreignness, and Islam). Yet at the same time, a wide range of subject positions have been drawn into the "war on terror" through federal government policies, including Arab Christians, Iranian Jews, Latinos/as, and Filipinos/as, women, and queer people, among others, illustrating that dominant U.S. discourses on "Islam" and "Muslims" are not only malleable and fluid but are arbitrary, fictional, and imaginary at best.[3] Here I draw upon Althusser's

1. Here I use Akhil Gupta and James Ferguson's term "anthropological locations." They define such "location work" as "an attentiveness to social, cultural, and political *location* and a willingness to work self-consciously at shifting or realigning our own location while building epistemological and political links with other locations" (1997).

2. Here I build upon Andrea Smith's notion of "racial logics." She argues against the assumption that all communities have been impacted by white supremacy in the same way. Instead, white supremacy operates through separate yet still related racial logics. Multiple logics operate depending on the context: "This framework does not assume that racism and white supremacy is enacted in a singular fashion; rather, white supremacy is constituted by separate and distinct, but still interrelated, logics" (2006, 67).

3. See Moallem (2002) for further analysis of discourses on "Islamic fundamentalism." She argues, for example, that discourses on "Islamic fundamentalism . . . [reduce] all Muslims to fundamentalists, and all fundamentalists to fanatical anti-modern traditionalists and terrorists,

(2003, 51; 1971, 121–73) definition of "the hailed individual." He argues that capitalism constitutes us as subjects by "interpellating" us—calling out to us in the way a policeman calls out to someone in the street. Althusser writes, "the hailed individual will turn around. By this mere one-hundred-and-eighty-degree physical conversation, he becomes a subject" (1971, 164). As Althusser's policeman creates a subject from the solitary walker in the street, one answerable to the law and to the state and system behind it, post–September 11 federal government and media discourses have created an arbitrary "potential terrorist" subject—intrinsically connected to "Islamic fundamentalism" and "terrorism."[4] I use the term "dominant U.S. discourses" to refer to systems of meaning about the "war on terror" produced among the federal government's policy makers, the defense industry, the corporate media, and neoconservative think tanks. In the demarcation of boundaries between good versus evil and between "those who are with us" and "those who are with the terrorists," dominant U.S. discourses on "terrorism" and "Islamic fundamentalism" have provided "definitions of patriotism, loyalty, boundaries and . . . belonging" (Said 2002, 578). They have also sparked nationalist sentiments that articulate subjects associated with "us" as those who are to be protected and those associated with "them" as those who are to be disciplined and punished.

In part 2, I explore the ways in which dominant U.S. discourses on terrorism were reproduced within the context of the post-9/11 backlash in the public sphere or in cases of harassment and hate crimes at school, at work, on the bus, and in the streets. I argue that the arbitrary, open-ended scope of the domestic "war on terror" emerged through the association between a wide range of signifiers such as particular names (e.g., Mohammed), dark skin, particular forms of dress (e.g., a headscarf or a beard) and particular nations of origin (e.g., Iraq or Pakistan) as signifiers of an imagined "Arab/Middle Eastern/Muslim" enemy.

---

even as it attributes a culturally aggressive and oppressive nature to all fundamentalist men, and a passive, ignorant, and submissive nature to all fundamentalist women.

4. Here I use Kent Ono's term, "potential terrorists." Ono argues that "potential terrorists" serves as a useful concept to begin to address political and media discourses that produce a creative, if fictional, 'network' or interconnection along racial, gender, national, sexual, political, and ideological lines. Hate crimes, surveillance by the repressive apparatus of the state, and surveillance and disciplining technologies have erected a powerful discursive barrier to full participation in society by those marked as 'potential terrorist'" (2005, 443).

In this sense, the category "Arab/Middle Eastern/Muslim" operated as a constructed category that lumps together several incongruous subcategories (such as Arabs and Iranians, including Christians, Jews, and Muslims, and all Muslims from Muslim-majority countries, as well as persons who are perceived to be Arab, Middle Eastern, or Muslim, such as South Asians, including Sikhs and Hindus).[5] Persons perceived to be "Arab/Middle Eastern/Muslim" were targeted by harassment or violence based on the assumption "they" embody a potential for terrorism and are thus threats to U.S. national security and deserving of discipline and punishment. Although these markers (name, skin color, dress, and nation of origin) were not the only signifiers that hailed individuals into associations with "Islamic fundamentalism" or "terrorism," they were among those most prevalent within my research participants' encounters with the post-9/11 backlash. While these signifiers were not mutually exclusive and operated relationally, particular signifiers were more salient than others, depending on the person or the situation. For example, in some contexts, a name such as Mohammed coupled with a beard signified the "Arab/Middle Eastern/Muslim" identity and in other contexts, it was nation of origin coupled with dark skin and a form of dress that signified the "Arab/Middle Eastern/Muslim."

I further argue that the post-9/11 backlash has been constituted by an interplay between two racial logics, cultural racism and nation-based racism (see footnote 3). I refer to "cultural racism" as a process of othering that constructs perceived cultural (e.g., Arab), religious (e.g., Muslim), or civilizational (e.g., Arab and/or Muslim) differences as natural and insurmountable.[6] Here, I build

---

5. The category "Arab/Middle Eastern/Muslim" as a signifier of the "enemy of the nation" was not produced after 9/11 but has permeated government and corporate media discourses for decades. After the attacks of September 11, 2001, the subcategory "South Asian" has been encompassed within dominant U.S. discourses on the "Arab/Middle Eastern/Muslim" enemy (Rana and Rosas 2006; Maira and Shihade 2006). Federal government policies, for example, tended particularly to target Arabs and South Asians, and hate crime incidents following 9/11 throughout the U.S. disproportionately targeted Arabs and South Asians, illustrating that Arabs and South Asians have been similarly associated with "Islamic fundamentalism," "terrorism," and the "enemy of the nation" in the context of the "war on terror." Because my research did not include a focus on South Asian communities, I will focus specifically on how Arab and Arab American research participants were perceived to be associated with the notion of an "Arab/Middle Eastern/Muslim" enemy, even though this term has taken on different form in other contexts.

6. See Moallem (2005), Balibar (1991), and Goldberg (1993).

upon Minoo Moallem's analysis of contexts in which religion may be considered "as a key determinant in the discourse of racial inferiority" (2005, 10) and Balibar's argument that "race," when coded as culture, can be constituted by a process that makes no reference to claims of biological superiority, but instead associates difference and inferiority with spiritual inheritance (1992, 25). In such instances, "culture can also function like a nature, and it can in particular function as a way of locking individuals and groups a priori into a genealogy, into a determination that is immutable and intangible in origin" (Balibar 1992, 22). As in European histories of anti-Semitism, histories of Islamophobia have deployed biological features in the racialization process. In this analysis, as in European histories of anti-Semitism, biological features are deployed, but "within the framework of cultural racism" (Balibar 1992, 22).[7] In other words, bodily stigmata become signifiers of a spiritual inheritance as opposed to a biological heredity (Balibar 1992, 22). In the context of my research, the term "cultural racism" refers to cases in which violence or harassment was justified on the basis that persons who were perceived to be "Arab/Middle Eastern/Muslim" were rendered as inherently connected to a backward, inferior, and potentially threatening Arab culture, Muslim religion, or Arab Muslim civilization.

I use the term "nation-based racism" to refer to the construction of particular immigrants as different than and inferior to whites based on the conception that "they" are foreign and therefore embody a potentiality for criminality and/or immorality and must be "evicted, eliminated, or controlled."[8] In the context of the "war on terror," the interplay between culture-based racism and nation-based racism has articulated subjects perceived to be "Arab/Middle Eastern/Muslim" not only as a moral, cultural, and civilizational threat to the "American" nation, but also as a security threat. The mapping of cultural racism onto nation-based racism has been critical in generating support for the idea that

7. See Stockton (1994), Rana and Rosas (2006), and Moallem (2005) for further analysis of cultural racism and the relationship between anti-Semitism and Islamophobia. Moallem, for example, argues that "this imputation of an intrinsic nature to a cultural or religious system has roots in European race theory, in particular, in the discourse of anti-Semitism" (10).

8. Although the construction of an Arab Muslim Other has permeated dominant U.S. national discourses for decades, it became increasingly pronounced—and expanded in scope—in the aftermath of September 11 (Ono and Sloop 2002, 35). See Abraham (1989), Joseph (1999), Saliba (1999), and Suleiman (1989) for analyses of the history of Arab American marginalization.

going to war "over there" and enacting racism and immigrant exclusion "over here" are essential to the project of protecting national security. Under the guise of a "war on terror," cultural and nation-based racism have operated transnationally to justify U.S. imperialist ambitions and practices as well as the targeting and profiling of persons perceived to be "Arab/Middle Eastern/Muslim" in the diaspora.[9]

Throughout my field sites, "racism" did not operate as a separate, mutually exclusive, axis of power. Rather, it intersected with multiple axes of oppression, such as class, gender, and sexuality. According to Linda Burnham, the idea of a simultaneity of oppressions "emerged among women of color feminists in fierce contention with the notion that racial identity trumps all other identities and that the struggle against racism should take precedence over all other forms of resistance to inequity" (2001, 9). My research illustrates that intersections between race, class, gender, and sexuality produced a range of engagements with "racism" among my research participants, depending on their social positioning. For example, the reproduction of government policies and media discourses in day-to-day interactions at work, on the bus, or on the streets were more violent and life threatening in working class urban locations than in upper-middle-class locations (Naber 2006). Because of their class privilege and the longer duration in which they had been in the United States, middle- to upper-class research participants had access to social, cultural, and economic privileges that allowed them to distance themselves from proximity to the "potential terrorists" compared to their working-class counterparts. Alternately, working-class immigrants were often perceived to be in closer proximity to "geographies of terror" (i.e., Muslim-majority nations) and were therefore perceived to be in closer proximity to the "potential terrorists" than their middle-class counterparts.[10] Throughout my field site, socioeconomic class intersected with race

9. See Robert Young for further analysis of the concept of "imperialism" (2001, 25–44). Also see Harvey (2003), who maintains that the New Imperialism represents U.S. efforts to resort to military power in the process of controlling the world's oil resources and to ensure continued U.S. dominance in the global arena. Also see Rashid Khalidi, *Resurrecting Empire* for a historical analysis of Western intervention and empire in the Middle East (2004).

10. Here I build upon Tadiar's theorization of racism in the context of the "war on terror." She argues, "from the dominant cultural logic of the U.S. state, terrorism embodies an other relation to death, and it is on this basis that racism operates against other peoples who are deemed close to this other relation to death epitomized by the would be suicide bomber" (2005).

and gender in that dominant discourses tended to construct working-class masculinities as agents of terrorism and working-class femininities as passive victims of "the terrorists."

RESEARCH METHODS

This essay is based on ethnographic research among Arab immigrants and Arab Americans in the San Francisco Bay Area between September 2002 and September 2003. Most of the research took place among two Arab/Arab American community networks, one that includes recent Arab Muslim immigrants and refugees from Iraq, Yemen, Palestine, and North Africa living in poverty and the other, middle- and upper-class professionals who are predominantly first and second generation and include Muslims and Christians from the Levant. The research entailed intensive interviews and participant observation with thirty board members representing eight religious, civil rights, and community-based organizations that serve Arabs/Arab Americans among their constituencies.[11] I conducted intensive interviews with six lawyers whose work was vital to community-based efforts in response to the anti-Arab/South Asian/Muslim backlash in the San Francisco Bay Area in the aftermath of September 11.[12] I also

11. I selected organizations that have played key roles in responding to the post–September 11 backlash, attracted the most members, and have the greatest membership size. I also selected organizations that were diverse, focusing on a range of issues that were educational, religious, cultural, and political and serving persons from various generations, socioeconomic class backgrounds, and countries or origin within the Arab world.

12. The lawyers who participated in this research worked on a wide range of issues and projects in solidarity with Arab and Muslim immigrant communities on a day-to-day basis. One lawyer, for example, was the co-chair of the Bay Area Arab American Attorneys Association and served via mayoral appointment on the San Francisco Human Rights Commission. The program director at the San Francisco Bay Area chapter of the National Lawyers Guild also participated in this research and helped to develop a "Know Your Rights" campaign. Several lawyers worked closely with special registration cases. Another lawyer helped organize a project that documented and monitored INS abuses in the city of San Francisco. A lawyer who was appointed as the Human Rights Commissioner of the city of San Francisco and participated in this research also organized a series of hearings where individuals targeted by the post-9/11 backlash narrated and recorded their stories.

conducted intensive interviews and participant observation among fifty community members from various class, generational, and religious backgrounds and various countries of origin in the Arab world.

Considering that the backlash had an impact not only on Arabs and Arab Americans, my research focused on the experiences of Arabs and Arab Americans as one among other entry points into interrogating the complex, nuanced ways in which the post–September 11 backlash operated. I thus conducted participant observation and open-ended interviews among diverse activists from various community-based organizations, multiracial coalitions, progressive organizations, and antiwar coalitions, including the American Arab Anti-Discrimination Committee, San Francisco Chapter; the Women of Color Resource Center; United Communities Against War and Racism; the National Lawyers Guild; Nosei; Asian Pacific Islanders for Community Empowerment; Asian Pacific Islanders Against War; La Raza Centro Legal; the Alliance of South Asians Taking Action; and the Committee for Human Rights in the Philippines.

HISTORICAL CONTEXT

On a global scale, the repeated framing of the aftermath of September 11 as an endless, fluid war has facilitated the Bush administration's conflation of diverse individuals, movements, and historical contexts such as bin Laden, Saddam Hussein, any and all forms of Palestinian resistance to Israeli occupation, Hizballah, Hamas, and al-Qaeda under the rubric "Islamic fundamentalists/Muslim terrorists."[13] It has also justified war on Afghanistan and Iraq, support for Israeli

13. The differences between Hizballah and al-Qaeda affirm this point. Hizballah is "a political party" and "a powerful actor in Lebanese politics" and "a provider of important social services" (Deeb 2006). According to Deeb, Hizballah's militia arose to battle Israel's occupation of southern Lebanon in 1982–2000 and to advocate for Lebanon's disenfranchised Shi'i Muslim community. Hizballah represents approximately 40 percent of the Lebanese population and has seats in the Lebanese government and a radio and a satellite TV station, as well as various social development programs. There is no international consensus that Hizballah is a terrorist organization, and the European Union does not list Hizballah as a terrorist organization. Al-Qaeda is an international alliance of militant Islamist organizations, a fringe group and, a diffuse movement, comprising individual nonstate actors or small cells operating independently.

occupation, Israel's war on Lebanon, and the transfer to the Philippines of U.S. troops who have enacted human rights violations against local people under the guise of "saving innocent people from terrorism." Within the geographic borders of the United States, the "war on terror" took on local form in the expansion of anti-immigrant discourses and practices beyond the axes of "illegal criminal" to "evil terrorist enemy within." On April 6, 2002, former attorney general John Ashcroft succinctly captured the federal government's framing of the aftermath of September 11 as a war against terrorists who are everywhere and anywhere with the following statement: "In this new war our enemy's platoons infiltrate our borders, quietly blending in with visiting tourists, students and workers. They move unnoticed through our cities, neighborhoods and public spaces.... Their tactics rely on evading recognition at the border and escaping detection within the United States" (Ashcroft 2002).

September 11–related immigration policies have targeted immigrants who fit amorphous characterizations of a "terrorist profile" through FBI investigations and spying, INS police raids, detentions, deportations, and interrogations of community organizations and activists. The INS targeted noncitizens from Muslim-majority countries as well as some individuals from Muslim-majority countries who were naturalized. These tactics were part of the federal government's implementation of a "wide range of domestic, legislative, administrative, and judicial measures in the name of national security and the war on terrorism" (Cainkar 2003, 1).[14] The "war on terror" also justified an intensification of anti-immigrant policies that affected a range of immigrant communities, particularly those historically racialized as nonwhite. For example, in the months following September 11 in San Francisco, the INS passed as local police in an effort to uphold Ashcroft's message that undocumented immigrants are the enemy, and members of local law enforcement are part of the solution. Reflecting on this period, Rosa Hernandez, a Latina community activist, reported in an interview that "the INS was engaging in random raids—at supermarkets, bus stops, and among unlicensed flower vendors." In

---

14. Cainkar argues: "These measures have included mass arrests, secret and indefinite detentions, prolonged detention of 'material witnesses,' closed hearing and use of secret evidence.... FBI home and work visits, seizures of property, removals of aliens with technical visa violations and mandatory special registration" (2003, 1).

February 2002, the federal government officially took over airport security. In the San Francisco Bay Area, this meant marking Filipino/a airport screeners as scapegoats in the attacks and laying them off en masse. Improving security meant replacing noncitizen workers with citizens who tended to be retired white military and police who received better pay, more benefits, and more respect. Several scholars and activists have added that the "war on terror" has legitimized an intensification of police brutality within working-class communities of color, exposed low-income students of color to unprecedented levels of military recruitment, and forced massive budget cuts that have disproportionately diminished social services and funding for schools in low-income communities of color.[15]

1. ANTI-IMMIGRANT LEGISLATION IN CALIFORNIA

Behtan Safeed,[16] a leading Iranian American immigrant-rights lawyer who represented more than six hundred clients in cases related to the post-9/11 backlash, summarized the impact of federal government policies on persons perceived to be Arab, Middle Eastern, South Asian, and/or Muslims as follows:

> They locked our men and our boys and our senior citizens away for the most ridiculous charges. A lot of them had valid visas. The edict that came from Attorney General Ashcroft, from the Department of Justice, was "guilty until proven innocent." No one who was held received a Notice to Appear. Even if they were served a bond for a Bond Hearing, it was going to be days—if not weeks—and in some cases months away, for no reason. It happened in stages: first came the PATRIOT Act; then came the first 5,000 men placed on a list; then came random FBI investigations; then came missing placed in lock down for 24 hours at a time while their families didn't know anything about them.

My research indicates that the FBI would either stop by a person's house without previous warning or arrange for a phone interview. In the Tenderloin, a

15. Rania Masri argues that "People of color communities comprise 60 percent of the U.S. military's front line: African Americans, Latinos, and, let us not forget, Native American" (2003).

16. I use pseudonyms to protect the confidentiality of research participants.

low-income neighborhood where several thousand recent Arab Muslim immigrants reside, many people received consecutive phone calls from the FBI.[17] On several occasions, the FBI went from building to building and did not explain that the interviews were voluntary. While lawyers, social service providers, and community activists who worked closely with the individuals and communities disproportionately targeted by 9/11-related legislation articulated the *kinds* of anti-immigrant measures that the federal government implemented with ease, their explanations of exactly *whom* these measures targeted were less explicit. The range of explanations they provided about exactly *who* was targeted, and the inconsistencies in their narratives, epitomizes this point. Consider the following three quotes. As Lana Salam,[18] an immigrant-rights lawyer and community activists explained, "I'd have to say that they focused on people with student visas and nonimmigrant visas—although it was also more broad-based and included people with green cards and U.S. citizenship. It also focused on known Muslim thinkers, writers, and clerics. It seemed focused mostly on Muslims—people who went to Friday prayers. I think they

17. The Tenderloin, where over 70 percent of the residents live in low-income households, is one of San Francisco's most impoverished neighborhoods. It is an urban inner city, densely inhabited, low-income neighborhood with many homeless people and single-resident-occupancy (SRO) hotels. Within San Francisco, the Tenderloin is where the greatest incidents of homicides, aggravated assaults, and drug use take place. Despite these statistics, over 25,000 people live in the Tenderloin. Most Arab Muslims living in the Tenderloin came to the United States from Iraq, Egypt, Tunis, Morocco, and Yemen. While no research exists on the number of Arab Muslims in the Tenderloin neighborhood, community activists agree that there are approximately 100 Yemeni families and over 1,500 Yemeni men who have citizenship or green cards and are in the country supporting their parents, siblings, wives, and/or children who live in Yemen. The majority of Arab Muslims in the Tenderloin are single men who share studio apartments with two to four other single men. In addition to working within the Tenderloin, I also conducted interviews and participant observation among a group of Iraqi refugees who had recently moved out of this neighborhood to Santa Clara, California, where they were granted better housing conditions through the Section 8 Certificate and Housing Program.

18. Lana Salam was the director of legal education and outreach for the American Arab Anti-Discrimination Committee directly after September 11 and played a key role in community education on legal topics relevant to a post-9/11 political landscape. She also organized a legal workshop on FBI questioning among local Arab American communities when the FBI starting questioning thousands of Arab men.

were looking for people with Islamic affiliations. I specifically recall that they interviewed Hamzah Yousef."[19]

Community leader and activist Ahmad Masri, a university lecturer and the director of two Muslim American organizations, explained, "Definitely, the policies impacted immigrants more than indigenous Muslims. That doesn't mean that in the long run the indigenous Muslims aren't going to be dragged into it, willingly or unwillingly. Among immigrants, the impact on Arabs was higher than other immigrant communities, with the exception of Pakistanis, who were also included in this." According to immigrant rights lawyer Behtan Safeed, "It was mostly Muslims [who] were detained, but there were Christians among them. There was an Iranian Armenian family. There were Jews among them. The gamut. The ones that look darker were more targeted. There was a particular age group I saw—twenty-somethings and forty-somethings, but I also saw sixteen-year-olds and I saw sixty-four-year-olds." These quotes reflect a broader pattern emergent throughout the San Francisco Bay Area within the first two years following 9/11. While particular persons were disproportionately targeted by federal government policies (most were Arab or South Asian and most were Muslim), the Bush administration's "terrorist profile" had the potential to single out a wide range of individuals, including Arab and Pakistani Muslims, non-Arab/non–South Asian Muslims; Christians and Jews; aliens, permanent residents, and citizens; and young men in addition to teenagers and the elderly.

A closer exploration of the process of special registration, part of the National Security Entry-Exit Registration System, exemplifies the arbitrary scope of the federal government's "terrorist profile." Special registration required nonresident men, such as students, visitors, and those conducting business in the U.S. from North Korea and twenty-four Muslim majority countries, to be fingerprinted, photographed, and interviewed.[20] According to Ashcroft, those required to register were "individuals of elevated national security concern who stay in the

19. Hamza Yusuf is a white American convert to Islam. In some cases, he is referred to as the "Great White Sheikh." See http://www.islamonline.net/english/views/2001/11/article8.shtml.

20. Under Special Registration, the U.S. Immigration and Customs Enforcement established mechanisms to track nonimmigrants who enter the United States each year by interviewing immigrants in person and restricting entry and departure to specially designated ports (see U.S. Immigration and Customs Enforcement 2006).

country for more than thirty days" (Ashcroft 2002). According to activists who monitored the process of Special Registration, the interviews entailed questions about the immigrants' family members and their names and addresses, their e-mail address, the names and addresses of their contacts in the U.S., and a form of identification other than their passport and immigration documents. Interviewers tended to ask how the person arrived in the United States and when as well as whether they have any connection to any "terrorist organizations" (Revolutionary Worker Online 2002). They asked about the interviewees' religious and political affiliations and about the mosques they attended. Interviewees were digitally photographed and fingerprinted—and the photo and prints were processed against various criminal and immigration service databases. Special registration resulted in the deportation of more than thirteen thousand individuals. Not one terrorist suspect was found in the process.[21]

The Bush administration purported that special registration would assist the federal government in locating "militant Islamic fundamentalists." That Iranian Jews were detained along with Muslims from Iran, Iraq, Libya, Sudan, and Syria during the first phase of Special Registration in Los Angeles (Jan. 27, 2003 and Feb. 7, 2003) is but one example of the arbitrary identity of groups linked to "militant Islam." Sources from the Iranian Jewish community said that up to a dozen Iranian Jews had been detained or arrested, though one attorney in Los Angeles had stated that he was trying to raise bail of $1,500 per person for thirty-five Iranian Jews. Moreover, eight of the Jewish detainees had moved from Iran to Israel and later came to the United States, and many held Israeli citizenship. Zvi Vapni, the Israeli deputy consul general in Los Angeles, said he had received complaints that Iranian Jews faced "very hard conditions," perhaps because of overcrowding, and had conveyed the consulate's concern to the INS (Fitleberg 2002).

Referencing the 9/11 attacks, Attorney General Ashcroft determined that "certain nonimmigrant aliens require closer monitoring." Thus, policy makers have named particular Muslims from particular countries of origin as those who fit this profile. Yet because the enforcement of such policies has been directed at such a broad range of identities, the question of exactly *who* these

---

21. See Rana and Rosas's argument that "'Muslim' has come to represent an ambiguous racial community that encompasses persons perceived to belong to the homogenous, fictional category, 'Arab-Middle Eastern-Muslim;' South Asians (including Christians, Hindus, Muslims and Sikhs), and possibly Latinas/os, and African Americans" (2006).

"immigrants" *are* remains unclear. On the one hand, the category "Muslim" is signified by fixed, solid referents (i.e., Muslim men from Muslim majority countries). On the other hand, it is open-ended and arbitrary in its potential to draw a wide range of subjects into association with "terrorism." Paralleling the Bush administration's "endless, fluid war," 9/11-related immigration policies have targeted persons who tend to "fit" the federal government's profile of a "potential terrorist" (i.e., Muslim immigrant men from Muslim majority countries), yet at the same time, they have rendered a range of subject positions as deserving of discipline and punishment under the guise of the "war on terror." This, in turn, facilitates any abuse or "defense" against them.

2. EMBLEMS OF TERRORISM: THE OPEN-ENDED TERRORIST ON THE STREETS

Paralleling federal government policies, day-to-day forms of harassment, violence, and intimidation in the public sphere also operated to hail a range of subject positions into discourses of "Islamic fundamentalism" and "terrorism." Consider the series of murders that took place within weeks after 9/11. On September 15, 2001, a Sikh man, Balbir Singh Sodhi, was gunned down in Mesa, Arizona, outside his gas station. According to Anya Cordell, who launched the *Campaign for Collateral Compassion* in February 2002 to bring attention to murders associated with September 11, Sodhi's killer spent the hours before the murder in a bar, bragging of his intention to "kill the ragheads responsible for September 11" (Hanania 2004). On September 15, 2001, a forty-six-year-old Pakistani, Waqar Hasan of Dallas, Texas, was shot to death in his convenience store. The man convicted of murdering him was also convicted of murdering Vasudev Patel days later in Mesquite, Texas. Anya Cordell explained that he admitted to authorities to blinding a third victim, a Bangladeshi, in between the murders of Hasan and Patel and that after his arrest he stated, "I did what every American wanted to do after September 11th but didn't have the nerve." On September 15, 2001, Adel Karas, a Coptic Christian grocer, was killed in his store in San Gabriel, California. On September 21, 2001, Ali Almansoop, a Yemeni American citizen and father of four, was murdered in his Detroit, Michigan, home (Hanania 2004). These murders took place within a broader context of a 1,600 percent increase in hate-based incidents against persons perceived to be Arab, Muslim, or South Asian in the United States (between 2000 to 2001).[22] These incidents illustrate how racialization within the context of the post-9/11 backlash operated throughout the United States to constitute South Asians from diverse religious backgrounds, Arab Christians, and Muslim immigrants from Muslim-majority countries as somehow intrinsically connected to Islamic fundamentalism and terrorism.

Among Arab immigrants and Arab Americans in the San Francisco Bay Area, September 11–related hate crimes and other forms of harassment in the public sphere disproportionately targeted persons who displayed what dominant government and corporate media discourses often constructed as emblems of a constructed "Arab/Middle Eastern/Muslim" identity, including particular kinds of names, appearances, or nations of origin that signified an association with the enemy of the nation. Such identity markers hailed multiple subject positions into the "war on terror" through hate crimes and various forms of violence, harassment, and intimidation in the public sphere—at school, on the bus, at work, at home, and on the streets.

Names and Naming: "Look, Mohammed the Terrorist Is Coming!"

Repeatedly throughout my research, participants' narratives on harassment in the public sphere were stories in which particular names operated as signifiers of an "Arab/Middle Eastern/Muslim" identity. Teachers and youth group leaders agreed that boys with names such as Mohammed or Osama were disproportionately harassed at school. Consider the following stories. Nayla, a Muslim American youth group leader, recalled an incident where school kids would frequently shout, "Look, Mohammed the terrorist is coming!" when a young boy named Mohammed would enter the playground. Amira, a college student, recalled reading the words, "I hate Mohammed. All Mohammeds should die," on a wall outside the Recreation and Sports Facilities Building at the University of California, Berkeley. Reflecting on difficulties that he and his wife faced in deciding whether or not to name their son Mohammed, Saleh, a small business owner, explained: "After September 11 no one would have thought about naming their son Mohammed in this country if they wanted him to be treated like

22. A press release posted on the American Arab Anti-Discrimination Committee website from Congresswoman's Marcy Kaptur's office states: "The FBI reports that the number of anti-Muslim incidents rose 1600% from 2000 to 2001, largely due to post-9/11 backlash" (Kaptur 2003).

a normal person. We thought about what would happen to our son in school, and how he would be discriminated against growing up. But we felt that this is our religion and our culture, and long before September 11 we decided that if we had a second son, we would name him Mohammed. We decided not to change what we stood for, but imagine what happens when your neighbor says, 'what is that cute little boy's name?' You say 'Mohammed' and they say, 'Oh . . . ' This is how September 11 impacted even the relationship between you and your neighbor."

Several Christian Arabs and Arab Americans with whom I interacted were similarly targeted based on associations between their name and the notion of a "potential enemy of the nation." In such cases, Christians were perceived to be Muslim because they had Arabic names, illustrating the ways that federal government and corporate media discourses that conflate the categories "Arab" and "Muslim" take on local form in the public sphere. A youth group leader at a Roman Catholic Arab American church reported that after their son Osama was repeatedly called "Muslim terrorist," his parents changed his name to "Sam." Recurring throughout the period of my research were similar stories of individuals who changed their Arabic names to anglicized names, including an Arab American Christian who changed his name from Fouad to Freddy after facing 9/11-related harassment. Misidentifications of Arab Christians as Muslims reify the absurd generalizations and misconceptions underlying hegemonic constructions of the category "Arab" or "Muslim." They also reify that encounters with racism are informed by fiction and comprise a wide variety of complexities and contradictions. As Amitava Kumar puts it, "In those dark chambers, what is revealed always hides something else" (2000, 74). In the cases of misidentified Arab Christians, the simple reality that not all Arabs are Muslim and not all Muslims are Arabs is hidden and erased from history.

Like federal government legislation, harassment against "potential terrorist men" in the public sphere operated within the logic of nation-based racism that considers discipline and punishment the "proper mechanism to set the tide of criminality intrinsic to them" (Ono and Sloop 2002, 33). Nation-based racism is not specific to the post-9/11 environment, but it has been critical to the justification of many cases of immigrant exclusion by the idea that citizens should be protected against "others" who are "potentially or already criminal" (33), or in this case, terrorists. Ono and Sloop argue that the post–Cold War period has witnessed a proliferation of the notion of the enemy of the nation and that discourse is constituted by the idea that "enemies threaten the moral, cultural, and political fabric of the nation state and must be evicted, eliminated, or controlled. . . . The production and proliferation of new enemies to blame, to oppose, and to conquer is part of a distinct contemporary culture" (35). Referring to histories of Asian immigrant exclusion, Lisa Lowe (1994, 55) writes that nation-based racism has operated through the construction of a binary opposition between patriot and enemy. After 9/11, in the process of legitimizing imperialist ambitions through appeals to nationalist narratives about protecting national security, dominant U.S. discourses have refashioned post-Cold War binaries from patriot versus enemy to those who are with us versus those who are with the terrorists.[23] Names signifying an "Arab/Middle Eastern/Muslim" identity rendered particular men and boys at once foreign, or alien, to the nation, but at the same time connected, in the most familial and instinctive terms, to "the terrorists." In this sense, nation-based racism conflates "Arab/Middle Eastern/Muslim" masculinities with an inherent potential for violence and terrorism and legitimizes the discipline and punishment of "Arab/Middle Eastern/Muslim" masculinities "over there" (in the countries the United States is invading) and "over here" (within the geographic borders of the U.S.). Moreover, that Saleh, in the narrative above, reconsidered whether to name his son Mohammed indicates that he came to understand that he was required to engage with the hegemonic conflation of names such as Mohammed with Muslim masculinity and terrorism. In this sense, the interpellation of subjects through hegemonic discourses produced disciplinary effects in them. While the conflation of the "Arab/Middle Eastern/Muslim" and "terrorism" brought into play dualistic mechanisms of exclusion (patriot vs. enemy/with us or against us), it simultaneously induced within individuals a state of consciousness that I refer to as "internment of the psyche" (Naber 2006). I use this term to refer to the ways in which engagements with racialization produced a sense of internal incarceration among my research participants that was emotive and manifested in the fear that at any moment one could be harassed, beaten up, picked up, locked up, or disappeared.

Although gender permeated nation-based racism through the conflation of particular names with Muslim masculinity and terrorism, a mapping of nation-based racism onto cultural racism also operated to articulate "Arab/Middle Eastern/Muslim" masculinity as inherently violent toward women. One cab driver

---

23. See Howell and Shryock (2003) for further analysis on the implications of the binary "those who are with us and those who are with terrorists" on Arab American identities and experiences.

told a story of his passengers' reaction to him after they read that his name was Mohammed: "Once, a woman got in my car. She looked at me, then read my name, then asked me if I was Muslim. When I said 'yes' she replied, 'how many girls have you killed today?'" In this case, a form of cultural racism that essentializes Muslimness as if the association between violence against women and Muslim masculinity is natural and insurmountable constitutes the articulation of Muslim masculinity as intrinsically connected to misogynist savagery. The woman's reaction to the cab driver reifies what Moallem refers to as "representations of Islamic fundamentalism in the West" that are "deeply influenced by the general racialization of Muslims in a neo-racist idiom which has its roots in cultural essentialism and a conventional Eurocentric notion of people without history."

Here, "religion" functions like a nature (Balibar 1999, 22) as "Mohammed," like the Osama and Fouad references above, becomes monstrously subversive, a metonymic source of sedition and danger within the nation, as well as to U.S. "interests" and to "American" bodies, white and nonwhite.

Appearances: Unveiling the Terrorist's Daughter

The intersection of race and gender was also apparent in the harassment of women who wore a headscarf. A general consensus among community leaders was that federal government policies disproportionately targeted men while hate crimes and incidents of harassment in the public sphere disproportionately targeted women. As Farah, a Muslim American woman community activist put it, "Women who wear *hijab* were more of a target because they're more visible than Muslim men in public. The awareness that they were in more danger and were more impacted than men could be seen by all of the events that were organized in solidarity with veiled women in response to the backlash. There were days of solidarity organized across the nation." Several cases in which employers fired women from their jobs for wearing headscarves instilled a sense of apprehension about the acceptability of discrimination against Muslim women in the public sphere among several of my research participants. As Manal, a university student explained, "We felt supported, but at the same time, there was a concern for our safety. I had never carried pepper spray. I started carrying pepper spray after 9/11 and was really being mindful of my surroundings. I remember the Muslim Student Association meetings—afterwards everyone would make sure that no one was walking alone to their cars." Several Muslim

American community leaders recalled cases in which women debated whether they should remove their scarves. As Amal, another university student put it, "I knew I had to prepare for at least some kind of backlash because I was visually identifiable. My mother, who doesn't cover, specifically told me 'Don't go outside for a month or two. Wait till things die down.' I was like, 'I shouldn't hide. I shouldn't be scared or restrain my lifestyle because of ignorance.'" In this sense, considerations of whether and to what extent one should wear or remove a headscarf or go out in public generated an "internment of the psyche" or the awareness that one must become habitually concerned about hegemonic misinterpretations and mistranslations.

While "Arab Muslim" masculinities were produced as the subjects of discourses that construct their primary and stable identity as violent agents of terrorism and/or misogyny, or the "true" enemy of the nation, "Arab Muslim" femininities, signified by the headscarf, were articulated as extensions of those practices.[24] In several cases, that headscarves signified an identification that transformed particular women into daughters or sisters of terrorists in general, or Osama or Saddam in particular, exemplifies one of the ways in which gender permeated nation-based racism in the context of the "war on terror." Lamia, a community activist summarized what she witnessed through her work among Arab Muslim youth in the Tenderloin, "After September 11, girls who wear *hijab* received lots of harassment on the bus, at school and on the street. People would try and pull their *hijab* off." The following excerpt from a group interview with Iraqi youth elucidates Lamia's point:

> *Maha:* "My sister was coming home from school one day and people were calling her, 'Osama's daughter.'"
>
> *Salma:* "At school, kids take off their shirts and put them on their heads and say, 'We look like Osama's daughter now. We look like you now.' Some kids would come up to us and say, 'Why don't you take it off? Are you still representing Osama?'"

24. For further analysis on representations of femininity as extensions of masculinity, "abject beings," or the construction of the feminine as objects that supply the site through which the phallus penetrates, see Butler (1993, 56–60). Also see Tadiar (2002, 5) for a discussion of the ways that women within a colonialist, patriarchal society are not only imprisoned within particular ideals about gender, but also function as useful objects that serve patriarchal, national, and international structures and processes.

In this narrative, young Arab Muslim girls are constructed as though patriarchal kinship ties are the sole determinants of their identities. Reduced to "daughters of Osama," they are transformed into the "property," "the harmonious extension" (Shohat and Stam 1994) of the enemy of the nation within, or symbols that connect others to the "real actors" or "terrorists" but who do not stand on their own (and lack agency). The "daughter of a terrorist" metaphor also articulates a condemnation of Muslim women for veiling.[25] Reifying the logic of nation-based racism that constructs a binary between us versus them and good, or moral Americans versus bad immoral potential criminal terrorists, Salma's peer not only asks her to "unveil" but also reduces her realm of possibilities to either "taking off her veil" or "representing Osama." For Salma's peer, either she is unveiled/with us, or she is with terrorism. In this sense, the "veil" serves as a boundary marker between "us" and "them," and as long as women remain "veiled" they remain intrinsically connected to "potential terrorists."

Dark-Skinned, Bearded Terrorists, and the "Queery-ing" of "Muslim Masculinities"

Several research participants reported incidents in which beards, coupled with dark skin and in some cases a particular form of religious dress, emerged as signifiers of "Islamic fundamentalism" or "terrorism." Salah Masri, director of one of the largest mosques in San Francisco, explained,

> I know this man who is a peaceful Tunisian Muslim that dresses in white robe with a long beard. He is extremely quiet and polite. He is a good engineer. He is an internet web designer. After September 11, we didn't see him at the *masjid* for a long time. When we asked about him, it turned out he didn't feel comfortable changing his clothes or shaving his beard so he decided to stay home. Some people didn't want to look Muslim. I know people who dyed their hair blond. One of them was a Turkish guy who dyed his hair blond because he thought he looked Arab or Middle Eastern. We had many cases of people shaving their beards or people who stopped attending the mosque. But why dye your hair?! He still looked Middle Eastern with it!

25. See Shohat and Stam for an analysis of colonialist discourses on "veiling." Ella Shohat and Robert Stam, in their critique of colonialist Hollywood films write, "The orient is . . . sexualized through the recurrent figure of the veiled woman, whose mysterious inaccessibility, mirroring that of the orient itself, requires Western unveiling to be understood" (1994, 149).

That Salah conflates "looking Muslim" with "looking Arab or Middle Eastern" epitomizes a consensus among many of my research participants that dominant U.S. discourses do not distinguish between "Arabs," "Middle Easterners," or "Muslims" and construct an image of an "Arab/Middle Eastern/Muslim look." Persons who closely resembled the corporate media's "Arab/Middle Eastern/Muslim look" were particularly vulnerable to federal government policies and harassment on the streets.[26] One immigrant-rights lawyer explained that the federal government went after "the CNN version of what a terrorist looks like. He was dark, Middle Eastern, and had a full beard. He was the typical terrorist looking guy—or at least the guy who CNN portrays as the terrorist. Timothy McVeigh is a terrorist, but he is not associated with terrorism because he does not look like the typical terrorist-looking guy." My research indicated that men who had beards, coupled with dark skin, were among those most severely concerned for their safety—particularly if they wore religious forms of dress perceived to be associated with Islam. That non-Muslim South Asian men such as Sikhs who wear turbans were repeatedly misidentified as Muslims (and in some cases killed) points to the ways that a range of signifiers can stand in as symbols of an "Arab/Middle Eastern/Muslim look." Cases such as these reify dominant U.S. distinctions between those who are with us and those who are with the terrorists by rendering particular kinds of bodies not only as unassimilable or "fundamentally foreign and antipathetic to modern American society and cultures" (Lowe 1996, 5), but also as threatening to national security and therefore legitimate targets of violence and harassment. Moreover, cases in which men considered shaving their beards or avoiding attendance at their mosque illustrate that while dominant discourses on "potential terrorists" often pulled particular bodies into associations with a violent "crazy" Muslim masculinity, they simultaneously produced an "internment of the psyche" that they themselves come to resist, transform, or reproduce.

On the streets, perpetrators of incidents of harassment often deployed sexualized tropes in targeting men whose appearances "fit" the "terrorist profile," reifying what Eman Desouky (2000) refers to as the "queery-ing" of Arab-Muslim subjectivities. Dominant U.S. discourses have often depicted the United States as feminist and gay-safe through comparisons between U.S. and Afghan

---

26. See Shaheen (1984) and Shohat and Stam (1994) for further analysis on the corporate media's representation of an Arab or Muslim "look."

views on gender and sexuality. Yet, as Puar and Rai explain, "the U.S. state, having experienced a castration and penetration of its capitalist masculinity, offers up narratives of emasculation as appropriate punishment for bin Laden, brown-skinned folks, and men in turbans" (2002, 10). A highly patriarchal and homophobic discourse has been central to the racialization of persons associated with "Islamic fundamentalism" and justifications for violence against them. In one case I learned of, hegemonic conflations between queerness, sexual deviancy, and the monstrous figure of "the terrorist" (2002, 126) underpinned the subjection of particular masculinities to physical or epistemic violence because they "appeared" to be Muslim. Consider the following community activist's narrative:

> A guy from Afghanistan called into the hate-crime hot-line. He had gone to help his friend whose car had broken down when he was doing some off-roading a couple of miles away from his house—which is also near a military base in Dublin. By the time his friend got out there to help him, there were two tow trucks out there. The tow truck drivers called the police because the men had beards so the drivers thought they were terrorists. They were near a reservoir and the tow truck drivers were saying things like, "Oh, okay . . . they're tapping the water." So they took them to the military base to interrogate them. Fifteen to twenty cops came. They all thought they were trying to contaminate the water. One of the guys had prayer beads with him and officers said quotes like, "your faggot beads. We're going to f——you up; we're going to [give you oral sex]." The officers were intimidating them.

In this narrative, the tow-truck drivers transform the Afghan men into terrorists vis-à-vis assumptions that conflate "the beard" with "Muslim masculinity" and "terrorism." Inscribing hegemonic discourses that "they" are trying to kill/penetrate "us" on the Afghan men's bodies, the tow-truck drivers transform them into terrorist threats/enemies within. Here, patriarchal, homophobic discourses of emasculation mark Islam—represented by the prayer beads—as "faggot," or not quite the right/straight kind of masculinity. The police's speech implicitly positions heterosexuality on the side of good and queerness on the side of evil. Moreover, as the police punish Muslim masculinities (read terrorists) with the threat of sodomy, a logic of militarized patriotism intensifies the normativity of heterosexuality. In this incident, as in the Abu Ghraib prison scandal, homophobia and racism intersect in the conceptualization that sexual degradation and the transformation of Muslim masculinities into "faggots" is an appropriate form of punishment.

Underlying this conceptualization is the heteronormative conflation of shame, humiliation, and homosexuality. Several LGBTST activists of color have produced alternative frameworks for understanding this conflation. Trishala Deb of the Audre Lorde Project argues that we need to ask ourselves what this latest chapter (Abu Ghraib) teaches us about the inevitable homophobia and racism in military culture as well as cultures of militarization (Deb and Mutis 2004, 7). She adds "that there are more than two genders and the subjugation of people who are any of those genders is not closer to femininity [or emasculization] but to dehumanization" (6).[27]

Nation of Origin and the Silencing of Political Dissent

My research indicated that emblems signifying particular nations of origin also placed persons into associations with the "potential terrorist" enemy of the nation. This process was based upon a logic that conflated particular nations with "Arabness," "Islam," and a potentiality for "terrorism." The signifier "nation of origin" often intersected with other emblems signifying the "Arab/Middle Eastern/Muslim" (such as name, skin color, facial hair, or headscarf). In particular, emblems representing "geographies of terror," or the nations that the Bush administration has referred to as terrorist-harboring countries or terrorist training grounds (e.g., Palestine or Iraq), tended to operate as signifiers of the enemy of the nation. Moreover, the potential for encountering harassment was often exacerbated when one was perceived to be an "Arab/Middle Eastern/Muslim" *and* simultaneously expressed solidarity with one or more of these nations. For example, Zainab, a Palestinian woman who wore a *kuffiyah* (a scarf representing Palestinian resistance) on a daily basis and posted a sticker of a Palestinian flag on a window near the front door of her home encountered some of the most severe forms of harassment I learned of throughout the period of my research. Zainab lived in the Mission District of San Francisco. She described her experience as follows: "I walked out [our door] and saw all this graffiti. I didn't

---

27. Trishala Deb argues that the military police and interrogation officials who oversaw these acts [of torture] might have intended to inflict what they perceived to be worst form of sexual degradation possible—which included what looks like gay sex (Deb and Mutis 2004, 5).

know. . . . Should I be afraid? angry? Then I looked at the sidewalk and saw 'Kill Arabs' in big blocks right in front of our house. The graffiti was all done in black spray paint. On top of the door, it said 'Die pig' in big block letters over where the Palestinian flag is. On the side wall were the words, 'Die pig.'" Afterwards, the perpetrator returned to her home five times. In one incident he threw feces and garbage all over her front door. "Whatever it is that he hits us with," she explained, "you can't leave. You can't open the door and get out, because it's just shit and garbage all over the place."[28]

For Zainab, the "war on terror" took on local form in that her public expression of Palestinian identity and political solidarity with Palestinian people put her in close proximity with the "terrorists." The perpetrator's articulation of violence against Zainab paralleled the Bush administration's rhetoric that violence is essential to patriotism, Americanness, and the protection of national security in the context of the "war on terror." In the ongoing hate crimes that took place in the two-year period following 9/11, vandalism and death threats emerged as critical venues for the articulation of nation-based racism against persons who were perceived to be intrinsically associated with "Islamic fundamentalism" and "terrorism" in the public sphere. Perpetrators deployed tactics "officially" banned by the state that simultaneously supported government discourses on militarized patriotism and war against the enemies of the nation—in this case, Palestinian Arabs.

Acts of harassment and intimidation against Arab and Arab American activists who participated in antiwar and/or Palestine solidarity movements exemplify the ways in which the targeting of activists who were perceived to be Arab/Middle Eastern/Muslim was influenced by an interplay between cultural and nation-based racism. This interplay set the stage for incidents of anti-Arab/Muslim racism coupled with political repression. On one university campus, for example, a series of peaceful demonstrations organized by an active Palestinian students' organization sparked an official university reaction that rendered members of the student group potentially "dangerous." Nadeem, a university student, recalling one of these demonstrations, explained,

28. With very little assistance from the local police, Zainab and her friend discovered who the perpetrator was by tape recording him in action. She discovered he lived a block away from her home. She continued to face resistance from the local police to put a restraining order on him or assist her with the case.

The police set up a barricade around us in the shape of a horseshoe so people would have to walk an extra 150 meters to get into the demonstration and so that they could protect people from us. The cops came, locked all the barricades together with plastic handcuffs and then his group of students stood outside the barricades shouting things like, "Sand nigger, camel jockey, f——ing terrorists, get the f—— out of here." Students from our group got upset and were shouting back things like, "F—— you, you know, blah, blah, blah." Later, the university president came out with a letter completely blasting the Palestinian students saying that in his fourteen years at this university, this was the most severe case of "lack of civility" that he has ever seen. A month later, the university imposed sanctions on our group and we were put under probation. We did not receive funding after that for a year.

Similar attacks targeted Arab and Arab American activists on other university campuses in the San Francisco Bay Area. Tamara, recalling an event on another university campus explained, "We were having a memorial for victims of the Israeli massacre of the refugee camp Jenin. Two people came over to disrupt the event. They were saying, 'Go blow yourself up' to a group of Arab American students who were there." This quote further illustrates the ways in which the silencing of political dissent, when directed against Arab student activists, took on specific form that connected them intrinsically to "the terrorists."

The difference between how official public discourses in the local media, among civil rights organizations, and among university officials represented white American and Arab American student involvement in the Palestine solidarity movement illustrates the racial logic underpinning the silencing of political dissent in the context of the "war on terror." In spring 2002, during a period of intense Israeli aggression against Palestinian civilians, two student groups on two different college campuses in the San Francisco Bay Area organized similar demonstrations in support of Palestinian people. The first group was composed of predominantly white students, and the second group was composed primarily of Arab students. The university tried to impose harsh punishments on the first group, including administrative detention and suspension. In this case, various civil rights groups quickly came to the student activists' support and framed the problem as an attack on political dissent on that campus. On the other campus, where the students were predominantly Arab, the same civil rights groups did not lend their support when the university imposed similar restrictions on the student organization. This response reflected a broader official discourse in that both universities and local media reports framed the tensions on the first campus as a free-speech issue while referring to the incidents on the second campus in terms of potentially dangerous Palestinian students. An immigrant-rights lawyer and community activists who worked with the Palestinian student group explained, "It was really easy to see the anti-Arab anti-Muslim sentiment in the university's assumptions that they were fighting the war on terrorism and that Palestinian students were dangerous supporters of terrorism."

In the cases above, nation-based racism was exacerbated in contexts where persons perceived to be "potential terrorists" by virtue of their name, appearance, or nation of origin engaged in public expressions of dissent, particularly against U.S. and/or Israeli policies in Arab homelands. As Tadiar argues, "from the dominant cultural logic of the U.S. state, terrorism embodies an other relation to death, and it is on this basis that racism operates against other peoples who are deemed close to this other relation to death (epitomized by the would be suicide bomber)" (2005). By framing Palestinian students as potentially dangerous and therefore deserving of disciplinary measures, dominant local discourses reified dominant corporate media and government discourses that position Palestinians in close proximity to "real terrorists" and thus legitimize statements such as "get out of here" and "go blow yourselves up." In referring to Palestinian students as "dangerous" and "lacking in civility," the university president reifies racialized representations that construct Palestinians as not only inherently violent, full of hate, and threatening to Israeli and U.S. national security, but also as backward and uncivilized. By justifying the targeting of students in terms of a civilizational discourse (i.e., their "lack of civility"), the university president deploys the logic of cultural racism that defines difference in terms of an "incompatibility of lifestyles and traditions" that are insurmountable. In this sense, a liberal politics of progress, legitimated by cultural racism, naturalizes the distinctions between self and Other, tradition and modernity, barbarism and civilization. Cultural racism and nation-based racism become critical to the structures of power through which the exclusion of particular Arabs and Arab Americans has functioned in a post-9/11 environment.

CONCLUSION

In the aftermath of September 11, 2001, in response to the backlash, the category "Arab, Muslim, South Asian" has been incorporated into liberal U.S.

multicultural discourses. Consider, for example, diversity initiatives that have operated to single out Arabs, Muslims, and South Asians as the *only* "targeted communities" in the post-9/11 moment (Lee 2002). In such instances, terms such as "targeted communities" have reinforced a multicultural rainbow where specific marginalized groups are associated with specific historical moments while occluding the long-term historical circumstances that produce oppression, marginality, and institutionalized racism, and overshadowing links between groups that have shared similar histories of immigrant exclusion and racism. That many liberal immigrant-rights organizations referred to anti-immigrant policies underlying the PATRIOT Act of 2001 as an "Arab, Muslim, and South Asian" issue and the "Border Protection" Bill HR4437 of 2006 as a Latino/a issue—even though both pieces of legislation affected Arabs, Muslims, South Asians, Latinos/as (and other immigrants as well as citizens) and even though the intensified anti-immigrant sentiment sparked by the aftermath of September 11 facilitated support for the HR4437—exemplifies this pattern.

Transgressing liberal multicultural approaches, many racial justice activists and scholars have agreed that while survivors of 9/11-related federal government policies and incidents of harassment in the public sphere tended to be Arab, Muslim, and South Asian, this is not an isolated case of group marginalization.[29] A new racial justice discourse thus emerged that called attention to anti-Arab/Muslim/South Asian racism; insisted that racial justice movements take the link

29. Among the widespread responses to the backlash among civil rights advocates, The New York City Commission of Human Rights published the report "Discrimination Against Muslims, Arabs, and South Asians in New York City since 9/11" (2003). In San Francisco, the organization Grantmakers concerned with Immigrants and Refugees published a report entitled, "Arab, Middle Eastern, Muslim, and South Asian Communities in the San Francisco Bay Area" to "inform the Bay Area foundation community about the most salient issues facing these communities and encourage foundations to support programs and strategies that respond to these issues" (Ahuja, Gupta, and Petsod 2004, 4). The U.S. Equal Employment Opportunity Commission issued a report entitled, "Questions and Answers about Workplace Rights of Muslims, Arabs, South Asians, and Sikhs" (2002). The national antiwar organization Not in Our Name, produced a documentary entitled, "'Under Attack:' Arab, Muslim and South Asian Communities Since 9/11" (2004) and a coalition of over two hundred individuals and organizations supported the first national day of solidarity with Muslim, Arab, and South Asian Immigrants (2002). The aftermath of September 11 also sparked new alliances between Arab American, Muslim American, and South Asian American organizations that joined forces in resisting the post–September 11 backlash against their communities and the expanding U.S.-led war in their homelands (Naber 2002).

between U.S.-led war in Muslim majority countries and the marginalization of Arabs, Muslims, and South Asians in the United States seriously; and linked the targeting of Arabs, Muslims, and South Asians to experiences of other communities with shared histories of oppression, including, but not limited to, Japanese Americans, Filipinos, Latinos/as, and African Americans. Despite these efforts, prevailing articulations of "race" within U.S. racial and ethnic studies tend to preclude comparative research and teaching on the links between the racialization of Arabs, Muslims, Middle Easterners, and South Asians and other communities that have been historically targeted by racism and state violence.

In the late 1960s, San Francisco State University was the site of the longest campus strike in the nation's history, spearheaded by the Black Students Union and the Third World Liberation Front (a coalition of the Black Students Union, the Latin American Students Organization, the Filipino-American Students Organization, and El Renacimiento, a Mexican American student organization). This movement demanded the expansion of the college's new Black Studies Department (the nation's first), the creation of a School of Ethnic Studies, and increased recruiting and admissions of minority students. On March 21, 1969, this strike officially came to an end with the establishment of the School of Ethnic Studies, which included a focus on Asian Americans, Latinos/as and Native Americans, and an expanded Black Studies Department (San Francisco State Univ. 2003). This movement, based on the strategic deployment of the terms "Third World people" and "people of color," legitimized the establishment and expansion of ethnic studies programs that place communities that have shared histories of oppression by the United States government at the center of study, analysis, activism, and empowerment. Yet this paradigm, which operates according to a 1960s understanding of what constitutes racism, limits our categories of analysis to those established during the height of student movements for ethnic studies in the 1960s. Contemporary articulations of this paradigm foreclose discussions on how the meaning of "race" has continued to shift and preclude analyses of how "racism" is constantly being remade. At the same time, many recent conversations within U.S. racial and ethnic studies have explored how research on emergent forms of racialization in relationship to both previous as well as new and current historical processes might contribute to conceptualizations of race and racism in a post-9/11 environment.[30]

30. See Ono (2005), Volpp (2003), and Maira and Shihade (2006).

In this chapter I sought to bring new questions to bear on the study of race and racism within U.S. racial and ethnic studies: What are the implications of continually reevaluating our understanding of racialized-gendered identities in light of new and changing historical moments? What are the possibilities for envisioning U.S. racial and ethnic studies in ways that remain connected to the 1960s student and civil rights struggles through which they were produced while becoming more attentive to current gendered racialization processes? How might becoming attentive to the gendered racialization of Arabs, South Asians, and/or Muslims contribute to explorations of the relationship between race, gender, sexuality, and empire or the structures of racism, sexism, and homophobia that operate against immigrants with whose homelands the United States is at war?

This chapter has reinforced existing theoretical approaches that tend to define U.S. race and ethnic studies that contend that "race" is malleable and shifting, that racial categories are socially and historically constructed, and that the construction of racial categories is a continuous process that takes on new and different form within different historical moments. It has also affirmed existing women of color feminist approaches that have called attention to differences within racialized groups (such as those of class, gender, sexuality, and religion) and contended that experiences of oppression that are shaped by both racism and sexism simultaneously cannot be subsumed within either a feminist framework that critiques sexism or an antiracist framework that is only critical of racism (Crenshaw 1991).[31] It has also illustrated that research on the gendered racialization of the "Middle Eastern/Muslim" or the "Arab/Muslim/South Asian" "enemy within" can generate important new questions, such as: To what extent does the rhetoric of an endless, fluid "war or terror" that "knows no boundaries" produce new forms of gendered racialization that are similarly arbitrary, open-ended, and transgress borders and particular geographic places?

31. I draw from Kimberlé Crenshaw's work on intersectionality. She argues that women of color often have to choose between participation in an antiracist movement or a feminist movement, yet the experiences of women of color mark intersections that cannot be captured *only* by a gender or race analysis that stand separate from each other. Crenshaw's work on the intersectionality transgresses this limitation by opening up a space for intersectional organizing/resistance (1991).

ELEVEN

Discrimination and Identity Formation in a Post-9/11 Era

A Comparison of Muslim and Christian Arab Americans

JEN'NAN GHAZAL READ

IN THE AFTERMATH of the terrorist attacks on September 11, 2001, the term "Arab American" has evolved into a catch-all category that inaccurately groups together persons of different national origins, ethnicities, and religious affiliations, all on the basis of physical characteristics thought to reflect "Arab." In reality, Arab Americans are a heterogeneous ethnic population that shares a cultural and linguistic heritage, tracing their ancestries to seventeen Arabic-speaking countries in northern Africa and western Asia. Compared to the U.S. adult population, Arab Americans are younger, more highly educated, have higher labor force participation rates, and earn higher incomes (U.S. Bureau of the Census 2000). Contrary to the stereotype that it is mostly an immigrant Muslim population, over one-half of Arab Americans are U.S.-born, 82 percent are U.S. citizens, and an estimated two-thirds are Christian, with the remaining third being Muslim (Read 2004a, 2004b; Zogby 2002). The proportion who are Muslim continues to rise, however, with immigration and domestic birth rates.

Such diversity in religious identity may have important implications for the incorporation of Arabs into American society, particularly after 9/11. Christian Arab Americans may be able to use their Christian identity as a bridge to the American mainstream, thereby distancing themselves from 9/11 and demonstrating that they are not terrorists or terrorist sympathizers (i.e., boundary work). Muslim Arab Americans, on the other hand, may be unable to maintain such boundaries because of their religious and ethnic out-group statuses (see

Lamont and Fournier 1992). The post-9/11 racialization of Middle Easterners may further disadvantage Muslim Arab Americans relative to Christian Arab Americans (hereafter "Muslim" and "Christian"), in part owing to differences in migration histories and physical appearances (Cainkar 2002a). Because Muslims are more likely to be newer immigrants with distinctive physical characteristics that separate them from white America, they may have fewer "ethnic options" than their Christian peers (Waters 1990).

This chapter examines this question by comparing the racial and ethnic identities of Muslims and Christians and assessing the relationship between multiple identities and their experiences of discrimination after September 11, 2001. Discrimination is an important issue to consider because it indicates the degree to which a group is marginalized in society. The data derive from a survey questionnaire that I administered to 335 Arab American congregants at an Arab church (n = 155) and Arab mosque (n = 180) in a metropolitan area in central Texas in fall 2002. The location is home to the largest Arab American community in the south, ranking ninth among Arab American communities nationwide. The research design is useful because it examines a geographic region that is often excluded in studies of Arab American populations, many of which focus on more dense and accessible Arab American communities in Dearborn, Detroit, and Chicago. This design is also useful because it allows for distinctions between Arab ethnicity and Muslim religion, which are often collapsed into synonymous components of culture in studies of Middle Eastern communities.

The chapter is organized in three sections. The first section provides the historical context for contemporary diversity in Arab American identity (i.e., Muslim and Christian) and offers a framework for theorizing about identity formation in the post-9/11 era. The next section provides details on the research questions and methodology, followed by empirical evidence on differences in Muslims' and Christians' racial and ethnic identities and experiences of discrimination. The chapter concludes by discussing the implications of the findings for the future incorporation and well-being of Arabs in American society.

HISTORICAL INFLUENCES ON CONTEMPORARY ARAB AMERICAN IDENTITY

Although research on Arab American identity formation is in its infancy, studies of other U.S. racial and ethnic populations provides a theoretical framework for understanding differences in identity construction among Christians and Muslims. In particular, prior studies establish the importance of historical and situational circumstances in defining immigrants' racial and ethnic identities (Chong 1998; Ebaugh and Chafetz 2000). Racial and ethnic identity is not automatically assumed on the basis of social category but is an emergent form of social organization that develops in response to external forces in society, such as host hostility and structural inequality. Societal conditions have likewise shaped the identity formations of Christian and Muslim Arab Americans.

In general terms, Arab Americans immigrated in two distinct waves, the first being predominantly Christian and the latter comprising mainly Muslims. The first wave began at the end of the nineteenth century and continued through World War I (Naff 1994). The majority of these early arrivals were working-class Christians from Greater Syria seeking better economic opportunities for their families. Like other immigrant sojourners of that era, most believed their immigration to be temporary and devoted little effort to assimilating into American life. Their Eastern Christian heritage served as a primary source of identity, and they built ethnic churches to provide a sense of solidarity and to sustain cultural traditions unique to their Christian Arab heritage (Kayal and Kayal 1975). Although Arab ethnic identity was an important part of individual identity, it was less salient than religious affiliation for these early Arab immigrants, a holdover from the Ottoman classification system that identified subjects by religious affiliation (Hooglund 1994).

Ultimately, sharing the religious tradition of the majority population facilitated their assimilation into white, mainstream American society. Their religious practices did not greatly distinguish them from Christianity, and intermarriage with other Christian ethnic groups became common, especially for Arab men (Samhan 2001). Simultaneously, encounters with U.S. immigration policies helped solidify their position as members of the white majority population—to avoid exclusionary Asian laws, they traced their Syrian ancestries to their Arab heritage, which gave them Caucasian racial status and eventually led to their being classified with European whites on the U.S. census, a practice that continues today (Samhan 1999).

The historical context was markedly different for the second wave of Arab immigration. In the three decades following World War II, roughly five hundred thousand Arabs came to the U.S. from twenty-two countries in North Africa and Southwest Asia. Although Christians continued to migrate in this wave, most of the arrivals were educated Muslims immigrating in response to political turmoil in the Middle East, such as the 1967 and 1973 Arab-Israeli wars. Others came as students to American universities and extended their stay permanently, often unable to return to their countries of origin for fear of political persecution (Suleiman 1994). These newer immigrants were more ethnically conscious and had stronger attachments to their nations of origin, arriving in the United States during an era of pan-Arab nationalism unknown to earlier immigrants (Suleiman and Abu-Laban 1989).

The process of assimilation has been more complex for Muslim immigrants compared to their Christian predecessors (Bilge and Aswad 1996). On the one hand, their educational achievements have encouraged integration into the American middle class. On the other hand, their status as a religious minority has militated against easy acculturation into mainstream society, particularly in a post-9/11 environment that has witnessed the racialization of Islam and of Muslim Americans. Nadine Naber argues in her introduction to this volume, racialization is a social and historical process by which racial categories are created, adopted, and transformed, and since 9/11, Arab and Muslim Americans have been lumped into a new racialized category that obscures the considerable diversity that exists within these populations. The ongoing war against terror globally, war in Iraq, and American attitudes toward Islam further exacerbate the racialization process, leaving many Muslim immigrants feeling alienated in their new homeland.

Although such diverse immigration experiences would seem to work against the development of a cohesive Arab ethnic community, there is evidence of increased ethnic solidarity among Arab Americans in times of heightened conflict and tension. In the aftermath of the 1967 Arab-Israeli war, for example, strong American support of Israel helped forge Arab American unity (Haddad 1991). For the first time, Christian and Muslim Arab Americans consciously chose to assert their common ethnicity by creating national organizations such as the National Association of Arab Americans to act as a political lobby to advance common Arab American interests, and the American Arab Anti-Discrimination Committee to combat negative images of Arabs and Muslims in the mass media (Majaj 1999a).

Although host hostility has generally increased group solidarity, it has periodically sharpened racial, religious, and ethnic boundaries among Arab Americans. Negative stereotypes of Muslims and Arabs have encouraged Christians to dissociate from their ethnic heritage to avoid prejudice and discrimination, while the racialization of more recent immigrants, most of whom are Muslim, has not offered Muslims the same options. The establishment of separate Muslim American organizations has further distinguished the Arab community along religious lines, offering Muslim Arabs alternative methods for expressing group grievances (Haddad 1994). Despite these distinctions, Christian and Muslim Arabs continue to demonstrate some degree of ethnic cohesion. For example, a nationwide poll of Arab Americans found that 89 percent of Christians and 94 percent of Muslims were "extremely proud" or "proud" of their ethnic heritage (Zogby 2000). Similarly, membership in national Arab American organizations remains high for Muslims and Christians of multiple generations.

OBJECTIVES AND METHODS

The above literature suggests that Arab Americans, like other immigrant groups, form their identities within the social contexts and boundaries of different historical periods. The terrorist attacks of September 11, 2001, introduced a new historical era in our society, one that will likely have long-term effects on Americans of all religious and ethnic backgrounds. Immigrants of Arab and Muslim origin have been particularly vulnerable to racial profiling and discrimination, which raises important questions about the effects of 9/11 on their identity and welfare.

There is some evidence that Muslim Arabs are more susceptible to racial profiling and discrimination than their Christian peers, in large part owing to the racialization of Muslim Americans in the aftermath of 9/11. For example, the Detroit Arab American Study finds that Muslims feel less secure than Christians after 9/11 and are more likely to feel that their religion is not respected by the American mainstream (Baker et al. 2004). There are also indications that Christian Arabs have greater latitude than Muslims in choosing their racial and ethnic identities (Zogby 2002). Besides these studies, few have explicitly compared the racial and ethnic identities of Muslims and Christians and none have tested the relationship between their identities and experiences of discrimination.

To examine these questions, this chapter draws on survey data collected from an Arab mosque and Arab church in central Texas in fall 2002, one year following the terrorist attacks of September 11. To protect the anonymity of the congregations and respondents, the exact locale will not be disclosed. Focusing on congregations is an effective method for examining the effects of discrimination on the ethnic and religious orientations of Arab Americans because the church and mosque are visible markers of identity. This method also provides a comparable basis for examining identity negotiation among Muslims and Christians because the latter group is hard to identify, as it is a largely assimilated population.

The church and mosque were selected based on similar demographic characteristics—primarily Arab congregations with two hundred to three hundred active families. Since there were non-Arab members in both religious communities, I screened survey participants with a standard question on Arab ancestry. The question asks where the following people were born: respondent, respondent's mother and father, and respondent's maternal and paternal grandparents. For greater comparability with the mosque, I focused on an Antiochian rather than a Coptic church because membership at Coptic churches is almost exclusively Egyptian, while Antiochian churches are more nationally diverse, comprising members from Syria, Lebanon, Palestine, and Jordan. To protect the anonymity of the respondents, I will use the generic terms mosque and church.

The survey questionnaire consisted of sixty-five closed- and open-ended questions that concentrated on the effects of 9/11 on Arab American identity and well-being. The questionnaire included several measures of ethnic identity, religious identity, and experiences of discrimination before and after 9/11, along with standard demographic measures, such as age, gender, and social class. The surveys were pretested on several groups of men and women at the church and mosque, and changes were made to the questions based on their feedback. The final survey was administered after prayer services at each location and took approximately twenty minutes to complete.

INTERSECTING IDENTITIES AND DISCRIMINATION

Given the variant migration histories of Muslims and Christians from the Middle East, we should expect to see differences in their subjective identification with their Arab heritage (e.g., Naff 1994). We might also expect to find that Christians have a stronger identification with white Americans and fewer encounters with discrimination, given their longer histories in the United States and shared status as religious majority. Table 11.1 examines these questions by comparing the racial and ethnic identities of Muslim and Christian respondents and examining their experiences of discrimination before and after September 11.

Table 11.1
Arab American Identity and Discrimination (%)

	Christian	Muslim
Nativity		
Foreign-born	45.8	82.8**
U.S.-born	54.2	17.2
Years residing in U.S.		
Less than 5	3.3	12.7**
5 to 14	26.3	41.8
15 or more	70.5	45.5
Subjective ethnic identity		
American	17.6	3.4**
Arab	56.8	59.0
Asian	1.4	28.7
Other	23.6	10.0
Ethnic meals per week		
None	16.1	5.1**
1 or 2	29.5	17.9
3 or more	54.3	77.0
Contact with Middle East		
Never	32.9	5.6**
A few times a year	28.3	36.9
More than once a month	25.0	53.1
Perceived racial category		
White	33.8	5.2**
Arab	25.2	54.3
Asian	0.7	13.3
Hispanic	17.9	16.8
Blacks	1.3	2.9
Don't know	21.2	7.5
Discrimination before 9/11		
Never	55.9	31.8**
Rarely	28.9	51.4
Fairly often	3.9	10.6
Very often	3.3	2.8

(continued)

Table 11.1
Arab American Identity and Discrimination (%) *(continued)*

	Christian	Muslim
Discrimination after 9/11		
Never	52.7	18.6**
Rarely	31.3	38.4
Fairly often	8.0	26.0
Very often	4.0	11.9
Ethnic Discrimination	31.6	58.9
Religious Discrimination	2.6	58.9**
N	155	180

Note: Variables not adding to 100 percent reflect missing data.
**$p<.01$.

Following known patterns of immigration to the United States over the past century, the Christians in this study are more likely than the Muslims to be native born, and of those who are foreign born, are more likely to have a longer duration of U.S. residency. They are also more likely to identify themselves subjectively as "American" or hyphenated American (listed in the "other" category). These results parallel those of the Detroit Arab American Study, where Christians were less likely than Muslims to accept the "Arab American" label (Baker et al. 2004).

Muslims, on the other hand, are more likely to identify themselves as "Arab" or "Asian," though it is worth noting that roughly an equal number of Christians consider themselves "Arab." Not surprisingly, Muslims have stronger ties to their ethnic identity, as evidenced by their greater frequency of cooking ethnic meals and contact with friends and family in the Middle East. These results indicate that Christians are more assimilated than their Muslim counterparts, in terms of both attitudes and behaviors.

In a telling question on perceived racial category, one-third of Christian respondents report that other people consider them "white," compared to only 5.2 percent of Muslims. Specifically, the survey question asked, "What group do you think *other* people think you belong to?" The response categories derived from the pretests were: white, black, Asian, Hispanic, Arab, don't know, and other. An additional one-fifth of Christians report that they are unsure of their racial

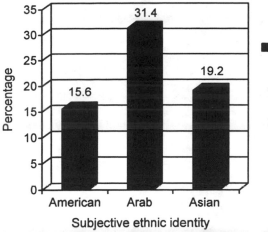

11.1. Ethnic Identity and Discrimination after 9/11

categorization, which may indicate that race is less salient than other aspects of their identity, or at minimum, that race is not a defining characteristic of their everyday experiences. Muslims, on the other hand, are much more likely to report that others perceive them as "Arab," Hispanic, or "Asian," with only a small fraction feeling that they pass as "white" Americans.

Corresponding to these differences in ethnic and racial identification, Muslims are also more likely to have experienced discrimination before 9/11, though a sizeable number of Muslims report having "rarely" or "never" experienced it. This result is in marked contrast to the post-9/11 question, where the number of Muslims who experienced discrimination doubled and tripled respectively for the categories "fairly often" and "very often." Christians only experienced a slight increase in discrimination after 9/11, and the vast majority still report rarely or never experiencing discrimination. An equal number of Muslims feel that the discrimination is on the basis of their ethnicity and religion, in part because they feel that Americans confuse the terms "Arab" and "Muslim."

Figures 11.1 and 11.2 assess in more detail the relationships between racial and ethnic identification and discrimination, and figures 11.3 and 11.4 examine the extent to which the relationships differ for Muslims and Christians. As seen in figure 11.1, one-third of respondents who subjectively identify as "Arab" report being discriminated against fairly or very often; this number is considerably higher than for any other group, and twice as high as those who consider themselves "American." Likewise, respondents who report that other people

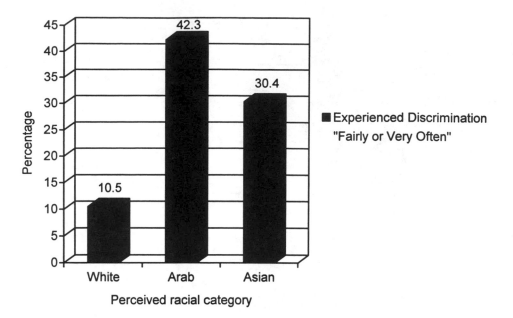

11.2. Racial Identity and Discrimination after 9/11

perceive them as Arab are significantly more likely to report being discriminated against relative to those who identify with other groups.

Respondents who self-identify or are perceived as "Asian" also report high levels of discrimination, while those who consider themselves "American" or "white" are least likely to have experienced discrimination in the aftermath of 9/11. The results in these figures clearly demonstrate that being an Arab in America, whether through subjective identification or ascription, is associated with higher levels of discrimination.

Figures 11.3 and 11.4 examine whether and how the relationship between identity and discrimination varies for Christians and Muslims. Figure 11.3 shows that Muslim respondents are more likely than Christians to experience discrimination, regardless of their subjective racial and ethnic identifications. For example, half of Muslims who identify themselves as "American" report high levels of discrimination, compared to only 7.7 percent of Christians who identify as "American." Moreover, the relationship between Arab identity and discrimination seen in figure 11.1 appears to be driven largely by the Muslim respondents—almost three times as many Muslims who identify as "Arab" report being discriminated against, compared to Christian Arabs. It is worth noting

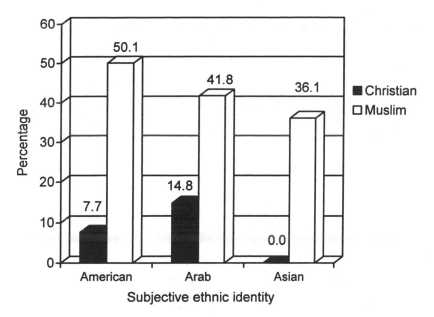

11.3. Ethnic Identity and Discrimination after 9/11 (Christian/Muslim)

that some of the categories contain a small number of respondents, so the magnitude of the differences between Christians and Muslims should not be overemphasized (e.g., only a small proportion of the Muslim respondents consider themselves American, so 50.1 percent reflects a small number). The important point is that Muslims, across the board, experience higher levels of discrimination than do their Christian counterparts.

Figure 11.4 paints a similar picture. Regardless of perceived racial category, Muslim respondents are more likely than Christians to report experiencing discrimination "fairly or very often." Taken together, figures 11.3 and 11.4 suggest that differences in racial and ethnic identification alone cannot explain the persistently higher levels of discrimination among Muslims relative to Christians. In other words, Muslims are uniformly disadvantaged in American society today, irrespective of their racial and ethnic identifications.

LOOKING TO THE FUTURE

The goal of this chapter was to compare the racial and ethnic identities of Muslims and Christians and assess the relationship between multiple identities

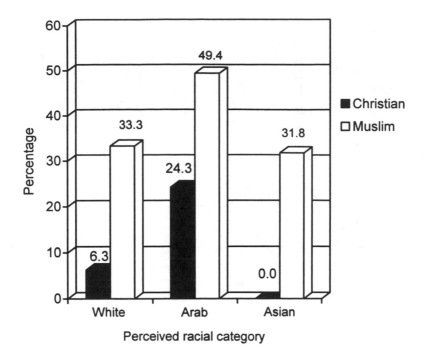

11.4. Racial Identity and Discrimination after 9/11 (Christian/Muslim)

and their experiences of discrimination after September 11, 2001. The analysis reveals that Muslim Arab Americans are more likely to define and perceive themselves as a minority group, while Christian Arab Americans appear to have greater latitude in affiliating with the majority white population. Correspondingly, Muslims are more susceptible to racial profiling and discrimination than their Christian peers, in part owing to their greater visibility and more recent immigrant status.

The findings also suggest that Christian Arab Americans are able to use their religious identity as a bridge to the cultural mainstream. Sharing the faith of the majority population facilitates their dissociation from the terror attacks of 9/11 by creating boundaries that separate them from "Arab" and "Muslim." Muslim Arab Americans, in contrast, are doubly marginalized by their ethnic and religious out-group statuses and are less able to use their identities as a bridge to American society.

These findings are consistent with and elaborate on Mary Waters's (1990) argument that white ethnic groups have more ethnic options than their racialized counterparts, who are assigned identities based on physical attributes. In this study, we have a case where ethnic options can vary *within* a group, based on religious affiliation and immigration history. As newer immigrants from diverse regions in the Middle East, Muslim Arabs may have fewer ethnic options than their Christian peers, many of whom are physically indistinguishable from white Americans.

Overall, results of this study underscore the need for additional research on America's emergent ethnic and religious populations, such as Arab Americans and U.S. Muslims. Mainstream sociological scholarship in religion, ethnicity, and immigration has been slow to document the experiences of these groups, despite their tremendous growth over the past few decades. Consequently, the social and economic adjustments of these communities remain less understood than those of other U.S. groups. Although not without limitations, this study points to the relevance of distinguishing between ethnicity and religion among persons of Middle Eastern descent, particularly in light of recent events.

TWELVE

Conclusion

Arab American Racialization

AMANEY JAMAL

THIS BOOK HAS PLACED THEORIES of racialization in conversation with Arab American studies. As this volume illustrates, the sources of Arab American racialization are both many and multifaceted. The racialization of Arab Americans is a dynamic process that encompasses the ways in which Arab Americans are differentiated yet also "accepted" in mainstream society. Arab American racialization is about the social construction of "Arab Americanness" in multiple contexts and the varied ways in which Arab Americans continue to negotiate their existence and respond to these different modalities.

Arab American racialization does not rely on phenotype alone, nor is it entirely contingent on the federal government's existing racial categories (i.e., the U.S. Census). How individual Arab Americans identify reveals that Arab Americans place themselves along multiple axes within the existing—and limiting—racial structures of U.S. society. Yet that is only part of the story when it comes to conceptualizing Arab Americans and "race." As many essays in this volume illustrate, dominant U.S. discourses and institutions have also positioned Arab Americans in terms of multiple, contradictory, and often ambiguous identities within existing racial structures.

The contributions in this volume repeatedly illustrate that within some contexts, Arab Americans have been positioned as "white but not quite." Other contributors have pointed to statistics that reveal that many Arab Americans do identify as white (Shryock). This statistic of "white identity" (for instance, 64 percent in the Detroit Arab American Study, 2003) is telling. First, it demonstrates that there is a "desire" among a significant majority of Arab Americans to situate themselves neatly within existing categories of racial identification. Some Arab Americans who can credibly identify as white might choose to see themselves as part of the dominant social structure in U.S. society, even while they may not always be accorded mainstream privileges linked with such identification. The Detroit Arab American Study reveals that 31 percent of Arab Americans identify as "other"—and among Muslim Arabs, that percentage is closer to 50 percent. This otherness could be a recognition that they don't fit neatly in any available racial classifications, are not accepted, or choose not to be identified as "white." These identifications are not based on phenotypical classifications or orientations. Rather, they are based on a series of interrelated processes whereby Arab Americans make sense of their own identity vis-à-vis existing hierarchies of race and how others see them in relation to these classifications. These identifications illustrate that even though the U.S. census continues to classify Arab Americans as "white," a solely "white" designation may not capture the diverse and complex ways that Arab American individuals experience "race."

What is absolutely compelling about the ways in which Arab Americans engage the racial markers that pervade U.S. society and the history of race relations in this country is the obvious limitations of the federal government's racial classifications. In this volume, some argue that "white" identification is built on the assumption of protected interests and security. Even while most Arabs identify as white, they are denied cultural citizenship. Still others have argued that this identification with whiteness has its own limitation. First of all, even though Arabs may choose to identify with whiteness, the "host society" may deny them that classification. And second, some Arabs and Arab Americans may not see themselves as white or experience "race" in terms of white privilege. Arab American whiteness presumes that Arab Americans are part of the dominant mainstream. Many of the contributions in this volume, however, have shown that while some Arab Americans claim whiteness, others have been denied this status or choose not to identify as white. These Arabs are not part or not accepted as part of the "white" superstructure, nor do they comfortably fit into other racial identity categories available to them. Where Arabs choose an identity other than white, they proclaim "Otherness."

ARAB AMERICAN OTHERNESS

This book illustrates that Arab American Otherness has been shaped by the ways that Arab Americans have been located within U.S. racial classification systems. The dichotomies of "white or nonwhite," "us or them," "American or enemy," "with us or against us": these are some of the binaries that construct Arab Americans within existing "racial" hierarchies in the United States. Within dominant U.S. discourses, the ideal Arab is one who consistently and repeatedly pays his allegiance to all things American, and one who is "with" the dominant discourse that prevails at any given time, even if that discourse is anti-Arab. If we look at the history of Arab American integration in the United States, it is rife with accounts of Arab Americans asserting their whiteness not only in relation to economic mobility and integration but also in relation to all things "American." In other words, for Arab Americans the words "white" and "American" are often experienced interchangeably.

Yet more recently, identification with white America has not resulted in Arab American acceptance as either white or American. Dominant representations of Arab Americans as un-American have only been exacerbated since 9/11. It is not lost on the average Arab that she does not neatly occupy a place within this white racial category. Yet, given the alternatives, some Arab Americans may argue that the white label has remained the one label that can protect Arab Americans from losing even the semblance of "American" status. Other Arab Americans may argue that gaining acceptance is not their objective and may instead reject the white identity label. Some Arab Americans may instead prioritize a vision that would entail ending anti-Arab racism and U.S.-led wars in their homeland. Therefore, they opt for identifying as persons of color as part of a strategy for participating in racial justice movements as antiracist/antiwar Arab Americans.

From the very onset of early immigration in the late 1880s, Arab racialization was solidified by markers of "outsider" status. Especially after World War II, when the United States became more involved in the Arab world, Arabs were consistently portrayed in popular representations as occupying the category of "other"—and too often, "enemy Other." It is this struggle to be accepted as an "ordinary citizen" that has dominated the lives of many Arab Americans. These same Arabs, along with other Arab Americans, have also been eagerly working toward ending U.S. military engagements in their countries of origin and the government and media's misrepresentation of Arab Americans.

The classification of "other" resonates much more strongly with Muslim Arab Americans than it does with Christian Arabs. Because Islam is not a major religion in the United States, and because the current war on terror has been widely perceived as a war against Islam, for Muslim Arab Americans the "non-American" status is all the more compounded. The Detroit Arab American Study found that Arab Muslim identification with otherness (at roughly 50 percent) was systematic among different immigrant and citizenship cohorts. On the other hand, Christian Arabs who had arrived earlier or were born in the United States and enjoy citizenship status were more likely to identify as white (Baker et al. 2004). However, identification by no means implies acceptance. Although the barriers to Americanness are more exacerbated for Arab Muslims, the same sources that stigmatize Arab Muslims are those that touch Arab Christian lives as well.

To Arabs, then, identifying as "other" as in the Detroit Arab American study, suggests marginalization, the lack of acceptance, the lack of comfortably fitting into any of the existent racial categories. Many of the processes of racialization and othering that have touched other minority groups extend to Arab Americans as well. Arab American racialization stems not only or even primarily from physical appearance but also from a deep and prolonged history of reduction to "Suspicious Arab."

Arab Americans—especially after 9/11—have not only experienced an increase in discrimination but also have seen the legal system turn against them. Not only is the denial of their Americanness more pervasive than ever, but the assumption of their guilt by ethnic association has never been more pronounced. Arabs and Muslims are seen and monitored as enemies residing within. Not all segments of the "mainstream," however, galvanize their efforts to treat Arabs as "enemies" within. While a third of Detroit Arabs reported receiving a gesture of support from a non–Middle Easterner after 9/11, significant percentages of Detroit Arabs also document a sense that their identities are not respected by American society (Baker et al. 2004). It is clear that although Arab Americans are the recipients of kind gestures from non-Arabs, there nevertheless exists an undeniable perception that Arabs are considered as suspicious Other.

It is this challenge of confronting a general environment that has been unwelcoming toward Arab Americans that provides altogether a more contextualized understanding of the label "other." Arabs neither are seen as white nor are they granted an officially defined minority status; rather, they stand outside all racial demarcations in an ambiguous, precarious position of Otherness compounded by existing policies and perceptions. Regardless, then, of the boxes Arabs check—whether white, black, or other—their racialization, which has resulted in a perception of Otherness, is real.

The post-9/11 environment has therefore reinforced Arab American existence in this elusive category of "other." September 11 has put the spotlight on Arabs as never before. To prove their loyalty to the state, they must denounce terrorism and fight a "war" that has entailed the monitoring of their own communities (Howell and Jamal forthcoming). In so doing, Arab Americans are not only asserting their "Americanness"; rather, the prevailing sentiment is that asserting loyalty, again and again, is one way to secure residential rights in the United States. Because dominant U.S. discourses and the media continue to portray Arabs as un-American, their inclusion in the war on terror is premised on the assumption that Arabs possess and have knowledge about terrorism that the Department of Homeland Security lacks. Hence, Arabs are seen as tools available for use and not American citizens situated on equal grounds. In this current "war on terror," most Arabs have not been able to address the sources of their marginalization; rather, their loyal involvement in helping fight the war on terror has reinforced the essential assumptions about that marginalization: they possess the propensities of suspicious enemies living within, un-loyal to America and thus not worthy of the Americanness enjoyed by "real Americans." Resulting in Otherness, racialization—as different than and inferior to "real" Americans—is a challenge that has contributed to further marginalization.

THE CHAPTERS in this volume have several commonalities worthy of highlighting. Primarily, all the chapters move beyond straightforward assimilationist models in the study of the integration of ethnic groups. That real barriers exist within the "host" society itself, relegating ethnic groups in "subordinate" classifications, even while Arab Americans themselves take pride in their identities, remains a key challenge to ethnic groups and in particular to Arab Americans. The chapters in this volume converge on a common theme, illustrating the ways in which processes of racialization have affected Arab American citizenship and patterns of civic engagement. Most of the contributors agree that racialization serves as one prism through which Arab Americans interact with the dominant society. These interactions are multifaceted, varied, and contingent on a plethora of factors. Yet there are noteworthy commonalities that have structured the racialization of Arab Americans. These commonalities include the construction of Arab Americans in terms of inferiority, suspicion, Otherness, and foreignness, and stem from a complicated history of U.S. intervention in the

Arab world. It is this reality that has paved the way to Arab American racialization. But the patterns of responses among Arab Americans to these racialization processes have not been monolithic. Some Arabs have embraced whiteness and not only pass as white but have benefited from this identity, while others have turned to "Otherness."

The chapters in this book document the historical roots and current trajectories of these racialization processes, the impact they have had on Arab Americans, and the varied ways in which Arab Americans continue to engage these racialization processes. This book's strength is that it brings the study of Arab Americans in direct dialogue with studies of "race" in the United States. By doing so, it offers ample empirical evidence that the process of othering is one where dominant elements in the society (often aided by the media and legal establishment) separate and distinguish themselves—proclaiming superiority—at the expense of the marginalized group. The challenge for Arab Americanists is to continue to uncover the ways in which the racialization process structures Arab American histories and experiences and their responses and reactions to these realities. By engaging in new conversations about the sources of Arab American identities (those freely chosen and those imposed by circumstance), we hope to generate new possibilities for future research.

WORKS CITED

INDEX

Works Cited

Abinader, Elmaz. 2000. "Children of Al-Mahjar: Arab American Literature Spans a Century." *U.S. Society and Values,* 1–8. Washington D.C.: U.S. Department of State. http://usinfo.state.gov/journals/itsv/0200/isje/abinader.html.

Abraham, Nabeel. 1989. "Arab-American Marginality: Mythos and Praxis." In *Arab Americans: Continuity and Change,* edited by Baha Abu-Laban and Michael Suleiman, 17–44. Belmont, Mass.: Assoc. of Arab-American Univ. Graduates Press.

———. 1994. "Anti-Arab Racism and Violence in the United States." In *The Development of Arab American Identity,* edited by Ernest McCarus, 155–214. Ann Arbor: Univ. of Michigan Press.

———. 1995. "Arab Americans." In *Gale Encyclopedia of Multicultural America,* edited by Judi Galens, Anna Sheets, and Robyn Young, 84–94. New York: Gale Research.

———. 2000. "To Palestine and Back." In *Arab Detroit: From Margin to Mainstream,* edited by Nabeel Abraham and Andrew Shryock, 425–62. Detroit: Wayne State Univ. Press.

Abraham, Nabeel, and Andrew Shryock, eds. 2000. *Arab Detroit: From Margin to Mainstream.* Detroit: Wayne State Univ. Press.

Abraham, Sameer, and Nabeel Abraham, eds. 1983. *Arabs in the New World: Studies on Arab-American Communities.* Detroit: Wayne State Univ., Center for Urban Studies.

Abu-Jaber, Diana. 1995. "Review: Food for Our Grandmothers: Writings by Arab-American and Arab-Canadian Feminists." *MESA Bulletin* 29, no. 1:103–4.

ACCESS Cultural Arts Program. 2002. *Understanding Arab Americans, the Arab World, and Islam.* Dearborn: ACCESS.

Agamben, Giorgio. 1998. *Homo Sacer: Sovereign Power and Bare Life.* Stanford, Calif.: Stanford Univ. Press.

———. 2000. *Means Without Ends: Notes on Politics.* Minneapolis: Univ. of Minnesota Press.

Agence France-Presse. 2006. "Lebanese Civilian Deaths Morally Not Same as Terror Victims—Bolton." July 17. http://www.afp.com (Feb. 6, 2007).

Ahmad, Muneer. 2002. "Homeland Insecurities: Racial Profiling the Day After 9/11."
Social Text 20, no. 3:101–15.

Ahuja, Sarita, Pronita Gupta, and Daranee Petsod. 2004. *Arab, Middle Eastern, Muslim and South Asian Communities in the San Francisco Bay Area: An Introduction to Grantmakers.* San Francisco: Asian American/Pacific Islanders in Philanthropy with Grantmakers Concerned with Immigrants and Refugees.

Aidi, Hisham. 2002. "Jihadis in the Hood: Race, Islam and the War on Terror." *Middle East Report* 224 (Fall). http://www.merip.org/mer/mer224/224_aidi.html.

———. 2003. "Let Us Be Moors: Islam, Race and 'Connected Histories.'" *Middle East Report* 229 (Winter). http://www.merip.org/mer/mer229/229_aidi.html.

Akash, Munir, and Khaled Mattawa, eds. 1999. *Post Gibran: Anthology of New Arab American Writings.* Syracuse: Jusoor, distr. by Syracuse Univ. Press.

Akram, Susan. 2002. "The Aftermath of September 11, 2001: The Targeting of Arabs and Muslims in America." *Arab Studies Quarterly,* Spring, 61–118.

Akram, Susan, and Kevin Johnson. 2002. "Race, Civil Rights, and Immigration Law After September 11, 2001: The Targeting of Arabs and Muslims." *NYU Annual Survey of American Law* 58:337.

Alba, R., and V. Nee. 1997. "Rethinking Assimilation Theory for a New Era of Immigration." *IMR* 31, no. 4:826–74.

———. 2003. *Remaking the American Mainstream: Assimilation and Contemporary Immigration.* Boston: Harvard Univ. Press.

Allen, Frank. 2000. "Review: *Grape Leaves.*" *Library Journal* 125, no. 6:105.

Alsultany, Evelyn. 2005. "The Changing Profile of Race in the United States: Racializing and Representing Arab and Muslim Americans Post-9/11." Ph.D. diss., Stanford Univ.

———. 2006. "From Ambiguity to Abjection: Iraqi-Americans Negotiating Race in the United States." In *The Arab Diaspora: Voices of an Anguished Scream,* edited by Zahia Smail Salhi and Ian Richard Netton, 127–42. London: Routledge.

Althusser, Louis. 1971. "Ideology and Ideological State Apparatuses." In *Lenin and Philosophy, and Other Essays,* translated by Ben Brewster, 127–86. New York: Monthly Review Press.

———. 2001. "Ideology and Ideological State Apparatuses (Notes Towards an Investigation)." In *Lenin and Philosophy, and Other Essays,* translated by Ben Brewster, 85–126. New York: Monthly Review Press.

———. 2003. *The Humanist Controversy and Other Writings, 1966–67.* Translated by G. M. Goshgarian. London: Verso.

American Arab Anti-Discrimination Committee (ADC). 1986. *Report on the FBI and Civil Rights of Arab Americans.* Washington, D.C.: ADC.

————. 1992. *1991 Report on Anti-Arab Hate Crimes: Political and Hate Violence Against Arab-Americans.* Washington, D.C.: ADC.

————. 2003. *Report on Hate Crimes and Discrimination Against Arab Americans: The Post–September 11 Backlash.* Washington, D.C.: ADC.

"American Arab Score FBI Agents for Continued Harassment." 1973. *American Syrian Lebanese Leader,* May 31.

American Civil Liberties Union (ACLU). 2003. "ACLU of Oregon Criticizes Use of Material Witness Law to Detain U.S. Citizen." Apr. 4. http://www.aclu.org/safefree/general/17325prs20030403.html.

American Civil Liberties Union of Northern California. 2002. *Caught in the Backlash: Stories from Northern California.* San Francisco: American Civil Liberties Union of Northern California.

Ang, Ien. 1991. *Desperately Seeking the Audience.* New York: Routledge.

————. 1995. *Living Room Wars: Rethinking Media Audiences for a Postmodern World.* New York: Routledge.

Ansara, James M. 1958. "Syrian-Lebanese Immigration to the United States." *National Herald,* Feb., 5ff.

Antonius, Rachad. 2002. "Un racisme 'respectable.'" In *Les relations ethniques en question: Ce qui a changé depuis de 11 Septembre 2001,* edited by Jean Renaud, Linda Pietrantonio, and Guy Bourgeault, 253–71. Montreal: Univ. of Montreal Press.

Aptheker, Bettina. 1982. *Woman's Legacy: Essays on Race, Sex, and Class in American History.* Amherst: Univ. of Massachusetts Press.

Arab American Institute (AAI). 1993a. "Statement to the House Subcommittee on Census, Statistics and Postal Personnel." Statement by deputy director Helen Samhan, June 30.

————. 1993b. *Surveillance and Defamation. Arab American Political Rights in Times of Crisis, A Special Report of the AAI.* Washington, D.C.: Arab American Institute.

————. 2006. Arab Americans: Demographics. Arab American Institute. http://www.aaiusa.org/arab-americans/22/demographics (Oct. 14, 2006).

Ashcroft, John. 2002. *Attorney General Prepared Remarks on the National Security Entry-Exit System.* Washington, D.C., June 6. http://www.usdoj.gov/archive/ag/speeches/2002/060502agpreparedremarks.htm (Feb. 8, 2007).

Aswad, Barbara C., comp. 1974. *Arabic Speaking Communities in American Cities.* [Staten Island, N.Y.:] Center for Migration Studies of New York/Association of Arab American Univ. Graduates.

Awad, Gary. 1981. "The Arab Americans: An Invisible Minority Awakens." *News Circle,* Mar., 31–32.

Bagby, Ihsan. 2004. *A Portrait of Detroit Mosques: Muslim Views on Policy, Politics, and Religion.* Clinton, Mich.: Institute for Social Policy and Understanding.

Baker, Lee D. 1998. *From Savage to Negro: Anthropology and the Construction of Race, 1896–1954.* Berkeley: Univ. of California Press.

Baker, Wayne, Sally Howell, Amaney Jamal, Ann Chih Lin, Andrew Shryock, Ron Stockton, and Mark Tessler. 2004. "Preliminary Findings from the Detroit Arab American Study." http://www.isr.umich.edu/news/arab-amer/final-report.pdf.

Balibar, Etienne. 1991. "Is There a 'Neo-Racism'?" In *Race, Nation, Class: Ambiguous Identities,* edited by Etienne Balibar and Immanuel Wallerstein, 17–28. London: Verso.

Banta, Martha. 1993. "Why Use Anthologies? Or One Small Candle Alight in a Naughty World." *American Literature* 65:330–34.

Banton, Michael P. 1977. *The Idea of Race.* London: Tavistock.

Barot, Rohit, and John Bird. 2001. "Racialization: The Genealogy and Critique of a Concept." *Ethnic and Racial Studies* 24, no. 4 (July):601–18.

Barrett, James R., and David Roediger. 1997. "Inbetween Peoples: Race, Nationality and the 'New Immigrant' Working Class." *Journal of American Ethnic History* 16, no. 3:3–44.

Bassiouni, M. Cherif, ed. 1974. *The Civil Rights of Arab-Americans: The Special Measures.* Belmont, Mass.: Arab-American Univ. Graduates.

Bawardi, Hani. 2006. Public lecture on early Arab American activism. Univ. of Michigan, Ann Arbor, Sept. 21.

Bayoumi, Moustafa. 2004. "A Bloody Stupid War." *Middle East Report* 231 (Summer):36–45.

Bazian, Hatem. 2004. "Virtual Internment: Arabs, Muslims, Asians, and the War on Terrorism." *Journal of Islamic Law and Culture* 9, no. 1 (Spring/Summer).

Beaty, Jerome, and J. Paul Hunter, eds. 1994. *New Worlds of Literature: Writings from America's Many Cultures.* New York: Norton.

Beck, E. M., and Stewart E. Tolnay. 1997. "When Race Didn't Matter: Black and White Mob Violence Against Their Own Color." In *Under Sentence of Death: Lynchings in the South,* edited by W. Fitzhugh Brundage, 132–54. Chapel Hill: Univ. of North Carolina Press.

Berkow, Ira. 2003. "Rower with Muslim Name Is an All-American Suspect." *New York Times,* Feb. 21, D.1, late edition, East Coast. http://proquest.umi.com/ (June 29, 2005).

Bernal, Martin. 1987. *Black Athena: The Afro-Asiatic Roots of Classical Civilization.* New Brunswick, N.J.: Rutgers Univ. Press. Cited in Rodriguez 2000, 35.

Bettencourt, B. Ann, Nancy Dorr, Kelly Charlton, and Deborah L. Hume. 2001. "Status Differences and In-group Bias: A Meta-analytic Examination of the Effects of

Status Stability, Status Legitimacy, and Group Permeability." *Psychological Bulletin* 127, no. 4:520–42.

Berger, V. 2002. "A Legacy of Racism." *National Law Journal* 24, no. 55.

Bilge, Barbara, and Barbara C. Aswad. 1996. "Introduction." In *Family and Gender among American Muslims: Issues Facing Middle Eastern Immigrants and Their Descendants*, edited by Barbara C. Aswad and Barbara Bilge, 1–16. Philadelphia: Temple Univ. Press.

Bishara, Kalil A. 1914. *The Origin of the Modern Syrian*. New York: Al-Hoda Publishing House.

Bonacich, E. 1973. "A Theory of Middleman Minorities." *American Sociological Review* 38 (Oct.):583–94.

———. 1980. "Middleman Minorities and Advanced Capitalism." *Ethnic Groups* 2:211–19.

Boullata, Issa J. 1990. "Book Review: *Grape Leaves*." *Middle East Journal* 44, no. 1:156.

Brodkin, Karen. 1998. *How the Jews Became White Folks and What That Says about Race in America*. New Brunswick: Rutgers Univ. Press.

Brown, Wesley, and Amy Ling, eds. 1993. *Visions of America: Personal Narratives from the Promised Land*. New York: Persea.

Brundage, W. Fitzhugh. 1993. *Lynching in the New South Georgia and Virginia, 1880–1930*. Urbana: Univ. of Illinois Press.

———, ed. 1997. *Under Sentence of Death: Lynchings in the South*. Chapel Hill: Univ. of North Carolina Press.

Burnham, Linda. 2001. "Introduction." In *Time to Rise*, edited by Linda Burnham, Maylei Blackwell, and Jung Hee Choi, 7–16. Berkeley: Women of Color Resource Center.

Bush, George W. 2005. "The President Discusses War on Terror," Norfolk, Va. Oct. 28. http://www.whitehouse.gov/news/releases/2005/10/20051028-1.html (Feb. 6, 2007).

Butler, Judith. 1993. *Bodies Matter: On the Discursive Limits of "Sex."* New York: Routledge.

———. 2004. *Precarious Life: The Powers of Mourning and Violence*. New York: Verso.

Cainkar, Louise. 1988. "Palestinian Muslim Women in the United States: Coping with Tradition, Change, and Alienation." Ph.D. diss., Northwestern Univ.

———. 2002a. "No Longer Invisible: Arab and Muslim Exclusion after September 11." *Middle East Report* 224 (Fall). www.merip.org/mer/mer224/224_cainkar.html.

———. 2002b. "The Treatment of Arabs and Muslims in Race and Ethnic Studies Textbooks." Paper presented at the Annual Meeting of the American Sociological Association.

———. 2003. "Targeting Muslims, at Ashcroft's Discretion," *Middle East Report Online*. Mar. 14. http://www.merip.org/mero/mero031403.html.

———. 2004a. "The Impact of 9/11 on Muslims and Arabs in the United States." In *The Maze of Fear: Security and Migration after September 11th,* edited by John Tirman, 215–39. New York: New Press.

———. 2004b. "The Impact of the September 11 Attacks and Their Aftermath on Arab and Muslim Communities in the United States." *GSC Quarterly* 13 (Summer/Fall). http://programs.ssrc.org/gsc/publications/quarterly13/cainkar.pdf.

———. 2004c. "Islamic Revival among Second-Generation Arab-Americans: The American Experience and Globalization Intersect." *Bulletin of the Royal Institute of Inter-Faith Studies* 6, no. 2:99–120.

———. Forthcoming. *Homeland Insecurity: The Arab/Muslim American Experience after 9/11.* New York: Russell Sage Foundation Press.

Capuzzo, Jill P. 2004. "Stalled Since 9/11, a Gathering Resumes with High Security." *New York Times,* Sept. 18, B.1, late edition, East Coast. http://proquest.umi.com/ (June 29, 2005).

Carby, Hazel V. 1987. *Reconstructing Womanhood: The Emergence of the Afro-American Woman Novelist.* New York: Oxford Univ. Press.

Carlton, Doyle E. 1929–32. Administrative correspondence, 1929–32. Series 204, box 16, folder 5. State Archives of Florida, Tallahassee.

"A Celebration of Arab Culture, History: *Food for Our Grandmothers: Writing by Arab-American and Arab-Canadian Feminists*" 1995. *Arab American News* 11:516.

Chirocos, T., and S. Eschholz. 2002. "The Racial and Ethnic Typification of Crime and the Criminal Typification of Race and Ethnicity in Local Television News." *Journal of Research in Crime and Delinquency* 39, no. 4:400–420.

Chong, Kelly H. 1998. "What It Means to Be Christian: The Role of Religion in the Construction of Ethnic Identity and Boundary among Second-Generation Korean Americans." *Sociology of Religion* 59, no. 3:259–86.

Christian, Barbara. 1995. "A Rough Terrain: A Case of Shaping an Anthology of Caribbean Women Writers." In *The Ethnic Canon: Histories, Institutions and Interventions,* edited by David Palumbo-Liu. Minneapolis: Univ. of Minnesota Press, 241–59.

Cichy, Rose. 1994. "Book Review: *Food for Our Grandmothers.*" *Library Journal* 119:16, 102.

Civantos, Christina. 1996. "The Middle East in North America: Questions of Identity in *Food for Our Grandmothers.*" *Stanford Electronic Humanities Review* 5, no. 1. http://www.stanford.edu/group/SHR/5-1/text/civantos.html.

Clines, Francis X. 2001. "Muslim Leader Presses Agenda of Understanding." *New York Times,* Oct. 3, B.8, late edition, East Coast. http://proquest.umi.com/ (June 29, 2005).

Coates, Rodney. 2004. "Critical and Ethnic Studies: Profiling and Reparations." *American Behavioral Scientist* 47, no. 7 (Mar.):873–78.

Cohen, Patricia. 2001. "Response to Attacks Splits Arabs in the West." *New York Times,* Sept. 29, A.9, late edition, East Coast. http://proquest.umi.com/ (June 29, 2005).

Collins, Patricia Hill. 1991. *Black Feminist Thought: Knowledge, Consciousness, and the Politics of Empowerment.* New York: Routledge.

Conklin, Nancy Faires, and Nora Faires. 1987. "'Colored' and Catholic: The Lebanese in Birmingham, Alabama." In *Crossing the Waters,* edited by Eric J. Hooglund, 69–84. Washington, D.C.: Smithsonian Institution Press.

Connelly, Marjorie. 2003. "There's Still a Chill in New York for Arab-Americans, Poll Says." *New York Times,* Sept. 14, late edition, East Coast. http://proquest.umi.com/ (June 29, 2005).

Crenshaw, Kimberlé. 1991. "Mapping the Margins: Intersectionality, Identity Politics, and Violence Against Women of Color." *Stanford Law Review* 43:1241–99.

Crenshaw, Kimberlé, Neil Gotanda, Gary Peller, and Kendall Thomas, eds. 1995. *Critical Race Theory: The Key Writings That Formed the Movement.* New York: New Press.

Dahab, F. Elizabeth, ed. 2002. *Voices in the Desert: An Anthology of Arabic Canadian Writers.* Toronto: Guernica.

Daher, Michael. 1995. "Book Review: *Food for Our Grandmothers.*" *Arab Studies Quarterly* 17, no. 3:85.

Danquah, Meri Nan-Ama, ed. 2000. *Becoming American: Personal Essays by First Generation Immigrant Women.* New York: Hyperion.

Davidson, Lawrence. 1999. "Debating Palestine: Arab-American Challenges to Zionism 1917–1932." In *Arabs in America: Building a New Future,* edited by Michael W. Suleiman, 227–40. Philadelphia: Temple Univ. Press.

Davis, Angela. 1981. *Women, Race, and Class.* New York: Random House.

Davis, Darren. 1995. "Exploring Black Political Intolerance." *Political Behavior,* Mar., 309–21.

Davis, Darren, and Brian Silver. 2004. "Civil Liberties vs. Security: Public Opinion in the Context of the Terrorist Attacks on America." *American Journal of Political Science,* Jan., 28–46.

Deb, Trishala, and Rafael Mutis. 2004. "Smoke and Mirrors: Abu Ghraib and the Myth of Liberation." *Colorlife! Magazine* (Summer). http://www.alp.org/colorlife/index .php (Feb. 6, 2006).

Debis, Cherien. 2001. "Arab and a Half." In *Mizna* 3, no. 3.

Deeb, Lara. 2006. "Hizballah: A Primer." *Middle East Report Online,* July 31. http:// merip.org/mero/mero073106.html.

de la Cruz, G. P., and Brittingham, A. 2003. *The Arab Population: 2000.* Washington, D.C.: U.S. Bureau of the Census.

Delgado, Richard, and Jean Stefancic. 2001. *Critical Race Theory: An Introduction.* New York: New York Univ. Press.

De Silva, Shelana. 2003. "Colorlines RaceWire: Special Registration Isn't Over Yet." Refuse and Resist!, Dec. 10. http://www.refuseandresist.org/detentions/art.php?aid=1204 (Feb. 6, 2006).

Desouky, Eman. 2000. *Re-que(e)rying the Queer: Imagining Queer Arab Women Through the Politics of Marginality and the Nation.* Master's thesis, Univ. of California, Santa Cruz.

Detroit Free Press. 2000. *100 Questions and Answers about Arab Americans.* Detroit: Knight Ridder.

di Leonardo, Micaela. 1994. "White Ethnicity, Identity Politics, and Baby Bear's Chair." *Social Text* 41:165–91.

Doane, Ashley W. and Eduardo Bonilla-Silva, eds. 2003. "Rethinking Whiteness Studies." In *White Out: The Continuing Significance of Racism,* edited by A. W. Doane and E. Bonilla-Silva, 3–18. New York: Routledge.

Douglas, Carol Anne. 1995. "Book Review: *Food for Our Grandmothers.*" *Off Our Backs* 25:10.

Dresch, Paul. 1995. "Race, Culture and—What? Pluralist Certainties in the United States." In *The Pursuit of Certainty: Religious and Cultural Formulations,* edited by Wendy James, 61–91. New York: Routledge.

Du Bois, W. E. B. 1903. *The Souls of Black Folk.* Bantam Books.

Ebaugh, Helen Rose, and Janet Saltman Chafetz. 2000. "Religion and the New Immigrants: Continuities and Adaptations." In *Religion and the New Immigrants: Continuities and Adaptations in Immigrant Congregations,* edited by Helen Rose Ebaugh and Janet Saltzman Chafetz. Walnut Creek, Calif.: AltaMira Press.

Edwards, Holly. 2000. "The Garments of Instruction from the Wardrobe of Pleasure: American Orientalist Painting in the 1870s and 1880s." In *Noble Dreams, Wicked Pleasures: Orientalism in America, 1870–1930,* edited by Holly Edwards and Brian T. Allen, 11–58. Princeton, N.J.: Princeton Univ. Press.

El Badry, Samia. 1994. "The Arab American Market." *American Demographics* 16, no. 1:22–30.

El Guindi, Fadwa. 2003. "Arab and Muslim American: Emergent Scholarship, New Visibility, Conspicuous Gap in Academe." *American Anthropologist* 105, no. 3:631–34.

Elia, Nada. 2002. "The 'White' Sheep of the Family: But *Bleaching* Is Like Starvation." In *This Bridge We Call Home: Radical Visions for Transformation,* edited by Gloria Anzaldua and Analouise Keating, 223–31. New York: Routledge.

Elkholy, Abdo A. 1969. "The Arab Americans: Nationalism and Traditional Preserva-
tions." In *The Arab Americans: Studies in Assimilation*, AAUG Monograph Series 1,
edited by Elaine C. Hagopian and Ann Paden, 3–17. Wilmette, Ill.: Medina Univ.
Press International.

Elnajjar, Ghada. 2002. "Arab American Women Poets Showcase Their Work." *U.S. Department of State: International Information Programs,* Nov. 18. http://usinfo.state
.gov/usa/islam/a111802.htm.

Fanon, Frantz. 1967. *Black Skin, White Masks.* New York: Grove Press.

Fay, Mary Ann. 1984. "Old Roots, New Soil." In *Taking Root, Bearing Fruit: The Arab
American Experience,* edited by James Zogby. Washington, D.C.: American Arab
Anti-Discrimination Committee.

Fetterley, Judith, and Joan Schulz. 1982. "A MELUS Dialogue: The Status of Women
Authors in American Literature Anthologies." *MELUS* 9, no. 3, 3–17.

Fields, B. J. 1990. "Slavery, Race, and Ideology in the United States of America." *New
Left Review* 181:95–18.

Finkleman, Paul. 2006. "Black Codes." In *Encyclopedia of African-American Culture and
History,* vol. 1, edited by Colin Palmer, 254–57. Detroit: Macmillan Reference.

Fischbach, Michael R. 1996. "Food For Our Grandmothers." *Journal of Palestine Studies*
25, no. 4:113.

Fishkin, Shelley Fisher. 1995. "Interrogating 'Whiteness,' Complicating 'Blackness': Re-
mapping American Culture." *American Quarterly* 47, no. 3, 428–66.

Fitleberg, Gary. 2002. "Iranian Jews and Muslims Detained in Los Angeles." *The Iranian,* Dec. 20. http://www.iranian.com/Features/2002/December/LA2/index.html
(Feb. 6, 2006).

Fliegelman, Jay. 1993. "Anthologizing the Situation of American Literature." *American
Literature* 65:334–38.

Forbes, Jack. 1990. "Undercounting Native Americans: The 1980 Census and the Ma-
nipulation of Racial Identity in the United States." *Wicazo Sa Review* 6, no. 1:2–26.

Foxman, Abraham H. 1993. ADL Info Helped HUAC in 1947 Witch-Hunts. *Middle East
Labor Bulletin* 4, no. 2. http://www.fpp.co.uk/docs/ADL/ADLitems/MELB0593
.html (Feb. 3, 2007).

Frankenberg, Ruth. 2001. "The Mirage of an Unmarked Whiteness." In *The Making and
Unmaking of Whiteness,* edited by B. B. Rasmussen et al., 72–96. Durham, N.C.:
Duke Univ. Press.

Friedman, Thomas L. 2005. "Giving the Hatemongers No Place to Hide," *New York
Times,* July 22. http://www.nytimes.com/2005/07/22/opinion/22friedman.html
?ex=1279684800&en=17fb5beb19b09d86&ei=5090&partner=rssuserland&emc=
rss%3CBR%3E.

Gabriel, Judith. 2001. "Emergence of a Genre: Reviewing Arab American Writers." *Al-Jadid* 34:4–6.

Gates, Henry Louis, Jr. 1985. "Writing 'Race' and the Difference It Makes." In *'Race,' Writing, and Difference,* edited by Henry Louis Gates, Jr., 1–20. Chicago: Univ. of Chicago Press.

———. 1991. "The Master's Pieces: On Canon Formation and Afro-American Tradition." In *The Bounds of Race: Perspectives on Hegemony and Resistance,* edited by Dominick La Capra, 17–38. Ithaca, N.Y.: Cornell Univ. Press.

———. 1992. *Loose Canons: Notes on the Culture Wars.* New York/Oxford: Oxford Univ. Press.

Genette, Gérard. 1972. *Figures III.* Paris: Seuil.

———. 1982. *Palimpsestes: La littérature au second degré.* Paris: Seuil.

Georgakas, D., and Surkin, M. 1998. *Detroit: I Do Mind Dying.* Cambridge: South End Press.

Gerges, Fawaz. 2003. "Islam and Muslims in the Mind of America." *The Annals of the American Academy of Political and Social Science,* July, 73–89.

Ghazoul, Ferial. 2000. "Building Bridges, Joining Streams." *Al-Ahram Weekly* 481, May 11–17. http://weekly.org.eg/2000/481/bk2_481.htm.

Giddens, Anthony. 1972. *Emile Durkheim: Selected Writings.* London: Cambridge Univ. Press.

Glaberson, William. 2001. "Interpreting Islamic Law for American Muslims." *New York Times,* Oct. 21, 1A.26, late edition, East Coast. http://proquest.umi.com/ (June 29, 2005).

Goldberg, David Theo. 1993. *Racist Culture.* Oxford and Cambridge: Blackwell.

Good, David L. 1989. *Orvie: The Dictator of Dearborn: The Rise and Reign of Orville L. Hubbard.* Detroit: Wayne State Univ. Press.

Goodstein, Laurie. 2001. "In U.S. Echoes of Rift of Muslims and Jews." *New York Times,* Sept. 12, A.12, late edition, East Coast. http://proquest.umi.com/ (June 29, 2005).

Goodstein, Laurie, and Gustav Niebuhr. 2001. "Attacks and Harassment of Arab-Americans Increase." *New York Times,* Sept. 14, A.14, late edition, East Coast.http://proquest.umi.com/ (June 29, 2005).

Gossett, Thomas F. 1997. *Race: The History of an Idea in America.* New York: Oxford Univ. Press.

Gourevitch, Alex. 2003. "Detention Disorder." *The American Prospect,* Jan. 31.

Graff, Gerald, and Jeffrey R. Di Leo. 2000. "Anthologies, Literary Theory, and the Teaching of Literature: An Exchange." *Symploke* 8, nos. 1–2:113–28.

Gualtieri, Sarah. 2001. "Becoming 'White': Race, Religion, and the Foundations of Syrian/Lebanese Ethnic Identity in the United States." *Journal of American Ethnic History* 20, no. 4:29–58.

———. 2004. "Strange Fruit? Syrian Immigrants, Extralegal Violence, and Racial Formation in the Jim Crow South." *Arab Studies Quarterly* 26, no. 3 (Summer):63–85.

Gupta, Akhil, and James Ferguson. 1997. "Discipline and Practice: 'The Field' as Site, Method, and Location in Anthropology." In *Anthropological Locations: Boundaries and Grounds of a Field Science,* edited by Akhil Gupta and James Ferguson, 1–46. Berkeley: Univ. of California Press.

Haddad, Yvonne Y. 1991. "American Foreign Policy in the Middle East and Its Impact on the Identity of Arab Muslims in the United States." In *The Muslims of America,* edited by Yvonne Y. Haddad, 217–35. Oxford: Oxford Univ. Press.

———. 1994. "Maintaining the Faith of the Fathers: Dilemma of Religious Identity in the Christian and Muslim Arab-American Communities." In *The Development of Arab-American Identity,* edited by Ernest McCarus, 61–84. Ann Arbor: Univ. of Michigan Press.

Hagopian, Elaine C. 2004. *Civil Rights in Peril: The Targeting of Arabs and Muslims.* Ann Arbor, Mich.: Pluto Press.

Hagopian, Elaine C., and Ann Paden. 1969. *The Arab Americans: Studies in Assimilation.* Wilmette, Ill.: Medina Univ. Press International.

Halbfinger, David M. 2001. "A Request for Patience If the Law Overreaches." *New York Times,* Sept. 24, B.9, late edition, East Coast.http://proquest.umi.com/ (June 29, 2005).

Hale, Grace Elizabeth. 1998. *Making Whiteness: The Culture of Segregation in the South, 1890–1940.* New York: Vintage.

Hall, Jacquelyn Down. 1979. *Revolt Against Chivalry: Jessie Daniel Ames and the Women's Campaign Against Lynching.* New York: Columbia Univ. Press.

Hall, Stuart. 1996. "Introduction: Who Needs 'Identity'?" In *Questions of Cultural Identity,* edited by Stuart Hall and Paul du Gay, 1–17. London/Thousand Oaks, Calif.: Sage.

———. 2000. "Racist Ideologies and the Media." In *Media Studies: A Reader,* edited by Paul Marris and Sue Thornham, 271–82. New York: New York Univ. Press.

Hammad, Suheir. 1996. *Born Palestinian, Born Black.* New York: Harlem River Press.

Hamod, H. S. 2003. "Arab American Poetry." *Ishmael Reed's Konch Magazine.* http://www.ishmaelreedpub.com/hamod6.html.

Hanania, Ray. 2004. *Fighting for the Last Victims of September 11.* http://www.hanania.com/hatevictims.html (Feb. 6, 2006).

Handal, Nathalie, ed. 2001. *The Poetry of Arab Women*. Northampton: Interlink.

Haney-López, Ian F. 1996. *White By Law: The Legal Construction of Race*. New York: New York Univ. Press.

Harden, Blaine. 2001. "For Many, Sorrow Turns to Anger and Talk of Vengeance." *New York Times*, Sept. 14, A.15, late edition, East Coast. http://proquest.umi.com/ (June 29, 2005).

Harrison, Faye V. 1995. "The Persistent Power of 'Race' in the Cultural and Political Economy of Racism." *Annual Review of Anthropology* 24:47–74.

Hartigan, J. 1999. *Racial Situations: Class Predicaments of Whiteness in Detroit*. Princeton, N.J.: Princeton Univ. Press.

Hartley, John. 1999. *The Uses of Television*. New York: Routledge.

Harvey, David. 2003. *The New Imperialism*. Clarendon Lectures in Geography and Environmental Studies. Oxford: Oxford Univ. Press.

Hasan, Aida. 2003. "Grape Leaves: A Book Review." Suite101.com, June 3. http://www.suite101.com/article.cfm/3810/41046.

Hassan, Salah. 2002a. "Arabs, Muslims, and Race in America: Arabs, Race, and the Post-September 11th National Security State." *Middle East Report* 32, no. 3:16–21.

———. 2002b. "Arabs, Race, and the Post-September 11 National Security State." *Middle East Report* 224. http://www.merip.org/mer/mer 224/224_hassan.html.

———. 2003. "Enemy Arabs." *Socialism and Democracy* Mar. 31. http://www.sdonline.org/33/salah_d_hassan.htm.

Hasso, Francis. 1987. "Conspiracy of Silence Against Arab Americans." *News Circle*, Feb./Mar., 26.

Hedges, Chris. 2002. "Muslims Return from Mecca with Joy, yet Concern." *New York Times*, Mar. 8, A.14, late edition, East Coast. http://proquest.umi.com/ (June 29, 2005).

Helal, Omeira, and Arsalan Iftikhar. 2003. "Pipes Nomination a Slap in the Face for Muslims," *San Francisco Chronicle*, May 11.

Helmbold, Lois Rita. 1998. "No Passing Zone." *Women's Review of Books* 15, no. 4.

Herrmann, Richard K., Philip E. Tetlock, and Penny S. Visser. 1999. "Mass Public Decisions to Go to War: A Cognitive-Interactionist Framework." *American Political Science Review* 93, no. 3:553–73.

Hersh, Seymour. 2004. "The Gray Zone: How a Secret Pentagon Program Came to Abu Ghraib." *New Yorker*, May 24.

Hing, Bill Ong. 2004. *Defining America Through Immigration Policy*. Philadelphia: Temple Univ. Press.

Hingham, John. 1994. *Strangers in the Land: Patterns of American Nativism, 1860–1925*. 2d ed. New Brunswick, N.J.: Rutgers Univ. Press.

Holt, Thomas C. 1995. "Marking: Race, Race-making, and the Writing of History." *American Historical Review* 100, no. 1:3.

———. 1997. Unpublished "Response to George Sanchez's 'Foreign and Female.'" Dean's Symposium, Univ. of Chicago, Nov. 7, 7.

———. 2000. *The Problem of Race in the Twenty-First Century.* Cambridge, Mass.: Harvard Univ. Press.

Hooglund, Eric J. 1987. "Introduction." In *Crossing the Waters: Arabic Speaking Immigrants in the United States Before 1940,* 1–14. Washington, D.C.: Smithsonian Institution Press.

———, ed. 1987. *Crossing the Waters: Arabic-Speaking Immigrants to the United States Before 1940.* Washington, D.C.: Smithsonian Institute Press.

hooks, bell. 1981. *Ain't I a Woman: Black Women and Feminism.* Boston: South End Press.

Houissa, Ali. 2000. "Review: Post Gibran." *Library Journal* 125, no. 6, 102.

Hourani, Albert. 1992. "Introduction." In *The Lebanese in the World: A Century of Emigration,* edited by Albert Hourani and Nadim Shehadi, 3–12. London: Center for Lebanese Studies.

Howard, Walter T. 1995. *Lynchings: Extralegal Violence in Florida During the 1930s.* Selinsgrove, Pa.: Susquehanna Univ. Press.

Howell, Sally. 2000a. "Cultural Interventions: Arab American Aesthetics Between the Transnational and the Ethnic." *Diaspora* 9, no. 1:59–82.

———. 2000b. "Politics, Pragmatism, and the 'Arab Vote': A Conversation with Maya Berry." In *Arab Detroit: From Margin to Mainstream,* edited by Nabeel Abraham and Andrew Shryock, 343–71. Detroit: Wayne State Univ. Press.

Howell, Sally, and Amaney Jamal. Forthcoming. "The Aftermath of the 9/11 Attacks among Arab Americans: Detroit Exceptionalism and the Limits of Political Incorporation." In *Citizenship and Crisis: Findings from the Detroit Arab American Study,* edited by Wayne Baker et al. New York: Russell Sage Foundation.

Howell, Sally, and Andrew Shryock. 2003. "Cracking Down on Diaspora: Arab Detroit and America's 'War on Terror.'" *Anthropological Quarterly* 76, no. 3:443–62.

Huddy, Leonie, Stanley Feldman, Charles Taber, and Gallya Lahav. 2005. "Threat, Anxiety, and Support of Antiterrorism Policies." *American Journal of Political Science* July, 593–608.

Huntington, Samuel. 1996. *The Clash of Civilizations and the Remaking of World Order.* New York: Free Press.

Hussaini, Hatem. 1974. "The Impact of the Arab-Israeli Conflict on Arab American Communities in the United States." In *Settler Regimes in Africa and the Arab World: The Illusion of Endurance,* AAUG Monograph Series 4, edited by Ibrahim

Abu-Lughod and Baha Abu-Laban, 201–20. Wilmette, Ill.: Medina Univ. Press International.

Ignatiev, N. 1995. *How the Irish Became White.* New York: Routledge.

Ingalls, Robert P. 1987. "Lynching and Establishment Violence in Tampa, 1858–1935." *Journal of Southern History* 53, no. 4:615.

Isaacs, Matt. 2000. "Spy vs. Spite." sfweekly.com, Feb. 2. http://www.sfweekly.com/2000 -02-02/news/spy-vs-spite.

Isikoff, Michael. 2003. "The FBI Says, Count the Mosques." *Newsweek,* Feb. 3.

Islamic Web. N.d. Population of Muslims Around the World. http://islamicweb.com/ begin/population.htm (Feb. 9, 2007).

Issawi, Charles. 1992. "The Historical Background of Lebanese Emigration, 1800–1914." In *The Lebanese in the World: A Century of Emigration,* edited by Albert Hourani and Nadim Shehadi, 13–32. London: Center for Lebanese Studies.

Jabara, Abdeen. 1998. "Special Report: RAWI (Radius of Arab-American Writers) Provides Creative Matrix for Writers Across America." *Washington Report on Middle East Affairs* (Jan.–Feb.): 34–35.

Jacobson, Matthew Frye. 1998. *Whiteness of a Different Color.* Cambridge, Mass.: Harvard Univ. Press.

Jaimes, Annette M. 1994. "American Racism: The Impact on American-Indian Identity and Survival." In *Race,* edited by Steven Gregory and Roger Sanjek, 41–61. New Brunswick, N.J.: Rutgers Univ. Press.

Jamal, Amaney. 2005. "The Determinants of Political Engagement and Participation of Muslim Americans." *American Politics Research* 33, no. 4:521–44.

———. 2005. "Mosques, Collective Identity and Gender Differences among Muslim Arab Americans." *Journal of Middle East Women's Studies* 1, no. 1:53–78.

Jamal, Amaney, and Sunaina Maira. 2005. "Muslim Americans and the War on Terror at Home and Abroad." *Middle East Journal* 58, no. 1:303–9.

Jarmakani, Amira. 2004. *Disorienting America: The Legacy of Orientalist Representations of Arab Womanhood in U.S. Popular Culture.* Ph.D. diss., Emory Univ., Atlanta, Ga.

Jentleson, Bruce. 1992. "The Pretty Prudent Public: Post-Vietnam American Opinion on the Use of Force." *International Studies Quarterly* 36, no. 1:49–74.

Jordan, June. 1996. "Eyewitness in Lebanon." *Progressive* 60, no. 8 (Aug.):13.

Joseph, Suad. 1994. "Problematizing Gender and Relational Rights: Experiences from Lebanon." *Social Politics* 1, no. 3, 271–85.

———. 1999a. "Against the Grain of the Nation—The Arab." In *Arabs in America: Building a New Future,* edited by Michael W. Suleiman, 257–72. Philadelphia: Temple Univ. Press.

———. 1999b. "Searching for Baba: Personal Notes on Rights and Responsibilities." In *Intimate Selving in Arab Families: Gender Self and Identity,* edited by Suad Joseph, 53–76. Syracuse: Syracuse Univ. Press.

Jusserand, J. 1923. Dispatch to R. Poincaré. Jan. 3. Levant 1918–1940, Syrie-Liban (SL), v. 407, Ministère des Affaires étrangères (MAE), Paris.

Kadi, Joanna, ed. 1994. *Food for Our Grandmothers: Writings by Arab-American and Arab-Canadian Feminists.* Boston: South End Press.

Kafka, Phillipa. 1989. "Another Round of Canon Fire: Feminist and Multi-Ethnic Theory in the American Literature Survey." *MELUS* 16, no. 2:31–45.

Kahf, Mohja. 1999. *Western Representations of the Muslim Woman: From Termagant to Odalisque.* Austin: Univ. of Texas Press.

Kaldas, Pauline, and Khaled Mattawa, eds. 2004. *Dinarzad's Children: An Anthology of Contemporary Arab American Fiction.* Fayetteville: Univ. of Arkansas Press.

Kaplan, Amy. 2003. "Homeland Insecurities: Transformations of Language and Space." In *September 11 in History: A Watershed Moment?* edited by Mary L. Dudziak, 55–69. Durham, N.C.: Duke Univ. Press.

Kaptur, Marcy. 2003. "Kaptur Bill Safeguards Civil Liberties for All: H. Res. 234 Seeks to Protect Against Religious, Ethnic Persecution." Press release by Congresswoman Marcy Kaptur (D-Ohio), May 15. http://www.adc.org/index.php?id=1803 (Feb. 8, 2007).

Katz, Judith. 1995. "Both Sides Now: *Lesbiot: Israeli Lesbians Tell Their Stories,* edited by Tracy Moore, and *Food for Our Grandmothers: Writings by Arab American and Arab Canadian Feminists,* edited by Joanna Kadi." *Lambda Book Report* 4, no. 10:24.

Kayal, Philip M., and Joseph M. Kayal. 1975. *The Syrian-Lebanese in America: A Study in Religion and Assimilation.* Boston: Twayne.

Kayyali, Randa. 2006. *The Arab Americans: New Americans.* Westport, Conn.: Greenwood Press.

Khalaf, Samir. 1987. "The Background and Causes of Lebanese/Syrian Immigration to the United States Before World War I." In *Crossing the Waters: Arabic-Speaking Immigrants in the United States Before 1940,* edited by Eric J. Hooglund, 17–35. Washington, D.C.: Smithsonian Institution Press.

Khalidi, Rashid. 2004. *Resurrecting Empire: Western Footprints and America's Perilous Path in the Middle East.* Boston: Beacon.

Khater, Akram Fouad. 2001. *Inventing Home: Immigration, Gender, and the Middle Class in Lebanon, 1870–1920.* Berkeley: Univ. of California Press.

Kiernan, Anna, ed. 2001. *Voices For Peace.* London: Scribner.

Kilcup, Karen L. 2000. "Anthologizing Matters: The Poetry and Prose of Recovery Work." *Symploke* 8, nos. 1–2: 36–56.

King, Peter H. 2005. "18 Years and Waiting for the Gavel to Fall." *Los Angeles Times,* June 29, A1.

Kumar, Amitava. 2000. *Passport Photos.* Berkeley: Univ. of California Press.

Lamont, Michele, and Marcel Fournier, eds. 1992. *Cultivating Differences: Symbolic Boundaries and the Making of Inequality.* Chicago: Univ. of Chicago Press.

Lauter, Paul. 1993. "On Revising the *Heath Anthology of American Literature.*" *American Literature* 65, no. 2: 327–30.

Lavie, Smadar, and Ted Swedenburg. 1996. "Introduction: Displacement, Diaspora, and Geographies." In *Displacement, Diaspora, and Geographies of Identity,* 1–27. Durham, N.C., and London: Duke Univ. Press.

Lawrence, Jill. 2005. "Parties' Issues Coincide with Parents' Issues." *USA Today,* May 31.

Lee, Kien S. 2002. "Building Intergroup Relations after September 11." *Analyses of Social Issues and Public Policy* 2, no. 1:131–41.

Lee, M. 2002. "US Evangelist Says Muslims 'Worse than Nazis.'" *Agence France Press.* Nov. 12.

Leland, John. 2004. "Tension in a Michigan City over Muslims' Call to Prayer." *New York Times,* May 5, A.20, late edition, East Coast. http://proquest.umi.com/ (July 1, 2005).

Lesser, Jeff. 1985–86. "Always 'Outsiders': Asians, Naturalization, and the Supreme Court." *Amerasia* 12, no. 1:83–100.

Levine, R. A., and Donald T. Campbell. 1972. *Ethnocentrism.* New York: Wiley.

Lewis, Neil A. 2002. "I.N.S. to Focus On Muslims Who Evade Deportation." *New York Times,* Jan. 9, A.12, late edition, East Coast. http://proquest.umi.com/ (June 29, 2005).

Lewis, Neil A., and Christopher Marquis. 2001. "Longer Waits for Arabs; Stir Over U.S. Eavesdropping." *New York Times,*. Nov. 10, A.1, late edition, East Coast. http://proquest.umi.com/ (accessed June 29, 2005).

Lind, W., and P. Weyrich. 2002. *Why Islam Is a Threat to America and the West.* Washington D.C.: Free Congress Foundation.

Lipsitz, George. 1998. *The Possessive Investment in Whiteness: How White People Profit from Identity Politics.* Philadelphia: Temple Univ. Press.

Little, Douglas. 2002. *American Orientalism: The United States and the Middle East since 1945.* Chapel Hill: Univ. of North Carolina Press.

Lowe, Lisa. 1996. *Immigrant Acts: On Asian American Cultural Politics.* Durham, N.C.: Duke Univ. Press.

Lutz, Catherine A., and Jane L. Collins. 1993. *Reading National Geographic.* Chicago: Univ. of Chicago Press.

MacIntosh, P. 1990. "White Privilege: Unpacking the Invisible Knapsack." *Independent School* 49, no. 2:31–35.

MacLean, Nancy. 1991. "The Leo Frank Case Reconsidered: Gender and Sexual Politics in the Making of Reactionary Populism." *Journal of American History* 78, no. 3:917–48.

Maira, Sunaina. 2002. *Desis in the House: Indian American Youth Culture in New York City*. Philadelphia: Temple Univ. Press.

Maira, Sunaina, and Magid Shihade. 2006. "Meeting Asian/Arab American Studies: Thinking Race, Empire, and Zionism in the U.S." *Journal of Asian American Studies* 9, no. 2:117–40.

Majaj, Lisa Suhair. 1996. "Arab American Literature and the Politics of Memory." In *Memory and Cultural Politics: New Approaches to American Ethnic Literatures*, edited by Amritjit Singh, Joseph T. Skerrett, Jr., and Robert E. Hogan, 267–90. Boston: Northeastern Univ. Press.

———. 1999a. "Arab-American Ethnicity: Locations, Coalitions and Cultural Negotiations." In *Arabs in America: Building a New Future*, edited by Michael Suleiman, 321–36. Philadelphia: Temple Univ. Press.

———. 1999b. "New Directions: Arab American Writing at Century's End." In *Post Gibran: Anthology of New Arab American Writing*, edited by Munir Akash and Khaled Mattawa, 66–77. Syracuse: Jusoor, distr. by Syracuse Univ. Press.

———. 2000. "Arab Americans and the Meaning of Race." In *Postcolonial Theory and the United States: Race, Ethnicity, and Literature*, edited by Amaritjit Singh and Peter Schmidt, 320–37. Jackson: Univ. of Mississippi Press.

Maksoud, Hala. 1994. "Food for Thought." *Ms.* 5, no. 3:74–75

Mamdani, Mahmood. 2004. *Good Muslim, Bad Muslim: America, the Cold War, and the Roots of Terror*. New York: Pantheon.

Mandel, Daniel. 2001. "Muslims on the Silver Screen," *Middle East Quarterly* (Spring). http://www.meforum.org/article/26.

Mankekar, Purnima. 1999. *Screening Culture, Viewing Politics: An Ethnography of Television, Womanhood, and Nation in Postcolonial India*. Durham, N.C.: Duke Univ. Press.

Marcuse, Herbert. 1969. "Repressive Tolerance." In *A Critique of Pure Tolerance*, edited by Robert Paul Wolff, Barrington Moore, Jr., and Herbert Marcuse, 95–137. Boston: Beacon. Accessed online at http://www.marcuse.org/herbert/pubs/60spubs/65repressivetolerance.htm.

Marger, Martin. 2003. *Race and Ethnic Relations*. Belmont, Calif.: Wadsworth.

Marshall, Rachelle. 1993. "Spy Case Update: The Anti-Defamation League Fights Back." *Washington Report on Middle East Affairs*, July/August, 20.

Masri, Rania. 2003. "Fog of War, Speech Given on April 5, 2003, at the 20th Annual Black Workers for Justice Banquet; Raleigh, N.C." Apr. 5. http://www.zmag.org/content/showarticle.cfm?ItemID=3433 (Feb. 6, 2006).

Massad, Joseph. 1993. "Palestinians and the Limits of Racialized Discourse." *Social Text* 34:94–114.

Massey, Douglas, and Nancy Denton. 1993. *American Apartheid: Segregation and the Making of the Underclass.* Cambridge, Mass.: Harvard Univ. Press.

Matar, N. I. 2000. *Turks, Moors, and Englishmen in the Age of Discovery.* New York: Columbia Univ. Press. Cited in Rana 2007.

Matloff, Judith. 2001. "When a Spouse Is Muslim, New Bonds, New Rifts." *New York Times,* Oct. 28, 14.4, late edition, East Coast. http://proquest.umi.com/ (June 29, 2005).

Mayer, Jane. 2005. "Annals of Justice: Outsourcing Torture." *New Yorker,* Feb. 14, 106.

McAlister, Melani. 2001. *Epic Encounters: Culture, Media, and U.S. Interests in the Middle East, 1945–2000.* Berkeley: Univ. of California Press.

McCarus, Ernest, ed. 1994. *The Development of Arab-American Identity.* Ann Arbor: Univ. of Michigan Press.

McClintock, Ann. 1995. *Imperial Leather: Race, Gender, and Sexuality in the Colonial Contest.* New York: Routledge.

McClosky, Herbert. 1964. "Consensus and Ideology in American Politics." *American Political Science Review,* June, 362–82.

McClosky, Herbert, and Alida Brill. 1983. *Dimensions of Tolerance: What Americans Believe about Civil Liberties.* New York: Basic Books.

McDonnel, Pat. 1987. "Mass Arrest of Seven Palestinians and a Kenyan Wife Shocked and Angered Arab-Americans." *News Circle* Feb.–Mar.:4–7.

McGovern, James R. 1982. *Anatomy of a Lynching: The Killing of Claude Neal.* Baton Rouge: Louisiana State Univ. Press.

Medina, Tony, and Louis Reyes Rivera, eds. 2001. *Bum Rush the Page.* New York: Three Rivers Press.

Melhem, D.H. 2001. "Gibran's *The Prophet:* Outside the Canon of American Literature." *Al-Jadid,* Summer, 10–11.

Merskin, Debra. 2004. "The Construction of Arabs as Enemies: Post-September 11 Discourse of George W. Bush." *Mass Communication & Society* 7, no. 2:157–75.

Metres, Philip. 2001. "Review: *Post Gibran.*" *Indiana Review* Spring, 140–41.

Miller, Toby. 1998. *Technologies of Truth: Cultural Citizenship and the Popular Media.* Minneapolis: Univ. of Minnesota Press.

Mills, Charles W. 1997. *The Racial Contract.* Ithaca, N.Y.: Cornell Univ. Press.

Mitchell, Timothy. 1988. *Colonising Egypt.* New York: Cambridge Univ. Press.

Moallem, Minoo. 2001. "Middle East Studies, Feminism, and Globalization." *Signs: Journal of Women in Culture and Society* 26, no. 4:1265–68.

———. 2002. "Whose Fundamentalism?" *Meridians: Feminisms, Race, Transnationalism* 2, no. 2:298–301.

———. 2005. *Between Warrior Brother and Veiled Sister: Islamic Fundamentalism and the Politics of Patriarchy in Iran.* Berkeley: Univ. of California Press.

Moallem, Minoo, and Iain A. Boal. 1999. "Multicultural Nationalism and the Poetics of Inauguration." In *Between Woman and Nation: Nationalisms, Transnational Feminisms, and the State,* edited by Caren Kaplan, Norma Alarcón, and Minoo Moallem, 243–63. Durham, N.C.: Duke Univ. Press.

Moore, Kathleen M. 1995. *al-Mughtaribun: American Law and the Transformation of Muslim Life in the United States.* Albany: State Univ. of New York Press.

———. 2002. "A Part of US or Apart from US? Post-September 11 Attitudes Toward Muslims and Civil Liberties." *Middle East Report* 224 (Fall):33.

Morris, Timothy. 1995. *Becoming Canonical in American Poetry.* Urbana/Chicago: Univ. of Illinois Press.

Morrison, Toni. 1993. *Playing in the Dark: Whiteness and the Literary Imagination.* New York: Vintage Books.

Morsy, Soheir. 1994. "Beyond the Honorary 'White' Classification of Egyptians: Societal Identity in Historical Context." In *Race,* edited by Steven Gregory and Roger Sanjek, 175–98. New Brunswick, N.J.: Rutgers Univ. Press.

Muaddi Darraj, Susan, ed. 2004. *Scheherazad's Legacy: Arab and Arab American Women on Writing.* Westport, Conn./London: Praeger.

Muñoz, Jose Esteban. 1999. *Disidentifications: Queers of Color and the Performance of Politics.* Minneapolis: Univ. of Minnesota Press.

Murray, Nancy. 2004. "Profiled: Arabs, Muslims, and the Post-9/11 Hunt for the 'Enemy Within.'" In *Civil Rights in Peril: The Targeting of Arabs and Muslims,* edited by Elaine Hagopian, 27–70. Ann Arbor, Mich.: Pluto Press.

Naber, Nadine. 1996. "The Most Invisibles of the Invisibles." *Middle East Women's Studies Review* 11:2.

———. 2000. "Ambiguous Insiders: An Investigation of Arab American Invisibility." *Ethnic and Racial Studies* 23, no. 1 (Jan.):37–61.

———. 2002. "So Our History Doesn't Become Your Future: The Local and Global Politics of Coalition Building Post September 11th." *Journal of Asian American Studies* 5, no. 3:217–42.

———. 2005. "Muslim First, Arab Second: A Strategic Politics of Race and Gender." *Muslim World* 95, no. 4:479–95.

———. 2006. "The Rules of Forced Engagement." *Cultural Dynamics* 18, no. 3:235–68.

Naff, Alixa. 1985. *Becoming American: The Early Arab Immigrant Experience.* Carbondale: Southern Illinois Univ. Press.

———. 1994. "The Early Arab Immigrant Experience." In *The Development of Arab-American Identity,* edited by E. McCarus, 23–35. Ann Arbor: Univ. of Michigan Press.

National Association for the Advancement of Colored People (NAACP). 1969. [1919]. *Thirty Years of Lynching in the United States 1889–1918.* New York: Negro Universities Press.

———. 1987. Part 7, The Anti-Lynching Campaign, 1912–1955, Series A "Anti-Lynching Investigative Files, 1912–1953," Reel 10, Univ. Publications of America, Inc.

NBC San Diego.com. 2005. "Marine General's Blunt Comments Draw Fire, Some Audience Members Clap." Feb. 1. http://www.nbcsandiego.com/news/4153541/detail.html.

Nelson, Bryce. 1973. "Mideast War Spurs Unprecedented Formation of Arab Groups in U.S." *Los Angeles Times,* Oct. 25, A12.

New York City Commission on Human Rights. 2003. *Discrimination Against Muslims, Arabs, and South Asians in New York City since 9/11.* New York: New York City Commission on Human Rights.

Ngai, Mae M. 1999. "The Architecture of Race in American Immigration Law: A Reexamination of the Reed Johnson Act of 1924." *Journal of American History* 66, no. 1:67–92.

———. 2004. *Impossible Subjects: Illegal Aliens and the Making of Modern America.* Princeton, N.J.: Princeton Univ. Press.

Nieves, Evelyn. 2001. "A New Minority Makes Itself Known: Hispanic Muslims." *New York Times,* Dec. 17, A.13, late edition, East Coast. http://proquest.umi.com/ (June 29, 2005).

Nimer, M. 2003. "Muslims in America after 9-11." *Journal of Islamic Law and Culture* 7, no. 2:1–36.

Nir, Ori. 2006. "Bush Riles Muslims With 'Islamic Fascist' Remark." *Jewish Daily Forward,* Aug 18.

Nisbet, E., and J. Shanahan. 2004. *MSRG Special Report: Restrictions on Civil Liberties, Views of Islam, and Muslim Americans.* Ithaca, N.Y.: Cornell Univ., The Media and Society Research Group.

Odell, J. H. 1980. Letter to Nabeel Abraham, President of AAUG, Mar. 3; "The Black American Project," box 33, *Archives of the AAUG,* Eastern Michigan Univ., Ypsilanti.

Omi, Michael and Howard Winant. 1994. *Racial Formation in the United States: From the 1960s to the 1990s.* New York: Routledge.

————. 1995. "Race in the Post–Civil Rights Movement Era." In *Origins and Destinies: Immigration, Race, and Ethnicity in American,* edited by Silvia Pedraza and Ruben G. Rumbaut, 470–78. New York: Wadsworth.

Ong, Aihwa. 2003. *Buddha Is Hiding.* Berkeley: Univ. of California Press.

Ono, Kent. 2005. "Asian American Studies after 9/11." In *Race, Identity and Representation in Education,* 2d ed., edited by Cameron McCarthy, Warren C. Richlow, Greg Dimitriadis, and Nadine Dolby, 439–51. New York: Routledge.

Ono, Kent A., and John M. Sloop. 2002. *Shifting Borders: Rhetoric, Immigration, and California's Proposition 187.* Philadelphia: Temple Univ. Press.

Orfalea, Gregory. 1988. *Before the Flames: A Quest for the History of Arab Americans.* Austin: Univ. of Texas Press.

Orfalea, Gregory, and Sharif Elmusa, eds. 2000. *Grape Leaves: A Century of Arab-American Poetry.* New York/Northampton: Interlink. (Orig. pub. 1988.)

Ortiz, Paul. 2005. *Emancipation Betrayed: The Hidden History of Black Organizing and White Violence in Florida.* Berkeley: Univ. of California Press.

Perlmann, Joel. 2001. "Race or People: Federal Race Classifications for Europeans in America, 1898–1913." Working Paper 230, Jerome Levy Economic Institute of Bard College, Jan., 4–13.

Peters, Issa. 2001. "Review: Post Gibran." *World Literature Today* 75, no. 1:187.

Portes, A. 1983. "Modes of Structural Incorporation and Present Theories of Labor Immigration." In *Global Trends in Migration: Theory and Research on International Population Movements,* edited by Mary M. Kritz, Charles B. Keely, and Silvano M. Tomasi, 279–97. Staten Island, N.Y.: Center for Migration Studies.

————. 1987. "The Social Origins of the Cuban Enclave Economy of Miami." *Sociological Perspectives* 30, no. 4, 340–72.

Prashad, Vijay. 2000. *The Karma of Brown Folk.* Minneapolis: Univ. of Minnesota Press.

————. 2002. *Everybody Was Kung Fu Fighting: Afro-Asian Connections and the Myth of Cultural Purity.* Boston: Beacon.

Prewitt, Kenneth. 2002. "Demography, Diversity, and Democracy: The 2000 Census Story." *Brookings Review* 20, no. 1:6–9.

Puar, Jasbir K., and Amit Rai. 2002. "Monster, Terrorist, Fag: The War on Terrorism and the Production of Docile Patriots." *Social Text* 20, no. 3:117–48.

Purdy, Matthew. 2001. "For Arab-Americans, Flag-Flying and Fear." *New York Times,* Sept. 14, A.14, late edition, East Coast. http://proquest.umi.com/ (June 29, 2005).

————. 2002. "On Arab-America's Main Street, New Flags and Old Loyalties." *New York Times,* Apr. 7, 1.29, late edition, East Coast. http://proquest.umi.com/ (June 29, 2005).

Rana, Junaid. 2007. "Islamophobia and Racism: On the Ethnology of the Muslim." *Souls* 9, no. 2.

Rana, Junaid, and Gilberto Rosas. 2006. "Managing Crisis." *Cultural Dynamics* 18, no. 3:219–34.

Rashmawi, Elias A. 1992. "A Journey Through the Palestinian Experience in the U.S. in the Company of the ADL: A Case Study in Subverting the U.S. Constitution and Intimidating Dissent." Paper circulated by author via e-mail.

Rasmussen, B. B., E. Klinenberg, I. J. Nexica, and M. Wray. 2001. "Introduction." In *The Making and Unmaking of Whiteness,* edited by B. B. Rasmussen, E. Klinenberg, I. J. Nexica, and M. Wray 1–24. Durham, N.C.: Duke Univ. Press.

Read, Brock. 2005. "Columbia U. Professor, Criticized for Views on Israel, Is Banned from Teacher-Training Program." *Chronicle of Higher Education,* Feb. 22.

Read, Jen'nan Ghazal. 2004a. *Culture, Class, and Work among Arab-American Women.* New York: LFB Scholarly Publishing.

———. 2004b. "Coming to America: The Effects of Nativity and Culture on Arab-American Women's Employment." *International Migration Review* 38, no. 4:52–77.

Revolutionary Worker Online. 2002. *Profiled and Persecuted: How the U.S. Government Is Terrorizing Immigrants from 20 Arab and Muslim Countries.* http://rwor.org/a/v24/1181-1190/1182/immigrants.htm (Feb. 6, 2006).

Rico, Barbara R., and Sandra Mano. 1991. *American Mosaic: Multicultural Readings in Context.* Boston: Houghton Mifflin.

Rodriguez, Clara E. 2000. *Changing Race: Latinos, the Census, and the History of Ethnicity in the United States.* New York: New York Univ. Press.

Roediger, David. 1991. *The Wages of Whiteness: Race and the Making of the American Working Class.* New York: Verso.

———. 1994. *Towards the Abolition of Whiteness: Essays on Race, Politics, and Working Class History.* London: Verso.

———. 2002. *Colored White: Transcending the Racial Past.* Berkeley: Univ. of California Press.

———. 2003. "Afterword: Du Bois, Race, and Italian Americans." In *Are Italians White?,* edited by J. Guglielmo and S. Salerno, 259–64. New York: Routledge.

———. 2005. *Working Toward Whiteness: How America's Immigrants Became White: The Strange Journey from Ellis Island to the Suburbs.* New York: Basic Books.

Rouse, Roger. 1995. "Thinking Through Transnationalism: Notes on the Cultural Politics of Class Relations in the Contemporary United States." *Public Culture* 7:353–402.

Rowe, M. Raven, ed. 2003. *Def Poetry Jam.* New York: Atria.

Sachs, Susan, and Blaine Harden. 2001. "A Family, Both Arab and Arab-American, Divided by a War." *New York Times,* Oct. 29, B.1, late edition, East Coast. http://pro quest.umi.com/ (June 29, 2005).

Sacks, Karen Brodkin. 1994. "How Did Jews Become White Folks?" In *Race,* edited by Steven Gregory and Roger Sanjek, 78–102. New Brunswick, N.J.: Rutgers Univ. Press.

Said, Edward. 1978. *Orientalism.* New York: Random House.

———. 1981. *Covering Islam: How the Media and the Experts Determine How We See the Rest of the World.* New York: Pantheon.

———. 1993. *Culture and Imperialism.* New York: Vintage.

———. 2001. "The Clash of Ignorance." *The Nation.* Oct. 4. http://www.thenation .com/doc/20011022/said (Feb. 9, 2007).

———. 2002. *Reflections on Exile and Other Essays.* Boston: Harvard Univ. Press.

Salaita, Steven. 2000. "Split Vision: Arab American Literary Criticism." *Al-Jadid* 32:14.

———. 2006. *Anti-Arab Racism in the USA: Where It Comes From and What It Means for Politics Today.* Ann Arbor, Mich.: Pluto Press.

Salem Manganaro, Elise. 1988. "Voicing the Arab: Multivocality and Ideology in Leon Uris' *The Hajj.*" *MELUS* 15, no. 4:3–13.

———. 2000–2001. "The Dynamics of Canon Formation: Arabic Literature in 'Translation.'" *Al-Abhath,* 48–49, 85–98.

Saliba, Najib E. 1992. *Emigration from Syria and the Syrian-Lebanese Community of Worcester, MA.* Ligonier, Pa.: Antakya Press.

Saliba, Therese. 1994. "Military Presences and Absences." In *Food for Our Grandmothers: Writings by Arab American and Arab Canadian Feminists,* edited by Joanna Kadi, 125–32. Boston: South End Press.

———. 1999. "Resisting Invisibility: Arab Americans in Academia and Activism." In *Arabs in America: Building a New Future,* edited by Michael Suleiman, 304–19. Philadelphia: Temple Univ. Press.

Samhan, Helen Hatab. 1987. "Politics and Exclusion: The Arab American Experience." *Journal of Palestine Studies* 16, no. 2:11–28.

———. 1999. "Not Quite White: Race Classification and the Arab-American Experience." In *Arabs in America: Building a New Future,* edited by Michael Suleiman, 209–26. Philadelphia: Temple Univ. Press.

———. 2001. "Arab Americans." *Grolier Multimedia Encyclopedia,* Danbury, Conn.: Grolier.

———. 2005. *A Definition of Arab Americans.* Arab American Institute. http://www .aaiusa.org/definition.htm (June 30, 2005).

San Francisco State Univ. 2003. *A History of SF State.* San Francisco: San Francisco State Univ. http://www.sfsu.edu/~100years/history/long.htm (Feb. 8, 2007).

Sanjek, Roger. 1994. "The Enduring Inequalities of Race." In *Race,* edited by Steven Gregory and Roger Sanjek, 1–18. New Brunswick, N.J.: Rutgers Univ. Press.

Saulny, Susan. 2002. "Demonstrations Highlight Deep Divisions over Growing Conflict in Middle East." *New York Times,* Apr. 6, B.5, late edition, East Coast. http://proquest.umi.com/ (June 29, 2005).

Saxton, Alexander. 1971. *The Indispensable Enemy.* Berkeley: Univ. of California Press.

Schrift, Alan D. 2000. "Confessions of an Anthology Editor." *Symploke* 8, no. 1–2:164–76.

Senechal de la Roche, Roberta. 1997. "The Sociogenesis of Lynching." In *Under Sentence of Death: Lynching in the South,* edited by W. Fitzhugh Brundage, 48–76. Chapel Hill: Univ. of North Carolina Press.

Shadroui, Gregory. 1991. "Book Review, *Grape Leaves: A Century of Arab American Poetry.*" *Washington Report on Middle East Affairs,* Mar., 73–76.

Shaheen, Jack. 1984. *The TV Arab.* Madison: Univ. of Wisconsin Press, Popular Press.

———. 2001. *Reel Bad Arabs: How Hollywood Vilifies a People.* New York: Olive Branch Press.

———. 2002. "Hollywood's Muslim Arabs." In *A Community of Many Worlds: Arab Americans in New York City,* edited by Kathleen Benson and Philip M. Kayal, 191–212. New York: Museum of the City of New York/Syracuse University Press.

———. 2003. "Bad Arabs: How Hollywood Vilifies a People." *The Annals of the American Academy of Political and Social Science* July, 160–75.

Shahid, Irfan. 2000. "Gibran and the American Literary Canon: The Problem of the Prophet." In *Tradition, Modernity and Postmodernity in Arabic Literature: Essays in Honor of Professor Issa J. Boullata,* edited by Kamal Abdel-Malek and Wael Hallaq, 321–34. Leiden: Brill.

Shakir, Evelyn. 1982. "Pretending to Be an Arab: Role Playing in Vance Bourjaily's *The Fractional Man.*" *MELUS* 91:7–21.

———. 1983. "Starting Anew: Arab-American Poetry." *Ethnic Forum* 3, no. 1–2:23–36.

———. 1993. "Coming of Age: Arab American Literature." *Ethnic Forum* 14, no. 2:64–80.

———. 1997. *Bint Arab: Arab and Arab American Women in the United States.* Westport, Conn.: Praeger.

———. 1998. "Mother's Milk: Women in Arab-American Autobiography." *MELUS* 15, no. 4:39–50.

Shalal-Esa, Andrea. 2002. "Diana Abu Jaber: The Only Response to Silencing Is to Keep on Speaking." *Al-Jadid* (Spring):4–6.

Shamieh, Betty. 2001. "Why I Am Afraid to Write This Poem." *Mizna* 3, no. 1.

Sheets, Hilarie M. 2001. "Stitch by Stitch, a Daughter of Islam Takes on Taboos." *New York Times,* Nov. 25, 2.33, late edition, East Coast. http://proquest.umi.com/ (June 29, 2005).

Shehadeh, Michele. 2000. Personal communication with Nadine Naber, Nov. 15.

Shohat, Ella. 1990. "Gender in Hollywood's Orient." *Middle East Report* 162 (Jan.–Feb):40–42.

———. 1998. "Introduction." In *Talking Visions: Multicultural Feminism in a Transnational Age,* edited by Ella Shohat, 1–62. Cambridge, Mass.: MIT Press.

———. 2001. "Area Studies, Transnationalism, and the Feminist Production of Knowledge." *Signs: Journal of Women in Culture and Society* 26, no. 4:1269–72.

———. 2006. "Gender and the Culture of Empire: Toward a Feminist Ethnography of the Cinema." In *Taboo Memories, Diasporic Voices,* 17–69. Durham, N.C.: Duke Univ. Press.

Shohat, Ella, and Robert Stam. 1994. *Unthinking Eurocentrism: Multiculturalism and the Media.* New York: Routledge.

Shryock, Andrew. 2000a. "Family Resemblances: Kinship and Community in Arab Detroit." In *Arab Detroit: From Margin to Mainstream,* edited by Nabeel Abraham and Andrew Shryock, 573–610. Detroit: Wayne State Univ. Press.

———. 2000b. "Public Culture in Arab Detroit: Creating Arab/American Identities in a Transnational Domain." In *Mass Mediations: New Approaches to Popular Culture in the Middle East and Beyond,* edited by Walter Armbrust, 32–60. Berkeley: Univ. of California Press.

———. 2004. "In the Double Remoteness of Arab Detroit: Reflections on Ethnography, Culture Work, and the Intimate Disciplines of Americanization." In *Off Stage/On Display: Intimacy and Ethnography in the Age of Public Culture,* edited by Andrew Shryock, 279–314. Palo Alto, Calif.: Stanford Univ. Press.

Shryock, Andrew, and Nabeel Abraham. 2000. "On Margins and Mainstreams." In *Arab Detroit: From Margin to Mainstream,* edited by Nabeel Abraham and Andrew Shryock, 15–35. Detroit: Wayne State Univ. Press.

Slade, Shelly. 1981. "Image of the Arab in America: Analysis of a Poll on American Attitudes." *Middle East Journal* 35 (Spring):2.

Smith, Andrea. 2006. "Heteropatriarchy and the Three Pillars of White Supremacy: Rethinking Women of Color Organizing." In *Color of Violence: The Incite! Anthology,* 66–73. Cambridge, Mass.: South End Press.

———. 2007. E-mail communication with Nadine Naber, Jan 10.

Smith, D. 2001. "When 'For a While' Becomes Forever." *Weekly Defense Monitor,* Oct. 2.

Smothers, Ronald. 1998. "Secret Evidence Standing in the Way of New Life for Some Immigrants." *New York Times,* Aug. 15, A11.

Sollors, Werner, ed. 1996. *Theories of Ethnicity: A Classical Reader.* New York: New York Univ. Press.

Spivak, Gayatri Chakravorty. 1999. *A Critique of Postcolonial Reason: Toward a History of the Vanishing Present.* Cambridge, Mass.: Harvard Univ. Press.

Stanley, Alessandra. 2002. "A Portrait of the Prophet Behind Islam." *New York Times,* Dec. 18, E.1, late edition, East Coast. http://proquest.umi.com/ (June 29, 2005).

Stathakis, Paula Maria. 1996. *Almost White: Greek and Lebanese-Syrian Immigrants in North and South Carolina, 1900–1940.* Ph.D. diss., Univ. of South Carolina.

Steet, Linda. 2000. *Veils and Daggers: A Century of* National Geographic's *Representation of the Arab World.* Philadelphia: Temple Univ. Press.

Steinfels, Peter. 2001. "Amid Islam's Complexity, Scholars Are Challenged to Influence Change Without Compromising." *New York Times,* Sept. 29, D.4, late edition, East Coast. http://proquest.umi.com/ (June 29, 2005).

Stockton, Ronald. 1994. "Ethnic Archetype and the Arab Image." In *The Development of Arab American Identity,* edited by Ernest McCarus, 119–53. Ann Arbor: Univ. of Michigan Press.

Struch, Naomi, and Shalom H. Schwartz. 1989. "Intergroup Aggression: Its Predictors and Distinctiveness from In-Group Bias." *Journal of Personality and Social Psychology* 56, no. 3:364–73.

Sugrue, T. J. 1996. *The Origins of the Urban Crisis: Race and Inequality in Postwar Detroit.* Princeton, N.J.: Princeton Univ. Press.

Suleiman, Michael. 1987. "Early Arab Americans: The Search for Identity." In *Crossing the Waters: Arabic-Speaking Immigrants to the United States,* edited by Eric Hoogland, 37–54. Washington D.C.: Smithsonian Institution Press.

———. 1989. "America and the Arabs: Negative Images and the Feasibility of Dialogue." In *Arab Americans Continuity and Change,* edited by Baha Abu-Laban and Michael Suleiman, 251–72. Washington, D.C.: Arab American Univ. Graduates.

———. 1994. "Arab Americans and the Political Process." In *The Development of Arab American Identity,* edited by Ernest McCarus, 37–60. Ann Arbor: Univ. of Michigan Press.

———. 1998. *The Arabs in the Mind of America.* Brattleboro, Vt.: Amana.

———, ed. 1999. "Introduction: The Arab Immigrant Experience." In *Arabs in America: Building a New Future,* edited by Michael Suleiman, 1–21. Philadelphia: Temple Univ. Press.

———. 2002. "Stereotypes, Public Opinion, and Foreign Policy: The Impact on Arab-American Relations." *Journal of Arab Affairs* (Apr.):147–66.

Suleiman, Michael W., and Baha Abu-Laban. 1989. "Introduction," In *Arab Americans: Continuity and Change,* edited by Baha Abu-Laban and Michael W. Suleiman, 1–13. Belmont, Mass.: Association of Arab-American Univ. Graduates.

Tadiar, Neferti. 2002. "Filipinas 'Living in a Time of War.'" In *Body Politics: Essays on Cultural Representations of Women's Bodies,* edited by Maria Josephine Barrios and Odine De Guzman, 2–18. Quezon City: Univ. of the Philippines Center for Women's Studies.

———. 2005. Comments made as part of the panel discussion "Race, Geopolitics, and Feminisms." Center for Cultural Studies, Univ. of California, Santa Cruz, May 13.

Takaki, Ronald. 1987. *From Different Shores: Perspectives on Race and Ethnicity in America.* New York: Oxford Univ. Press.

Tebeau, Charlton W. 1971. *A History of Florida.* Coral Gables, Fla.: Univ. of Miami Press.

Terry, Janice. 1985. *Mistaken Identity.* Washington, D.C.: American-Arab Affairs Council.

———. 1999. "Community and Political Activism among Arab Americans in Detroit." In *Arabs in America: Building a New Future,* edited by Michael Suleiman, 241–54. Philadelphia: Temple Univ. Press.

Tessler, Mark, and Dan Corstange. 2002. "How Should Americans Understand Arab Political Attitudes: Combating Stereotypes with Public Opinion Data from the Middle East." *Journal of Social Affairs* (Winter):13–34.

Trinh T. Minh-ha. 1989. *Woman, Native, Other: Writing Postcoloniality and Feminism.* Bloomington: Indiana Univ. Press.

Truzzi, Oswaldo. 1997 "The Right Place at the Right Time: Syrians and Lebanese in Brazil and the United States: A Comparative Approach." *Journal of American Ethnic History* 16, no. 2:1–34.

Tsao, Fred, and Rhoda Rae Gutierrez. 2003. *Losing Ground.* Chicago: Illinois Coalition for Immigrant and Refugee Rights.

Twain, Mark. 1984 [1869]. *The Innocents Abroad: Roughing It.* New York: Viking. Cited in Little 2002.

U.S. Bureau of the Census. 1920. Manuscript Census of Population. National Archives Microfilm Publication; 14th Census of the United States; Los Angeles Public Library.

———. 1930. Manuscript Census of Population. National Archives Microfilm Roll T626-308, 15th Census of the United States. downloaded from http://content.gale.ancestry.com.

———. 1933. 15th Census of the United States, Reports by States: 1930 (Florida). Washington, D.C.: GPO.

———. 1943. 16th Census of the United States: 1940, Population (Florida), v. 2. Washington, D.C.: GPO.

———. 2000. Census of Population and Housing. Public-use microdata samples. Washington, D.C.: GPO.

———. 2001. *Overview of Race and Hispanic Origin.* Census 2000 Brief. Washington, D.C.: U.S. Census Bureau.

———. 2003. *The Arab Population, 2000.* Census 2000 Brief. Washington, D.C.: U.S. Census Bureau.

U.S. Congress. 1929. *Congressional Record.* 71st Cong., 1st sess., Apr. 29, 638.

U.S. Congress. 1948. Senate, Committee on the Judiciary, *Crime of Lynching.* Washington, D.C.: GPO.

U.S. Department of Homeland Security. 2003. "Fact Sheet: US-VISIT Program." May 19.

U.S. Department of Justice. 2002. *Attorney General Prepared Remarks on the National Security Entry-Exit Registration System.* http://www.usdoj.gov/archive/ag/speeches/2002/060502agpreparedremarks.htm (Feb. 6, 2006).

———. 2004. *The September 11 Detainees.* Inspector General Report. Washington D.C.: GPO.

U.S. Equal Employment Opportunity Commission. 2002. *Questions and Answers about Workplace Rights of Muslims, Arabs, South Asians, and Sikhs.* Washington D.C.: Equal Employment Opportunity Commission.

U.S. House Judiciary Committee. 1981. Report No. 97-264, "Need for Legislation." Oct. 2.

U.S. Immigration and Customs Enforcement. 2006. "What Is Special Registration?" http://www.ice.gov/pi/specialregistration/archive.htm (Feb. 8, 2007).

U.S. Immigration and Naturalization Service. 1943. "The Eligibility of Arabs to Naturalization." *INS Monthly Review* 1:15.

———. N.d. Memo HQINS 70/28 from Johnny Williams, Executive Associate Commissioner, Office of Field Operations.

Valente, Judith. 1977. "Arab Americans Sue Marriott Corp., Alleging Job Discrimination." *Washington Post,* Apr. 28, VA 12.

Vandrick, Stephanie. 1995. "Book Review, *Food for Our Grandmothers.*" *Feminist Teacher* 9, no. 2:98–104.

Visweswaran, Kamala. 1994. *Fictions of Feminist Ethnography.* Minneapolis: Univ. of Minnesota Press.

Volpp, Leti. 2003. "The Citizen and the Terrorist." In *September 11 in History: A Watershed Moment?* edited by Mary L. Dudziak, 147–62. Durham, N.C.: Duke Univ. Press.

Wade, Corey. 2001. "Memoirs of a White Arab American." *Mizna* 3, no. 3.

Wakin, Daniel. 2004. "Even Muslims on the Move Stop at Prayer Time." *New York Times,* May 28, B.1, late edition, East Coast. http://proquest.umi.com/ (June 29, 2005).

Waldrep, Christopher. 2002. *The Many Faces of Judge Lynch: Extralegal Violence and Punishment in America.* New York: Palgrave Macmillan.

Ware, V. 2002. "Outworldly Knowledge: Toward a "Language of Perspicuous Contrast." In *Out of Whiteness,* edited by V. Ware and L. Back, 15–32. Chicago: Univ. of Chicago Press.

Warren, Kenneth. 1993. "The Problems of Anthologies, or Making the Dead Wince." *American Literature* 65:338–42.

Waters, Mary. 1990. *Ethnic Options.* Berkeley: Univ. of California Press.

———. 1999. *Black Identities: West Indian Immigrant Dreams and American Realities.* Cambridge, Mass.: Harvard Univ. Press.

Wayne, Leslie. 2004. "Arabs in U.S. Raising Money to Back Bush." *New York Times,* Feb. 17, A.1, late edition, East Coast. http://proquest.umi.com/ (June 29, 2005).

West, Stan. 2000. "An Afrocentric Look at the Arab Community." *Mizna* 2, no. 3:20–22.

White, Deborah Gray. 1985. *Ar'n't I a Woman? Female Slaves in the Plantation South.* New York: Norton.

Wilgoren, Jodi. 2001a. "Islam Attracts Converts by the Thousands, Drawn Before and After Attacks." *New York Times,* Oct. 22, B.10, late edition, East Coast. http://proquest.umi.com/ (June 29, 2005).

———. 2001b. "Struggling to Be Both Arab and American." *New York Times,* Nov. 4, 1B.1, late edition, East Coast. http://proquest.umi.com/ (June 29, 2005).

Williams, Brackette F. 1996. *Women Out of Place: The Gender of Agency and the Race of Nationality.* New York/London: Routledge.

Winant, Howard. 1994. *Racial Conditions: Politics, Theory, Comparisons.* Minneapolis: Univ. of Minnesota Press.

———. 2001. *The World Is a Ghetto.* New York: Basic Books.

Worth, Robert. 2002. "Gay Muslims Face a Growing Challenge Reconciling Their Two Identities." *New York Times,* Jan. 13, 1.30, late edition, East Coast. http://proquest.umi.com/ (June 29, 2005).

Wright, L. 1994. "One Drop of Blood." *New Yorker,* July 24.

Wu, Duncan. 1997. "Editing Student Anthologies: The Burning Question." *Romanticism on the Net* http://www.erudit.org/revue/ron/1997/v/n7/005757ar.html (Apr. 30).

Yadegar, Rebecca. 1995. "Arab-American/Arab-Canadian Anthology: An International Perspective." *Sojourner: The Women's Forum* 20:12.

Young, Robert. 2001. *Postcolonialism: An Historical Introduction.* Oxford: Blackwell.

Zangrando, Robert L. 1980. *The NAACP Crusade Against Lynching, 1909–1950.* Philadelphia: Temple Univ. Press.

Zogby, James, ed. 1984. *Taking Root, Bearing Fruit: The Arab-American Experience.* Washington, D.C.: American Arab Anti-Discrimination Committee.

————. 2000. "What Ethnic Americans Really Think." Zogby Culture Polls. Feb. 10–15. New York: Zogby International.

————. 2001. *"Rediscovering" Arab Americans.* Nov. 12. http://www.aaiusa.org/washington-watch/1587/w111201.

Zogby, John. 1990. *Arab American Today: A Demographic Profile of Arab Americans.* Washington, D.C.: The Arab American Institute.

————. 2002. Arab American Institute/Zogby Group Poll. October 11th. Washington, D.C.: Arab American Institute.

Zoghby, Mary. 1988. "Review: *Grape Leaves: A Century of Arab American Poetry.*" *MELUS* 15, no. 4:91–101.

Index

Italic page numbers denote figures and tables.